THE
TEMPEST

William Shakespeare

Grace Tiffany, Editor
Western Michigan University

J. J. M. Tobin, General Editor
University of Massachusetts-Boston

WADSWORTH
CENGAGE Learning

Australia • Brazil • Japan • Korea • Mexico • Singapore • Spain • United Kingdom • United States

WADSWORTH
CENGAGE Learning™

Evans Shakespeare Series:
The Tempest
Grace Tiffany, Editor
J. J. M. Tobin, General Editor

Senior Publisher: Lyn Uhl

Publisher/Exectutive Editor:
Michael Rosenberg

Development Editor:
Michell Phifer

Assistant Editor: Erin Bosco

Editorial Assistant: Rebecca
Donahue

Media Editor: Janine Tangney

Senior Marketing Manager:
Melissa Holt

Marketing Communications
Manager: Glenn McGibbon

Content Project Manager:
Aimee Chevrette Bear

Art Director: Marissa Falco

Print Buyer: Betsy Donaghey

Rights Acquisition Specialist,
Text: Katie Huha

Rights Acquisition Specialist,
Images: Jennifer Meyer Dare

Production Service: MPS Limited,
a Macmillan Company

Cover Designer: Walter Kopec

Text Designer: Maxine Ressler

Cover Image: Antony Sher as
Prospero and Atandwa Kani
as Ariel in a 2009 joint Baxter
Theatre/Royal Shakespeare
Company production of *The
Tempest*, Cape Town, South
Africa. (Corbis)

Compositor: MPS Limited,
a Macmillan Company

For product information and
technology assistance, contact us at **Cengage Learning
Customer & Sales Support, 1-800-354-9706**

For permission to use material from this text
or product, submit all requests online at
www.cengage.com/permissions.
Further permissions questions can be emailed to
permissionrequest@cengage.com.

Library of Congress Control Number: 2010942813

ISBN-13: 978-0-495-91125-8

ISBN-10: 0-495-91125-9

Wadsworth
20 Channel Center Street
Boston, MA 02210
USA

Cengage Learning is a leading provider of customized
learning solutions with office locations around the globe,
including Singapore, the United Kingdom, Australia,
Mexico, Brazil, and Japan. Locate your local office at:
international.cengage.com/region

Cengage Learning products are represented in Canada by
Nelson Education, Ltd.

For your course and learning solutions, visit
www.cengage.com

Purchase any of our products at your local college store
or at our preferred online store **www.cengagebrain.com.**

Printed in the United States of America
1 2 3 4 5 6 7 14 13 12 11

Other titles in the *Evans Shakespeare Editions*
from Cengage Learning

As You Like It
Heather Dubrow, Volume Editor

Hamlet
J. J. M. Tobin, Volume Editor

King Lear
Vincent F. Petronella, Volume Editor

Macbeth
Katherine Rowe, Volume Editor

Measure for Measure
John Klause, Volume Editor

A Midsummer Night's Dream
Douglas Bruster, Volume Editor

Richard III
Nina Levine, Volume Editor

The Winter's Tale
Lawrence F. Rhu, Volume Editor

TABLE OF CONTENTS

Modern Essays

LIST OF ILLUSTRATIONS

In memory of James E. Robinson, whose class inspired
me to become a Shakespeare scholar

ABOUT THIS SERIES

J. J. M. Tobin

THE EVANS Shakespeare Editions are individual editions of essential plays by William Shakespeare, edited by leading scholars to provide college and university students, advanced high school students, and interested independent readers with a comprehensive guide to the plays and their historical and modern contexts.

The volume editor of each play has written an introduction to the play and a history of the play in performance on both stage and screen. Central sources and contexts for the play are included, and each editor also has surveyed the critical commentary on the play and selected representative influential essays to illuminate the text further. A guide to additional reading, viewing, and listening concludes the volume and will continue the reader's relationship with the play.

Each volume includes an overview of Shakespeare's life and the world of London theater that he inhabited. Our goal for these editions is that they provide the reader a window into Shakespeare and his work that reminds us all of his enduring global influence.

The text for these plays comes from *The Riverside Shakespeare*, edited with notes and textual commentary by the late Gwynne Blakemore Evans. Evans was known for his unrivaled scholarly precision, and his *Riverside* text is an essential and much-admired modern edition of Shakespeare. The Evans Shakespeare Editions preserve the *Riverside* line numbering, which is the numbering used in the invaluable *Harvard Concordance to Shakespeare* by Marvin Spevack.

Beyond his scholarly work, Evans was a generous mentor to many of the editors in this series and a tremendous influence on all of us. His kind-hearted nature made it impossible for him truly to dislike anyone. However, despite an identification with the most traditional and canonical of cultural texts, he reserved a raised eyebrow and stern words for those whose politics lacked empathy and understanding for the full diversity of human experience. In this attitude too, as in all his writing and teaching, it was evident that he was a scholar who understood Shakespeare. This series is dedicated to his memory.

SHAKESPEARE'S LIFE

J. J. M. Tobin

S HAKESPEARE WAS a genius, but he was no unreachable ivory-tower poet. Instead, Shakespeare was a young man from the provinces who made good in the big city of London. Just when and how he came from the provinces remains a mystery. He was born in 1564, the eldest son of an initially quite successful father whose position as alderman and then bailiff (mayor) of the town of Stratford allowed his son to attend the local Latin Grammar School. There, Shakespeare received an education that, contrary to some critics' belief, provided him with the historical perspective and verbal flexibility that helped define his writing.

The schoolboy grew into a young man who married an older woman, Anne Hathaway, and became the father of a daughter and a set of twins, a boy and a girl, by the age of twenty-one. The boy, Hamnet, would die before his twelfth birthday. When the playwright's father, John Shakespeare, only recently recovered from two decades of legal and financial difficulties, died in 1601, having earlier secured the coat of arms of a gentleman (Duncan-Jones 90–102), Shakespeare was left in Stratford with a family of four women: his wife, his two daughters, and his mother, Mary, née Arden. Shakespeare's own familial experiences, from the fluctuations of his father's fortunes, to the strong influence of several female relatives, to the tragic loss of a beloved son, doubtless added heart and depth to the incisive portrayals of characters that he created in his plays and poems.

Accordingly, given the fact that all description is necessarily selective, Shakespeare often had in mind his own experiences when he chose narrative and dramatic sources for the foundation of his comedies, histories, and tragedies. The few facts of his life that survive are open to all sorts of interpretations, some of which reveal more about the interpreter than about the facts themselves, while others carry with them a greater degree of likelihood. A few critics have noted that Shakespeare was the eldest boy in a patriarchal world, the first surviving child born in a time of plague after the infant deaths of two siblings. As a child, he doubtless saw and remembered his father dressed in the furred scarlet gown of a bailiff in 1568, going about his appointed supervisory tasks, a figure both familiar as a person and strangely exalted as an official, and as Stephen Greenblatt has noted, all by means of a costume (Greenblatt 30–31). He was likely to have been the indisputable favorite of his mother, acquiring a self-confidence that often leads young men with even a modicum of talent on to success.

Richard Wheeler has pointed out that Shakespeare's choice of source material in which a female is disguised as a boy, best illustrated in *Twelfth Night*, has psychological roots in the playwright's wish to have repaired the loss of his son, Hamnet, whose twin sister, Judith, remained a constant reminder of the absent boy (Wheeler 147–53). Finally, although his marriage and fatherhood indicate some clear grounds for heterosexuality, Shakespeare also wrote beautiful poems about a young man, and his plays often feature male bonding and pathetic male isolation when the bond is broken by marriage, as in the instances of Antonio and Bassanio in *The Merchant of Venice* and a second Antonio and Sebastian in *Twelfth Night*. These scenarios offer putative evidence of at least homosociability.

Of course, over-reliance on causal links between the playwright and the experiences of his creations would logically have Shakespeare a conscience-stricken killer like Claudius or Macbeth, a disoriented octogenarian like Lear, and a suicidal queen like Cleopatra—interpretative leaps that even the most imaginative critic is unwilling to make.

Between the birth of the twins in February 1585 and the writer Robert Greene's allusion to Shakespeare as an actor-turned-playwright in September 1592, there is no hard evidence of his whereabouts, although many theories abound. Perhaps he was a schoolmaster in the country; perhaps he was attached to the household of a Catholic landowner in Lancashire. Certainly one of the most plausible theories is that Shakespeare joined the traveling theatrical troupe called the Queen's Men in 1587 as it passed through Stratford and then came to London as a member of their company. If so, he joined an exciting theatrical world with competition for the entertainment dollar among several companies with plays written by both authors who were university graduates and a minority who were not. It was a world that on its stages carefully reflected the political issues and events of the moment, but did so indirectly because of restrictions created by governmental censorship and by the potential dangers posed by a personal response to criticism by the powerful men of the time.

These dramas were composed for a public audience of mixed class and gender, from work-cutting apprentices to lords of the realm and every possible class gradation in between. They were also performed occasionally for a private audience of higher status in smaller indoor venues.

The London of these plays was a fast-growing city, even in a time of plague, full of energy, color, commerce, varieties of goods, animals, and people of all social degrees. The population numbered perhaps 200,000 by the end of the sixteenth century. It was governed by a Lord Mayor and a municipal council quite concerned about issues of crowd control, the spread of disease, crime, and the fallout of all three in neighborhoods either just at the edge of their partial jurisdiction, Shoreditch in the north and Southwark, Bankside, in the south, or fully within it, like the Blackfriars. Playhouses, three-tiered amphitheaters, and the earlier open-plan inn-yards with galleries above, brought together all three of these problems and more, and they were threatened constantly with restriction by the authorities, who also had the subtle financial desire of taxing players whose performances were not protected by aristocratic patronage.

By the time he joined the newly formed Lord Chamberlain's Men in 1594, Shakespeare had already written his first four history plays (*1, 2, & 3 Henry VI* and *Richard III*), the farcical comedies *The Taming of the Shrew* and *The Comedy of Errors*, and the grotesquely interesting tragedy *Titus Andronicus*. Many, but certainly not all, of his 154 sonnets were also written in the mid-1590s. When the Lord Chamberlain's Men moved into the newly constructed Globe theater in late 1599, having had five good years at the Theatre and the nearby Curtain in Shoreditch, Shakespeare had scripted four more history plays, *King John, Richard II,* and *1 & 2 Henry IV* (and part of a fifth play, *Edward III*), six comedies, including *The Two Gentlemen of Verona, Love's Labour's Lost,* three of the five so-called "golden comedies" (*A Midsummer Night's Dream, The Merchant of Venice,* and *Much Ado About Nothing*), and *Romeo and Juliet,* the tragic companion to *A Midsummer Night's Dream.*

The opening season at the Globe doubtless included the last of the English history plays written solely by Shakespeare, *Henry V,* the pastoral comedy both debunking and idealistic, *As You Like It,* and the most frequently taught of the plays focused on Roman history, *Julius Caesar.* Before the death of Queen Elizabeth in late March of 1603, Shakespeare had certainly written his most famous play, *Hamlet,* his most intensely claustrophobic tragedy, *Othello,* the bourgeois domestic comedy *The Merry Wives of Windsor,* the last of the "golden comedies," which we find alloyed with both satire and melancholy, *Twelfth Night,* and the uniquely powerful satirical comedy *Troilus and Cressida,* as well as the enigmatic poem about martyrdom, *The Phoenix and Turtle.*

Outbreaks of the plague affected Shakespeare both as a dramatist and as a poet, for the virulence of the disease, when deaths reached more than fifty a week in London, forced the authorities to close the theaters in order to restrict contagion. Shakespeare was thus left with added time free from the incessant pressure to produce dramatic scripts, and he then composed his two Ovidian narrative poems, *Venus and Adonis* (1593) and *The Rape of Lucrece* (1594). The most extended theater closings were from June 1592 to May 1594 and from March 1603 to April 1604, but there were other, briefer closings. The plague was an abiding and overpowering presence in the lives and imaginations of the poet and his audiences.

After the accession in 1603 of James VI of Scotland as James I of England, when the Lord Chamberlain's Men became the King's Men, and before the company activated for themselves the lease in 1608 of the Blackfriars, a smaller, indoor theater that was to draw a higher and more homogeneous class of spectator, Shakespeare created his other great tragedies, *King Lear, Macbeth, Antony and Cleopatra,* and *Coriolanus,* as well as the bitter *Timon of Athens* (although there is no record of its ever having been performed), and the two "bed-trick" plays, *All's Well That Ends Well* and *Measure for Measure,* comedies in which a lecherous man is fooled by the substitution of one woman for another in the darkness of the night. For that indoor spectacle-friendly Blackfriars theater, Shakespeare wrote the romances *Pericles, Cymbeline, The Winter's Tale,* and *The Tempest,* with their wondrous atmospheres and radiant daughters. By 1611, Shakespeare was moving into partial retirement, co-authoring with John Fletcher, his younger colleague and successor as principal playwright of the King's Men, *Henry VIII, The Two Noble Kinsmen,* and, probably, the lost *Cardenio.*

The division of his plays into these categories—comedies, histories, tragedies, and romances—reminds us that the first step taken by the playwright (indeed any playwright) was to determine the basic genre or kind of play that he wished to write, however much he might expand its boundaries. Genre creates expectations in the mind of the audience, expectations that no dramatist of the time was willing to frustrate. Regarding kind, Polonius tells us with unconscious humor of the versatility of the players who come to Elsinore: "The best actors in the world, either for tragedy, comedy, history, pastoral, pastoral-comical, historical-pastoral, tragical-historical, tragical-comical-historical-pastoral" (2.2.396–399). In that boundary-blurring, increasingly capacious definition of genre, he also informs us of Shakespeare's own gift in all kinds of writing and the fact of his often combining many of these genres in a single work. When, at the end of Plato's *Symposium,* Socrates argues that logically, the greatest tragic writer should also be the greatest comic writer, he was prophetic of Shakespeare, even if he doesn't go on to argue that these principles of tragedy and comedy could and should be connected in the same play. And Shakespeare indirectly repays Socrates for his prophecy by alluding to the philosopher's death in Mistress Quickly's description of the dying Falstaff in *Henry V,* 2.3.

Shakespeare is Shakespeare because of a combination of philosophical tolerance, psychological profundity, and metaphoric genius; that is, he is generous-minded, aware of what makes people tick, and is able to express himself more vividly and memorably than anyone else in the language. And it is his language that truly sets him apart, while simultaneously creating some occasional static in the mind of the modern reader.

There are six areas of this problematic language worth special attention: word choice, false friends, allusions, puns, iambic rhythm, and personification. Shakespeare's vocabulary has words that are no longer part of today's language, chiefly because they refer to things and concepts no longer in use, such as "three-farthings," coins of small value, in the Bastard's metaphoric "Look where three-farthings goes" (*King John*, 1.1.143). Such terms are easily understood by looking at the footnotes, or by checking *The Oxford English Dictionary* or a Shakespearean lexicon, like that of Schmidt; C. T. Onions's *A Shakespeare Glossary;* or *Shakespeare's Words,* by David and Ben Crystal. More difficult are false friends, words spelled the same as words we use today but that have different meanings. One example of this issue is "brave," which as an adjective in the sixteenth and early seventeenth centuries meant primarily "splendid" or "glorious," as in Miranda's expression of awe and excitement in *The Tempest*: "O *brave* new world/That has such people in't" (5.1.183–84), or "virtue," which in Shakespeare's language usually means "strength or power," as in Iago's argument for personal responsibility to Roderigo and the latter's lament that "it is not in my *virtue* to amend it [being in love with Desdemona]":"*Virtue?* A fig! 'tis in ourselves that we are thus or thus" (*Othello*, 1.3.318–20).

Equally problematic, but just as easily understood by reference to footnotes, are instances of classical and biblical allusion, where Shakespeare assumes a recognition by all or some of the audience of glancing references to Greek and Roman deities, frequently to elements in that most abiding narrative in Western literature, the Trojan War, as well as historical and legendary figures, as in Hamlet's "My father's brother, but no more like my father/Than I to *Hercules*" (1.2.152–53) or his subconscious reminder in the graveyard of the fact that his father was the victim of fratricide, "How the knave jowls it to the ground, as if 'twere *Cain's* jaw-bone" (5.1.76–77).

More difficult at times are Shakespeare's puns—plays on words, sometimes comedic and sometimes intentionally non-comedic, but in each case designed to bring more than one meaning in a single word to the attention of the audience and the reader. Shakespeare's puns are almost always thematically significant, revelatory of character, or both, and attention to the possibilities of the presence of punning can only increase our understanding and pleasure in the lines. There are such simple etymological puns as "lieutenant," the military title of Cassio in *Othello*, where the word is defined as one who holds the place of the captain in the latter's absence—exactly the fear Othello has about the relationship that he imagines exists between his wife, Desdemona, and Lieutenant Cassio. There are also puns that fuse the physical and the moral, as in Falstaff's comment that his highway robbery is condoned by the goddess of the moon, "under whose *countenance* we steal" (*1 Henry IV*, 1.2.29), where the word "countenance" means both "face" and "approval." Falstaff's pun is in prose, a good example of how Shakespeare, commonly regarded as the greatest of English poets and dramatists, wrote often in prose, which itself is full of the linguistic devices of poetry.

When Shakespeare was writing in verse, he used iambic pentameter lines, ten syllable lines with five feet, or units, of two syllables each, in the sequence of short–long or unstressed–stressed. Consider, for example, Romeo's "But soft,/what light/through yond/er win/

Fig. 1. Joseph Fiennes as William Shakespeare fighting through writer's block in the film *Shakespeare in Love*: a handsome dramatist without the receding hairline of contemporary portraits and busts.

dow breaks?" (*Romeo and Juliet*, 2.2.1), or Antony's "If you/have tears/prepare/to shed/them now" (*Julius Caesar*, 3.2.169).

Scanning the rhythm of these lines is made easier by our knowledge that Shakespeare and the English language are both naturally iambic and that proof of the correct rhythm begins with marking the stress on the final syllable of the line and moving right to left. The rhythm with the emphasized syllables will lead the actor delivering the lines to stress certain words more than others, as we imagine Shakespeare to have intended, even as we know that stage delivery of lines with an unexpected stress can create fruitful tension in the ear of the audience. For example, Barnardo's "It was about to speak when the cock crew" (*Hamlet*, 1.1.147) is a pentameter line, but the expected iambic rhythm is broken in the last two feet, especially in the sequentially stressed final two syllables, which by their alliteration and double stress combine in form to underscore the moment of interruption in the play's narrative. Such playing off the expected is part of Shakespeare's arsenal of verse techniques.

In addition to these issues of unknown terms, false friends, allusions chiefly classical and biblical, meaningful puns, and verse rhythm itself, there is the metaphoric language that is the glory of Shakespeare, but each instance of this feature demands careful unpacking. Consider the early example of Romeo's personifying Death as an erotic figure keeping Juliet as his mistress, linking the commonly joined notions of love and death: "Shall I believe/That unsubstantial Death is amorous,/And that the lean abhorred monster keeps/Thee here in dark to be his paramour?" (5.3.102–05). This link already had been anticipated by the Chorus in the prologue to the play, which speaks of "The fearful passage of their death-marked love" (1.6).

More compactly, later in his career, Shakespeare will have Hamlet, in prose, combine Renaissance and medieval views in similes and metaphors, comparisons with and without "like" or "as," in order to describe the multifaceted nature of man: "...how like an angel in apprehension, how like a god! The beauty of the world; the paragon of animals; and yet to me what is this quintessence of dust?" (*Hamlet*, 2.2.306–08). Macbeth in his play will argue against his wife's view that a little water will cleanse his guilty hands: "No; this my hand will rather/The multitudinous seas incarnadine,/Making the green one red" (2.2.58–60). Here Shakespeare has been careful to combine the mouth-filling hyperbole and its Latinate terms "multitudinous" and "incarnadine" (an illustration of the technique that he had learned from Christopher Marlowe) with a crystal-clear synonymous expression, "Making the green one red," for the benefit of all in the theater, even as everyone hears the hypnotically mellifluous line that comes before it.

Sometimes Shakespeare scorned the opportunity to use high-flown language, even when one might expect it most, as in the Roman play *Antony and Cleopatra*, when the queen uses a noun as a verb in her bitter image of herself live on the Roman stage played by a child actor, "And I shall see/Some squeaking Cleopatra *boy* my greatness/I'th' posture of a whore" (*Antony and Cleopatra*, 5.2.219–221). Shakespeare gives to Cleopatra's handmaiden Charmian the least hyperbolic expression in a context linking the erotic and funereal (analogous to that situation described by Romeo), "Now boast thee, death, in thy possession lies/A *lass* unparallel'd" (5.2.315–16), where the simple pastoral monosyllable charms the audience, which all along had sensed the antithesis of the playful girl within the cunningly imperious and imperial queen.

While nothing can fully explain the development of this language, its raw material comes largely from Shakespeare's reading, as do the basic elements of plot and character. The same man who was to save and increase his money and property in London and Stratford was, as a craftsman, equally economical, preferring to alter and expand upon material given to him in the literary sources that lie behind all his compositions rather than to create from experience alone. He is the chief counter-example to Polonius's admonition "Neither a borrower nor a lender be" (*Hamlet* 1.3.75)—Shakespeare is a world-class borrower, but one who reshapes and transforms the borrowed materials.

Certainly he had a most retentive memory and could and did recall, at times subconsciously, both single expressions and rather lengthy passages from his reading. "It is often as if, at some deep level of his mind, Shakespeare thought and felt in quotation," as Emrys Jones has noted (Jones 21). Dryden's comment that Shakespeare "needed not the spectacles of books to read Nature; he looked inwards and found her there" ignores Shakespeare's conscious manipulations of his reading as a chief source for his achievement. Nevertheless, Dryden gives us the basic image useful for picturing Shakespeare's genius. The playwright's metaphorical spectacles had two lenses, one of which was focused on life as he knew it and one on the writings of his predecessors and contemporaries: historians both classical and English, proto-novelists, poets, pamphleteers, and essayists, and playwrights who had in their own ways dealt with themes that interested him.

It is by looking at what Shakespeare himself perused that we see his manipulative genius at work, omitting, adding, preserving, and qualifying those plots, motifs, and images viewed through one lens of his binoculars. An important question is just how much of the original theme and significance is brought over in the creative borrowing, a question made more difficult to answer by the fact that in the composition of his plays, Shakespeare often modified and sometimes even inverted the gender and number of the persons in the original material. See, for example, the model in the story of Cupid and Psyche from Apuleius' *The Golden Asse* (1566), where Psyche almost murders Cupid, for the description of the deaths of the little princes in *Richard III*, as well as for the presentation of the murder of Desdemona in *Othello*. The closer one looks at this source and the affected passage, the more one sees that the young man from Stratford, despite being accused by his London-educated colleague and rival Ben Jonson of having "small Latin and less Greek," was a sufficiently good Latinist to check the translation of Apuleius that he was using against the original, even as he would later check Golding's translation of the *Metamorphoses* against Ovid's Latin for use in *The Tempest*.

We don't know the workplace of Shakespeare, the desk or table where he kept his books, nor do we know for certain who provided him with these volumes, some of which were quite expensive, such as Holinshed's *Chronicles*, North's *Plutarch*, and bibles, both Bishops' and Geneva. But, if we imagine a bookshelf above his desk and envision the titles that he might have ordered there chronologically, we would first see the classics, most importantly Ovid and Virgil; then the Bible, especially Genesis, the Gospel of St. Matthew, and the Book of Revelation; medieval and Renaissance writers, including Chaucer and Erasmus; and then his own immediate predecessors and colleagues, especially Thomas Kyd, Christopher Marlowe, Robert Greene, and Thomas Nashe. Sometimes the most unlikely source can provide a motif or a character, but for more important ideas, we may note what he would have learned from four exemplary volumes on this imagined shelf.

From Seneca, the Roman philosopher, tutor to the emperor Nero and playwright of closet tragedies (that is, of plays meant to be read in the study rather than performed on stage), Shakespeare learned to balance a sensational theme—fratricide and incest—with a plot structured with care and characters subtly developed with an attitude quite fatalistic. From Plutarch, the Greek historian who wrote parallel lives of Greek and Roman leaders, he learned the importance of the nature of the private man when serving in public office and how that nature is revealed in small gestures with large significance—what James Joyce, the "spiritual son" of Shakespeare, would later refer to as "epiphanies." From Machiavelli, the notorious early-sixteenth-century political theorist, or from the image of Machiavelli, he saw what he had already known about the role of deception and amorality in political life. From Michel de Montaigne, the sixteenth-century father of the essay, he added to his already operative skepticism, a capacity to question received notions about the consistency of the "self" and the hierarchical place of human beings in creation.

Fig. 2. Later, on other writers' bookshelves, would be Shakespeare's own First Folio (1623), containing thirty-six plays, half of them appearing in print for the first time. It does not, however, include any of the longer poems or sonnets.

To enjoy Shakespeare, it is not at all necessary to understand the sources that he mined, but to study Shakespeare, the better to appreciate the depth and complexity of the work, it is extremely useful to examine the foundations upon which he has built his characters and plots. We can trace, for example, the many constituent elements that have gone into the creation of Falstaff, who, together with Hamlet, is the most discussed of Shakespeare's creations. The elements include, among still others, the Vice of the morality plays; the rogue from Nashe's *The Unfortunate Traveller;* the *miles gloriosus* or cowardly braggart warrior from the Roman comic playwright (and school text) Plautus; the cheerful toper from the Bacchus of Nashe's *Summer's Last Will and Testament;* parodically, the Protestant martyr Sir John Oldcastle from Foxe's *Book of Martyrs;* and even the dying Socrates of Plato's *Phaedo.* Not that Falstaff is at all times all these figures, but in the course of his career in four plays, alive in *1 & 2 Henry IV,* dying offstage in *Henry V,* and radically transformed in *The Merry Wives of Windsor,* he is each of them by turn and counterturn, and still so much more than the mere sum of all these literary, dramatic, and historical parts.

In terms of giving voice to multiple perspectives, to characters of different ages, genders, colors, ethnicities, religions, and social ranks, Shakespeare is unrivaled. No other playwright, then or since, makes other selves live while simultaneously concealing his own self or selves, a talent described by Keats as "negative capability." Shakespeare was also an actor; that is, a person interested in imitating imaginary persons. He was thus doubly a quite creative mimic. Some of the selves mimicked are versions of the "Other," those foreigners or aliens from around the world, including Africans (Aaron, Morocco, Othello), Jews (Shylock, Tubal, Jessica), Frenchmen and Frenchwomen (the Dauphin, Joan of Arc, Margaret of Anjou), non-English Britons (Irish: Macmorris; Scots: Jamy; Welsh: Fluellen), as well as such other continental Europeans as Spaniards (Don Armado) and Italians (including several Antonios), to say nothing of the indefinable Caliban.

Some of his topics, his subjects for dramatic treatment, came often from already set pieces at school, as Emrys Jones, among others, has shown. For example, a set question to be answered, pro and con, was, should Brutus have joined the conspiracy to assassinate Caesar, the answer to which helps create the tensions in *Julius Caesar* (Jones 16). Such an on-the-one-hand and on-the-other school exercise became part of Shakespeare's dramatic strategy, where plays provide the tension created by opposites and the consequent rich ground for multiple interpretations by readers and audiences. There were also sources in earlier stage productions, including plays about Romeo and Juliet, King John, King Lear, and Hamlet. Marlowe especially provided structures to imitate and diverge from in his plays of a weak king (*Edward II*) and of several extraordinary ambitious characters, among whom are a villainous Jew (*The Jew of Malta*), and a rhetorical conqueror (*Tamburlaine*), brilliant efforts which become in Shakespeare's hands the still more dramatic *Richard II, The Merchant of Venice,* and *Henry V.*

Shakespeare's borrowing was frequent and pervasive, but his creative adaptations of those raw materials have made him ultimately not just a borrower but in fact the world's greatest lender, giving us four hundred years of pleasure and providing countless artists, whether painters, novelists, film directors, or even comic book writers, with allusive material. Of course, we would happily surrender our knowledge of a number of these borrowings if only we could have some sense of the quality of the voice of the leading man Richard Burbage, of the facial expressions of the comic actor Will Kemp, the sounds of the groundlings' responses to both the jokes and the set soliloquies, and the reactions of both Queen Elizabeth, who allegedly after watching *1 & 2 Henry IV* wanted to see Falstaff in love, and King James, who doubtless loved the image of his ancestor Banquo in *Macbeth.*

Shakespeare's last years before his death in April 1616 were spent back in Stratford. Although little is known of that time, we are left with the enigmatic coda to his life: his will, in which he famously left to his wife, Anne Hathaway Shakespeare, "the second-best bed"—it is unclear whether it was a cruel slight or a fondly personal bequest. Care of his estate went to his elder daughter, Susannah, while a lesser inheritance went to his wayward younger daughter, Judith, and any children she might have. He died a landowner, a family man, and a once well-known playwright. His will did not cite what has become his greatest legacy—the plays and poems that we read today—but the clues that these works leave about his life, and certainly the testament to his talent that they represent, are more valuable than even the most detailed autobiography. To be sure, however, the local boy who made good, worked hard, had flaws, and lived a complicated family life has more in common with many of his readers, then and now, than does the iconic Shakespeare, who has been mistakenly portrayed as a distant genius paring his fingernails while creating many of the greatest works in world literature.

ELIZABETHAN THEATER

J. J. M. Tobin

MASS ENTERTAINMENT today has become ever more fractured as technology provides myriad ways to take in a film (and myriad ways for Hollywood to try to make money). Movie theaters now have to compete with home theaters and couches in a way they never had to before in order to put people in the seats. The attractions of high-definition screens and stereo surround-sound are not the draw they once were now that individuals can access such technology in their own homes, and stadium seating and chair-side concessions don't make up the difference. The appeal of first-run films is fading too, now that movies go to DVD in a matter of weeks and are also available for immediate streaming through a Netflix subscription. All of these technologies, however, whether enjoyed in the cinema or at home, contribute to the moviegoer's sensation of being transported to another time and place (a journey, moreover, that lasts not much longer than an hour and a half). Hard to imagine, then, that a little over four hundred years ago, when the battle for the entertainment dollar took place on the stage rather than the screen, most members of the Elizabethan audience gladly stood for more than two hours without benefit of a padded seat, buttered popcorn, or Junior Mints (although they did have dried fruit and nuts), or the pause button in order to watch the plays of Shakespeare and his fellow dramatists performed. The legendary plays we read today on these pages were once the sixteenth- and early-seventeenth-century equivalents of the *Harry Potter* series or *Avatar*—artistic creations to be sure, but first and foremost moneymakers for their producers.

Theatrical performances in Elizabethan England took place all over the country in a wide variety of venues. As we know from the work of A. Gurr and others, if we put aside the sites used by touring companies like the Queen's Men of the 1580s (to which Shakespeare himself may have been attached), the guildhalls and marketplaces in cities and towns like Norwich, Bristol, and Stratford, or the halls of the universities of Oxford and Cambridge, and instead concentrate on London itself, we see that there were five basic performance locales (Gurr, esp. 115 ff.). There were, of course, the inns and inn-yards, in large part roofed against the weather and useful especially during the winter months.

The most celebrated of these inns in the history of London theater were the Bel Savage, the Bull, and the Cross Keys, these latter two on the same London street. These were the locations most frequently of concern to the mayor and other municipal authorities anxious about unruly crowds and increased chances of plague contagion, until 1594, when it was declared by the Lord Chamberlain of the Queen's court that there would be only two adult companies—his own, the Lord Chamberlain's Men (Shakespeare's group), and his father-in-law's, the Lord Admiral's Men, troupes that would upon the succession of King James be called the King's Men and Prince Henry's Men—and they would not perform anymore in city inns.

Second, there were two indoor halls, one in a building abutting St. Paul's Cathedral, not too far from the Bel Savage Inn, and the other in the refectory of the old Blackfriars monastery, each used by the children's companies of boys who put on plays with adult political and moral themes. Shakespeare and his company in 1596 had hoped to use the Blackfriars because Blackfriars was a liberty—that is, a district that, for reasons of its religious history, was independent of the secular control of the sheriff—but were refused by a powerful NIMBY (not in my backyard) movement of influential residents. They then leased the building to a second generation of a children's company and had to wait until 1608 to take possession of what would turn out to be both a "tonier" and quite lucrative theatrical space.

Third were the dining halls of the Inns of Court, the London law schools or, perhaps, more accurately, legal societies, where noteworthy performances of *The Comedy of Errors* (Gray's Inn) and *Twelfth Night* (the Middle Temple) took place. There, special audiences with their appetite for contemporary satire allowed for the lampooning of particular individuals whose traits and foibles would be represented by grimace, gesture, voice imitation, and even clothing, as in the case of Dr. Pinch in *The Comedy of Errors*, Malvolio in *Twelfth Night*, and Ajax in *Troilus and Cressida*. When these plays were moved to the larger public stage, the personalized elements could be withdrawn and the characters could continue as general, non-specifically humorous figures.

Fourth was the Queen's court itself (after the death of Elizabeth in 1603, it became the King's court), where at Christmastide, the major companies would be invited to perform for the pleasure of the monarch. Indeed, throughout the long period of tension between the city authorities and the court, the justification for allowing the players to perform their craft in public was that they needed to practice in order to be ready at year's end to entertain the monarch. This argument assumed a quite disproportionate ratio of practice to performance, but it was a convenient semi-fiction that seemed to satisfy all concerned. These court performances were rewarded financially by the Master of the Revels and were less expensive than other kinds of royal entertainment, including masques with elaborate scenery and complicated production devices, the high costs of which later contributed to the downfall of Charles I, James's son and successor. Legend has it that Queen Elizabeth so enjoyed some of the performances featuring the character of Falstaff that she wished to see him in love, a comment which was allegedly the stimulus for *The Merry Wives of Windsor*, which was said to have been written in two weeks, the better to satisfy the queen's request. A close look at the multiple sources used in the creation of this middle-class comedy suggests that the legend may be well founded.

Last, there are the purpose-built amphitheaters, beginning with James Burbage's the Theatre (1576) in Shoreditch, just to the north of the city limits; and the Curtain (1578) nearby. To the south, across the Thames, were the Rose (1587), the site of the Lord Admiral's company and most notably the performances of Christopher Marlowe's plays; the Swan (1596); the Globe (1599), built with the very timbers of the Theatre transported across the river in the winter of 1598 after the twenty-one-year lease on the old property had expired and several subsequent months of renting; and, back to Shoreditch in the north, the Fortune (1600), explicitly built in imitation of the triple-tiered Globe.

There was competition for the same audience in the form of bull-baiting, bear-baiting and cockfighting, and also simple competition for attention from such activities as royal processions, municipal pageants, outdoor sermons, and public executions with hangings, eviscerations, castrations, and quarterings, not to mention the nearby temptation of the houses ("nunneries") of prostitution. Nonetheless, these theatrical structures proved that, if you build it, they will come.

And come they did, with hundreds of performances each year of thirty or more plays in repertory for each company, plays of chronicle history, romance, tragedy (especially revenge tragedy), satire, and comedy (slapstick, farcical, situational, verbal, and, from 1597, "humorous"; that is, comedy dependent upon characters moved by one dominant personality trait into behavior mechanical and predictable, almost monomaniacally focused). The two major companies could and did perform familiar plays for a week or more before adding a new play to the repertory. A successful new play would be performed at least eight times, according to Knutson, within four months to half a year (Knutson 33–34). New plays were house-fillers, and entrance fees could be doubled for openings. When sequels created a two-part play, performances were only sometimes staged in proper sequence, even as moviegoers will still watch on cable *Godfather II* or *The Empire Strikes Back* without worrying that they have not just seen *The Godfather* or *Star Wars*.

S. PAULES CHURCH
THAMESIS
The Bear Gardne
The Globe

Fig. 3. Part of J. C.Visscher's view of London (c. 1616 or slightly earlier) looking north from the Bankside and showing the Beargarden theater and, to the right, the Globe theater (or possibly the Swan).

The players seemed willing to play throughout the week and throughout the year, but municipal officials repeatedly insisted that there be no performances on Sundays and holy days and holidays, nor during Lent. These demands had some effect, although their repetition by the authorities clearly suggests that there were violations, with performances on occasional Sundays, even at court, on some holidays, and on some days in Lent.

Of course, even though almost half of Shakespeare's plays had already been performed at the Theater and elsewhere, we think of the Globe, open for business probably in the late summer of 1599, as the principal venue for Shakespeare's work, perhaps with *As You Like It* the first production. The current New Globe on the Bankside in Southwark, erected in careful imitation of what we know to have been the methods and materials of the sixteenth century, allows for a twenty-first-century experience analogous to that of the Elizabethan theatergoer. It may be that the diameter of the current theater, of one hundred feet, is a bit too wide, and that seventy-two feet is rather closer to the exact diameter of not only the Globe but several of these late-sixteenth-century London theaters. If so, the judgment that such Elizabethan theaters could hold between 2,000 and 3,000 people suggests that spectators, particularly the groundlings—those who had paid a penny to stand throughout the two-to-three hour performance—were packed in cheek by jowl.

The geometry of the Globe itself is that of a polygon, but it appears circular. From a distance, one would know that a play was to be performed that day by the presence of a flag flying high above the tiring house, the dressing area for the actors. Once inside the building, the theatergoer would note the covered stage projecting from an arc of the circle almost to the center of the uncovered audience space, such that the groundlings would be on three sides of the stage, with those in the front almost able to rest their chins on the platform which was raised about five feet from the floor. This stage was not raked—that is, inclined or tilted towards the audience—as it often is in modern theaters today. Raking both creates better sightlines and potentially affects stage business, as in the case of a fallen Shylock in productions of *The Merchant of Venice*, who at one point struggled in vain to stand on a pile of slippery ducats (gold coins). This move is made even more difficult by the slight incline. However, instead of raking the stage, the Rose, and perhaps the Globe and the Fortune, had the ground on which the audience stood slightly raked (Thomson 78–79), to the great advantage of those in the back of the theater.

Behind the stage, protected by a backdrop on the first level, was the tiring house where the actors dressed and from which they came and went through two openings to the left and right. There were few surprise entrances in the Elizabethan theater, as the audience could always see before them the places of entry. Covering the upper stage and a large part of the outer stage would be the "heavens," supported by two columns or pillars behind which characters could hide in order to eavesdrop and which could serve metaphorically as trees or bushes. The underside of the "heavens" was adorned with signs of the zodiac, the better to remind the audience that all the world is a stage. At the back of the stage in the center, between the two openings of exit and entrance, was a discovery space within which, when a curtain was drawn, an additional mini-set of a study, a bed, or a cave could be revealed.

From below the stage, figures, especially ghosts, could ascend through a trapdoor, and mythological deities could be lowered from above. From the second tier of the galleries, still part of the tiring house, characters could appear as on battlements or a balcony. Music was a very great part of Elizabethan theater, and musicians would be positioned sometimes on that second level of the tiring house. Less musical but still necessary sound effects, say one indicating a storm and thunder, were achieved by such actions as the offstage rolling of a cannonball down a metal trestle or repeated drumming.

Although the groundlings were the closest to the talented actors, for those members of the audience who wished to sit in the galleries (Stern, esp. 212–13) and were willing to pay more money for the privilege, there would have been the comfort of the familiar, as V. F. Petronella has pointed out, inasmuch as these galleries included rooms not unlike those in the domestic buildings near the Globe. However, the familiar was balanced with the rare via the figures on the stage who represented kings, nymphs, fairies, and ghosts, personages not usually found in the Southwark area (Petronella, esp. 111–25). These audiences themselves came from a great range of Elizabethan society, male and female, from aristocrats to lowly apprentices, with all gradations of the social spectrum in between. The late Elizabethan and early Jacobean period is so special in theatrical history in part because of the work of a number of gifted playwrights, Shakespeare preeminent among them, but also in part because of the inclusive nature of the audiences, which were representative of the society as a whole.

When the King's Men in 1609 began to perform in the smaller, indoor Blackfriars theater while still continuing at the Globe in the summer months, they were able to charge at Blackfriars five or six times the entry fee at the Globe for productions that pleased a grander and wealthier group, but at the cost of having a more socially homogeneous audience. Although the Blackfriars was a more lucrative venue,

Shakespeare's company still profited from productions at the Globe, to the degree that when the Globe burned down during a performance of *Henry VIII* on June 29 1613, the company immediately set about rebuilding the structure so that it could reopen the very next year. One wonders whether Shakespeare came down from semi-retirement in Stratford for the new opening or was already in London working yet again in collaboration with John Fletcher, his successor as principal playwright of the King's Men.

In the more heterogeneous atmosphere at the Globe, whether the first or second version, audiences watched action taking place on a platform of about twelve hundred square feet, a stage which could be the Roman forum at one moment, the senate house at another, and a battlefield at still another. Yet the audience was never at a loss in recognizing what was what, for the dramatist provided place references in the dialogue between and among characters (and some plays may also have featured signs indicating place). The action was sometimes interrupted by informative soliloquies, speeches directed to the audience as if the character speaking on the stage were totally alone, whether or not he or she actually was. By convention, what was said in a soliloquy was understood to be the truthful indication of the character's thoughts and feelings. These soliloquies must have been in their day somewhat analogous to operatic arias—plot-useful devices, but also stand-alone bravura exercises in rhetorical display. Othello's "flaming minister" speech (5.2.1–22) is a good example of the show-stopping effect of the soliloquy, and Edmund's defense of bastardy in *King Lear* (1605; 1.2.1–22), in a passage of identical length, seldom fails to elicit applause at the last line even from today's audiences, who otherwise are accustomed not to interrupt the flow of a performance.

The actors and the audience were proximate and visible to each other during these daylight performances, putting them on more intimate terms than is the case in theaters today. Performers were dressed onstage in contemporary Elizabethan clothing, with the kings and dukes wearing specially purchased, costly garments whose fate as they grew worn and tattered was to outfit the clowns with social pretensions. There were also attempts to provide historical atmosphere when needed with helmets, shields, greaves and togas appropriate to the ancient world. Perhaps as few as ten men and four boys, who would play the women's roles in this all-male theatrical world, could perform all sixteenth-century plays. The boys would remain with the company until their voices cracked, and some then became adult members of the company when places became available. They were apprentices in a profession where the turnover was not great—a bonus to the dramatist who could visualize the actor who would be playing the character he was creating but not so advantageous for a young actor looking for a permanent place within a stable group. Because plays were very seldom performed in an uninterrupted run, actors needed powerful memories. It was a time when the aural rather than the visual understanding was much greater than in our own time, but even so, the capacity of actors to hold in their heads a large number of roles from many different plays was extraordinary, and new plays were constantly being added to the repertory.

Even as one man in his time plays many parts, so did Shakespeare's company of actors. The skills and particular strengths of these actors must have given Shakespeare a great deal of confidence about the complexity of the roles that he could ask them to create. Such an element of the familiar increased the pleasure of the audience when it could recognize the same actor behind two different characters whose similarity might now be perceived. Celebrated instances of doubling include, in *A Midsummer Night's Dream*, Theseus/Oberon and Hippolyta/Titania; and, in *Hamlet*, Polonius/First Gravedigger and, most strikingly, the Ghost/Claudius. The audience would likewise be affected by their experience with an actor in a current play having performed in a previous play that they had also seen. One example of this link between roles that allows the audience to anticipate the plot comes in *Hamlet,* when Polonius tells us of his having played Caesar. Caesar, of course, was killed by Brutus in Shakespeare's *Julius Caesar.* The actor now playing Polonius had played Caesar previously in *Julius Caesar,* and in that production, he was killed by Brutus, played by Richard Burbage (son of James). In this performance of *Hamlet*, Burbage was playing Hamlet, and he would shortly kill Polonius, in a repeat of history.

The theater is the most collaborative of enterprises. We should think of Shakespeare as a script-writer under considerable pressure to provide material for his colleagues, all of whom viewed the play to come as a fundamentally money-making project. Shakespeare had multiple advantages beyond his inherent verbal and intuitive gifts. Not only did he write for a group of actors whose individual talents he could anticipate in the composition of his characters, but the script that he was creating was often a response to recent successes by rival companies with their own revengers, weak and strong English kings, and disguised lovers.

The performances themselves relied greatly on the power of the audience's imagination to fill in what was missing because of the limitations of the Elizabethan stage, as the self-conscious Prologue in *Henry V* (1599) makes clear by appealing to the audience to imagine whole armies being transported across the sea. Other Elizabethan dramatists did attempt to be "realistic" in ways that are laughable even beyond the well-intended efforts of Quince, Bottom, and the other Mechanicals in *A Midsummer Night's Dream* (1596). Consider, as noted by G. B. Evans, Yarrington's *Two Tragedies in One* (1594–c. 1598), 2.1: "When the boy goeth in to the shop, Merry striketh six blows on his head and, with the seventh, leaves the hammer sticking in his head; the boy groaning must be heard by a maid, who must cry to her master." Three scenes later, a character "Brings him forth in a chair with a hammer sticking in his head" (Evans 71). Such grossly imperfect efforts increasingly gave way to conventional signals expressive of the limitations of the stage. Four or five men with spears and a flag could represent an army, and a single coffin could represent a whole graveyard. While the Globe stage lacked scenery as we know it, it was not lacking in props. Not only were there a trapdoor grave and a bank of flowers, but also a good number of handheld props like swords, torches, chalices, crowns, and skulls, each a real object and potentially a symbol.

Sometimes convention and symbolism gave way to nature in the case of live animals. Men in animal skins are safer, of course, but some animals, like dogs and bears, are trainable. It is certain that Crab, the dog in the *Two Gentlemen of Verona* (1595–96), was "played" by a true canine, and it is quite likely that the bear that pursues Antigonus in *The Winter's Tale* was only sometimes a disguised human being; but at other times, it was a bear, managed but real, possibly even a polar bear reared from the time of its capture as a cub. Further reflection on the known dangers associated with working with bears and our knowledge of the props listed in *Henslowe's Diary* of 'j beares skyne' (Henslowe 319) suggest that Elizabethan actors were more comfortable with artificial bears, thereby avoiding any sudden ursine aggression, revenge for all the suffering their colleagues had endured at the bear-baiting stake.

The authorities whose powers of censorship were real and forceful did not worry much about whether animals were live onstage or not, but they did care about theological issues being discussed explicitly and about urban insurrection, as we know from the strictures applied to *The Book of Sir Thomas More*, a manuscript play in which Shakespeare most probably had a hand. For all their apparent sensitivity to political issues, the government seems not to have interfered with plays that show the removal—or even the murder—of kings, although the scene of the deposing of Richard in *Richard II* (1596) was thought too delicate to be printed during the lifetime of Queen Elizabeth, who recognized Richard as a parallel figure and pointedly said: "I am Richard the Second, know ye not that?" Scholars debate whether some of these potent themes regarding right versus might, illegitimate succession, and successful usurpation were recognized imperfectly by the government and so escaped into performance if not always into print. Another theory is that the authorities allowed the audiences to be excited and then pacified by these entertaining productions, a release of energies that returned the audience at the play's end to an unchanged social and political reality.

While it is now customary to refer to this reality as part of the Early Modern Period, it is still important to remember that the two main cultural forces of the time, the Renaissance and the Reformation, came together in a perfect storm of new ideas about values. The Renaissance brought us the rebirth of classical culture and an emphasis on the dignity of human beings, and the Reformation stripped levels of interpretative authority in favor of the individual's more direct reliance on Scripture. These new ideas, sometimes in concert and sometimes in tension, have led increasingly over four hundred years to our current distant but clearly related theories of skepticism and pragmatism.

It is just as important to remember that when James Burbage built his theater in 1576, he was not so much interested in the idea of the dignity of human beings or in the proper interpretation of Scripture as in the making of money. When his son, Richard, and his son's friend and partner, William Shakespeare, and their fellow shareholders were creating and performing their scripts, they were counting the house above all else. Theater was an essential part of the entertainment industry, and for some, it was especially lucrative. If a man was an actor, he made a little bit of money; if a playwright, a little more; if a shareholder in the company that put on the play, a very great deal more; and if a householder in the building in which the plays were performed, even more still. Shakespeare was all four, and as we read his scripts, we should remember that the artist was also a businessman, interested in the box office as much as or more than any hard-to-imagine immortality. The Elizabethan theater was the forerunner of the multiplex, a collaborative, secular church in which the congregation/audience focused on the service before them, and Shakespeare and his fellows focused on both the service and the collection plate.

And yet with all the primary focus on material gain, Shakespeare and his competitors and collaborators were aware of the cultural importance and historical traditions of drama itself. Their own work continued myths and rituals that had begun in Athens and elsewhere more than two thousand years ago. It may well be true, as Dr. Samuel Johnson famously said, that no man but a blockhead ever wrote for anything but money, and Mozart might have been partially correct when he said that good health and money were the two most important elements in life. Yet we also know that just because a work has been commissioned doesn't rule out the presence of beauty and truth, as indeed Mozart's own works reveal. Michelangelo was paid by Pope Julius II to paint the Sistine Chapel, but nobody thinks of the fee the artist earned when she or he looks at the creation of Adam or the expulsion of Adam and Eve from the Garden of Eden. Shakespeare's career in the Elizabethan theatrical world turned out to be quite lucrative, but given the many profound reasons for which we read and study *A Midsummer Night's Dream, King Lear,* and *The Tempest* today (among so many other plays and poems), we see that the dramatist who created these works and gained so much material success was nevertheless grossly underpaid.

WORKS CITED

Crystal, David and Ben Crystal. *Shakespeare's Words.* London: Penguin, 2002. Print.

Duncan-Jones, Katherine. *Ungentle Shakespeare: Scenes from His Life.* London: Arden Shakespeare-Thomson, 2001. Print.

Evans, G. Blakemore. *Elizabethan-Jacobean Drama.* London: A&C Black, 1988. Print.

Foakes, R. A., ed. *Henslowe's Diary.* 2nd ed. Cambridge: Cambridge UP, 2002. Print.

Greenblatt, Stephen. *Will in the World: How Shakespeare Became Shakespeare.* New York: Norton, 2004. Print.

Gurr, Andrew. *The Shakespearean Stage 1574–1642.* 3rd ed. Cambridge and New York: Cambridge UP, 1992. Print.

Jones, Emrys. *The Origins of Shakespeare.* Oxford: Clarendon, 1977. Print.

Knutson, Rosalyn. *The Repertory of Shakespeare's Company, 1594–1603.* Fayetteville: U of Arkansas P, 1991. Print.

Onions, C. T. *A Shakespeare Glossary.* Oxford: Clarendon, 1911. Print.

Petronella, Vincent F. "Shakespeare's Dramatic Chambers." *In the Company of Shakespeare: Essays on English Renaissance Literature in Honor of G. Blakemore Evans.* Eds. Thomas Moisan and Douglas Bruster. Madison and London: Fairleigh Dickinson and Associated UPs, 2002. 111–38. Print.

Schmidt, Alexander. *Shakespeare Lexicon.* Berlin: Georg Reimer, 1902. Print.

Stern, Tiffany. "'You that walk i' in the Galleries': Standing and Walking in the Galleries of the Globe Theater." *Shakespeare Quarterly* 51 (2000): 211–16. Print.

Thomson, Peter. *Shakespeare's Professional Career.* Cambridge: Cambridge UP, 1992. Print.

Wheeler, Richard P. "Deaths in the Family: The Loss of a Son and the Rise of Shakespearean Comedy." *Shakespeare Quarterly* 51 (2000): 127–54. Print.

ABBREVIATIONS

F1, F2, etc. First Folio, Second Folio, etc.
conj. conjecture
ed. editor, edition
l(l). line(s)
om. omit(s), omitted
s.d(d). stage direction(s)
s.p(p). speech-prefix(es)
subs. Substantially

KEY TO WORKS CITED IN EXPLANATORY AND TEXTUAL NOTES

Reference in explanatory and textual notes is in general by last name of editor or author. Not included in the following list of works so cited are this edition and its editor or editions of the play or special studies referred to in the selected bibliography appended to the "Note on the Text" following the play.

BULLEN, Arthur H., ed., *Works,* 1904-7 (10 vols.)

BULLOUGH, Geoffrey, *Narrative and Dramatic Sources of Shakespeare,* 1957-73 (7 vols.)

CAMBRIDGE, *Works,* ed. W. G. Clark and W. A. Wright, 1863-66 (9 vols.); ed. W. A. Wright, 1891-93 (9 vols.)

CAPELL, Edward, ed., *Works,* [1768] (10 vols.)

COLLIER, John P., ed., *Works,* 1842-44 (8 vols.); 1853; 1858 (6 vols.)

COLLIER MS, *Perkins' Second Folio,* 1632 (Huntington Library)

CRAIG, William J., ed., *Works,* 1891

DANIEL, P. A., *Notes and Conjectural Emendations,* 1870

DAVENANT-DRYDEN, John Dryden and William Davenant, *The Tempest: or The Enchanted Island,* 1669

DYCE, Alexander, ed., *Works,* 1857 (6 vols.); 1864-67 (9 vols.); 1875-76 (9 vols.)

HANMER, Thomas, ed., *Works,* 1743-44 (6 vols.); 1745; 1770-71 (6 vols.)

JOHNSON, Samuel, ed., *Works,* 1765 (2 eds., 8 vols.); 1768 (8 vols.)

KNIGHT, Charles, ed., *Works,* 1838-43 (8 vols.); 1842-44 (12 vols.)

MALONE, Edmond, ed., *Works,* 1790 (10 vols.)

MUNRO, John, ed., *Works* (The London Shakespeare), 1958 (6 vols.)

NEILSON, William A., ed., *Works,* 1906

NEILSON-HILL, W. A. Neilson and C. J. Hill, *Works,* ed. 1942

POPE, Alexander, ed., *Works,* 1723-25 (6 vols.); 1728 (8 vols.)

RANN, Joseph, ed., *Works,* 1786-[94] (6 vols.)

ROWE, Nicholas, ed., *Works,* 1709 (2 eds., 6 vols.); 1714 (8 vols.)

SISSON, Charles, ed., *Works,* 1954

STEEVENS, George, ed., *Works,* 1773 (with Samuel Johnson, 10 vols.); 1778 (10 vols.); 1793 (15 vols.)

THEOBALD, Lewis, ed., *Works,* 1733 (7 vols.); 1740 (8 vols.); 1757 (8 vols.)

WARBURTON, William, ed., *Works,* 1747 (8 vols.)

WHITE, Richard Grant, ed., *Works,* 1857-66 (12 vols.); 1883 (6 vols.)

WILSON, John Dover (with A. Quiller-Couch et al.), ed., *Works* (New Cambridge), 1921-66 (39 vols.)

INTRODUCTION

SOME MEANINGS OF THE PLAY

"WE ARE such stuff/As dreams are made on," says the magician Prospero in *The Tempest's* fourth act. He has just dismissed the actors of an elaborate masque he has staged for his daughter, Miranda, and her betrothed, Prince Ferdinand. The actors, he has said, are "spirits" who now melt into "thin air." Having played their parts, they dissolve as "the great globe itself" one day will (4.1.148ff).

To many scholars, directors, and playgoers, those lines have signaled Shakespeare's own poignant farewell to the theater. Their idea is bolstered by the fact that *The Tempest*, widely thought the last play written by Shakespeare alone, was first produced near the time of Shakespeare's retirement to Stratford, and preceded his death by just a few years. Those circumstances invite us to view the play at least in part as a poetic comment on the playwright's lifelong relation to his art and to his audience. And indeed, much additional language and action in the play support such an approach to it. The great storm of *The Tempest's* first scene strands a group of seafaring Italian noblemen on a desert beach. As they look about, their comments call attention to the bare floor or raised stage on which they, the actors, stand, and to the familiar Shakespearean theme of viewers' imaginative power to control what they see on that stage. To hopeful Gonzalo, who looks with an "eye of green," the island-stage is "lush and lusty" (2.1.56, 53); to sour Antonio and Sebastian the place is a foul-smelling "fen" (2.1.49). Prospero's epilogue reinforces the suggestion that the perceptions and will of an audience propel the play, for in that final speech he tells us that he "dwell[s]/In this bare island" only "by [our] spell" (Epi. 7-8).

Within the play, the medium by whom Prospero exercises his art is his servant Ariel, in whom spirit and nature combine. Ariel's name is Hebrew for "Lion of God," suggesting some otherworldly ministry. Yet he is immersed in this world's physical reality, able to transform himself into fire, water, air, or earth. Of these four elements Renaissance cosmologists, following the Golden Age Greek philosopher Empedocles, thought all organic nature was composed. Ariel "flame[s]" on a sinking ship, "tread[s] the ooze/Of the salt deep," and "run[s] upon the sharp wind" and "in the veins o'th'earth" (1.1.198, 252-55). Yet music flows like water from this natural spirit. Sometimes he sings and plays a flute; at other times his entrances are marked by off-stage melodies (s.dd. 1.2.375, 2.1.297, 3.3.83). Indeed, Ariel's and Prospero's turbulent yet finally harmonious alliance dramatizes Shakespeare's complex fusion of his own art with nature. In *The Sea and the Mirror*, the great twentieth-century poet W. H. Auden invoked Prospero's relationship to Ariel as a metaphor for all artists' struggles to express truth through make-believe. Yet in *The Tempest*, the bond between mage and nature-spirit more specifically represents the relation between the playwright and the live actors who literally embody his work. In the playhouse, as in few other locations, artifice and reality—art and nature—are one.

The exaggerated artificiality of *The Tempest*'s genre assists this metatheatrical theme. Like *Cymbeline*, *Pericles*, and *The Winter's Tale*, *The Tempest*, written in late 1610 or 1611, is a romance, a type of play that was popular in England in the second decade of the seventeenth century. Romance plots involved miraculous, providential reunions between lost lovers and family members, as well as obviously fake stage contrivances, like the lowering of the god Jupiter from the ceiling by means of a clearly visible rope in Shakespeare's *Cymbeline* (1609-10). Certainly Blackfriars, Shakespeare's company's new indoor theater, was equipped with the requisite stage machinery for such effects, to the probable enjoyment of Shakespeare, who enjoyed highlighting the phoniness of theatrical tricks even as he exploited them. Perhaps the clearest instance of such Shakespearean highlighting occurs in *The Tempest*, in Prospero's aforementioned interruption of the fourth-act wedding masque. The masque, a popular courtly form of Jacobean theater, was in a sense a heightened, stylized, concentrated romance, involving elaborate stage machinery that produced spectacular effects. Crowd-pleaser Shakespeare brings his motley audience a taste of this aristocratic entertainment, with an in-play masque that features the goddesses Iris, Juno, and Ceres, who combine to bless Miranda's and Ferdinand's impending nuptials. It is probably because of its wedding masque that *The Tempest* was staged early in 1613, as part of the court celebration of King James's daughter Elizabeth's marriage to Frederick, the Elector Palatine. Yet *The Tempest*'s masque is halted mid-way by "playwright" Prospero, who finds that it distracts him from other business unfolding in his island-theater. "The minute of their plot is almost come," he says, speaking of his slave Caliban's rebellion, of which Ariel has warned him and to which he must attend (4.1.141-42). Whatever comment the 1613 *Tempest* production might have made about English royal marriages, Prospero's abrupt words here would seem always to return the play's theme from politics to art, and specifically to a focus on the creator

Fig. 4. Costume sketch of an airy, fire-bearing spirit for a 1613 court masque.

of staged fictions and his many obligations. After the masque and at other times, Prospero's comment on the need for haste ("What is the time o'th'day?" [1.2.239]; "At this hour" [3.3.24]; "How's the day?" [5.1.3]) underscore *The Tempest*'s actual brevity. At a little over two thousand lines, it is one of Shakespeare's shortest plays. Prospero's hurriedness also makes humorously plain the playwright's struggle to order and conclude what *Romeo and Juliet*'s Chorus calls "the two-hours' traffic of [the] stage" (Pro. 12) within a reasonable period of time.

Indeed, *The Tempest* seems designed not only to conclude Shakespeare's *oeuvre*, but to reverse the direction of some of his earlier plots. It has been widely noted that Shakespeare's romances–*Cymbeline*, *Pericles*, *The Winter's Tale*, and *The Tempest*–revisit and overturn the sad outcomes of his greatest tragedies. In *The Tempest*, *Hamlet*'s usurping monarch Claudius is remembered both in Prospero's villainous brother Antonio and in the treacherous King Alonso, who has collaborated in the "thrust[ing]" of Prospero from Milan (5.1.205). Both *Hamlet*'s Claudius and *The Tempest*'s Alonso are struck by guilt pangs, but while Claudius, unable to repent, goes unforgiven to his doom, Alonso is graced with both the will to confess his evil and Prospero's ultimate pardon. Similarly, the regicidal plotting of *The Tempest*'s

Antonio and Sebastian recapitulates but reconfigures Macbeth's private conversations with Banquo. Alone, having listened to Macbeth, Banquo wonders whether the witches might also "set [him] up in hope" (*Macbeth* 3.1.10). Similarly, Sebastian finds his ambition fired by a friend's treacherous example and tantalizing arguments. *The Tempest*'s "*Macbeth*" plot ends comically, as king-killing is thwarted by the appearance of magic Ariel. The spirit simply wakes up loyal lord Gonzalo, who rouses Alonso before his enemies can perform the crime.

The Tempest includes other backward-looking "quotations" of Shakespeare's earlier work. Towards its conclusion, Prospero's boasts of his magical achievements remind us of Shakespeare's prior dramatic successes. The elves of *A Midsummer Night's Dream*, the battles of the history plays, the storm of *King Lear*, and the fearsome ghosts of *Hamlet*, *Macbeth*, *Richard III*, and *Julius Caesar* are evoked in one of Prospero's last speeches (which Shakespeare adapted from Medea's boast in the seventh book of Ovid's *Metamorphoses*). There Prospero refers to "elves" that cavort by "moonshine," to "roaring war," to "dread rattling thunder," and to "graves" that "at [his] command/Have wak'd their sleepers." We may also hear Shakespeare's pun on his own name in Prospero's lines, "Jove's . . . oak/. . . Have I made *shake*, and by the *spurs* plucked up/The pine and cedar" (5.1.33-48, my emphasis). These lines, and the play, end with Shakespeare's renunciation of theatrical art. "[T]his rough magic," he has Prospero proclaim in act five, "I here abjure" (ll.50-51). From Stratford, Shakespeare would contribute to the writing of *Henry VIII* and *The Two Noble Kinsmen*, plays composed with his younger colleague John Fletcher. Both those plays—even, by some accounts, *The Winter's Tale*, which was wholly composed by Shakespeare—post-date *The Tempest*. Yet Prospero's lines were a harbinger of Shakespeare's withdrawal from the theater world. They predicted his coming departure.

Compelling though this allegorical reading is, of course, it lays bare only one thread of *The Tempest*'s complex tapestry. Deeply concerned with the relationships among author, nature, and art, the play also explores larger themes of hurt and forgiveness, of the mutual obligations of rulers and subjects, and of the wondrousness of new English encounters with unfamiliar lands and peoples.

To begin with the last: *The Tempest* is widely considered the only Shakespeare play to touch the shores of what was, to the Renaissance English, the New World. Prospero's island may lie in the Mediterranean, yet the storm-tossed mariners' ship is preserved in a "nook" somewhere near the "Bermoothes" (Bermudas, 1.2.229), West Atlantic islands whose name would have been known to readers of popular Jacobean travel writings. Those writings tended toward the fantastic, or at least the amazing. In the early sixteenth century, Thomas More had mocked the travelogue in his short work *Utopia*, which described the discovery of a strange, apparently ideal community whose Latin name meant, ironically, "Nowhere." Shakespeare echoes More's mockery of utopian travel dreams in Gonzalo's fanciful notion of the ideal "commonwealth" he would create on Prospero's island, free of "treason, felony,/Sword, pike, knife," and "gun" (2.1.148ff). (Gonzalo's musings are immediately followed by the drawn swords and attempted treason of two of his listeners, Antonio and Sebastian.) But Shakespeare's *Tempest* also honors authentic accounts of New World journeys. Some of those later travelers' tales spread rumors that the Bermudas in particular were haunted, a notion which persists to this day in tales of modern ships and planes lost in the Bermuda Triangle. However, the 1610 *Discovery of the Barmudas, Otherwise Called the Isle of Devils* told not just of spooky disappearances, but of the miraculous delivery of two vessels in the Bermudas' vicinity. In that pamphlet the sailor Sylvester Jourdain described his time with a Virginia Company fleet that left Plymouth, England, on June 2, 1609, for the newly founded Jamestown colony. Although most of the fleet sank in a storm, Jourdain's bark and one other ship grounded on the shores of the Bermudas, where the men found enough wood, fresh water, and food to sustain them through the winter and enable them to make repairs. The lucky sailors came successfully to Jamestown the following May, and from thence sailed back to England. Their story was an important source of *The Tempest*'s action and moral meaning. Jourdain's account moves from the sailors' apparent devastation to their actual redemption, a pattern retraced by *The Tempest*, wherein Prince Ferdinand's lost father King Alonso and, indeed, all the missing sailors are not sunk and drowned, but lost and found, subjected to a "sea change/Into something rich and strange" (1.2.401-02). Even Duke Prospero's unwilling twelve-year exile on the wild island is proven a blessing of sorts. It has been a time of penance, an occasion to school his stubborn heart to forgive his enemies and to practice the arts of governance he had neglected in Milan.

Yet such is the moral complexity of *The Tempest* that Prospero's strict rule of the island seems not just compensation for past neglect, but an occasion for his fresh sin. We see this paradox most clearly in Prospero's treatment of Caliban, the one character who is native to the island. Through the pair's master-slave relationship Shakespeare seems, at least to twenty-first century eyes, either to champion or expose Old World explorers' and settlers' oppressions and enslavements of the inhabitants of lands colonized by Europeans. Indeed, since 1950 some dramatic and novelistic adaptations of *The Tempest*, such as

Aimé Césaire's *Une Tempête* and George Lamming's *Water with Berries*, have criticized colonialism by transforming Caliban to an oppressed Caribbean islander and Prospero to an exploitative agent of empire. Many post-colonial critical discussions of the original *Tempest* have charged the play itself with complicity in a like grim seventeenth-century program of European imperialism. Yet, conversely, many late-twentieth-century productions of the play have shown us a visionary work critical of the growing European exploitation of New World peoples, through various dramaturgical choices described in this volume's section on the play's performance history. That directors have successfully staged the play as this kind of critique is due to the fact that *The Tempest*'s raw script discloses and generates doubts about colonialism, when carefully read. Imperial ambition is gently mocked in the play's dialogue, not least by Sebastian's reduction of Ancient Imperial Rome's founding hero to a mundane fellow called "widower Aeneas" (2.1.80).

CHARACTERS AND RELATIONSHIPS

In keeping with its critique of imperialism—or of domineering behavior—*The Tempest*'s language limits our approval for governor Prospero's treatment of the islanders, especially Caliban. Careful reading—or listening—shows us that although Prospero calls Caliban "beast" (4.1.140), the island native is a complex and suffering human being. Caliban's name, as some critics point out, is an anagram for "cannibal," but it is not "cannibal," nor does Caliban show any signs of the cannibalism seventeenth-century Europeans associated with New World natives. Instead, he eats "water with berries in it," "pig-nuts" (possibly acorns) and "filberts," and rock "scamels," whatever they are (1.2.334, 2.2.167-72). His expertise at harvesting island delicacies is crucial to Prospero, who has enlisted Caliban's services since his own arrival. Caliban's pig-nut-digging fingers will also prove useful to shipwrecked Stephano and Trinculo, who, like Prospero before them, exploit Caliban's knowledge and skills in their attempt to control the island. The actions of Stephano and Trinculo, who employ the servant-monster in their plot to murder Prospero and seize Miranda and the whole island "state" (3.2.6), parodies European exploitation of New World natives to gain land, natural resources, and silver and gold. Trinculo initially imagines taking Caliban to England and charging people "silver" to see him, since there, folk who "will not give a doit to relieve a lame beggar" will "lay out ten to see a dead Indian" (2.2.30ff).

Shakespeare's exposure of Prospero's oppressiveness is subtler. First treated, by Caliban's own account, as Prospero's cherished dependent, Caliban is now jailed in a cave and forced to carry wood. At first we may think these penalties deserved since, as Caliban freely admits, he once sought (in Prospero's words) "to violate/The honor" of Prospero's real child, Miranda (1.2.347-48). Yet the feral Caliban, we soon learn, was ignorant even of language until taught it by Miranda, and could not initially have understood the abstract concept of violation, nor the even more abstract word "honor," by which Prospero means Miranda's virginity. Thus the attempted rape seems more likely to have stemmed from untaught natural impulse than from considered evil, and even some Renaissance playgoers might have found its punishment excessive (if, for a father, understandable. Prospero's determination to guard his daughter from further wild erotic assault is made clear in act 4, not only by his lecture to Ferdinand but by his banning of Venus and Cupid from the young couple's wedding masque [4.1.14ff, 92ff]). It is true that the once-naïve Caliban has become considerably more intellectually sophisticated since the attempted rape, since he regrets its failure in politic terms: had it succeeded, he might have "peopled . . ./This isle with Calibans" and wrested control of it back from Prospero (1.2.350-51). But he has a credible claim, if not to Miranda, at least to the island. He was, after all, there first. His defiant statement, "This island's mine by Sycorax my mother" (1.2.331), is not quickly dismissable from the consideration of those respectful of lineal property rights, as modern audiences tend—and Jacobean audiences tended—to be. Caliban is apparently no mere savage animal, but—when sober—a wily intellectual adversary.

A hallmark of Prospero's character is his inability correctly to judge the characters of others. In the past he "[o]'er-priz'd" his false brother, Antonio, and he once calls quick Ariel "dull thing" (1.2.92, 285). It is in keeping with his limited perception that he does not fully understand Caliban. Our sense that he does not is heightened by Caliban's words about himself. Although Prospero thinks him a monster "on whose nature/Nurture can ne'er stick" (4.1.188-89), Caliban ultimately repents of having worshipped "dull fool" Stephano, and vows to be "wise" and "seek for grace" (5.1.296-98). Even before this well-reasoned promise, Caliban's humanity is made clear through his language. He is largely ruled by his belly—"I must eat my dinner" is his sixth line (1.2.330)—but he speaks blank verse (and sings). His poetry reveals his imaginative power. Indeed, it is through Caliban's rich descriptions that the magic island is most vividly presented to the audience's minds. Caliban knows of the "bogs, fens," and "flats" of the place, of the spirits who appear like "fire-brand[s] . . . in the dark," and of the "adders," "cloven-tongue[d]," who "hiss [him] into madness" (2.2.2, 6, 13-14).

The lines with which he calms the nervous Stephano and Trinculo are among the most evocative and poignant of the play:

Be not afeard, the isle is full of noises,
Sounds, and sweet airs, that give delight and hurt not.
Sometimes a thousand twangling instruments
Will hum about mine ears; and sometime voices,
That if I then had wak'd after long sleep,
Will make me sleep again, and then in dreaming,
The clouds methought would open, and show riches
Ready to drop upon me, that when I wak'd
I cried to dream again.

(3.2.135-43)

Angry, comforting, longing, lustful, murderous, awake to beauty, and able to dream, Caliban displays the puzzling mixture of darkness and light that is the core of humanness. Prospero calls him "devil" (4.1.188), but Prospero calls all his enemies devils (e.g., 3.3.36). He regards Caliban as mere "earth" (1.2.314), but of earth, the Bible told Shakespeare, all of us were made, and for earth (*adamah* in Hebrew) man was first named. Perhaps it is Prospero's glimpse of his own image in Caliban that provokes both the duke's harshness towards his slave and his late grudging confession concerning him: "This thing of darkness/I acknowledge mine" (5.1.275-76).

Prospero's harshness toward his daughter is trickier to fathom. In many performances of *The Tempest*, Prospero is gruff in his first long speech, commanding Miranda to listen quietly to the narrative in which he explains their presence on the island, a near-monologue whose 162-line length might tax the patience of any fifteen-year-old. (At its end the girl sleeps, and some stagings of the scene have wryly implied that it is not her father's magic but his long-windedness that produces this "good dullness" [1.2.185].) Later Prospero rebukes her harshly when she attempts to intercede with him for Ferdinand, whom he chides and then enchants. Just before the three clash, Prospero has told the audience, in an aside, that he must "uneasy make" Ferdinand's wooing, lest the prince's "too light winning" of his daughter "[m]ake the prize light" (1.2.452-53). This excuse, however, has failed to mollify some feminist scholars, who have objected to Prospero's treatment of his daughter as a possession he has created: a doll to dangle before lovestruck Prince Ferdinand so as to engineer a royal marriage, that through her Prospero's "issue/Should become kings of Naples," restoring Prospero's loss and then some (5.1.205-06). Feminist critics are also put off by Prospero's near-obsessive concern for Miranda's virginity, his characterization of his daughter as "Poor worm" (3.1.31), and the offensive words with which he rejects her plea for Ferdinand: "What, I say,/My foot my tutor?" (1.2.470). Actors often dilute Prospero's anger by saying these lines archly or with a wink to the audience. In a 2000 London Globe production, a woman—the director, Vanessa Redgrave—played Prospero, and thus deeply compromised his paternalism. A film and at least one stage *Tempest* have since gone farther down this road, making Prospero "Prospera," Miranda's mother. Yet paternal Prospero's fond tyranny over his daughter is necessary to his character. It comports with his driving impulse to control all the beings of the island—for it is not only crude Caliban but noble Ferdinand, gentle Ariel, and even the airy spirits of the wedding masque who taste his impatience and his ire.

Prospero's first speech tempts us to see his later quelling of both Miranda's mild complaints and Caliban's more serious revolt as compensation for past laxness. It is, after all, through strict rule of the island that he shows himself capable of the governance skills he lacked in Milan, where—in his self-flattering remembrance—he devoted himself to "the bettering of my mind," to his "state grew stranger," and made possible his brother's usurpation of his dukedom (1.2.89ff). To educated members of Shakespeare's seventeenth-century audience, Prospero's reference to his past failure bespoke his having abused the traditional Renaissance moral choice of a life that was active, contemplative, or voluptuous. We might see Prospero's immersion in his books as his choice of voluptuous pleasure—books do constitute that for some—or we might more charitably view Prospero's reading as a contemplative choice, since books spur reasoned thought and, at times, religious devotion. Still, Prospero, as Milan's governor, has erred in choosing anything but an active life, and has compounded his error by engaging in a suspect version of the contemplative one, whereby he pursues "secret studies" (1.2.77), or sorcery, rather than prayer and moral philosophy or devotional readings. A few early-modern aristocrats, notably the famed astrologer John Dee, dabbled in the occult and experimented with alchemy, but English moralists and the general public regarded these practices as devil's play: the sort of "black" art that *The Tempest* associates with the dead witch Sycorax, whose spells once imprisoned Ariel in a tree. Still, paradoxically, Jacobeans loved fictions of "white" magic practiced by good wizards in the golden worlds of romances. Thus Shakespeare's audience might well have accepted that Shakespeare's imaginary wizard Prospero, schooled by exile in a likewise imaginary locale, could turn his powers to the good, redeeming old errors by actively overseeing his strange realm with benevolent artistry. By those Jacobeans and by us, Prospero's governing work on the island might be seen as healthful penitence and the delayed performance of duty.

Still, as we've seen, Prospero's governorship has a dark side. Prospero wants, impossibly, to "new create" the very souls of his unwilling subjects (1.2.81). Caliban's sustained defiance and Sebastian's and Antonio's lack of repentance show that he cannot do so: that Providence, not Prospero, will guide events. Prospero's failures reveal the hubris of his effort to *be* Providence. The duke's frustrated attempts to control his island-subjects also mirror other characters' struggles to reconcile their longings for unfettered power with their obligations to accept the rule of higher authorities.

The Tempest's first scene exposes that tension. The play opens with a storm which, pounding the ship, levels the human hierarchy of king, lords, and sailors so that all look evenly powerless in the face of natural forces. "Where is the master, bos'n?," Antonio asks, meaning the captain. "Do you not hear him?," the Boatswain replies, meaning the wind. An argument ensues in which the lords insist on their authority, while the Boatswain points out that their rank counts for nothing in the present crisis. "Use your authority," he jeers. "[I]f you can command these elements to silence . . . we will not hand a rope more." In the end Gonzalo agrees, and warns his fellow lords, "our case is as theirs" (1.1.12-55). The men are not natural lords but natural subjects.

It is, of course, Ariel who, embodying nature as the storm, controls the men's experience here. He will do this again later in the play by charming them to sleep, waking them at will, and finally terrifying them with a spirit-lecture in act three. But *The Tempest*'s second scene shows that airy Ariel is himself controlled by Prospero. Though Ariel's elemental nature calls him to disembodiment, to "the air at freedom" (4.1.265), Prospero reveals Ariel's history of entrapment, first in the "cloven pine" where the witch Sycorax bound him (1.2.277), and now in the forms in which Prospero demands Ariel serve him to repay him for liberation from that wooden prison. Prospero's and Ariel's master-servant relationship is, of course, more complex than it initially appears. I have said that Prospero's relation to his "tricksy spirit" (5.1.226) represents the dramatist's own tricky task of harnessing nature to perform his art. Prospero's and Ariel's relation also suggest humans'—or Western humans'—general struggle to control the natural forces in their environment, and Ariel's grudging but ultimately willing submission to Prospero may appear to suggest the rightness of a hierarchy which makes humans the lords of nature. Yet at the play's end Ariel is free and Prospero's "charms are all o'erthrown" (Epi. 1). The fleetingness of Prospero's wizardly rule shows Shakespeare's skepticism about humankind's final authority over the natural world, as has the fearful tempest that began the play. The skepticism is grounded in an old description of the weakness of human sailors next to the strength of storm-master God. Psalm 107 reads, "For he commandeth and raiseth the stormie winde, and it lifteth up the waves thereof. [Sailors] mount up to the heaven, and descend to the deepe, so that their soule melteth for trouble. They are tossed to and fro, and stagger like a drunken man, and all their cunning is gone. Then they cry unto the Lord in their trouble, and he bringeth them out of their distresse. He turneth the storme to calme, so that the waves thereof are still. When they are quieted, they are glad, and he bringeth them unto the haven, where they would be" (verses 25-30, Geneva). Prospero employs Ariel both to imperil and to rescue the seamen in *The Tempest*. But the Bible-literate Jacobeans would have understood the powers of both Prospero and Ariel to be allowed and, finally, circumscribed by God.

Caliban is mere "earth" to Ariel's volatile mix of earth, water, fire, and air, but he, too, enacts the paradox of freedom qualified by bondage. Caliban angrily recalls the lost liberty of his first years on the island, in the time before Prospero's and Miranda's arrival. Now, he tells Prospero, "I am all the subjects that you have, / Which first was mine own king" (1.2.341-42). Yet, though he longs for release from the "hard rock" where Prospero has chained him (1.2.343), when escape presents itself Caliban proves unable to conceive of freedom except as an alternative, superior kind of confinement. Gone now is the vision of the absolute liberty of his solitary island years. When he is discovered by the shipwrecked butler Stephano, purveyor of "celestial liquor," Caliban's first instinct is to kneel and beg the domineering fellow to "be [his] god" (2.2.149). (This interplay may constitute Shakespeare's reference to Europeans' eagerness to exploit New World natives' weakness for alcohol, and certainly forms his wry joke about the enslaving power of drink.) Caliban's situation here is akin to that of Ariel, whose harsh confinement in the cloven pine Prospero has transformed, not yet to the "air at freedom," but to a more capacious servitude. Caliban imagines a similar progress when, drunkenly celebrating with his new friends Stephano and Trinculo, he sings to the absent Prospero, "'Ban, 'Ban, Ca-Caliban, / Has a new master, get a new man!" and adds, "freedom, high-day! High-day, freedom!" as a chorus (2.2.184-87).

Of course, events mock his choice of a new master. That Caliban mistakes the comically degenerate Stephano for a god shows his weak judgment. But nowhere does *The Tempest* condemn Caliban's—or any character's—choice to serve *someone*, nor does the play affirm any ideal of a person's liberation from all constraints. Although Prospero fails to note Caliban's transformation, we see the monster finally enlightened by the insight that there are moral distinctions among masters, that he has chosen badly, and, indeed, that *choice* of a master is possible. Throughout the play Caliban's greater enslavement has been to what Renaissance and classical thinkers called passions, meaning both strong emotions and carnal impulses. He initially heeds Prospero out of fear: "I must obey," he says, since Prospero's "art is of such pow'r/It would control my dam's god, Setebos" (1.2.372-373). Lust and, possibly, calculation have impelled him to assault Miranda, and now he follows Stephano for the rapture imparted by European liquor and for the angry dream of revenge against Prospero that Stephano pledges to make real. After their revenge scheme crashes on the rocks—more accurately, when it dumps the conspirators in a pool of "horse-piss" (4.1.199)—Caliban finds himself finally able to obey a superior (though imperfect) master, no longer out of fear, but by rational decision. "I'll be wise hereafter," he tells Prospero. "What a thrice double ass/Was I to take this drunkard for a god,/And worship this dull fool!" (5.1.296-98).

Prince Ferdinand is both Caliban's analogue and his opposite. Indeed, Prospero invites us to compare the two when he tells the love-struck Miranda, as she stares goggle-eyed at the prince, "To th' most of men this is a Caliban" (1.2.481). Shakespeare follows the scene wherein Caliban defects to Stephano's service with the one in which Ferdinand replaces Caliban as Prospero's log-bearer, and shows that, like the poor monster, who finds temporary liberation in serving Stephano, Ferdinand finds freedom in his new enslavement. Ferdinand's motive is not vengeful, but erotic. In the tradition of the Petrarchan poet, subdued by amorous desire for an idealized woman, Ferdinand describes how his love for Prospero's daughter converts thralldom to bliss. "This my mean task," he says, "Would be as heavy to me as odious, but/The mistress which I serve quickens what's dead,/And makes my labors pleasures" (3.1.4-7). A love-slave, he tells Miranda, "for your sake/Am I this patient log-man" (3.1.67). Ferdinand, of course, is civil while Caliban is not, and Shakespeare would have us see that his civility helps him take pleasure in what for Caliban was drudgery. Ferdinand is content to enjoy platonic conversation with Miranda and, unlike lustful Caliban, to honor what Prospero calls Miranda's "virgin knot" (4.1.15). Rationally understanding that his liberation will come in time, he finds joy in service, and bears out the adage sung (ironically) by drunken Stephano: "Thought is free" (3.2.123). Still, Ferdinand's ultimate goal is disturbingly similar to Caliban's earlier one. He is smitten by Miranda's appearance before his "ears have . . . drunk a hundred words/Of [her] tongue's uttering" (to adapt *Romeo and Juliet*'s poetry once more [*RJ* 2.2.58-59]). That fact confirms that, like the monster, he is chiefly driven by carnal desire for Miranda, although, as a product of Prospero's own culture, he knows the principles of civility and honors the restraining rituals that will enable him to win her. Audiences—and

Miranda—may hope, but not know, that Ferdinand's moral education will impel him to continue to treat her well once time tempers eros—when, in Auden's bittersweet words, Miranda is as "familiar" to Ferdinand "as a stocking," and is herself no longer "lovesick" (p. 133). Right now, of course, it works in Ferdinand's favor that he, unlike poor Caliban, is "honor'd with/A human shape" and thus able to make Miranda "sig[h] for" him (1.2.283–84, 447)—though, of course, as her father points out, she hasn't seen many non-monster-men yet.

When Miranda is finally confronted with the other Europeans, her naïve worshipfulness recapitulates Caliban's foolish veneration of Stephano, and casts our backward doubt on her and Ferdinand's mutual romantic idolatry of one another. "How many goodly creatures are there here!" she gushes, describing a group that includes the murderous knaves Antonio and Sebastian and sinful old King Alonso. "O brave new world . . . !" "'Tis new to thee," her father drily responds (5.1.182-84). Unlike Ferdinand and Miranda, charmed and charming young lovers, Prospero knows that worship and even ultimate trust are improperly bestowed on anything human. Doubtless the short wedding masque of act four and the longer presentation of Ferdinand's and Miranda's betrothal complimented Princess Elizabeth and her groom, the Elector Palatine, when *The Tempest* was played at court in 1613. But to compliment is not always to flatter. The play includes but is not a formal masque, in which Jacobean playwrights conventionally combined moral advice with praise for the virtues of the aristocratic or royal patrons who were watching. (Significantly, since *The Tempest*'s own internal masque is aborted, all such praise is marred.) By its many exposures of misplaced reverence—from the storm-tossed travelers' reliance first on their own authority and then on that of their helpless captain, to Caliban's foolish worship of Stephano, to the awed admiration Miranda bestows on the guilty Italians—Shakespeare's play reminds its audience of the dangers of confusing humans with God.

BONDAGE AND LIBERTY

Prospero knows human moral limitations from his own experience of exile and thralldom. For the play makes plain that Prospero, like Caliban, is a prisoner. First self-fettered to books in his Milanese cell, he is now trapped not only on the island but in his own vengeful anger towards Antonio and Alonso. His freedom arrives when, like that "thing of darkness," Caliban, he can master his emotion with reason. "[W]ith my nobler reason, 'gainst my fury/Do I take part," he finally decides, once the noblemen have been shamed and imprisoned by Ariel (5.1.26-27). The line explains the necessary paradox of Prospero's harshness. His strictness has been needed by the islanders, some of whom would have raped or murdered without it. But Prospero's rigor has also proven his moral flaw. The play's insistence on his—and all humans'—imperfection prevents us from justifying his rigor in ideological terms: that is, from attributing his occasionally domineering behavior to the righteousness of the Christian European ruler. Prospero's pride and wrath are human sin. He knows it, or comes to know it over the course of the play.

Prospero's opening speech introduces us to his propensity for wrath. Speaking to Miranda, he puzzlingly alternates terms of endearment ("my dear one," "cherubin") with testy outbursts ("Dost thou attend me?" "Thou attend'st not!" [1.2.17, 152; 78, 87]). Individual performances of the play sometimes justify Prospero's chiding with a bored, teenage gum- (or scamel?-) chewing Miranda whose attention visibly wanders during her father's long explanation of how the pair of them came to be on the island, an understandable directorial choice, as noted before. Still, the script offers little evidence that Miranda is not listening raptly to the story, for whose unfolding she claims to have begged. "Your tale, sir, would cure deafness," she says now (1.2.106). In fact, Prospero's anger during their dialogue erupts not at anything Miranda does, but at a memory that plagues his own "beating mind" (4.1.163). His guilt and embarrassment over his loss of his dukedom are clear in his self-castigating words, as he confesses that as duke, he, "poor man," "to [his] state grew stranger" (1.2.109, 76). But his emotion bursts forth most strongly whenever he names the perpetrator of his deepest injury: his treacherous brother, Antonio, who usurped his dukedom with the support of King Alonso of Naples. "Thy false uncle—dost thou attend me?," "[H]e was/The ivy which had hid my princely trunk,/And suck'd my verdure out on't. Thou attends not!" "Hence his ambition growing—/Dost thou hear?" (1.2.77ff). Prospero has intended this long speech as proof that his magical storm-attack on King Alonso's ship, which bears Antonio, was done "in care of" his daughter, but the anger which boils over during his tale-telling hints at a darker motivation: revenge. This opening near-monologue complicates his character, so that even before we hear Caliban's complaints against him, we cannot regard Prospero as a wholly benevolent *white* magician (my word-play is intentional). Instead, he seems a spiritually wounded man grappling with seething resentment. Were *The Tempest* a tragedy rather than a romance, Prospero's task would be to stoke rather than to conquer that resentment. But Prospero isn't Hamlet. He inhabits a play that, like others of its romance genre, advances toward a final scene in which those thought dead are joyously recovered, and old wounds are not avenged but forgiven. Thus Prospero's ability to bless his enemies is crucial to the play's comic outcome. Forgiveness may not be integral to his recovery of his dukedom, but it is necessary to his recovery of himself.

Forgiveness is also necessary to Alonso's, Antonio's, and Sebastian's self-recovery, a possibility that is opened to them by Ariel but fully embraced only by Alonso. Ariel chides the "three men of sin," threatening them with eternal suffering unless they undergo "heart's sorrow" and live "a clear life ensuing" (3.3.81-82). Alonso's contrition follows immediately. He calls his guilt "monstrous! monstrous!" and admits that Ariel's accusations have "base[d] his trespass" against Prospero (3.3.95ff). His awakened conscience prompts thoughts of suicide, from which Prospero's forgiveness and the restoration of his son redeem him. Shakespeare frames Prospero's mercy in terms which stress not only the self-knowledge but the self-possession it imparts to mercy's recipients. "[T]hey shall be themselves," Prospero tells Ariel (5.1.32). Gonzalo later exults that all the men have "found [them]selves" on the "poor isle; . . ./When no man was his own" (5.1.210-13).

As Ariel has directed, "heart's sorrow" is the inescapable route to both the ability to forgive and the repentance that enables the receipt of forgiveness. In this play more than any other, Shakespeare relies on the precepts of the sixteenth-century French moral philosopher Montaigne to dramatize the progress of mercy. Montaigne wrote of the necessity to "insinuate [ourselves] into [others'] places" in order to see our own darkness reflected in others' pain and sinfulness" (1:243). Imaginative empathy breeds compassion; compassion breeds repentance and forgiveness. Thus Alonso's pain at the perceived loss of his son Ferdinand is the "heart's sorrow" that enables him vicariously to feel the pain he caused Prospero, and that empathy prompts his penitence and his pledge to live a "clear life ensuing."

Prospero finds empathy more difficult. Early in the play, Miranda demonstrates her greater ability to feel others' suffering. Of the shipwrecked sailors, she laments, "O! I have suffered/With those that I saw suffer," and she begs her father to allay the tormenting storm (1.2.5-6). Later, Ariel's intercession will be needed to motivate Prospero's pity for his enemies, who are now frightened and confined in a grove. He does this by sketching word-images of their pain and fear, laying stress on how Gonzalo's "tears run down his beard like winter's drops/ From eaves of reeds" (5.1.16-17). Underlying Ariel's speech is Montaigne's confession, "There is nothing sooner moveth teares in me, than to see others weepe" (2:119). To witness sorrow is to risk compassion. "[I]f you now beheld them," Ariel tells Prospero, "your affections would become tender" (5.1.18-19). His plea shames the wizard, who responds,

> Hast thou, which art but air, a touch, a feeling
> Of their afflictions, and shall not myself,
> One of their kind, that relish all as sharply
> Passion as they, be kindlier mov'd than thou art?
>
> 5.1.21-24

The dialogue's emphasis on the power of spectacle and verse to stimulate compassion strongly argues for the deep moral power of theater, which works hearts and minds. Fantastic Ariel first appears costumed "*like a harpy*" (s.d. 3.3.53) to chide the "men of sin" and stimulate their remorse. He then makes Prospero see his pitiful enemies' "wrack" in his mind (like the Chorus in Shakespeare's famously metatheatrical *Henry V*, who tells the Globe audience to "eche out" Henry's soldiers's condition "with [their] mind[s]" [3.Cho.35]). A catalyst for both repentance and compassion, Ariel is a "comforter" (5.1.58), which is what Christ calls the intercessory Holy Spirit that interprets sinners' groans and sighs (John 14:26, Ro. 8:26). "Comforter" is also a word used in *The Tempest* to describe dreamful sleep (2.1.196), a metaphor for playgoing which Shakespeare loved all his life, and to which he returns in *The Tempest*'s fourth act: "We are such stuff/As dreams are made on, and our little life/Is rounded with a sleep" (4.1.156-58). Unlike the degrading and delusory "comfort" of Stephano's wine-bottle (2.2.45, 55), which leads only to drunken vainglory, the comfort afforded by theatrical "dream" is a holy balm that heals human resentment, by giving watching and listening minds a means to sympathize with others' misfortunes. Ariel, here analogous to tragicomic drama itself, is the instrument that produces this human harmony.

But not necessarily. Forgiveness is a choice, and nowhere does *The Tempest* suggest that mercy, even when assisted by the compassionate imagination, is something easily bestowed. Prospero "relish[es]" passion "sharply" even as he struggles to acknowledge the like sharp pains of his foes. His lines to Ariel express the inner struggle between vicious and virtuous impulses that Montaigne saw as the defining human conflict. The lines' revelation of that struggle—of the fact that forgiveness is hard—also helps us understand the imperfect nature of the pardon Prospero will finally grant his enemies. Forgiveness is a difficult alchemy, achieved by degrees. Thus in the play's last scene Prospero is charitable to Alonso, but less so, as we have seen, to Caliban, as well as to the man whose betrayal embittered him most and longest: his brother, Antonio. "For you, most wicked sir, whom to call brother/ Would even infect my mouth, I do forgive/Thy rankest fault," he tells Antonio (5.1.130-32). Antonio, for his part, seems uninterested in Prospero's friendship, and less regenerate than Caliban. The last scene presents him not kneeling, like Alonso, in repentance, but scheming, like Trinculo, to display Caliban to curious Europeans for money. The end of *The Tempest* is something like its beginning. At start and finish the play stresses the universality of human imperfection, and the consequent general need for divine mercy. Even Prospero—though he is better than most of the play's Europeans—is no Christ.

That he is not a mask of God is made clear not only by his enduring anger towards Antonio but by the play's early juxtaposition of a first scene staging his potency and a second one showing his human weaknesses. When, in scene one, the Boatswain jeers that Gonzalo, the "councillor," cannot calm the storm that tosses them (1.1.21), the bitter jest invokes not only the psalm's description of God's overlordship but the image of the counselor who controlled the waves of Galilee (Luke 8:22-25). Superficially, the reference implies a correspondence between Christ and the sublunary master of *this* storm, Prospero. But the second scene mocks that analogy by dramatizing the distance between Prospero and Christ, showing through Prospero's narrative his past moral failures and dramatizing his present lack of patience (with Miranda), lack of compassion (for the sailors), and lack of humility ("Thy father was . . . [a] prince of power" is the proud claim with which Prospero launches his tale [1.2.54-55]). Shakespeare's careful depiction of his protagonist's own moral flaws makes sense of Prospero's plea to the audience in the epilogue. That plea is not only a request for release from the "magic island" the stage has been. It is also a request for forgiveness, of which even Prospero–and, by implication, even Shakespeare–stands in need.

WATER-WORDS AND SEA CHANGES

Something should be said of the great system of water and nautical images that flows through the play, and that helps Prospero express his last request. The play progresses from the stage enactment of a storm at sea, where sailors pray for deliverance, to Prospero's description of the literal sea-journey that brought him and Miranda to the island twelve years before, in a "rotten carcass of a butt," exposed to sea and wind (1.2.146). Ariel then sings of the "sea-change" undergone by King Alonso: "Full fadom [fathom] five thy father lies . . ./ Of his bones are coral made:/Those are pearls that were his eyes" (1.2.397ff). Here the transforming action of flowing water is evoked to suggest the spiritual change sea-sufferings will effect in the king, if not in the other sea-swallowed men, Antonio and Sebastian, who remain, to borrow Sebastian's phrase, unrepentant "standing water" (2.1.221). Stephano's celestial liquor is a false water that clouds his and Caliban's thinking; later, the "foul lake" into which Ariel leads them provides a salutary dunking that sobers Caliban's judgment (4.1.183). Likewise, Prospero's highborn enemies' gradual self-knowledge approaches like the sea: "Their understanding/Begins to swell, and the . . . tide/Will shortly fill the reasonable [shores]" (5.1.79-81). Miranda and Ferdinand are more pleasurably immersed in the self-dissolving experience of romantic attraction, which Prospero likens to the storm itself. When Alonso asks him when he "lost [his] daughter," Prospero enigmatically responds, "In this last tempest" (5.1.153). Most profoundly, salt water is both the symbol and the means of the shame which precipitates repentance and forgiveness. Prospero recalls having "deck'd the sea with drops full salt"—tears—on his journey to the island (1.2.155), and Alonso longs to drown himself in despair over his loss of Ferdinand and to expiate his guilt for betraying Prospero. Although Gonzalo is innocent of that betrayal, still, confined in the island grove, "his tears run down his beard like winter's drops," and Ariel's description of Gonzalo's weeping helps move Prospero to sympathy (5.1.16ff). Finally, the epilogue returns us to the dangerous seafaring of the play's first scene, as Prospero uses the threat of shipwreck to figure his woeful condition without forgiveness, born of—and borne by—prayer.

> Gentle breath of yours my sails
> Must fill, or else my project fails,
> Which was to please. Now I want
> Spirits to enforce, art to enchant,
> And my ending is despair,
> Unless I be reliev'd by prayer,
> Which pierces so, that it assaults,
> Mercy itself, and frees all faults.
>> As you from crimes would pardon'd be,
>> Let your indulgence set me free.
>   (Epi. 11-20)

This last speech joins nautical imagery to a reference to the pre-Reformation Catholic practice by which the living purchased indulgences to limit the Purgatorial sufferings of the dead. Thus in the end Prospero, who has vowed that once back in Milan "every third thought shall be [his] grave" (5.1.312), steers *The Tempest*'s light comic mood toward a more sober reflectiveness, invoking ultimate endings and the mutual assistance we each require to pass from this life with grace.

It's pretty to think of Shakespeare playing the role of Prospero just once, prior to his final retirement. No external evidence suggests that he did. Yet, even so, Prospero is clearly as much a figure of the playwright as he is, at the end, an abstract of all humankind. Only a few years after this play's creation Shakespeare died of causes unknown to us. We may wonder whether weakness or illness gave him the intimations of his own mortality that the play's ending reflects. More happily, we may find repeated in Prospero's final words and actions *The Tempest*'s overwhelming emphasis on even late life's ever-possible renewal through imaginative compassion, assisted by art. In Prospero's last scenes, Shakespeare uses his own stagecraft to convey the experience of loss, even that of the necessary personal loss, through relinquishment, of art itself. Yet Prospero/Shakespeare does not finally destroy his magic book, but drowns it, and buries his broken staff "fadoms" deep (5.1.55): the sea measure. And, as the play has shown us, a thing plunged fathoms deep does not die, but suffers a sea-change into something rich and strange.

So *The Tempest* lives on, not only in contemporary post-colonial stagings, but in radical adaptations across nations and cultures to other art forms, from poetry to plays, from fiction to film. Examples of twentieth-century poems honoring *The Tempest* include—along with Auden's *The Sea and the Mirror*—parts of T. S. Eliot's *The Waste Land*, expatriate American Modernist H. D.'s "The Tempest," and contemporary poet Robin Kirkpatrick's "After Prospero." The play's dramatic adaptations began during the Restoration, with William Davenant and John Dryden's creation of *The Enchanted Island*. Three hundred years later, Aimé Césaire's *Une Tempête* was staged on the Caribbean island of Martinique. In Tokyo in 2001, performance artist Chin Woon Ping gave *The Tempest* a wry feminist response, appearing in her *Psycho Wracks* as the witch Sycorax dressed in a Western man's business suit and lecturing her audience on global history. A host of wildly distinct *Tempest*-inspired novels includes George Lamming's aforementioned post-colonial complaint, *Water with Berries* (1971), Rachel Ingall's 1983 *Mrs. Caliban*, Grace Tiffany's *Ariel* (2005), and Briton Aldous Huxley's 1932 futurist classic, *Brave New World*. Huxley's science-fiction Shakespeare may have influenced the American film director Fred Wilcox, whose 1956 *Forbidden Planet* shot *The Tempest*'s characters into outer space. Recent decades have given birth to new movie adaptations of the work, like American Paul Mazursky's comic *Tempest* (1982), in which Prospero (John Cassavetes) is a Manhattan architect self-exiled to a Greek island with his disaffected teenaged daughter (Molly Ringwald) and a lusty Greek goatherd named "Kalibanos" (Raúl Júlia). *Prospero's Books*, a surreal film directed nine years later by Briton Paul

Greenaway, substitutes gorgeous images for most of Shakespeare's dialogue. What remains is said by sweet-voiced nonagenarian John Gielgud, who speaks not only Prospero's lines but everyone else's, too.

Productions of Shakespeare's actual play, of course, continue apace, forging new meanings from *The Tempest's* old themes of imagination's deft transmutations of pain to forgiveness, of bondage to liberation. We and generations yet unborn inherit Prospero's rich, strange legacy.

Grace Tiffany

PERFORMANCE HISTORY

ORIGINAL CONDITIONS OF PRODUCTION

THE DATE of *The Tempest's* first performance is not known. The first staging on record, noted in the Revels Office accounts of Shakespeare's own time, occurred in 1611 at Whitehall before King James, most likely in the royal Banqueting House. A second command performance in May, 1613, in honor of the princess Elizabeth's marriage to Frederick, the Elector Palatine (alluded to in the above introduction), suggests that the monarch and his family liked the play. It is easy to see why. Certainly in its act four presentation of winged goddesses followed by dancing yokels, *The Tempest* offered instances of the stately and the antic masque, both of which kinds of spectacle enchanted the Stuarts. (Just as *The Tempest's* masque gave Shakespeare's lower-class audience members a taste of aristocratic entertainments, masques featuring rural rustics gave aristocrats a sense of the commoners' delights.) The fact that the Revels accounts mark only two royal performances to prove the play's early theatrical existence might prompt us to think it was made primarily for a lordly audience, and thus structured for the halls at various court venues. But in fact, *The Tempest* was written for everyone. Theater historians almost unanimously agree that the play was designed to showcase—or be showcased by—Blackfriars, The King's Men's indoor, roofed public playhouse north of the Thames, which had only recently opened for business. After all, Blackfriars boasted pulleys and ropes to facilitate flying spirits and goddesses. And nothing suggests that *The Tempest* was not also performed at the open-air Globe in its early years, particularly in summer.[1] The Blackfriars musicians were "already famous," in Christine Dymkowski's words (5), and the play's reliance on music suggests Shakespeare had these artists' assistance in mind, particularly when he created the tuneful Ariel. And, as Andrew Gurr notes, the balcony at the Globe was easily converted into a "music room" (*The Shakespeare Company*, 37), so the Blackfriars consort could supply *The Tempest's* players as easily there, on the south side of Thames, as they could at Blackfriars.

The Tempest's early incarnations may then be imagined as taking place on the wooden stage of the Globe or Blackfriars, where the naked scaffold stood for what was truly a "bare island" (Epi.8). Early Modern theater audiences were accustomed to observing plays' invisible geographical settings with an inward eye, and to listening intently to dialogue to "see" where characters were. (As noted in this volume's introduction, Shakespeare sports in *The Tempest* with the stage-island's variant appearances in different minds. To some it's a "desert," to others "lush," "lusty," and "green" [2.1.35, 53–54].) The sparseness of the scene focused eyes on key props: Prospero's book, robe, and staff; the log toted by Ferdinand; the would-be regicides' drawn swords; Stephano's bottle. The play's most elaborate Jacobean prop was a table on which was glued false food of wood or plaster, to be flipped over quickly by an actor in order to make Prospero's enemies' spirit-banquet disappear (s.d. 3.3.53).

At Blackfriars as well as at the Globe, actors entered and exited through two doors at the rear of the thrust stage. Between these doors was a curtained discovery space with its own off-stage entrance, used when Prospero drew the curtain to reveal Ferdinand and Miranda inside playing chess in the play's last scene (s.d. 5.1.172). (Miranda, of course, was played by a boy, as were all female characters during this period.) We know not only the manner of entries and exits, but something of some of Shakespeare's actors' costumes and face-paint. Prospero, who was probably played by lead actor Richard Burbage, most likely wore a robe stitched with arcane cabalistic symbols (Dymkowsi, 118). The actor who played earthy Caliban had his face and arms smirched with umber, a convention for stage devils, who in England were already starting to be conflated, in proto-racist fashion, with stage-Moors, or North Africans.[2] (Audiences would have noted that Caliban's mother was from Argier, or Algiers.) Ariel's visual differences were registered in sound and costume rather than by a radically distinct way of appearing and disappearing. Music played amply on Shakespeare's stage to mark Ariel's stage entrances, but like Caliban and all the play's other characters (save the flying spirits in the masque), Ariel did not fly, but walked (or ran) through one of two doorways at the rear of the thrust stage (though more gracefully than Caliban would have come and gone, of course). An exception occurred when Ariel briefly appeared to Prospero's enemies as a harpy, whose costume both Gurr and Gabriel Egan suppose was "a kind of 'car' into which the actor was strapped and then lowered over the [vanishing banquet] table in a prone position" (Egan, 65). "*Enter Ariel invisible,*" the First Folio's initial stage direction concerning Ariel, is a puzzler, but it's been shown that the first Ariel, a boy named John Rice, feigned invisibility in a "close-fitting" sea-nymph outfit replete with a "collection of aquatic adornments," like shells (Egan, 70). The harpy-harness fitted easily over the sea-shape, requiring no costume change for the disappearing banquet scene (*The Tempest* 3.3).

That scene, like that of the shipwreck in the play's loud opening, called for thunder. This noise was supplied by loud drumming and by bowling balls rolled in a metal trough in the theater's upper gallery, an early example of the extension of a play's fictive location into the house itself. Although artists in ensuing centuries—and Victorian theater directors—would delight in visually presenting every detail of a storm-tossed ship shaken by waves and thunderbolts, Shakespeare's players enacted the storm through off-stage sounds and choreographed on-stage staggers. Still far in the future was the convention of variable lighting, which would have cast the play's audience in shadow during the opening storm, and also allowed for darkness, lit only by torches, on the stage itself. Plays at the Globe were performed in broad daylight, and those at Blackfriars, while staged at night, used uniform lighting (mostly by candles) for playing and seating areas. Thus audience members could see each other as well as the players.

At all playing venues–even the pricier and presumably higher-toned Blackfriars, and palaces—Renaissance audiences were rowdy compared to us, but not nearly as riotous and criminal as the anti-theatrical moralists of the day claimed.[3] Pickpockets circulated in all

Fig. 5. Victorian artist Walter Crane's rendition of Shakespeare's storm, from "Eight Illustrations to Shakespeare's *Tempest*" (1894).

crowds in Shakespeare's day, but, as Gurr observes, only "one pick-pocket in seven of those convicted at the Middlesex sessions was caught at a playhouse" (*The Shakespearean Stage,* 224): a modest pro-portion. The most obnoxious behavior was exhibited, not by thieves or lower-class Londoners who paid a penny to sit in the yard, but by the "gallants" (the disdainful word appears frequently in the writings of playwrights themselves) who sat in high-priced boxes or even on the stage, cracking nuts loudly and distracting other patrons from the performances.[4] Shakespeare's *A Midsummer Night's Dream* mocks the habit of such upper-class watchers' rude interpolations into the dia-logue (*MND* 5.1). Even the early-modern moralists complained not only of the circulation of thieves and prostitutes in the Globe's yard, but that at all public playing sites "you shall see such heaving, and shoving, such itching and shouldering [of well-dressed young men], to sit by women; such care for their garments, that they be not trod on . . . such ticking, such toying . . . that it is a right comedie." Thus vary-ing degrees of audience concentration were focused on the Jacobean *Tempest,* though it is likely that the play's rapid pace, spectacular effects, and—of course—ear-catching poetry held most folks' attention.

PRODUCTIONS OF THE TEMPEST FROM THE RESTORATION THROUGH THE EARLY TWENTIETH CENTURY

The Tempest remained a popular romance in England–essentially un-changed in dialogue, though its musical component grew—through the second, third, and fourth decades of the seventeenth century, until the mid-century Interregnum put a halt to all plays. When English theaters reopened in 1660 after the parliament-imposed interruption, however, Shakespeare's play was soon supplanted by *The Enchanted Island* (1667), the adaptation by John Dryden and William Davenant which substituted newer poetry and nautical language and a great number of visual effects for much of the play's original dialogue. *The Enchanted Island*'s Restoration dialogue implied a connection between Prospero's usurping brother Antonio and Oliver Cromwell, and be-tween Prospero himself and Charles II. However, the *Island*'s more famous alterations of Shakespeare were not politically minded but spectacular. Instead of Shakespeare's bare, thrust island-scaffold, a prosce-nium stage, initially hidden by a curtain, was used for the new comedy. As the orchestra played the curtain rose to reveal an elaborate moving frontispiece: "a thick Cloudy Sky, a very Rocky Coast, and a Tempes-tuous Sea in perpetual Agitation. This Tempest . . . has many dreadful objects in it, as several Spirits in horrid shapes flying down amongst the

Sailors, then rising and crossing in the Air. And when the Ship is sinking, the whole House is darken'd, and a shower of Fire falls upon 'em. This is accompanied with Lightning, and several Claps of Thunder." The dialogue among storm-tossed sailors and noblemen was greatly reduced, indeed drowned out by sound, when they appeared. This expansion of spectacle at the expense of dialogue was a hallmark of the entire adaptation. In *The Enchanted Island's* later Restoration and early eighteenth-century productions "one triumph of spectacular staging succeeded another, but the text throughout" was "severely shortened," as Stanley Wells writes (349). Audience attention was directed elsewhere. Thomas Shadwell, producing the Dryden-Davenant version at Dorset Gardens in 1674, included an Ariel who flew in from the sun, a "chorus of devils," and "a ballet of winds." The music of the famed composer Henry Purcell was added to Shadwell's London production in 1695. Samuel Pepys, the inveterate Restoration playgoer, wrote rapturously of the dances and "curious . . . Musique" in *Island* (8:521–22).

Shakespeare's actual play did not disappear entirely from view during the Restoration and eighteenth century, but even on the rare occasions when it was staged it lay "buried well beneath layers of immediate appeal," to quote Katherine Scheil. These layers included "masques" (more of them), "songs, flyings, and dancing" (64). Stage splendor was the taste of the age, and ocular and auditory pleasures were enhanced by the fact that after 1660, real women rather than boys played the roles of Miranda and of numerous singing, dancing spirits. As Wells observes, "Shakespeare was being translated into a different medium from that in which he wrote: drama was replaced by spectacular mime; the play came close to the condition of a ballet" (349).

Not until 1757 did *The Tempest* regain popularity on British stages (including those in America). It did so thanks to the great actor and theater impresario David Garrick, who restored most of Shakespeare's original dialogue to the play and jettisoned newer lines. Still, the play had suffered a sea-change. A curious feature of the Restoration adaptation that also marked eighteenth-century *Tempest* productions was the diminishment of Caliban, on whom much of the comedy centered for Shakespeare's audience, as it does for us. Dryden and Davenant had added to their play's cast of characters one "*Hippolito*, one that never saw Woman, right heir of the Dukedom of *Mantua*," an island "natural" whose presence meant Caliban could no longer "signify humanity in a state of nature," as Alden T. and Virginia Mason Vaughan have observed. The Vaughans attribute the reduction of Caliban to the age's taste for "manners and artificial follies" rather than rough, lumbering clownishness (178–79). With Garrick's restoration, Caliban moved closer back to the foreground, but performance notes of Garrick's and others' productions suggest that the nuances of his character were not realized. Garrick's Caliban was directed to speak always with a "rough, malignant costiveness of expression," and in 1789, John Philip Kemble cut his most poignant lines (which end "in dreaming,/The clouds methought would open, and show riches/Ready to drop upon me, that when I wak'd/I cried to dream again" [3.2.140-43]) so as not to complicate his crudeness and engender audience sympathy for him (Dymkowski, 50, 254n122-30).

The thoroughly crude Caliban persisted into the early nineteenth century, provoking complaints from Romanticists who found depth in the suffering character as Shakespeare had written him. James Boaden criticized the actor John Emery's Caliban not only for speaking with a Yorkshire accent but for lacking "poetry." "Caliban is not a vulgar creation," Boaden wrote (qtd. in Vaughan, 179). But in 1838, when William Macready went beyond Garrick's *Tempest* rehabilitation to restore Shakespeare's full text, a more complex Caliban returned to the scaffold. George Bennett, a skilled tragic actor, achieved pathos in his portrayal of the "demi-devil" (5.1.272), not least by hurling himself at Prospero in a fury in his first scene, only to be thrown painfully to earth by the master's wizardly wand. In later Victorian productions Caliban's character stirred anthropological interest in directors and audiences who were intrigued by Darwin's theory. Two notable productions featured a Caliban who, rather than a demi-devil, seemed a missing link between animals and humans. At Stratford-upon-Avon in 1873, Frank Benson wore a "half-monkey, half-coco-nut" costume, carried a real fish in his mouth (*Mainly Players*, 97, 179), and "chattered, showed his teeth, and swung from branches," in the words of Herbert Coursen (148). Benson studied caged apes at the zoo to prepare for the role, and ended up so convincing that a stagehand reportedly asked, "What 'appens to monkey at t'end of show?" (qtd. Dymkowski, 53). The 1904 Caliban of Herbert Beerbohm Tree, as he appears in a famed painting, is a monkeyish humanoid, a "clawed, shaggy creature of pointed tooth and ear, clad in animal skins with a necklace of shells and bones" (Rundle, 53. See also color plate 3 of this edition). The choices of Benson, a star, and Tree, the manager of his London company, to play Caliban rather than (as had Garrick, Kemble, and Macready) Prospero indicates the near-tragic stature both accorded the part. Tree's Caliban possessed the final moments of the play, as, seated on a rock alone on the island, he reached out to Prospero's departing ship in a gesture of futile longing for a more civilized world. In these portrayals of Caliban, anthropological interests and Romantic reappraisals of this curious character were combined.

The late Victorian period saw the start of a departure from visually ornate and mechanically spectacular productions of *The Tempest*, or

Fig. 6. "Caliban on a Branch," or "Elf," depicts the monster as imagined by French painter Odilon Redon (1881).

Réunion des Musées Nationaux / Art Resource, NY

rather, of a bifurcation of performance styles into the fancier and the simpler (in J. C. Trewin's words, the "spangled or plain" [*Going*, 274]). Throughout the nineteenth century in both Britain and America, elaborate stage sets had predominated. (An 1854 production in New Orleans contained "fifteen . . . sets, including the rocky pass, the interior and exterior of the cave of Prospero, the deep glen, the dragon tree, and the crag-crowned beach" [Roppolo, 123], and in 1857 Charles Kean brought a working ship with a crew of thirty onto his stage.) By the turn of the century, plainer staging options had gradually become thinkable once more. Shakespeare's own career-long celebration of the audience's power and responsibility imaginatively to project spectacle onto the bare stage was echoed, surprisingly, by George Bernard Shaw—generally no fan of Shakespeare's romantic fantasies—who was moved by William Poel's retro-Jacobean staging of *The Tempest* in 1897 to say "the best scenery you can get will only destroy the illusion created by the poetry" (qtd. Coursen, 146). Poel—who simply let the "singer's gallery" represent the storm-tossed ship, rather than relying on painted flats or an elaborate stage construction—did make use of electric lighting, whose invention had made possible a great variety of "lightning" effects. Poel's stage, however, was relatively unadorned.

In the early twentieth century, such minimalist representations of the ship and of Prospero's island became commoner. The storm might be "a swaying lantern on a toppling mast" (Trewin, *Shakespeare*, 32), the island a plain stage marked by a large rock. Dymkowski describes twentieth-century stage designers' tendency to "create mood or meaning," largely through color, "rather than to re-create place" (116), a movement encouraged by the influential Harley Granville-Barker, whom some critics called a "Post-Impressionist" director (Bate and Jackson, 126), but whom later theater aficionados might have called a conceptualist. The modern taste for striking symbolism rather than naturalism in staging *The Tempest*, partly inaugurated by Granville-Barker's general approach to Shakespeare, would ultimately yield Peter Brook's Ariel (1968), who entered with a model of a ship on his head, and Tony Tripp's stage set of a disk of sand on which sat a sculpture of Prospero's head (Melbourne, 1990). A much earlier example of Granville-Barker's conceptualist influence was John Drinkwater's 1915 production in Birmingham, in which splashes of grey and blue for sea and island were reflected in Caliban's and Ariel's costumes and sharply contrasted with by the red outfits of the "intrusive court" (Dymkowski 117, 158).

Drinkwater's starkly modern, highly conceptual, color-based design presented a "plain" and modern contrast to Tree's "spangled" early-Edwardian production, which had featured a stage crowded with props and a rigged ship. But the two productions were alike in the sympathy they promoted for Caliban. Twentieth-century *Tempest*s would vary between such presentations of Caliban as an unfairly disenfranchised native and/or missing link and others which accentuated his fantastic and quasi-supernatural (demi-devilish) quality through costuming and makeup (like Harcourt Williams's 1930 production at the Old Vic, in which Caliban, with a face like a "Mongolian devil-mask," resembled an "ogre in a Japanese fairy-tale," according to theater critic Ivor Brown [qtd. Dymkowski, 158]). In 1926, Henry Bayton's Caliban was a scaly fish-man. Productions that made Caliban look like an earth- or fish-monster implied his complementarity with Ariel, his analogue and opposite. Wearing diaphanous, sometimes white-winged costumes, wielding power over lightning, and often soaring above the stage in wire-borne entries and exits, Ariel was air and fire to Caliban's earth and water.

Increasingly in the twentieth century Ariel was performed by women—the practice had become occasional by 1900—who presented an additional, gender counterpoint to ruggedly male Calibans. Such casting choices were not proto-feminist but retrograde, as, stripping Ariel of the androgyny he'd possessed when played by boys, they registered and promulgated stereotypical associations of delicacy with women and toughness with men. Thus it was in Miranda's enactments, not Ariel's, that twentieth-century audiences saw the greatest expansion of the role of women (or of woman) in the play. Nineteenth-century Mirandas had been delicate, flowery, submissive, and not of particular interest to audiences who worshipped (for example) Ellen Terry's fiery Lady Macbeth. However, in the first decades of the twentieth-century, while the soft Miranda remained in evidence on various stages, bolder, more assertive, and even rebellious Mirandas began to appear (or reappear). In 1926, director Henry Baynton's thoroughly modern Miranda was a flapper with a boyish haircut, long beads, and a short dress. This kind of Miranda talked louder, and more. Directors and adapters since the Restoration had transferred Miranda's angry speech to Caliban ("Abhorred slave . . . !" [1.2.351ff]) after Prospero's revelation of Caliban's rape attempt to Prospero himself, on the presumption that it was indecorous for Miranda even to be involved in this conversation. But beginning with Lena Ashwell's 1925 London production, that spirited speech went to the daughter, as Shakespeare—or his compositor—had

© Hulton–Deutsch Collection/CORBIS

Fig. 7. A delicate late-Victorian Miranda with her Ferdinand in an early twentieth-century production of *The Tempest* at London's Court Theater.

intended. Succeeding decades saw peevish Mirandas who chewed gum or yawned during Prospero's long first speech, tomboy Mirandas who climbed stage trees, and even randy Mirandas who literally jumped on their Prince Ferdinands when they appeared. In Pip Simmons's 1988 production, Miranda stayed mostly naked throughout the performance and engaged in frequent mock intercourse with various characters. The lustiness with which she said, "O brave new world/ That has such people in't!" (5.1.183–84) can be imagined.

How have stage Prosperos treated their daughters and other island subjects? Throughout *The Tempest*'s stage history the more common Prospero has been the compassionate, humane, and long-suffering duke, who expresses even his anger with righteous dignity, self-control, and confident authority. Dryden's and Davenant's Prospero was dignified in his righteous wrath toward his enemies, and consistently gentle with his daughter. The nineteenth-century Prosperos Kean, Kemble, and Macready spoke warmly and affectionately to their Mirandas throughout the initial long dialogue in scene two, delivering lines like "Dost thou hear?" in mildly chiding or concerned rather than vexed tones of voice. Frequently, father and daughter embraced, and in all these productions Prospero at some point physically guided his child around the stage (particularly when casting his sleeping spell on her). Kean and his contemporary the American actor-manager Augustin Daly blithely waved their wands to repel Caliban's threatening advances in the play's second scene, and forgave their enemies at play's end without pause, as though that outcome had been determined from the beginning.

THE LATER TEMPEST: EXPERIMENTATION AND RECOVERY

A very recent twist on–and, to an extent, reversion to—the homely Prospero has been the literally maternal Prospero, played by a woman, as in Vanessa Redgrave's 2000 London production at the Globe (mentioned in this volume's introduction). Redgrave seemed a "sweet eccentric" (O'Connor and Goodland, 1409). In 2003, Blair Brown's "Prospera," directed by Emily Mann in Princeton, New Jersey, was a tougher "woman of power," but still a decidedly warm and affectionate mom (Genzlinger). On stage, such gender experimentation with Prospero has been rare. Most directors have remained rightfully intrigued by Prospero as the protective father whom Shakespeare created, though the testy, often controlling side of this father was for some time lost in sentimental portrayals of the good eighteenth-century or Victorian papa. Post-Renaissance directors and actors began to recuperate the flawed Prospero in the late nineteenth century, around the same time Caliban's moral complexity became newly clear to them. Not surprisingly, nonplussed reviewers found one of the first "angry" Prosperos, that of Stephen Phillips in Frank Benson's 1891 Stratford production, surprisingly harsh. However, as the twentieth century arrived and progressed, testy Prosperos became, though never universal, much more common ("reflecting," in Dymkowski's words, "both the influence [on theatrical practices] of Freud in investigating psychological processes and of Stanislavsky in scrutinizing subtextual nuances" [17]). The most successful early-twentieth-century enactor of this more complex and variable Prospero was John Gielgud, who in several performances of the role between 1930 and 1974 played a world-weary exile, disappointed, dictatorial, and struggling against bitterness. Gielgud's "bare-chested despot" (so-called in a reference to Peter Brook's 1957 production [*Guardian*, 5/21/88]) moved painfully from harshness to hard-won magnanimity in the final scene. In productions by Clifford Williams and Peter Brook (Stratford-upon-Avon, 1963), John Hirsch (Canada, 1982), Braham Murray (Manchester, 1990), and Christopher Plummer (Canada, 2010) Prospero's recounting of the story of their exile to Miranda revealed an undercurrent of bad temper and anxiety, which, in the modern Mirandas, provoked defensiveness. The imperfect Prosperos of the twentieth century also shouted with real temper rather than paternal strictness at Ariel when reminding the spirit of the reasons for his servitude. In Ron Daniels's 1982 Stratford-upon-Avon production, it was Prospero (Derek Jacobi) rather than Ariel who seemed "moody" (1.2.244).

Nowhere has Prospero's sometimes ungovernable anger been more evident than in his interactions with Caliban. Productions imparting a racist or classist inflection to Prospero's dislike of his slave have been abundant since, beginning at mid-twentieth century, representations of Caliban as an oppressed man of color or disenfranchised peasant displaced the "missing link" Calibans of directors like Frank Benson and Herbert Beerbohm Tree. Canada Lee was the first black actor to play Caliban, in 1945 in New York. While the casting of Lee and, subsequently, other actors of color in the role of a monster had racist overtones—especially in 1940s America—still, as decades passed, many Calibans of color and their directors used the role to indict not the monster but the Europeans who had made him one. Richard Digby Day's 1972 production at Regent's Park featured Caliban as a New World "Mohican" Indian whose dignity was eroded by his contact with the Europeans' liquor (O'Connor and Goodland, 1361). In Jonathan Miller's 1970 production at London's Mermaid Theater, Caliban was an Uncle Tom, hiding his fear of Prospero's superior might by grinning and groveling. That in this production Ariel too was played

by a black actor suggested (albeit vaguely) another possible response—
that of spiritual transcendence of bondage and suffering—to white
European oppression. In 1978 in Milan, Giorgio Strehler's Caliban was
a strong, beautiful black man whose first appearance—one dark, sin-
ewy arm after another emerging from his dug-out cave—signaled his
dangerousness and his power, a paradoxical message that was both ra-
cially respectful and, in a way, racist. Indeed, mixed racial messages have
been a hallmark of many productions which have used Caliban (or
Ariel) and Prospero to signify a New World or African and European
encounter. In Gerald Freedman's 1979 Stratford, Connecticut, production, Caliban was a stereotype. He had rhythm and sang his rebellion-
ditty to a catchy jazz melody. In 1995 in Sydney, Australia, however,
Aboriginal actor Kevin Smith more successfully portrayed the anger
and degradation of a dispossessed people, strutting in a loincloth and
a Redcoat jacket, staggering from the effects of English alcohol, and
trying vainly to explain his island's musical traditions to his tin-eared
European companions. In George Wolfe's 1995 Central Park production, *Star Trek*'s famed Patrick Stewart, playing Prospero, doffed his hat
to Caliban in the last scene to apologize for his injustices. In Brisbane,
Australia, in 1999, director Simon Phillips gave a local habitation to *his*

© Robbie Jack/Corbis

Fig. 8. John Kani as Caliban
and Atandwa Kani as Ariel in
a 2009 joint Baxter Theatre/
Royal Shakespeare Company
production of *The Tempest* in
Cape Town, South Africa.

anti-imperialist vision of the play. Phillips's Prospero was a white eighteenth-century settler, bent on exploiting the wealth of a continent rather than a mere island. Ariel and (as in the 1995 Sydney production) Caliban were Aborigines.

Other modern productions have experimented with proletarian and even female Calibans. In Czech director Liviu Ciulei's 1981 production in Minneapolis, Jan Triska played the slave in droopy grey pants, a vest, and a cap, looking like a Slavic peasant or Russian serf. In a 1986 production of Aimé Césaire's adaptation of *The Tempest, Une Tempête*, in Avignon, Marilu Marini played the part in sackcloth. These two productions respectively reveal the occasional use of the play to expose and critique class and gender oppression. Yet no other form of "minority" casting has been as successful and widespread with regard to Caliban as color-casting.

However, in a kind of post–post-colonialist staging trend, many recent productions have downplayed or muted the play's racial conflicts, turning back toward traditional representations of Prospero as benevolent ruler and Caliban as fantastic freak. In Rupert Goold's 2006 Royal Shakespeare production in Ann Arbor, Michigan—famed for its unusual representation of the magic island as Arctic and freezing— the same Patrick Stewart who in 1995 had shamefacedly off-capped to a black, human Caliban now seemed unrepentant toward his slave, whose obnoxiousness justified Prospero's anger. In this production's last act, Stewart as Prospero sternly reprimanded the rapacious servant, a rascally fish-monster played by a white actor. Still, despite such reversions to traditional representations of the Prospero-Caliban relation, most modern performances of *The Tempest* still contain an element of post-colonial criticism, not because of conceptual direction, but because the play's own once-latent critique of colonialism is more immediately evident to twenty-first century audiences than it used to be, and less in need of a director's emphasis.

As though in recognition of this advance, many late-twentieth- and twenty-first-century productions have re-embraced the fantastical as opposed to the historical when they have come to stage this play. Ariel's eerie non-humanness has been reclaimed in productions like Rupert Goold's, mentioned above, which portrayed the sprite as an impassive, white-faced ghost in a dark, floor-length, vaguely military coat. (Playgoers at the Goold production might have been forgiven for briefly supposing they had stumbled into a performance of *Hamlet*.) The Ariel in Sam Mendes's 1993-94 Stratford-upon-Avon/London production was described by a critic as "robotic": urging Prospero to let his affections become tender, he delivered his line "Mine would, sir, were I human" in "efficient tones of service" rather than a voice

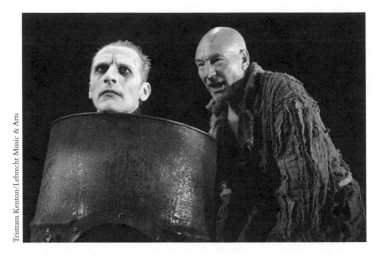

Tristram Kenton/Lebrecht Music & Arts

Fig. 9. Patrick Stewart as Prospero and Julian Bleach as Ariel in a Royal Shakespeare Company production of *The Tempest* in Ann Arbor, Michigan, in 2006.

suggesting human empathy (Holland, 203-04). Ariel's alien nature was more successfully expressed in Barbara Gaines's 2002 Chicago Shakespeare Repertory production. Gaines's Ariel flew much of the time, performing aerial flips (pun unintentional), and looked with detached fascination at all displays of human affection. In a brilliant piece of stage-work, in the middle of Ariel's sprightly pledge to Prospero to bring spirits for the masque "with mop and mow," Ariel caught sight of Miranda and Ferdinand snuggling on a swing and fell silent. Only after gazing at the betrothed pair intently for a moment did he turn back to Prospero and ask, "Do you love me, master? no?"

Caliban's otherworldliness is not eerie Ariel's, but, like the airy sprite's, it is increasingly seen. Fewer productions now pin on Caliban the badge of a specific historically oppressed or colonized people. More frequently, contemporary Calibans are individuals, bizarre and near-magically monstrous (and indeed, fish-monster Calibans never completely went out of style). In Adrian Noble's 1998 Newcastle production, Caliban was a beast of nature with a shell from which he had to be pulled like a snail (O'Connor and Goodland, 1404). Likewise, Caliban in Liam Steel's 2009 London open-air production "slither[ed] like a lizard inside a dark, mollusk-encrusted hunchback and tail," according to one reviewer (Hutera).

Sometimes staging strongly suggests that both Caliban and Ariel are psychological projections. Many productions since the 1990s, exploiting the play's metatheatricalism, have used sets or tricks that suggest that Caliban and Ariel and sometimes all the play's characters are

Fig. 10. A scaly Caliban and a sax-playing Trinculo in Liam Steel's 2009 Regent's Park production of *The Tempest*.

emanations of Prospero/Shakespeare's authorial consciousness. (Recall Tony Tripp's 1990 production in Melbourne, alluded to above, in which a huge bust of Prospero loomed over a sandy base like a head on Easter Island.) In 2010 the broad suggestion of Prospero as artist was still popular: in Stratford, Ontario, Christopher Plummer as Prospero bade farewell to an Ariel who turned instantly (via a darkening and subsequent lighting of the theater) into a playwright's floating quill pen, which sailed upward and disappeared into the recesses of the theater. *The Tempest* as artist's psychodrama, according to theater critic Nigel Cliff, is a "modish idea" (qtd. in O'Connor and Goodland, 1409). Still, director Sam Mendes has twice sailed along its metatheatrical tack to critical acclaim. In his 1993-94 Royal Shakespeare Company production at Stratford (and London), Prospero stood on a ladder at stage rear, watching the various events he had orchestrated unfold between him and the audience. Trinculo, played as a northern English ventriloquist bearing a Charlie McCarthy-like dummy-Trinculo, functioned hilariously to illustrate what Mendes called the director's inability "to control his actors": when Ariel, at Prospero's command, tried to speak through Trinculo, he ended up possessing the dummy rather than the man. "Nobody is a willing subject," Mendes explained in an interview (Bate and Rasmussen, 129). In Mendes's 2010 Brooklyn production at the Brooklyn Academy of Music, Mendes made the Prospero-playwright analogy even more explicit, though the later production featured a stronger Prospero who exhibited mastery over his shadowy players. In Brooklyn, the magic island was a mere circle of sand, around which were ranged the "props and musicians" who helped Prospero "conjure his enchantments," according to theater critic John Lahr. Prospero sat "close to the circle, watching the events that he ha[d] set in motion." Other actors came alive only when they entered the circle, and were "mute, absent presences" at other times, "seated upstage." At the close of the play, after having "restored the other characters to their senses," Prospero stood before the audience "as an almost ordinary citizen," asking "to be released" himself. To Lahr, the meaning was clear: "Shakespeare, the compulsive magician, is finally freed from the spell he cast."

Fig. 11. David Bradley played Trinculo as a ventriloquist in Sam Mendes's 1993 Royal Shakespeare Company production at the Barbican.

THE TEMPEST *ON FILM*

That few filmed versions of *The Tempest* have ever been made is probably owing to two facts aptly summarized by David Bevington, Anne Marie Welsh, and Michael Greenwald in their enormously helpful *Shakespeare: Script, Stage, and Screen*. First, "Because the text relies on poetic descriptions to establish the isle's magic, the primarily visual media of film and television render Shakespeare's words superfluous." Second, "The play's ultimate magic rests in a theatrical—as opposed to cinematic—rendering of the text. We know that film and television can create magic through electronic gimmickry, but there is something even more compelling when such feats are created in a space shared with the audience" (859).

Such *Tempest* films as exist, or existed, are—or were—mostly adaptations. The first of these, made in England, was Percy Stow's 1908 production, for which Langford Reed wrote the screenplay: subtitles like "To humble Prince Ferdinand, Prospero sets him to log-shifting" appear for the audience. Silent film demanded that all dialogue be radically reduced, and in conformance with the restrictions as well as the opportunities of the medium, Stow expanded the play's visually represented events, so that Prospero's and Miranda's arrival on the island is dramatized rather than narrated. Something is thereby gained in the area of narrative continuity, but of course, Shakespeare's dramatization of character shaped by painful remembering is lost (along with his dialogue). Filmed in open air, on water and land, the 1908 movie essayed some cinematographic gimmicks, like turning Ariel into a monkey. Yet it did homage to the theater by including stage sets, and thus achieved what Judith Buchanan calls an "ambiguity of styles" (27).

An American film version of the play directed by Edwin Thanhouser closely followed the Clarendon film, in 1911. This film, (perhaps) unfortunately, was lost in a fire at Thanhouser's warehouse. Little is known about it, though one film historian notes that "[c]omment at the time said that the film added little to the company's reputation" (Sammons, 144). *La Tempête*, a French adaptation, was made in 1912, and has also been lost, though its recorded plot clearly marks it a version of Shakespeare's story. A looser adaptation, though one in English, was made in America in 1921. Entitled *The Tempest*, the American film's plot involves a young man lost at sea during a storm. Arriving somehow at an island, the man falls in love with the lighthouse-keeper's daughter.

The invention of talkies made possible an actual film of the play, featuring Shakespeare's own dialogue spoken by actors. The first of these was made in 1939 for BBC Television, and starred a young Peggy Ashcroft as Miranda. A second BBC *Tempest* was made in 1956. Across the Atlantic, in 1960, Hallmark created a ninety-minute version of the play, directed by George Schaefer, for NBC Television. The film starred Lee Remick as Miranda and Richard Burton, not as Ferdinand, as one would expect, but as an unusually good-looking and smooth-voiced Caliban. Burton was said to have made audible the intellectual aspect of Caliban's mind. While no great experimentation with the television medium was attempted by this film—it was essentially a filmed theatrical performance—in play were a few tricks of the camera, including the reduction of Ariel to Tinkerbell proportions.

As part of its Shakespeare Plays Series, the BBC made a third *Tempest* in 1980, employing John Gorrie as director. Like most films in this series, Gorrie's *Tempest* is designed generally to simulate a Renaissance playhouse performance rather than to capitalize on the potential of the filmic medium. Nevertheless, like ABC in 1960, the BBC could not resist doing tricky things with tricksy Ariel, whose "mysterious appearances are effected in chroma-key, much as a TV weatherman is superimposed over a map" (Bevington, Welsh, Greenwald, 859). In 1992 the BBC aired its fourth and most successful *Tempest*, an eerily beautiful animated, greatly shortened version of the play for children, directed by Stanislov Sokolov. Well worth watching on Youtube, where it now resides, this three-part *Tempest* features a shimmering, musical island peopled with rich-voiced, marionette-like characters, including a green-faced Prospero and a froggy Caliban. Finally, in 2010, a big-budget Hollywood *Tempest* was made, by Miramax. Filmed on Hawaii's black volcanic beaches, the movie is visually gorgeous and beautifully acted. Director Julie Taymor's transformation of Prospero to a woman (played by Helen Mirren) is attended by surprisingly few alterations of the script.

In 2006, a Los Angeles studio, Shout! Factory, produced a riveting prison documentary called *Shakespeare Behind Bars* which should be ranked among the best treatments of The *Tempest* using film. Under Hank Rogerson's direction, the documentary alternates between interviews with prisoners at a Kentucky penitentiary and scenes from *The Tempest* in rehearsal and, ultimately, performance by these same men. Guided by Shakespeare director Curt Tofteland, the prison inmates allow their own contrition and struggles with guilt and vengefulness to emerge in their portrayals of the play's characters.

An early, talkie-era film as well as some later twentieth-century *Tempest* adaptations deserve comment here. In 1932, *Island of Lost Souls,* starring Charles Laughton, blended plot elements of *The Tempest* and of H. G. Wells's creepy short story *The Island of Dr. Moreau* (1896) to create a darker vision of the Prospero-Miranda relation. In the film the Miranda analogue is a woman named Lota, the Frankenstein-like Dr. Moreau's perfect creation. When Moreau introduces Lota to a shipwrecked sailor, it is for experimental purposes. Fred Wilcox's *Forbidden Planet* (1956) also exploits the science-fiction possibilities of *The Tempest*, reimagining Prospero as the scientist "Dr. Mobius," who dwells on a remote planet with his daughter Altaira and an Ariel-type assistant, Robby the Robot, as well as an invisible monster. Leslie Nielson (he of later *Naked Gun* fame) plays Commander Adams, a Ferdinand type who falls in love with Altaira. *Forbidden Planet*—which later inspired one of the more memorable Star Trek episodes—probes the psychological subtext of Prospero's relationship with Caliban. The film culminates in Dr. Mobius's acknowledgment that on his planet, the feared monster is really his own dark subconscious impulses. As Shakespeare might say, "This thing of darkness I acknowledge mine."

Critics are divided over whether the most outrageous film adaptation of *The Tempest* is *Tempest: by William Shakespeare, as Seen Through the Eyes of Derek Jarman* (1980) or Peter Greenaway's *Prospero's Books* (1991). Jarman's film includes a view of the witch Sycorax breast-feeding her grown son Caliban, and replaces Prospero's wedding masque with a blues rendition of "Stormy Weather." Trinculo is a drag queen. In *Prospero's Books*, a robed or sheeted John Gielgud happily inhabits an island crowded with sexy spirits, evoking images of Emperor Tiberius on the isle of Capri. While Shakespeare's dialogue is only selectively spoken in *Prospero's Books*, Greenaway's camera exults in images. We see the books, which include not only volumes devoted to games, utopias, and the mystical properties of water, but Shakespeare's own *The Tempest*, which is placed by hand at the head of the First Folio in the film's last scene. Also, Ariel creates the storm by peeing on the ship, and everybody's naked.

Perhaps the adaptation most true to *The Tempest*'s theme of forgiveness and reconciliation within families is Paul Mazursky's 1982 *Tempest*, called by Douglas Bruster "the first postmodern Shakespeare film" (26) and briefly described in this volume's prior section. In Mazursky's film, a jaded New York architect named Phil (John Cassavetes) voluntarily removes himself, his appalled daughter Miranda (Molly Ringwald), and his girlfriend Aretha (Susan Sarandon, a stand-in for Ariel) to a Greek island. There they encounter a funny Caliban (Raúl Júlia), who plays music for his goats and speaks English he's learned from American television. On the island, Miranda loses her glumness, learns to do physical work, and begins to breach the gap between herself and her father. "Show me the magic," Phil says on the island, and it unfolds around him. Exhibiting heretofore unguessed-at powers, he conjures up a storm to bring some of his corporate enemies to the isle, where he makes them duly miserable. But the bigger surprise, and deeper magic, comes when Antonia, his estranged wife (Geena Rowlands), enters the scene. With Antonia Phil achieves a measure of mutual forgiveness for their shared betrayal—in this case, romantic betrayal—by the end of the film. After his experience performing in *Prospero's Books*, John Gielgud is said to have commented that for all his skill with montage and other forms of cinematographic wizardry, Peter Greenaway didn't quite seem to grasp the point of Shakespeare's play. Mazursky did.

NOTES

1. Leeds Barroll has recently suggested that legal disputes over noise and other issues delayed the opening of Blackfriars until as late as 1610 or 1611—around the date of *The Tempest*'s creation—and that therefore even Shakespeare's late plays were mainly performed at the Globe.
2. See Hornback, chapter 2, on the racist clown tradition.
3. See Alfred Harbage, 17-18, on how Shakespeare's audiences have been maligned.
4. See, for example, the sixth chapter of Thomas Dekker's *The Gull's Hornbook* (1609), "How a Gallant Should Behave Himself in a Playhouse."

WORKS CITED FOR INTRODUCTION AND PERFORMANCE HISTORY

Auden, W. H. *Selected Poems.* New York: Vintage Books, 1979. Print.

Bate, Jonathan, and Russell Jackson. *Shakespeare: An Illustrated Stage History.* Oxford, U.K.: Oxford UP, 1996. Print.

_____, and Eric Rasmussen. "The Director's Cut: Interviews with Peter Brook, Sam Mendes, and Rupert Goold." William Shakespeare. *The Tempest.* Ed. Jonathan Bate and Eric Rasmussen. NY: Random House, 2008. 120-35. Print.

Bevington, David, and Anne Marie Welsh and Michael L. Greenwald. *Shakespeare: Script, Stage, Screen.* NY: Pearson, 2006. Print.

Bruster, Douglas. "The Postmodern Theater of Mazursky's *Tempest.*" *Shakespeare, Film, Fin de Siècle.* Ed. Mark Thornton Burnett and Romana Wray. London: Macmillan, 2000. 26-29. Print.

Buchanan, Judith. *Shakespeare on Film.* Harlow, U.K.: Pearson, 2005. Print.

Coursen, Herbert. *The Tempest: A Guide to the Play.* Westport, Connecticut: Greenwood Press, 2000. Print.

Dymkowski, Christine. Intro. and notes. William Shakespeare, *The Tempest.* Shakespeare in Production series. Ed. Christine Dymkowski. Cambridge, U.K.: Cambridge UP, 2000. Print.

Dekker, Thomas. *The Gull's Hornbook.* London: 1609. Print.

Dryden, John, and William Davenant. *The Enchanted Island.* New Variorum edition. Ed. H. H. Furness. Philadelphia: 1892, reprinted 1964. Print.

Egan, Gabriel. "Ariel's Costume in the Original Staging of *The Tempest.*" *Theater Notebook* 51:2 (1997): 62-71. Print.

The 1599 Geneva Bible. Facsimile. Ozark, MO: L. L. Brown, 2003. Print.

Genzlinger, Neil. "A Woman of Power Was a Vowel Away." *New York Times*: February 9, 2003. Print.

Gosson, Stephen. *Plays Confuted in Five Actions.* London: 1582. Print.

Gurr, Andrew. *The Shakespeare Company, 1594-1642.* Cambridge, U.K.: Cambridge UP, 2004. Print.

—————. *The Shakespearean Stage 1574-1642.* Cambridge, U.K.: Cambridge UP, 1992. Print.

Harbage, Alfred. *Shakespeare's Audience.* NY: Columbia UP, 1941. Print.

Holland, Peter. "Shakespeare Performances in England, 1992-1993." *Shakespeare Survey* 47 (1994): 181-208. Print.

Hornback, Robert. *The English Clown Tradition from the Middle Ages to Shakespeare.* Studies in Renaissance Literature series. Rochester, NY: D. S. Brewer, 2009. Print.

Hutera, Donald. "*The Tempest* at Regent's Park London NW1." *Times Online:* June 16, 2009. Web.

Lahr, John. "Big Magic: 'The Tempest' and 'Clybourne Park.'" *The New Yorker* (March 8, 2010): 78-79. Print.

Mainly Players. London: Thornton Butterworth, 1926. Print.

Montaigne, Michel. *Montaigne's Essays.* Trans. John Florio. Ed. L. C. Harmer. 3 vols. London: Everyman's Library-Dent, 1965. Print.

O'Connor, John, and Katharine Goodland. *A Directory of Shakespeare in Performance: 1970-2005.* Vol. 1: Great Britain. New York: Palgrave Macmillan, 2007. Print.

Pepys, Samuel. *The Diary of Samuel Pepys.* Ed. Robert Latham and William Matthews. 11 vols. London: Bell and Hyman, 1970-83. Print.

Rogerson, Hank, dir. *Shakespeare Behind Bars.* Los Angeles, CA: Shout! Factory, 2006. DVD.

Roppolo, Joseph Patrick. "Shakespeare in New Orleans, 1817-1865." *Shakespeare in the South.* Ed. Philip C. Kolin. Jackson: UP of Mississippi, 1983. 112-127. Print.

Rundle, Erika. "Caliban's Legacy: Primate Drama and the Performance of Species." *TDR: The Drama Review* 51:1 T193 (Spring 2007): 49-66. Print.

Sammons, Eddie. *Shakespeare: A Hundred Years on Film.* Oxford, U.K.: Scarecrow Press, 2004. Print.

Scheil, Katherine West. *The Taste of the Town: Shakespearian Comedy and the Early Eighteenth-Century Theater.* Lewisburg, PA: Bucknell UP, 2003. Print.

Shakespeare, William. *The Riverside Shakespeare.* Ed. G. Blakemore Evans. Boston: Houghton Mifflin, 1974. Print.

—————. *The Norton Facsimile of the First Folio of Shakespeare.* Ed. Charlton Hinman. New York: Norton, 1968. Print.

Trewin, J.C. *Going to Shakespeare.* London: Allen and Unwin, 1978. Print.

—————. *Shakespeare on the English Stage 1900-1964: A Survey of Productions.* London: Barrie and Rockliff, 1964. Print.

Vaughan, Alden T. and Virginia Mason. *Shakespeare's Caliban: A Cultural History.* Cambridge, U.K.: Cambridge UP, 1991. Print.

Wells, Stanley. "Problems of Stagecraft in 'The Tempest'." *New Theater Quarterly* 10:40 (November, 1994): 348-357. Print.

THE
TEMPEST

NAMES OF THE ACTORS

ALONSO, *King of Naples*
SEBASTIAN, *his brother*
PROSPERO, *the right Duke of Milan*
ANTONIO, *his brother, the usurping Duke of Milan*
FERDINAND, *son to the King of Naples*
GONZALO, *an honest old councillor*
ADRIAN *and* FRANCISCO, *lords*
CALIBAN, *a salvage and deformed slave*
TRINCULO, *a jester*
STEPHANO, *a drunken butler*
MASTER OF A SHIP
BOATSWAIN
MARINERS
MIRANDA, *daughter to Prospero*
ARIEL, *an airy spirit*
IRIS
CERES
JUNO   } *SPIRITS*
NYMPHS
REAPERS
[*Other* SPIRITS *attending on Prospero*]

THE SCENE: [*A ship at sea;*] *an uninhabited island*

Act I

SCENE I

A tempestuous noise of thunder and lightning heard.
Enter a SHIP-MASTER *and a* BOATSWAIN.

MASTER Boatswain!
BOATSWAIN Here, master; what cheer?
MASTER Good; speak to th' mariners. Fall to't,
  yarely, or we run ourselves aground. Bestir, bestir.

                                   Exit.

              Enter MARINERS.

BOATSWAIN Heigh, my hearts! cheerly, cheerly, my   5
  hearts! yare, yare! Take in the topsail. Tend to th'
  master's whistle.—Blow till thou burst thy wind, if
  room enough!

      Enter ALONSO, SEBASTIAN, ANTONIO, FERDINANDO,
                  GONZALO, *and others.*

ALONSO Good boatswain, have care. Where's the
  master? Play the men.   10
BOATSWAIN I pray now keep below.
ANTONIO Where is the master, bos'n?
BOATSWAIN Do you not hear him? You mar our labor.
  Keep your cabins; you do assist the storm.
GONZALO Nay, good, be patient.   15

Words and passages enclosed in square brackets in the text above are either emendations of the copy-text or additions to it. The Textual Notes immediately following the play cite the earliest authority for every such change or insertion and supply the reading of the copy-text wherever it is emended in this edition.

Names of the Actors. **salvage:** savage.

1.1. Location: On a ship at sea.   **3. Good:** An acknowledgment of the boatswain's reply. The punctuation differentiates this from line 15's *good*, which means "good fellow."   **4: yarely:** smartly, nimbly.   **7–8: Blow . . . enough.** He addresses the storm. **if room enough:** so long as we have sea-room, i.e., space in which to maneuver without going aground.   **10. Play:** ply, urge on (?).

BOATSWAIN When the sea is. Hence! What cares these
roarers for the name of king? To cabin! silence!
trouble us not.

GONZALO Good, yet remember whom thou hast aboard.

BOATSWAIN None that I more love than myself. You are   20
a councillor; if you can command these elements
to silence, and work the peace of the present, we will
not hand a rope more. Use your authority. If you cannot,
give thanks you have liv'd so long, and make
yourself ready in your cabin for the mischance of   25
the hour, if it so hap.—Cheerly, good hearts!—Out of
our way, I say.   *Exit.*

GONZALO I have great comfort from this fellow. Methinks
he hath no drowning mark upon him, his complexion
is perfect gallows. Stand fast, good Fate,   30
to his hanging, make the rope of his destiny our cable,
for our own doth little advantage. If he be not born to
be hang'd, our case is miserable.   *Exeunt.*

Enter BOATSWAIN.

BOATSWAIN Down with the topmast! yare! lower, lower!
bring her to try with main-course. (*A cry within.*)   35
A plague upon this howling! they are louder than the
weather, or our office.

Enter SEBASTIAN, ANTONIO, *and* GONZALO.

Yet again? What do you here? Shall we give o'er and
drown? Have you a mind to sink?

SEBASTIAN A pox o' your throat, you bawling, blasphemous,   40
incharitable dog!

BOATSWAIN Work you then.

ANTONIO Hang, cur! hang, you whoreson, insolent
noisemaker! We are less afraid to be drown'd than
thou art.   45

---

17. roarers: (1) turbulent waves; (2) rowdies.   **21. councillor:** member of the King's council.   **22. the present:** the present occasion; but *present* may be a mistake for *presence*, i.e., the King's presence or presence chamber.   **28–30: Methinks . . . gallows.** Alluding to the proverb "He that is born to be hanged need fear no drowning."   **29–30. complexion:** appearance (as reflecting his temperament).   **31–32. make . . . advantage:** make the rope that will hang him our anchor chain, since our actual one now does us little good.   **35. bring . . . maincourse:** keep her close to the wind by means of the mainsail.   **37. office:** duties.

GONZALO I'll warrant him for drowning, though the
  ship were no stronger than a nutshell, and as leaky as
  an unstanch'd wench.
BOATSWAIN Lay her a-hold, a-hold! Set her two courses
  off to sea again! Lay her off.   50

Enter MARINERS *wet.*

MARINERS All lost! To prayers, to prayers! All
  lost!   [*Exeunt.*]
BOATSWAIN What, must our mouths be cold?
GONZALO The King and Prince at prayers, let's assist them,
  For our case is as theirs.
SEBASTIAN   I am out of patience.   55
ANTONIO We are merely cheated of our lives by drunkards.
  This wide-chopp'd rascal—would thou mightst lie drowning
  The washing of ten tides!
GONZALO   He'll be hang'd yet,
  Though every drop of water swear against it,
  And gape at wid'st to glut him.
    A confused noise within: "Mercy on us!"—   60
  "We split, we split!"—"Farewell, my wife and children!"—
  "Farewell, brother!"—"We split, we split, we split!"
                                        [*Exit Boatswain.*]
ANTONIO Let's all sink wi' th' King.
SEBASTIAN Let's take leave of him.   *Exit* [*with Antonio*].
GONZALO Now would I give a thousand furlongs of sea   65
  for an acre of barren ground, long heath, brown [furze],
  any thing. The wills above be done! but I would fain
  die a dry death.   *Exit.*

SCENE 2

Enter PROSPERO *and* MIRANDA.

MIRANDA If by your art, my dearest father, you have
  Put the wild waters in this roar, allay them.
  The sky it seems would pour down stinking pitch,
  But that the sea, mounting to th' welkin's cheek,

---

46. warrant him for: guarantee him against. **49. a-hold:** a-hull, close to the
wind. **49–50. Set . . . sea:** i.e., set her mainsail and foresail so as to get her out to
sea. **56. merely:** utterly. **57. wide-chopp'd:** wide-jawed. **58. ten tides:** Pirates
were hanged on shore and left until three tides had washed over them. **60. gape . . .
him:** open its mouth to the widest to gulp him down. **66. heath . . . furze:** heather . . .
gorse (plants that grow in poor soil). **67. fain:** gladly. **1.2. Location:** An island. Before
Prospero's cell. **1. art:** magic. **4. welkin's:** sky's. **cheek:** (1) face; (2) side of a grate.

Dashes the fire out. O! I have suffered   5
With those that I saw suffer. A brave vessel
(Who had, no doubt, some noble creature in her)
Dash'd all to pieces! O, the cry did knock
Against my very heart. Poor souls, they perish'd.
Had I been any God of power, I would   10
Have sunk the sea within the earth or ere
It should the good ship so have swallow'd, and
The fraughting souls within her.
PROSPERO   Be collected,
No more amazement. Tell your piteous heart
There's no harm done.
MIRANDA   O woe the day!
PROSPERO   No harm: 15
I have done nothing, but in care of thee
(Of thee my dear one, thee my daughter), who
Art ignorant of what thou art, nought knowing
Of whence I am, nor that I am more better
Than Prospero, master of a full poor cell,   20
And thy no greater father.
MIRANDA   More to know
Did never meddle with my thoughts.
PROSPERO   'Tis time
I should inform thee farther. Lend thy hand,
And pluck my magic garment from me. So,
                    Lays down his mantle.
Lie there, my art. Wipe thou thine eyes, have comfort.   25
The direful spectacle of the wrack, which touch'd
The very virtue of compassion in thee,
I have with such provision in mine art
So safely ordered that there is no soul—
No, not so much perdition as an hair   30
Betid to any creature in the vessel
Which thou heardst cry, which thou saw'st sink. Sit down,
For thou must now know farther.
MIRANDA   You have often

---

6. brave: splendid.   **11. or ere:** before.   **13. fraughting:** forming the cargo. **collected:** composed.   **14. amazement:** terror. **piteous:** pitying.   **19. more better:** of higher rank (common Elizabethan double comparative). **20. full:** very.   **21. no greater:** i.e., of no loftier position than is implied by his "full poor cell." **22. meddle with:** mingle with, enter.   **26. wrack:** shipwreck.   **27. virtue:** essence. **28. provision:** foresight.   **29. soul—:** The sentence changes its course in what follows, but the sense is plain.   **30. perdition:** loss.   **31. Betid:** happened.

Begun to tell me what I am, but stopp'd
And left me to a bootless inquisition, 35
Concluding, "Stay: not yet."
PROSPERO   The hour's now come,
The very minute bids thee ope thine ear.
Obey, and be attentive. Canst thou remember
A time before we came unto this cell?
I do not think thou canst, for then thou wast not 40
Out three years old.
MIRANDA   Certainly, sir, I can.
PROSPERO By what? by any other house, or person?
Of any thing the image, tell me, that
Hath kept with thy remembrance.
MIRANDA   'Tis far off;
And rather like a dream than an assurance 45
That my remembrance warrants. Had I not
Four, or five, women once that tended me?
PROSPERO Thou hadst; and more, Miranda. But how is it
That this lives in thy mind? What seest thou else
In the dark backward and abysm of time? 50
If thou rememb'rest aught ere thou cam'st here,
How thou cam'st here thou mayst.
MIRANDA   But that I do not.
PROSPERO Twelve year since, Miranda, twelve year since,
Thy father was the Duke of Milan and
A prince of power.
MIRANDA   Sir, are not you my father? 55
PROSPERO Thy mother was a piece of virtue, and
She said thou wast my daughter; and thy father
Was Duke of Milan, and his only heir
And princess no worse issued.
MIRANDA   O the heavens,
What foul play had we, that we came from thence? 60
Or blessed was't we did?
PROSPERO   Both, both, my girl.
By foul play (as thou say'st) were we heav'd thence,
But blessedly holp hither.
MIRANDA   O, my heart bleeds

---

35. bootless inquisition: useless inquiry. **41. Out:** fully. **45. assurance:** certainty. **46. remembrance warrants:** memory guarantees. **50. backward ... time:** abyss of the past. **56. piece:** masterpiece. **virtue:** chastity. **59. no worse issued:** no less noble in birth. **63. blessedly holp:** providentially helped.

To think o' th' teen that I have turn'd you to,
Which is from my remembrance! Please you, farther.　　65
PROSPERO　My brother and thy uncle, call'd Antonio—
　　I pray thee mark me—that a brother should
　　Be so perfidious!—he whom next thyself
　　Of all the world I lov'd, and to him put
　　The manage of my state, as at that time　　70
　　Through all the signories it was the first,
　　And Prospero the prime duke, being so reputed
　　In dignity, and for the liberal arts　　·
　　Without a parallel; those being all my study,
　　The government I cast upon my brother,　　75
　　And to my state grew stranger, being transported
　　And rapt in secret studies. Thy false uncle—
　　Dost thou attend me?
MIRANDA　　　　　　　　Sir, most heedfully.
PROSPERO　Being once perfected how to grant suits,
　　How to deny them, who t' advance, and who　　80
　　To trash for overtopping, new created
　　The creatures that were mine, I say, or chang'd 'em,
　　Or else new form'd 'em; having both the key
　　Of officer and office, set all hearts i' th' state
　　To what tune pleas'd his ear, that now he was　　85
　　The ivy which had hid my princely trunk,
　　And suck'd my verdure out on't. Thou attend'st not!
MIRANDA　O, good sir, I do.
PROSPERO　　　　　　　　I pray thee mark me.
　　I, thus neglecting worldly ends, all dedicated
　　To closeness and the bettering of my mind　　90
　　With that which, but by being so retir'd,
　　O'er-priz'd all popular rate, in my false brother
　　Awak'd an evil nature, and my trust,
　　Like a good parent, did beget of him
　　A falsehood in its contrary, as great　　95
　　As my trust was, which had indeed no limit,

64. teen: sorrow, trouble. **turn'd you to:** reminded you of.　**65. from:** out of.
71. signories: city states.　**72. prime:** chief, first in rank.　**79. perfected:** expert in.　**81. trash for overtopping:** check because of his having become too powerful. (*Tiffany*) Two images are combined here: *trash* = check a hunting dog from going too fast; *overtopping* = growing too high.　**82. or:** either.
83. key: (1) key to office; (2) tuning key.　**85. that:** so that. (*Tiffany*)
87. verdure: vigor, vitality. **on't:** of it.　**90. closeness:** seclusion.　**92. O'er-priz'd
. . . rate:** had greater worth than any vulgar evaluation would place upon it.
94. good parent: That a good parent often bred a bad child was proverbial.

A confidence sans bound. He being thus lorded,
Not only with what my revenue yielded,
But what my power might else exact—like one
Who having into truth, by telling of it,   100
Made such a sinner of his memory
To credit his own lie—he did believe
He was indeed the Duke, out o' th' substitution,
And executing th' outward face of royalty
With all prerogative. Hence his ambition growing—   105
Dost thou hear?
MIRANDA   Your tale, sir, would cure deafness.
PROSPERO To have no screen between this part he play'd
And him he play'd it for, he needs will be
Absolute Milan—me (poor man) my library
Was dukedom large enough: of temporal royalties   110
He thinks me now incapable; confederates
(So dry he was for sway) wi' th' King of Naples
To give him annual tribute, do him homage,
Subject his coronet to his crown, and bend
The dukedom yet unbow'd (alas, poor Milan!)   115
To most ignoble stooping.
MIRANDA   O the heavens!
PROSPERO Mark his condition, and th' event, then tell me
If this might be a brother.
MIRANDA   I should sin
To think but nobly of my grandmother.
Good wombs have borne bad sons.
PROSPERO   Now the condition.   120
This King of Naples, being an enemy
To me inveterate, hearkens my brother's suit,
Which was, that he in lieu o' th' premises,
Of homage, and I know not how much tribute,
Should presently extirpate me and mine   125
Out of the dukedom, and confer fair Milan
With all the honors on my brother; whereon,

---

97. sans: without. lorded: i.e., established in a position of power. 99-102. like one .
. . lie: like one who has, by the telling of his lie, made his memory such a sinner unto
truth that it credited that lie. (*Tiffany*) 100. into: unto, against (*into truth* modifies
sinner). 102. To: as to. 103. out: as a result. 107-8. To have no . . . for: So as to
have no separation between acting as Duke and being Duke. (*Tiffany*) 109. Absolute Milan: actual Duke of Milan. 110. temporal royalties: practical administra-
tion. 111. confederates: makes alliance. 112. dry: thirsty. sway: power, influence.
(*Tiffany*) 117. condition: agreement. (*Tiffany*) event: outcome. 123. lieu . . .
premises: return for the pledge. 125. presently extirpate: immediately remove.

A treacherous army levied, one midnight
Fated to th' purpose, did Antonio open
The gates of Milan, and i' th' dead of darkness   130
The ministers for th' purpose hurried thence
Me and thy crying self.
MIRANDA   Alack, for pity!
I, not rememb'ring how I cried out then,
Will cry it o'er again. It is a hint
That wrings mine eyes to't.
PROSPERO   Hear a little further,   135
And then I'll bring thee to the present business
Which now's upon's; without the which this story
Were most impertinent.
MIRANDA   Wherefore did they not
That hour destroy us?
PROSPERO   Well demanded, wench;
My tale provokes that question. Dear, they durst not,   140
So dear the love my people bore me; nor set
A mark so bloody on the business; but
With colors fairer painted their foul ends.
In few, they hurried us aboard a bark,
Bore us some leagues to sea, where they prepared   145
A rotten carcass of a butt, not rigg'd,
Nor tackle, sail, nor mast, the very rats
Instinctively have quit it. There they hoist us,
To cry to th' sea, that roar'd to us; to sigh
To th' winds, whose pity, sighing back again,   150
Did us but loving wrong.
MIRANDA   Alack, what trouble
Was I then to you!
PROSPERO   O, a cherubin
Thou wast that did preserve me. Thou didst smile,
Infused with a fortitude from heaven,
When I have deck'd the sea with drops full salt,   155
Under my burthen groan'd, which rais'd in me

---

134. **hint:** occasion.   135. **wrings:** (1) constrains; (2) extracts moisture from.
137. **now's upon's:** now is upon us. (*Tiffany*)   138. **impertinent:** irrelevant.
143. **With ... ends:** undertook to accomplish the same end by less violent
means.   144. **In few:** In a few words. (*Tiffany*)   146. **butt:** tub.   151. **Did
... wrong:** only added to our discomfort.   155. **deck's:** (1) adorned; (2) covered.   156. **which:** i.e., Miranda's smile.

An undergoing stomach, to bear up
Against what should ensue.

MIRANDA   How came we ashore?

PROSPERO By Providence divine.
Some food we had, and some fresh water, that   160
A noble Neapolitan, Gonzalo,
Out of his charity, who being then appointed
Master of this design, did give us, with
Rich garments, linens, stuffs, and necessaries,
Which since have steaded much; so of his gentleness,   165
Knowing I lov'd my books, he furnish'd me
From mine own library with volumes that
I prize above my dukedom.

MIRANDA   Would I might
But ever see that man!

PROSPERO   Now I arise.   [*Puts on his robe.*]
Sit still, and hear the last of our sea-sorrow: 170
Here in this island we arriv'd, and here
Have I, thy schoolmaster, made thee more profit
Than other princes can, that have more time
For vainer hours, and tutors not so careful.

MIRANDA Heavens thank you for't! And now I pray you, sir,   175
For still 'tis beating in my mind, your reason
For raising this sea-storm?

PROSPERO   Know thus far forth:
By accident most strange, bountiful Fortune
(Now my dear lady) hath mine enemies
Brought to this shore; and by my prescience   180
I find my zenith doth depend upon
A most auspicious star, whose influence
If now I court not, but omit, my fortunes
Will ever after droop. Here cease more questions.
Thou art inclin'd to sleep; 'tis a good dullness,   185
And give it way. I know thou canst not choose.

                              [*Miranda sleeps.*]

Come away, servant, come; I am ready now,
Approach, my Ariel. Come.

157. undergoing stomach: 1. moral strength to undergo hardship. (The stomach was considered the seat of courage.) 2. intestinal fortitude to combat seasickness. (*Tiffany*) 165. steaded: been of use. gentleness: character proper to one of high birth and cultivation. 167. volumes: i.e., books of magic. 172. more profit: profit more. 173. princes: The title "prince" could be used to honor either sex. 179. my dear lady: i.e., favorable to me. 181. zenith: height of fortune. 182. influence: power (astrological term). 183. omit: ignore. 185. dullness: sleepiness. 187. Come away: come here.

Enter ARIEL.

ARIEL All hail, great master, grave sir, hail! I come
　　　 To answer thy best pleasure; be't to fly,　　　　　　　190
　　　 To swim, to dive into the fire, to ride
　　　 On the curl'd clouds. To thy strong bidding, task
　　　 Ariel, and all his quality.
PROSPERO　　　　　　　　　　Hast thou, spirit,
　　　 Perform'd to point the tempest that I bade thee?
ARIEL To every article.　　　　　　　　　　　　　　　　　195
　　　 I boarded the King's ship; now on the beak,
　　　 Now in the waist, the deck, in every cabin,
　　　 I flam'd amazement. Sometime I'ld divide,
　　　 And burn in many places; on the topmast,
　　　 The yards and boresprit, would I flame distinctly,　　200
　　　 Then meet and join. Jove's lightning, the precursors
　　　 O' th' dreadful thunder-claps, more momentary
　　　 And sight-outrunning were not; the fire and cracks
　　　 Of sulphurous roaring the most mighty Neptune
　　　 Seem to besiege, and make his bold waves tremble,　　205
　　　 Yea, his dread trident shake.
PROSPERO　　　　　　　　　　　My brave spirit!
　　　 Who was so firm, so constant, that this coil
　　　 Would not infect his reason?
ARIEL　　　　　　　　　　　　Not a soul
　　　 But felt a fever of the mad, and play'd
　　　 Some tricks of desperation. All but mariners　　　　　210
　　　 Plung'd in the foaming brine, and quit the vessel;
　　　 Then all afire with me, the King's son, Ferdinand,
　　　 With hair up-staring (then like reeds, not hair),
　　　 Was the first man that leapt; cried, "Hell is empty,
　　　 And all the devils are here."
PROSPERO　　　　　　　　　　 Why, that's my spirit!　　215
　　　 But was not this nigh shore?
ARIEL　　　　　　　　　　　　Close by, my master.
PROSPERO But are they, Ariel, safe?
ARIEL　　　　　　　　　　　　Not a hair perish'd;

---

193. quality: (1) skill; (2) cohorts, minor spirits under him.　**194. to point:**
in detail.　**196. beak:** prow.　**200. boresprit:** bowsprit. **distinctly:** in separate places.　**207. coil:** uproar.　**209. of the mad:** such as madmen have.
212. Then . . . me: Many editors repunctuate lines 211–12 so as to make this phrase
modify *vessel* rather than *son*.　**213. up-staring:** upstarting (*Tiffany*), standing
on end.

On their sustaining garments not a blemish,
But fresher than before; and as thou badst me,
In troops I have dispers'd them 'bout the isle.   220
The King's son have I landed by himself,
Whom I left cooling of the air with sighs,
In an odd angle of the isle, and sitting,
His arms in this sad knot.
PROSPERO   Of the King's ship,
The mariners, say how thou hast dispos'd,   225
And all the rest o' th' fleet.
ARIEL   Safely in harbor
Is the King's ship, in the deep nook, where once
Thou call'dst me up at midnight to fetch dew
From the still-vex'd Bermoothes, there she's hid;
The mariners all under hatches stowed,   230
Who, with a charm join'd to their suff'red labor,
I have left asleep; and for the rest o' th' fleet
(Which I dispers'd), they all have met again,
And are upon the Mediterranean float
Bound sadly home for Naples,   235
Supposing that they saw the King's ship wrack'd,
And his great person perish.
PROSPERO   Ariel, thy charge
Exactly is perform'd; but there's more work.
What is the time o' th' day?
ARIEL   Past the mid season.
PROSPERO At least two glasses. The time 'twixt six and now   240
Must by us both be spent most preciously.
ARIEL Is there more toil? Since thou dost give me pains,
Let me remember thee what thou hast promis'd,
Which is not yet perform'd me.
PROSPERO   How now? moody?
What is't thou canst demand?
ARIEL   My liberty.   245
PROSPERO Before the time be out? No more!
ARIEL   I prithee,

---

218. sustaining garments: garments that bore them up in the water.   **224. in . . .
knot:** i.e., crossed thus (Ariel illustrates with a gesture). Crossed arms indicated
melancholy.   **227. nook:** inlet, small bay.   **229. still-vex'd Bermoothes:** always
stormy Bermuda islands.   **231. with a charm:** by means of a magic spell. **their
suff'red labor:** the labor they have endured.   **234. float:** flood, sea.   **239. mid
season:** noon.   **240. glasses:** hourglasses.   **242. pains:** duties, chores.   **243. remember:** remind.

Remember I have done thee worthy service,
Told thee no lies, made thee no mistakings, serv'd
Without or grudge or grumblings. Thou didst promise
To bate me a full year.
PROSPERO   Dost thou forget   250
From what a torment I did free thee?
ARIEL   No.
PROSPERO Thou dost; and think'st it much to tread the ooze
Of the salt deep,
To run upon the sharp wind of the north,
To do me business in the veins o' th' earth   255
When it is bak'd with frost.
ARIEL   I do not, sir.
PROSPERO Thou liest, malignant thing! Hast thou forgot
The foul witch Sycorax, who with age and envy
Was grown into a hoop? Hast thou forgot her?
ARIEL No, sir.
PROSPERO   Thou hast. Where was she born?
Speak. Tell me.   260
ARIEL Sir, in Argier.
PROSPERO   O, was she so? I must
Once in a month recount what thou hast been,
Which thou forget'st. This damn'd witch Sycorax,
For mischiefs manifold, and sorceries terrible
To enter human hearing, from Argier   265
Thou know'st was banish'd; for one thing she did
They would not take her life. Is not this true?
ARIEL Ay, sir.
PROSPERO This blue-ey'd hag was hither brought with child,
And here was left by th' sailors. Thou, my slave,   270
As thou report'st thyself, was then her servant,
And for thou wast a spirit too delicate
To act her earthy and abhorr'd commands,
Refusing her grand hests, she did confine thee,
By help of her more potent ministers,   275
And in her most unmitigable rage,
Into a cloven pine, within which rift
Imprison'd, thou didst painfully remain
A dozen years; within which space she died,
And left thee there, where thou didst vent thy groans   280

250. **bate:** remit.   256. **bak'd:** hardened.   261. **Argier:** Algiers.   272. **for:** because.   274. **hests:** commands.

As fast as mill-wheels strike. Then was this island
(Save for the son that [she] did litter here,
A freckled whelp, hag-born) not honor'd with
A human shape.
ARIEL   Yes—Caliban her son.
PROSPERO Dull thing, I say so; he, that Caliban   285
Whom now I keep in service. Thou best know'st
What torment I did find thee in; thy groans
Did make wolves howl, and penetrate the breasts
Of ever-angry bears. It was a torment
To lay upon the damn'd, which Sycorax   290
Could not again undo. It was mine art,
When I arriv'd and heard thee, that made gape
The pine, and let thee out.
ARIEL   I thank thee, master.
PROSPERO If thou more murmur'st, I will rend an oak
And peg thee in his knotty entrails till   295
Thou hast howl'd away twelve winters.
ARIEL   Pardon, master,
I will be correspondent to command
And do my spriting gently.
PROSPERO   Do so; and after two days
I will discharge thee.
ARIEL   That's my noble master!
What shall I do? say what? what shall I do?   300
PROSPERO Go make thyself like a nymph o' th' sea; be subject
To no sight but thine and mine, invisible
To every eyeball else. Go take this shape
And hither come in't. Go. Hence with diligence!
                               Exit [Ariel].   305
Awake, dear heart, awake! Thou hast slept well,
Awake!
MIRANDA   The strangeness of your story put
Heaviness in me.
PROSPERO   Shake it off. Come on,
We'll visit Caliban my slave, who never
Yields us kind answer.
MIRANDA   'Tis a villain, sir,
I do not love to look on.
PROSPERO   But as 'tis,   310

---

281. mill-wheels: i.e., the clappers on mill-wheels. **292. gape:** open wide.
295. his: its. **297. correspondent:** obedient. **307. Heaviness:** drowsiness.

We cannot miss him. He does make our fire,
Fetch in our wood, and serves in offices
That profit us. What ho! slave! Caliban!
Thou earth, thou! speak.
CALIBAN (*Within.*)   There's wood enough within.
PROSPERO Come forth, I say, there's other business for thee.   315
Come, thou tortoise, when?

Enter ARIEL *like a water-nymph.*

Fine apparition! My quaint Ariel,
Hark in thine ear.
ARIEL   My lord, it shall be done.   *Exit.*
PROSPERO Thou poisonous slave, got by the devil himself
Upon thy wicked dam, come forth!   320

Enter CALIBAN.

CALIBAN As wicked dew as e'er my mother brush'd
With raven's feather from unwholesome fen
Drop on you both! A south-west blow on ye,
And blister you all o'er!
PROSPERO For this, be sure, to-night thou shalt have cramps,   325
Side-stitches, that shall pen thy breath up; urchins
Shall, for that vast of night that they may work,
All exercise on thee; thou shalt be pinch'd
As thick as honeycomb, each pinch more stinging
Than bees that made 'em.
CALIBAN   I must eat my dinner.   330
This island's mine by Sycorax my mother,
Which thou tak'st from me. When thou cam'st first,
Thou strok'st me and made much of me, wouldst give me
Water with berries in't, and teach me how
To name the bigger light, and how the less,   335
That burn by day and night; and then I lov'd thee
And show'd thee all the qualities o' th' isle,
The fresh springs, brine-pits, barren place and fertile.
Curs'd be I that did so! All the charms

311. miss: do without.   **316. when:** a common expression of impatience.
317. quaint: clever, ingenious.   **323. south-west:** southwest wind, thought to
bring pestilence.   **326. urchins:** hedgehogs; here, goblins in the shape of hedgehogs.   **327. for . . . work:** during that long and desolate period of darkness during
which they are permitted to perform their mischief. It was thought that malignant spirits lost their power with the coming of day.   **330. 'em:** i.e., cells of the
honeycomb.

Of Sycorax, toads, beetles, bats, light on you!   340
For I am all the subjects that you have,
Which first was mine own king; and here you sty me
In this hard rock, whiles you do keep from me
The rest o' th' island.

PROSPERO   Thou most lying slave,
Whom stripes may move, not kindness! I have us'd thee   345
(Filth as thou art) with human care, and lodg'd thee
In mine own cell, till thou didst seek to violate
The honor of my child.

CALIBAN O ho, O ho, would't had been done!
Thou didst prevent me; I had peopled else   350
This isle with Calibans.

MIRANDA   Abhorred slave,
Which any print of goodness wilt not take,
Being capable of all ill! I pitied thee,
Took pains to make thee speak, taught thee each hour
One thing or other. When thou didst not, savage,   355
Know thine own meaning, but wouldst gabble like
A thing most brutish, I endow'd thy purposes
With words that made them known. But thy vild race
(Though thou didst learn) had that in't which good natures
Could not abide to be with; therefore was thou   360
Deservedly confin'd into this rock,
Who hadst deserv'd more than a prison.

CALIBAN You taught me language, and my profit on't
Is, I know how to curse. The red-plague rid you
For learning me your language!

PROSPERO   Hag-seed, hence!   365
Fetch us in fuel, and be quick, thou'rt best,
To answer other business. Shrug'st thou, malice?
If thou neglect'st, or dost unwillingly
What I command, I'll rack thee with old cramps,
Fill all thy bones with aches, make thee roar   370
That beasts shall tremble at thy din.

CALIBAN   No, pray thee.
[*Aside.*] I must obey. His art is of such pow'r,
It would control my dam's god, Setebos,

---

345. stripes: lashes. **346. human:** humane. **351.** s.p. **Mir:** Some editors
make Prospero the speaker. **358. vild:** vile. **race:** nature. **364. rid:** destroy.
366. thou'rt best: you had better. **369. old:** i.e., such as old people have.
370. aches: Pronounced *aitches.*

And make a vassal of him.

PROSPERO   So, slave, hence!   *Exit Caliban.*

    Enter FERDINAND; *and* ARIEL, *invisible, playing and singing.*

ARIEL['S] SONG

Come unto these yellow sands,   375
   And then take hands:
Curtsied when you have, and kiss'd,
   The wild waves whist:
Foot it featly here and there,
   And, sweet sprites, [the burthen bear].   380
Hark, hark!
     Burthen, dispersedly, [*within*]. Bow-wow.
The watch-dogs bark!
     [*Burthen, dispersedly, within.*] Bow-wow.
Hark, hark, I hear   385
The strain of strutting chanticleer:
Cry [*within.*] Cock-a-diddle-dow.

FERDINAND Where should this music be? I' th' air, or th' earth?
   It sounds no more; and sure it waits upon
   Some god o' th' island. Sitting on a bank,   390
   Weeping again the King my father's wrack,
   This music crept by me upon the waters,
   Allaying both their fury and my passion
   With its sweet air; thence I have follow'd it,
   Or it hath drawn me rather. But 'tis gone.   395
   No, it begins again.

ARIEL['S] SONG

Full fadom five thy father lies,
   Of his bones are coral made:
Those are pearls that were his eyes:
   Nothing of him that doth fade,   400
But doth suffer a sea-change
Into something rich and strange.
Sea-nymphs hourly ring his knell:
     Burthen [*within*]. Ding-dong.
Hark now I hear them—ding-dong bell.   405

---

373. dam's: mother's. (*Tiffany*)   **374. s.d. invisible:** Ariel is of course visible to the audience but he wears a costume which by convention makes him invisible to other persons on the stage, except Prospero.   **378. whist:** being hushed. **379. featly:** nimbly.   **380. the burthen bear:** bear the burden, i.e., the bass undersong.   **382. dispersedly:** from several directions.   **393. passion:** emotion. (*Tiffany*)   **397. fadom:** fathom.

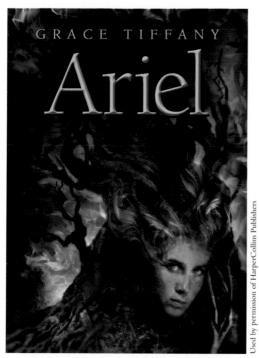

Pl. 1. The cover of *Ariel*, a modern novel by Grace Tiffany, suggests the androgynous nature of this *Tempest* character, who may represent human or divine creative energies, the artistic imagination, or the powers intrinsic to the natural world. *Ariel*—which provides a fictional pre-history for the character—is one of many "spin-offs" or adaptations of *The Tempest*, a work which has appealed more to fantasy and science-fiction authors than has any other Shakespeare play.

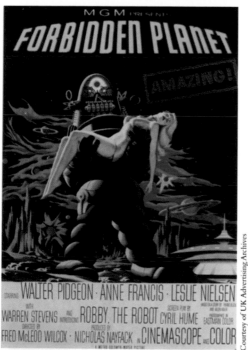

Pl. 2. This poster advertised one of the more radical modern adaptations of Shakespeare's play, Fred Wilcox's 1956 *Forbidden Planet*, which would become a cult film. In it Prospero, Shakespeare's main character, has become "Dr. Mobius," a slightly mad scientist, and Ariel is replaced by "Robby the Robot."

Pl. 3. The famed British actor and director Herbert Beerbohm Tree played Caliban in 1904 at His Majesty's Theater in London. Charles A. Buchel's 1904 painting depicting Tree's somewhat simian Caliban shows the influence of Darwin's theory on Tree's interpretation of the character.

Pl. 4. This poster advertising Tree's production catered to early twentieth-century English audiences' interest in fairies. Although in the play Ariel is referred to as "he," this distinctly feminine image of the spirit suggests the androgyny of the character, who was played in this instance by Viola Tree, the director's daughter.

FERDINAND The ditty does remember my drown'd father.
　This is no mortal business, nor no sound
　That the earth owes. I hear it now above me.
PROSPERO The fringèd curtains of thine eye advance,
　And say what thou seest yond.
MIRANDA　　　　　　　　What, is't a spirit?　　　　410
　Lord, how it looks about! Believe me, sir,
　It carries a brave form. But 'tis a spirit.
PROSPERO No, wench, it eats, and sleeps, and hath such senses
　As we have—such. This gallant which thou seest
　Was in the wrack; and but he's something stain'd　　415
　With grief (that's beauty's canker), thou mightst call him
　A goodly person. He hath lost his fellows,
　And strays about to find 'em.
MIRANDA　　　　　　　　　I might call him
　A thing divine, for nothing natural
　I ever saw so noble.
PROSPERO　　　　　[Aside.] It goes on, I see,　　　420
　As my soul prompts it. Spirit, fine spirit, I'll free thee
　Within two days for this.
FERDINAND　　　　　　　Most sure, the goddess
　On whom these airs attend! Vouchsafe my pray'r
　May know if you remain upon this island,
　And that you will some good instruction give　　425
　How I may bear me here. My prime request,
　Which I do last pronounce, is (O you wonder!)
　If you be maid, or no?
MIRANDA　　　　　　　No wonder, sir,
　But certainly a maid.
FERDINAND　　　　　　My language? heavens!
　I am the best of them that speak this speech,　　430
　Were I but where 'tis spoken.
PROSPERO　　　　　　　　How? the best?
　What wert thou, if the King of Naples heard thee?
FERDINAND A single thing, as I am now, that wonders
　To hear thee speak of Naples. He does hear me,

---

408. owes: owns. 409. advance: raise. 412. brave: excellent, splendid. 415.
but: except that. something stain'd: somewhat disfigured. 416. canker: worm
that eats blossoms. 423. airs: i.e., the music he has heard. 426. prime: first, most
important. 428. maid: i.e., a human maiden, not a goddess. 429. maid: virgin.
(Tiffany) 430. best: first in rank. 433. single: solitary (because he thinks that he
and the King are one and the same), but he probably has in mind also the senses
"deserted" and "helpless."

And that he does I weep. Myself am Naples, 435
Who with mine eyes (never since at ebb) beheld
The King my father wrack'd.
MIRANDA   Alack, for mercy!
FERDINAND Yes, faith, and all his lords, the Duke of Milan
And his brave son being twain.
PROSPERO   [*Aside.*] The Duke of Milan
And his more braver daughter could control thee, 440
If now 'twere fit to do't. At the first sight
They have chang'd eyes. Delicate Ariel,
I'll set thee free for this.—A word, good sir,
I fear you have done yourself some wrong; a word.
MIRANDA Why speaks my father so ungently? This 445
Is the third man that e'er I saw; the first
That e'er I sigh'd for. Pity move my father
To be inclin'd my way!
FERDINAND   O, if a virgin,
And your affection not gone forth, I'll make you
The Queen of Naples.
PROSPERO   Soft, sir, one word more. 450
[*Aside.*] They are both in either's pow'rs; but this swift business
I must uneasy make, lest too light winning
Make the prize light.—One word more: I charge thee
That thou attend me. Thou dost here usurp
The name thou ow'st not, and hast put thyself 455
Upon this island as a spy, to win it
From me, the lord on't.
FERDINAND   No, as I am a man.
MIRANDA There's nothing ill can dwell in such a temple.
If the ill spirit have so fair a house,
Good things will strive to dwell with't.
PROSPERO   Follow me.— 460
Speak not you for him; he's a traitor.—Come,
I'll manacle thy neck and feet together.
Sea-water shalt thou drink; thy food shall be
The fresh-brook mussels, wither'd roots, and husks

---

435. Naples: King of Naples. **436. at ebb:** dry (a part of the continued sea-imagery in the play). **439. his brave son:** Not mentioned elsewhere in the play. **440. control:** refute. **442. chang'd eyes:** exchanged loving looks. **444. done . . . wrong:** An ironically polite way of charging him with lying. **452. uneasy:** difficult. **452–53. light . . . light:** easy . . . lightly esteemed. **457. on't:** of it.

Wherein the acorn cradled. Follow.
FERDINAND   No,   465
  I will resist such entertainment till
  Mine enemy has more pow'r.
    He draws, and is charmed from moving.
MIRANDA   O dear father,
  Make not too rash a trial of him, for
  He's gentle, and not fearful.
PROSPERO   What, I say,
  My foot my tutor? Put thy sword up, traitor,   470
  Who mak'st a show but dar'st not strike, thy conscience
  Is so possess'd with guilt. Come, from thy ward,
  For I can here disarm thee with this stick,
  And make thy weapon drop.
MIRANDA   Beseech you, father.
PROSPERO Hence! hang not on my garments.
MIRANDA   Sir, have pity,   475
  I'll be his surety.
PROSPERO   Silence! one word more
  Shall make me chide thee, if not hate thee. What,
  An advocate for an impostor? Hush!
  Thou think'st there is no more such shapes as he,
  Having seen but him and Caliban. Foolish wench,   480
  To th' most of men this is a Caliban,
  And they to him are angels.
MIRANDA   My affections
  Are then most humble; I have no ambition
  To see a goodlier man.
PROSPERO [*To Ferdinand.*] Come on, obey:
  Thy nerves are in their infancy again   485
  And have no vigor in them.
FERDINAND   So they are.
  My spirits, as in a dream, are all bound up.
  My father's loss, the weakness which I feel,
  The wrack of all my friends, nor this man's threats
  To whom I am subdu'd, are but light to me,   490
  Might I but through my prison once a day
  Behold this maid. All corners else o' th' earth

---

469. gentle: of high birth. **fearful:** cowardly.   **470. foot:** i.e., subordinate (Miranda).   **472. ward:** position of defense.   **476. I'll be his surety:** I'll vouch for him. (*Tiffany*)   **481. To:** in comparison with.   **482. affections:** inclinations.   **485. nerves:** sinews.   **487. spirits:** vital powers.

Let liberty make use of; space enough
Have I in such a prison.
PROSPERO   [*Aside.*] It works. [*To Ferdinand.*] Come on.—
    Thou hast done well, fine Ariel! [*To Ferdinand.*] Follow me.   495
    [*To Ariel.*] Hark what thou else shalt do me.
MIRANDA   Be of comfort,
    My father's of a better nature, sir,
    Than he appears by speech. This is unwonted
    Which now came from him.
PROSPERO   Thou shalt be as free
    As mountain winds; but then exactly do   500
    All points of my command.
ARIEL   To th' syllable.
PROSPERO   [*To Ferdinand.*] Come, follow.
    [*To Miranda.*] Speak not for him.   *Exeunt.*

496. do me: do for me.

Act 2

Enter ALONSO, SEBASTIAN, ANTONIO, GONZALO,
ADRIAN, FRANCISCO, *and others.*

GONZALO Beseech you, sir, be merry; you have cause
(So have we all) of joy; for our escape
Is much beyond our loss. Our hint of woe
Is common: every day some sailor's wife,
The masters of some merchant, and the merchant   5
Have just our theme of woe; but for the miracle
(I mean our preservation), few in millions
Can speak like us. Then wisely, good sir, weigh
Our sorrow with our comfort.
ALONSO   Prithee peace.
SEBASTIAN He receives comfort like cold porridge.   10
ANTONIO The visitor will not give him o'er so.
SEBASTIAN Look, he's winding up the watch of his wit, by
and by it will strike.
GONZALO Sir—
SEBASTIAN One. Tell.   15
GONZALO When every grief is entertain'd that's offer'd,
Comes to th' entertainer—
SEBASTIAN A dollar.
GONZALO Dolor comes to him indeed, you have spoken
truer than you purpos'd.   20
SEBASTIAN You have taken it wiselier than I meant you
should.
GONZALO Therefore, my lord—

2.1. Location: Another part of the island. **3. hint:** occasion. **5. masters . . .
the merchant:** chief officers of some merchant vessel, and the owner of it.
9. with: against. **10. porridge:** There is an underlying pun on *peace* (line
9) and *pease,* i.e., peas, a common ingredient of porridge. **11. visitor:** minister who visits the sick and bereaved, i.e., would-be comforter, here Gonzalo.
15. Tell: count. **17. entertainer:** sufferer. Sebastian puns on the sense "innkeeper."
18. dollar: a continental coin. **19. Dolor:** sorrow.

ANTONIO Fie, what a spendthrift is he of his tongue!
ALONSO I prithee spare. 25
GONZALO Well, I have done. But yet—
SEBASTIAN He will be talking.
ANTONIO Which, of he or Adrian, for a good wager,
first begins to crow?
SEBASTIAN The old cock. 30
ANTONIO The cock'rel.
SEBASTIAN Done. The wager?
ANTONIO A laughter.
SEBASTIAN A match!
ADRIAN Though this island seem to be desert— 35
SEBASTIAN Ha, ha, ha!
ANTONIO So: you're paid!
ADRIAN Uninhabitable, and almost inaccessible—
SEBASTIAN Yet—
ADRIAN Yet— 40
ANTONIO He could not miss't.
ADRIAN It must needs be of subtle, tender, and delicate
temperance.
ANTONIO Temperance was a delicate wench.
SEBASTIAN Ay, and a subtle, as he most learnedly deliver'd. 45
ADRIAN The air breathes upon us here most sweetly.
SEBASTIAN As if it had lungs, and rotten ones.
ANTONIO Or, as 'twere perfum'd by a fen.
GONZALO Here is every thing advantageous to life. 50
ANTONIO True, save means to live.
SEBASTIAN Of that there's none, or little.
GONZALO How lush and lusty the grass looks! How
green!
ANTONIO The ground indeed is tawny. 55
SEBASTIAN With an eye of green in't.
ANTONIO He misses not much.
SEBASTIAN No; he doth but mistake the truth totally.
GONZALO But the rariety of it is—which is indeed almost
beyond credit— 60

30. **old cock:** i.e., Gonzalo. **31. cock'rel:** i.e., Adrian. **35. desert:** deserted, un-inhabited. (*Tiffany*) **36. Ha, ha, ha:** Antonio wins the bet, since Adrian spoke first. The winner was entitled to a laugh, and though he gets one from Sebastian, most editors reverse the speech prefixes for lines 36 and 37, because of "you're paid." (*Tiffany*) **43. temperance:** climate. Antonio puns on the word as a girl's name. **55. tawny:** parched tan or yellow. **59. rariety:** Perhaps this spelling indicates an unusual pronunciation of the word by Gonzalo, which Sebastian mimics.

SEBASTIAN As many vouch'd rarieties are.
GONZALO That our garments, being (as they were)
   drench'd in the sea, hold notwithstanding their freshness
   and glosses, being rather new dy'd than stain'd
   with salt water.   65
ANTONIO If but one of his pockets could speak, would
   it not say he lies?
SEBASTIAN Ay, or very falsely pocket up his report.
GONZALO Methinks our garments are now as fresh as
   when we put them on first in Afric, at the marriage   70
   of the King's fair daughter Claribel to the King of Tunis.
SEBASTIAN 'Twas a sweet marriage, and we prosper well
   in our return.
ADRIAN Tunis was never grac'd before with such a   75
   paragon to their queen.
GONZALO Not since widow Dido's time.
ANTONIO Widow? a pox o' that! How came that
   widow in? Widow Dido!
SEBASTIAN What if he had said "widower Aeneas" too?   80
   Good Lord, how you take it!
ADRIAN "Widow Dido," said you? You make me
   study of that. She was of Carthage, not of Tunis.
GONZALO This Tunis, sir, was Carthage.
ADRIAN Carthage?   85
GONZALO I assure you, Carthage.
ANTONIO His word is more than the miraculous harp.
SEBASTIAN He hath rais'd the wall, and houses too.
ANTONIO What impossible matter will he make easy
   next?   90
SEBASTIAN I think he will carry this island home in his
   pocket, and give it his son for an apple.
ANTONIO And sowing the kernels of it in the sea,
   bring forth more islands.
GONZALO Ay.   95
ANTONIO Why, in good time.

---

61. vouch'd: vouched for. (*Tiffany*) **68. pocket up:** conceal, suppress. One who
failed to challenge a lie or an insult was said to "pocket up" the injury. **76. to:**
for. **84. This ... Carthage:** Tunis and Carthage were separate cities, though not
far apart. **87. miraculous harp:** the legendary harp of Amphion, which raised the
walls of Thebes. Gonzalo's error has created a whole new city. **95. Ay:** Probably
a reassertion of the identity of the two cities. Antonio responds with a sarcastic
expression of approbation.

GONZALO Sir, we were talking that our garments seem
  now as fresh as when we were at Tunis at the marriage
  of your daughter, who is now queen.
ANTONIO And the rarest that e'er came there.   100
SEBASTIAN Bate, I beseech you, widow Dido.
ANTONIO O, widow Dido? Ay, widow Dido.
GONZALO Is not, sir, my doublet as fresh as the first
  day I wore it? I mean, in a sort.
ANTONIO That "sort" was well fish'd for.   105
GONZALO When I wore it at your daughter's marriage?
ALONSO You cram these words into mine ears against
  The stomach of my sense. Would I had never
  Married my daughter there! for coming thence,
  My son is lost and (in my rate) she too,   110
  Who is so far from Italy removed
  I ne'er again shall see her. O thou mine heir
  Of Naples and of Milan, what strange fish
  Hath made his meal on thee?
FRANCISCO   Sir, he may live.
  I saw him beat the surges under him,   115
  And ride upon their backs. He trod the water,
  Whose enmity he flung aside, and breasted
  The surge most swoll'n that met him. His bold head
  'Bove the contentious waves he kept, and oared
  Himself with his good arms in lusty stroke   120
  To th' shore, that o'er his wave-worn basis bowed,
  As stooping to relieve him. I not doubt
  He came alive to land.
ALONSO   No, no, he's gone.
SEBASTIAN Sir, you may thank yourself for this great loss,
  That would not bless our Europe with your daughter,   125
  But rather loose her to an African,
  Where she, at least, is banish'd from your eye,
  Who hath cause to wet the grief on't.
ALONSO   Prithee peace.
SEBASTIAN You were kneel'd to, and importun'd otherwise
  By all of us, and the fair soul herself   130

---

101. Bate: except. **104. in a sort:** sort of. (*Tiffany*) **107–8. You . . . sense:** The image is of force-feeding. (*Tiffany*) **110. rate:** opinion. **121. his wave-worn basis:** the shore's foundation hollowed by the action of the sea. (*Tiffany*) **126. loose:** With second (perhaps primary) sense "lose," often spelled *loose.*

Weigh'd between loathness and obedience, at
Which end o' th' beam should bow. We have lost your son,
I fear for ever. Milan and Naples have
Moe widows in them of this business' making
Than we bring men to comfort them.   135
The fault's your own.
ALONSO   So is the dear'st o' th' loss.
GONZALO My Lord Sebastian,
The truth you speak doth lack some gentleness,
And time to speak it in. You rub the sore,
When you should bring the plaster.
SEBASTIAN   Very well.   140
ANTONIO And most chirurgeonly.
GONZALO It is foul weather in us all, good sir,
When you are cloudy.
SEBASTIAN   Fowl weather?
ANTONIO   Very foul.
GONZALO Had I plantation of this isle, my lord—
ANTONIO He'd sow't with nettle-seed.
SEBASTIAN   Or docks, or mallows.   145
GONZALO And were the king on't, what would I do?
SEBASTIAN Scape being drunk, for want of wine.
GONZALO I' th' commonwealth I would, by contraries,
Execute all things; for no kind of traffic
Would I admit; no name of magistrate;   150
Letters should not be known; riches, poverty,
And use of service, none; contract, succession,
Bourn, bound of land, tilth, vineyard, none;
No use of metal, corn, or wine, or oil;
No occupation, all men idle, all;   155
And women too, but innocent and pure;
No sovereignty—
SEBASTIAN   Yet he would be king on't.

131–32. **Weigh'd ... bow:** weighed in the scale her unwillingness to marry and her duty of obedience to her father, to see which would prevail. **134. Moe:** more. **136. dear'st:** most heartfelt. **139. time:** appropriate occasion. **140. plaster:** healing ointment. (*Tiffany*) **141. chirurgeonly:** like a surgeon. **143. Fowl:** Sebastian's pun returns to the imagery of lines 28–31. **144. plantation:** colonization, but the following speakers take up the word in the sense "planting." **148. contraries:** the opposite of what is customary. **149. traffic:** business, trade. **151. Letters:** learning, literacy. **152. service:** servanthood, serving of some by others. **succession:** inheritance, hereditary privilege. **153. Bourn:** boundary, i.e., division of land among individual owners. **tilth:** tillage. **154. corn:** grain.

ANTONIO The latter end of his commonwealth forgets
  the beginning.
GONZALO All things in common nature should produce   160
  Without sweat or endeavor: treason, felony,
  Sword, pike, knife, gun, or need of any engine,
  Would I not have; but nature should bring forth,
  Of it own kind, all foison, all abundance,
  To feed my innocent people.   165
SEBASTIAN No marrying 'mong his subjects?
ANTONIO None, man, all idle—whores and knaves.
GONZALO I would with such perfection govern, sir,
  T' excel the golden age.
SEBASTIAN   'Save his Majesty!
ANTONIO Long live Gonzalo!   170
GONZALO   And—do you mark me, sir?
ALONSO Prithee no more; thou dost talk nothing to me.
GONZALO I do well believe your Highness, and did it to
  minister occasion to these gentlemen, who are of such
  sensible and nimble lungs that they always use to
  laugh at nothing.   175
ANTONIO 'Twas you we laugh'd at.
GONZALO Who, in this kind of merry fooling, am
  nothing to you; so you may continue, and laugh at nothing still.
ANTONIO What a blow was there given!   180
SEBASTIAN And it had not fall'n flat-long.
GONZALO You are gentlemen of brave mettle; you
  would lift the moon out of her sphere, if she would
  continue in it five weeks without changing.

      Enter ARIEL [*invisible*], *playing solemn music.*

SEBASTIAN We would so, and then go a-batfowling.   185
ANTONIO Nay, good my lord, be not angry.
GONZALO No, I warrant you, I will not adventure my discretion
  so weakly. Will you laugh me asleep, for I am very heavy?
ANTONIO Go sleep, and hear us.   190
      [*All sleep except Alonso, Sebastian, and Antonio.*]

---

162. pike: spear. **engine:** instruments of war. **164. it:** its. **foison:** plenty.
169. 'Save: God save. **173. minister occasion:** give opportunity. **174. sensible
and nimble:** sensitive and lively. **181. And:** if. **flat-long:** with the sword blade
flat, not on edge. **185. a-batfowling:** bird-hunting with sticks (*bats*) at night. He
suggests that they would use the moon as their lantern. **187–88. adventure . . .
weakly:** risk my reputation for good sense by getting angry at such superficial
fellows. **190. hear us:** i.e., listen to our laughter.

ALONSO What, all so soon asleep! I wish mine eyes
  Would, with themselves, shut up my thoughts. I find
  They are inclin'd to do so.
SEBASTIAN   Please you, sir,
  Do not omit the heavy offer of it.
  It seldom visits sorrow; when it doth,   195
  It is a comforter.
ANTONIO   We two, my lord,
  Will guard your person while you take your rest,
  And watch your safety.
ALONSO   Thank you. Wondrous heavy.
                              [*Alonso sleeps. Exit Ariel.*]
SEBASTIAN What a strange drowsiness possesses them!
ANTONIO It is the quality o' th' climate.
SEBASTIAN   Why   200
  Doth it not then our eyelids sink? I find not
  Myself dispos'd to sleep.
ANTONIO   Nor I, my spirits are nimble.
  They fell together all, as by consent;
  They dropp'd, as by a thunder-stroke. What might,
  Worthy Sebastian, O, what might—? No more—   205
  And yet methinks I see it in thy face,
  What thou shouldst be. Th' occasion speaks thee, and
  My strong imagination sees a crown
  Dropping upon thy head.
SEBASTIAN   What? art thou waking?
ANTONIO Do you not hear me speak?
SEBASTIAN   I do, and surely   210
  It is a sleepy language, and thou speak'st
  Out of thy sleep. What is it thou didst say?
  This is a strange repose, to be asleep
  With eyes wide open—standing, speaking, moving—
  And yet so fast asleep.
ANTONIO   Noble Sebastian,   215
  Thou let'st thy fortune sleep—die, rather; wink'st
  Whiles thou art waking.
SEBASTIAN   Thou dost snore distinctly,
  There's meaning in thy snores.
ANTONIO I am more serious than my custom; you

---

194. omit ... offer: neglect the opportunity sleepiness provides. **207. speaks thee:** speaks to thee. (*Tiffany*) **216. wink'st:** keep your eyes shut.

Must be so too, if heed me; which to do,   220
  Trebles thee o'er.
SEBASTIAN   Well; I am standing water.
ANTONIO I'll teach you how to flow.
SEBASTIAN   Do so. To ebb
  Hereditary sloth instructs me.
ANTONIO   O!
  If you but knew how you the purpose cherish
  Whiles thus you mock it! how, in stripping it,   225
  You more invest it! Ebbing men, indeed,
  Most often, do so near the bottom run
  By their own fear or sloth.
SEBASTIAN   Prithee say on.
  The setting of thine eye and cheek proclaim
  A matter from thee; and a birth, indeed,   230
  Which throes thee much to yield.
ANTONIO   Thus, sir:
  Although this lord of weak remembrance, this
  Who shall be of as little memory
  When he is earth'd, hath here almost persuaded
  (For he's a spirit of persuasion, only   235
  Professes to persuade) the King his son's alive,
  'Tis as impossible that he's undrown'd,
  As he that sleeps here swims.
SEBASTIAN   I have no hope
  That he's undrown'd.
ANTONIO   O, out of that no hope
  What great hope have you! No hope, that way, is   240
  Another way so high a hope that even
  Ambition cannot pierce a wink beyond,
  But doubt discovery there. Will you grant with me
  That Ferdinand is drown'd?
SEBASTIAN   He's gone.
ANTONIO Then tell me,

---

221. Trebles thee o'er: triples your fortune. **223. Hereditary sloth:** natural laziness. **224. cherish:** enrich. **226. invest:** dress up. **229. setting:** fixed look. **231. throes:** causes labor pains. **232. this lord:** i.e., Gonzalo. **of weak remembrance:** having a short memory (perhaps alluding to Gonzalo's lapse in identifying Tunis with Carthage); with following shift to the sense "remembered only briefly after death." **234. earth'd:** buried. **235–36. only . . . persuade:** has no function except to persuade. Gonzalo is a privy councillor. **240. that way:** i.e., with respect to Ferdinand's being undrowned. **242. pierce a wink:** penetrate by so much as even a glimpse. The metaphor seems mixed. (*Tiffany*) **243. doubt discovery there:** is uncertain of seeing clearly even there.

Who's the next heir of Naples?
SEBASTIAN   Claribel.   245
ANTONIO She that is Queen of Tunis; she that dwells
    Ten leagues beyond man's life; she that from Naples
    Can have no note, unless the sun were post—
    The Man i' th' Moon's too slow—till new-born chins
    Be rough and razorable; she that from whom   250
    We all were sea-swallow'd, though some cast again
    (And by that destiny) to perform an act
    Whereof what's past is prologue, what to come
    In yours and my discharge.
SEBASTIAN   What stuff is this? How say you?
    'Tis true, my brother's daughter's Queen of Tunis,   255
    So is she heir of Naples; 'twixt which regions
    There is some space.
ANTONIO   A space whose ev'ry cubit
    Seems to cry out, "How shall that Claribel
    Measure us back to Naples? Keep in Tunis,
    And let Sebastian wake." Say this were death   260
    That now hath seiz'd them, why, they were no worse
    Than now they are. There be that can rule Naples
    As well as he that sleeps; lords that can prate
    As amply and unnecessarily
    As this Gonzalo; I myself could make   265
    A chough of as deep chat. O that you bore
    The mind that I do! what a sleep were this
    For your advancement! Do you understand me?
SEBASTIAN Methinks I do.
ANTONIO   And how does your content
    Tender your own good fortune?
SEBASTIAN   I remember   270
    You did supplant your brother Prospero.
ANTONIO   True.
    And look how well my garments sit upon me,
    Much feater than before. My brother's servants
    Were then my fellows, now they are my men.

---

247. Ten . . . life: thirty miles farther than a lifetime's journey. **248. note:** news. **post:** messenger. **250. from:** coming from. **251. cast:** (1) cast up; (2) cast as actors. **254. discharge:** performance. **257. cubit:** measure of about 20 inches. **259. Measure us:** i.e., travel over the cubits. **Keep:** Stay. (*Tiffany*) **260. wake:** i.e., awake to fortune. **265–66. make . . . chat:** train a jackdaw to speak as wisely as he. **269. content:** inclination. **270. Tender:** regard. **273. feater:** more gracefully.

SEBASTIAN But, for your conscience? 275

ANTONIO Ay, sir; where lies that? If 'twere a kibe,
   'Twould put me to my slipper; but I feel not
   This deity in my bosom. Twenty consciences,
   That stand 'twixt me and Milan, candied be they,
   And melt ere they molest! Here lies your brother, 280
   No better than the earth he lies upon,
   If he were that which now he's like—that's dead,
   Whom I with this obedient steel, three inches of it,
   Can lay to bed for ever; whiles you, doing thus,
   To the perpetual wink for aye might put 285
   This ancient morsel, this Sir Prudence, who
   Should not upbraid our course. For all the rest,
   They'll take suggestion as a cat laps milk;
   They'll tell the clock to any business that
   We say befits the hour.

SEBASTIAN   Thy case, dear friend, 290
   Shall be my president: as thou got'st Milan,
   I'll come by Naples. Draw thy sword. One stroke
   Shall free thee from the tribute which thou payest,
   And I the King shall love thee.

ANTONIO   Draw together;
   And when I rear my hand, do you the like, 295
   To fall it on Gonzalo.

SEBASTIAN   O, but one word. [*They talk apart.*]

Enter ARIEL [*invisible*]*, with music and song.*

ARIEL My master through his art foresees the danger
   That you, his friend, are in, and sends me forth
   (For else his project dies) to keep them living.

                        Sings in Gonzalo's ear.

     While you here do snoring lie, 300
     Open-ey'd conspiracy
       His time doth take.
     If of life you keep a care,
     Shake off slumber, and beware.
       Awake, awake! 305

ANTONIO Then let us both be sudden.

---

276. kibe: swelling or ulcer. (*Tiffany*)   **277. put me to:** make me wear.   **279. Milan:** the dukedom of Milan.   **285. wink:** sleep. **for aye:** forever. (*Tiffany*)   **287. upbraid:** scold us for. (*Tiffany*)   **288. suggestion:** evil prompting.   **289. tell . . . to:** i.e., agree that the time sorts with.   **291. president:** precedent.   **296. fall it:** let it fall.   **302. time:** opportunity.

GONZALO [*Waking.*]   Now, good angels
  Preserve the King! [*Wakes Alonso.*]
ALONSO Why, how now, ho! Awake? Why are you drawn?
  Wherefore this ghastly looking?
GONZALO   What's the matter?
SEBASTIAN Whiles we stood here securing your repose,   310
  Even now, we heard a hollow burst of bellowing
  Like bulls, or rather lions. Did't not wake you?
  It strook mine ear most terribly.
ALONSO   I heard nothing.
ANTONIO O, 'twas a din to fright a monster's ear,
  To make an earthquake; sure it was the roar   315
  Of a whole herd of lions.
ALONSO   Heard you this, Gonzalo?
GONZALO Upon mine honor, sir, I heard a humming
  (And that a strange one too) which did awake me.
  I shak'd you, sir, and cried. As mine eyes open'd,
  I saw their weapons drawn. There was a noise,   320
  That's verily. 'Tis best we stand upon our guard,
  Or that we quit this place. Let's draw our weapons.
ALONSO Lead off this ground, and let's make further search
  For my poor son.
GONZALO   Heavens keep him from these beasts!
  For he is sure i' th' island.
ALONSO   Lead away.   325
ARIEL Prospero my lord shall know what I have done.
  So, King, go safely on to seek thy son.   *Exeunt.*

SCENE 2

Enter CALIBAN *with a burthen of wood. A noise of
thunder heard.*

CALIBAN All the infections that the sun sucks up
  From bogs, fens, flats, on Prosper fall, and make him
  By inch-meal a disease! His spirits hear me,
  And yet I needs must curse. But they'll nor pinch,
  Fright me with urchin-shows, pitch me i' th' mire,   5

---

310. securing: guarding. **313. strook:** struck. **319. cried:** called out.
2.2. Location: Another part of the island. **3. By inch-meal:** inch by inch. Cf.
piecemeal. **5. urchin-shows:** sights of goblins in the shape of hedgehogs.

Nor lead me, like a fire-brand, in the dark
Out of my way, unless he bid 'em; but
For every trifle are they set upon me,
Sometime like apes that mow and chatter at me,
And after bite me; then like hedgehogs which   10
Lie tumbling in my barefoot way, and mount
Their pricks at my footfall; sometime am I
All wound with adders, who with cloven tongues
Do hiss me into madness.

Enter TRINCULO.

                                        Lo, now lo,
Here comes a spirit of his, and to torment me   15
For bringing wood in slowly. I'll fall flat,
Perchance he will not mind me.
TRINCULO Here's neither bush nor shrub to bear off any
    weather at all. And another storm brewing, I hear it
    sing i' th' wind. Yond same black cloud, yond   20
    huge one, looks like a foul bumbard that would shed
    his liquor. If it should thunder as it did before, I know
    not where to hide my head. Yond same cloud cannot
    choose but fall by pailfuls. What have we here?
    a man or a fish? dead or alive? A fish, he smells   25
    like a fish; a very ancient and fish-like smell; a kind of,
    not-of-the-newest poor-John. A strange fish! Were I
    in England now (as once I was) and had but this fish
    painted, not a holiday fool there but would give a piece
    of silver. There would this monster make a man;   30
    any strange beast there makes a man. When they will
    not give a doit to relieve a lame beggar, they will lay
    out ten to see a dead Indian. Legg'd like a man; and
    his fins like arms! Warm, o' my troth! I do now let
    loose my opinion, hold it no longer: this is no fish,   35
    but an islander, that hath lately suffer'd by a thunderbolt.
    [*Thunder.*] Alas, the storm is come again! My

6. **like a fire-brand:** in the shape of a will-o'-the-wisp, or floating fire. Will-o'-the-wisps, thought to be spirits, were the result of nighttime phosphorescence caused by swamp gas. (*Tiffany*) 9. **mow:** make faces. 13. **wound:** twined about. 17. **mind:** notice. 18. **bear off:** ward off. 21. **bumbard:** bombard, leather bottle. 22. **his:** its. 27. **poor-John:** cheap dried fish. 29. **painted:** i.e., on a sign hung outside a booth at a fair to attract customers, with the monster exhibited within. 30. **make a man:** make a man's fortune, with obvious punning sense "be indistinguishable from an Englishman." 32. **doit:** coin of trifling value. 34. **o' my troth:** by my faith. 35. **hold it:** hold it back.

best way is to creep under his gaberdine; there is no
other shelter hereabout. Misery acquaints a man with
strange bedfellows; I will here shroud till the dregs of   40
the storm be past.

       Enter STEPHANO, *singing,* [*a bottle in his hand*].

STEPHANO "I shall no more to sea, to sea,
      Here shall I die ashore—"
This is a very scurvy tune to sing at a man's funeral.
Well, here's my comfort. *Drinks.*   45
(*Sings.*) "The master, the swabber, the boatswain, and I,
    The gunner and his mate,
Lov'd Mall, Meg, and Marian, and Margery,
    But none of us car'd for Kate;
    For she had a tongue with a tang,
    Would cry to a sailor, 'Go hang!'   50
She lov'd not the savor of tar nor of pitch,
Yet a tailor might scratch her where e'er she did itch.
    Then to sea, boys, and let her go hang!"
This is a scurvy tune too; but here's my comfort.   55
                              Drinks.

CALIBAN Do not torment me! O!

STEPHANO What's the matter? Have we devils here? Do
you put tricks upon's with salvages and men of Inde?
Ha? I have not scap'd drowning to be afeard now of
your four legs; for it hath been said, "As proper a   60
man as ever went on four legs cannot make him give
ground"; and it shall be said so again while Stephano
breathes at' nostrils.

CALIBAN The spirit torments me! O!

STEPHANO This is some monster of the isle with four legs,   65
who hath got (as I take it) an ague. Where the devil
should he learn our language? I will give him some
relief, if it be but for that. If I can recover him, and
keep him tame, and get to Naples with him, he's a
present for any emperor that ever trod on neat's-leather.   70

CALIBAN Do not torment me, prithee. I'll bring my
wood home faster.

---

38. gaberdine: loose cloak of coarse material. **58. put tricks upon's:** delude us with a conjuror's or showman's devices. **salvages:** savages. **Inde:** India.
60–61. As . . . legs: Stephano adapts a proverbial expression by substituting *four*
for *two. Proper* = handsome. *Give ground* = retreat. (*Tiffany*) **68. recover:** cure.
(*Tiffany*) **70. neat's-leather:** cowhide.

STEPHANO He's in his fit now, and does not talk after the
wisest. He shall taste of my bottle; if he have never
drunk wine afore, it will go near to remove his fit.   75
If I can recover him, and keep him tame, I will not take
too much for him; he shall pay for him that hath him,
and that soundly.

CALIBAN Thou dost me yet but little hurt; thou wilt
anon, I know it by thy trembling. Now Prosper works   80
upon thee.

STEPHANO Come on your ways. Open your mouth; here
is that which will give language to you, cat. Open your
mouth; this will shake your shaking, I can tell you,
and that soundly. You cannot tell who's your friend.   85
Open your chaps again. [*Caliban drinks.*]

TRINCULO I should know that voice; it should be—but
he is drown'd; and these are devils. O, defend me!

STEPHANO Four legs and two voices; a most delicate
monster! His forward voice now is to speak well   90
of his friend; his backward voice is to utter foul
speeches and to detract. If all the wine in my bottle
will recover him, I will help his ague. Come. [*Caliban
drinks again.*] Amen! I will pour some in thy other
mouth.   95

TRINCULO Stephano!

STEPHANO Doth thy other mouth call me? Mercy, mercy!
This is a devil, and no monster. I will leave him, I have
no long spoon.

TRINCULO Stephano! If thou beest Stephano, touch me,   100
and speak to me; for I am Trinculo—be not afeard—thy
good friend Trinculo.

STEPHANO If thou beest Trinculo, come forth. I'll pull
thee by the lesser legs. If any be Trinculo's legs, these
are they. Thou art very Trinculo indeed! How   105
cam'st thou to be the siege of this moon-calf? Can he
vent Trinculos?

TRINCULO I took him to be kill'd with a thunder-stroke.

76–77. I will . . . much: whatever I can take for him won't be too much.
77. hath: gets. **79–80. thou wilt anon:** i.e., you will hurt me more very
soon. **82–83. here . . . cat:** Alluding to the proverb "Liquor will make a cat
talk." **86. chaps:** jaws. **89. delicate:** ingenious. **99. long spoon:** Alluding to the proverb "He must have a long spoon that will eat with the devil."
106. siege: excrement. **moon-calf:** monstrosity, creature born misshapen because
of lunary influence.

But art thou not drown'd, Stephano? I hope now thou
art not drown'd. Is the storm overblown? I hid   110
me under the dead moon-calf's gaberdine for fear of the
storm. And art thou living, Stephano? O Stephano,
two Neapolitans scap'd!
STEPHANO Prithee do not turn me about, my stomach is
not constant.   115
CALIBAN [*Aside.*] These be fine things, and if they be
    not sprites.
That's a brave god, and bears celestial liquor.
I will kneel to him.
STEPHANO How didst thou scape? How cam'st thou
hither? Swear by this bottle how thou cam'st   120
hither—I escap'd upon a butt of sack which the sailors
heav'd o'erboard—by this bottle, which I made of the
bark of a tree with mine own hands since I was cast
ashore.
CALIBAN I'll swear upon that bottle to be thy true subject,   125
for the liquor is not earthly.
STEPHANO Here; swear then how thou escap'dst.
TRINCULO Swom ashore, man, like a duck. I can swim
like a duck, I'll be sworn.
STEPHANO Here, kiss the book. [*Passing the bottle.*]   130
Though thou canst swim like a duck, thou art made like
a goose.
TRINCULO O Stephano, hast any more of this?
STEPHANO The whole butt, man. My cellar is in a rock by
th' sea-side, where my wine is hid. How now, mooncalf?   135
how does thine ague?
CALIBAN Hast thou not dropp'd from heaven?
STEPHANO Out o' th' moon, I do assure thee. I was the
Man i' th' Moon, when time was.
CALIBAN I have seen thee in her, and I do adore thee.   140
My mistress show'd me thee, and thy dog, and thy bush.
STEPHANO Come, swear to that; kiss the book. I will
furnish it anon with new contents. Swear.

[*Caliban drinks.*]

---

116. and if: if. **121. butt of sack:** barrel of Spanish wine. **128. Swom:**
swam. **130. kiss the book:** Trinculo has taken his oath on the bottle, not on the
customary Bible. Stephano means "Take a drink." **139. when time was:** once
upon a time. **141. dog . . . bush:** The man in the moon was placed there in punishment for gathering firewood on Sunday. He carries a "bush" of sticks and has a
dog. See *MND* 3.1.59-60 and 5.1.35-36. (*Tiffany*)

TRINCULO By this good light, this is a very shallow
　　monster! I afeard of him? A very weak monster!　　　　145
　　The Man i' th' Moon? A most poor credulous monster!
　　Well drawn, monster, in good sooth!
CALIBAN I'll show thee every fertile inch o' th' island;
　　And I will kiss thy foot. I prithee be my god.
TRINCULO By this light, a most perfidious and drunken　　150
　　monster! When's god's asleep, he'll rob his bottle.
CALIBAN I'll kiss thy foot. I'll swear myself thy subject.
STEPHANO Come on then; down, and swear.
TRINCULO I shall laugh myself to death at this puppy-headed
　　monster. A most scurvy monster! I could find　　　　155
　　in my heart to beat him—
STEPHANO Come, kiss.
TRINCULO But that the poor monster's in drink. An
　　abominable monster!
CALIBAN I'll show thee the best springs; I'll pluck thee
　　　　berries;　　　　　　　　　　　　　　　　　　　160
　　I'll fish for thee, and get thee wood enough.
　　A plague upon the tyrant that I serve!
　　I'll bear him no more sticks, but follow thee,
　　Thou wondrous man.
TRINCULO A most ridiculous monster, to make a wonder　　165
　　of a poor drunkard!
CALIBAN I prithee let me bring thee where crabs grow;
　　And I with my long nails will dig thee pig-nuts,
　　Show thee a jay's nest, and instruct thee how
　　To snare the nimble marmazet. I'll bring thee　　　　170
　　To clust'ring filberts, and sometimes I'll get thee
　　Young scamels from the rock. Wilt thou go with me?
STEPHANO I prithee now lead the way without any more
　　talking. Trinculo, the King and all our company else
　　being drown'd, we will inherit here. Here! bear　　　175
　　my bottle. Fellow Trinculo, we'll fill him by and by again.
CALIBAN [Sings drunkenly.] Farewell, master; fare-
　　well, farewell!
TRINCULO A howling monster; a drunken monster!

---

147. **Well drawn:** that's a good long draught you've taken. **sooth:** truth.　**167.**
crabs: crab apples.　**168. pig-nuts:** acorns. (*Tiffany*)　**170. marmazet:** marmo-
set (a small monkey).　**172. scamels:** Meaning unknown, but apparently either
shellfish or rock-inhabiting birds. Some editors emend to *sea-mels,* i.e., sea-mews.

CALIBAN   No more dams I'll make for fish,   180
   Nor fetch in firing
   At requiring,
   Nor scrape trenchering, nor wash dish.
   'Ban, 'Ban, Ca-Caliban
   Has a new master, get a new man.   185
  Freedom, high-day! high-day, freedom! freedom, high-
 day, freedom!
STEPHANO   O brave monster! lead the way.   *Exeunt.*

---

180. dams: barriers to pen fish. (*Tiffany*)   **181. firing:** firewood. (*Tiffany*)
183. trenchering: trenchers, wooden plates.

Act 3

SCENE I

Enter FERDINAND *bearing a log.*

FERDINAND There be some sports are painful, and their labor
  Delight in them [sets] off; some kinds of baseness
  Are nobly undergone; and most poor matters
  Point to rich ends. This my mean task
  Would be as heavy to me as odious, but   5
  The mistress which I serve quickens what's dead,
  And makes my labors pleasures. O, she is
  Ten times more gentle than her father's crabbed;
  And he's compos'd of harshness. I must remove
  Some thousands of these logs, and pile them up,   10
  Upon a sore injunction. My sweet mistress
  Weeps when she sees me work, and says such baseness
  Had never like executor. I forget;
  But these sweet thoughts do even refresh my labors,
  Most [busil'est] when I do it.

              Enter MIRANDA, *and* PROSPERO
              [*at a distance, unseen*].

MIRANDA   Alas, now pray you   15
  Work not so hard. I would the lightning had
  Burnt up those logs that you are enjoin'd to pile!
  Pray set it down, and rest you. When this burns,
  'Twill weep for having wearied you. My father
  Is hard at study; pray now rest yourself,   20
  He's safe for these three hours.
FERDINAND   O most dear mistress,

3.1. Location: Before Prospero's cell. **1. are painful:** that are laborious.
1–2. their . . . off: their difficulty both postpones and adorns (two meanings of
"sets off") delight in victory or achievement. (*Tiffany*) **2. baseness:** menial activ-
ity. **6. quickens:** brings to life. **8. crabbed:** crabby. (*Tiffany*) **11. sore injunction:** harsh command. **13. like:** such, i.e., such a noble. **15. Most . . . it:** when
I am working hardest. **19. weep:** i.e., exude resin.

The sun will set before I shall discharge
What I must strive to do.
MIRANDA   If you'll sit down,
  I'll bear your logs the while. Pray give me that,
  I'll carry it to the pile.
FERDINAND   No, precious creature,   25
  I had rather crack my sinews, break my back,
  Than you should such dishonor undergo,
  While I sit lazy by.
MIRANDA   It would become me
  As well as it does you; and I should do it
  With much more ease, for my good will is to it,   30
  And yours it is against.
PROSPERO   [*Aside.*] Poor worm, thou art infected!
  This visitation shows it.
MIRANDA   You look wearily.
FERDINAND No, noble mistress, 'tis fresh morning with me
  When you are by at night. I do beseech you—
  Chiefly that I might set it in my prayers—   35
  What is your name?
MIRANDA   Miranda.—O my father,
  I have broke your hest to say so.
FERDINAND   Admir'd Miranda,
  Indeed the top of admiration! worth
  What's dearest to the world! Full many a lady
  I have ey'd with best regard, and many a time   40
  Th' harmony of their tongues hath into bondage
  Brought my too diligent ear. For several virtues
  Have I lik'd several women, never any
  With so full soul but some defect in her
  Did quarrel with the noblest grace she ow'd,   45
  And put it to the foil. But you, O you,
  So perfect and so peerless, are created
  Of every creature's best!
MIRANDA   I do not know
  One of my sex; no woman's face remember,
  Save, from my glass, mine own; nor have I seen   50
  More that I may call men than you, good friend,

---

32. visitation: (1) visit; (2) attack of plague (carrying on the medical figure in *infected*). **37. hest:** command. **Admir'd Miranda:** A pun, since *Miranda* = admired, i.e., wondered at. **40. best regard:** highest approval. **42, 43. several:** particular. **45. ow'd:** owned. **46. foil:** (1) contrast; (2) defeat.

And my dear father. How features are abroad
I am skilless of; but by my modesty
(The jewel in my dower), I would not wish
Any companion in the world but you;   55
Nor can imagination form a shape,
Besides yourself, to like of. But I prattle
Something too wildly, and my father's precepts
I therein do forget.
FERDINAND   I am, in my condition,
    A prince, Miranda; I do think, a king   60
    (I would, not so!), and would no more endure
    This wooden slavery than to suffer
    The flesh-fly blow my mouth. Hear my soul speak:
    The very instant that I saw you, did
    My heart fly to your service, there resides,   65
    To make me slave to it, and for your sake
    Am I this patient log-man.
MIRANDA   Do you love me?
FERDINAND O heaven, O earth, bear witness to this sound,
    And crown what I profess with kind event
    If I speak true! if hollowly, invert   70
    What best is boded me to mischief! I,
    Beyond all limit of what else i' th' world,
    Do love, prize, honor you.
MIRANDA   I am a fool
    To weep at what I am glad of.
PROSPERO   [Aside.] Fair encounter
    Of two most rare affections! Heavens rain grace   75
    On that which breeds between 'em!
FERDINAND   Wherefore weep you?
MIRANDA At mine unworthiness, that dare not offer
    What I desire to give; and much less take
    What I shall die to want. But this is trifling,
    And all the more it seeks to hide itself,   80
    The bigger bulk it shows. Hence, bashful cunning,
    And prompt me, plain and holy innocence!
    I am your wife, if you will marry me;
    If not, I'll die your maid. To be your fellow

---

52. abroad: elsewhere. **53. skilless:** ignorant. **59. condition:** rank. **63. blow:** defile. **69. kind event:** favorable outcome. **70. hollowly:** insincerely. **70–71. invert ... to mischief:** turn ... to ill fortune. **71. boded:** destined. **79. want:** be without. **84. maid:** handmaiden. **fellow:** mate.

You may deny me, but I'll be your servant,   85
Whether you will or no.
FERDINAND   My mistress, dearest,
And I thus humble ever.
MIRANDA   My husband then?
FERDINAND Ay, with a heart as willing
As bondage e'er of freedom. Here's my hand.
MIRANDA And mine, with my heart in't. And now farewell   90
Till half an hour hence.
FERDINAND   A thousand, thousand!
                    Exeunt [Ferdinand and Miranda severally].
PROSPERO So glad of this as they I cannot be,
Who are surpris'd [withal]; but my rejoicing
At nothing can be more. I'll to my book,
For yet ere supper-time must I perform   95
Much business appertaining.   *Exit.*

SCENE 2

Enter CALIBAN, STEPHANO, *and* TRINCULO.

STEPHANO Tell not me. When the butt is out, we will
drink water—not a drop before; therefore bear up and
board 'em. Servant-monster, drink to me.
TRINCULO Servant-monster? the folly of this island!
They say there's but five upon this isle: we are three   5
of them; if th' other two be brain'd like us, the state
totters.
STEPHANO Drink, servant-monster, when I bid thee.
Thy eyes are almost set in thy head.
TRINCULO Where should they be set else? He were a   10
brave monster indeed if they were set in his tail.
STEPHANO My man-monster hath drown'd his tongue in
sack. For my part, the sea cannot drown me; I swam,
ere I could recover the shore, five and thirty leagues off
and on. By this light, thou shalt be my lieutenant,   15
monster, or my standard.

91. thousand: i.e., thousand farewells.   93. withal: with it, i.e., by it. "Who" is
the subject of "are surprised," and "Who" refers to "they." (*Tiffany*)   3.2. Location:
Another part of the island.   1. out: empty.   2–3. bear . . . 'em: stand firm and
attack. Stephano uses naval jargon as an encouragement to drink.   4. folly of:
low level of intellect on.   9. set: sunk out of sight. Trinculo puns on the sense
"placed."   16. standard: standard-bearer.

TRINCULO Your lieutenant if you list, he's no standard.

STEPHANO We'll not run, Monsieur Monster.

TRINCULO Nor go neither; but you'll lie like dogs, and
    yet say nothing neither.   20

STEPHANO Moon-calf, speak once in thy life, if thou beest
    a good moon-calf.

CALIBAN How does thy honor? Let me lick thy shoe.
    I'll not serve him, he is not valiant.

TRINCULO Thou liest, most ignorant monster, I am in   25
    case to justle a constable. Why, thou debosh'd fish
    thou, was there ever man a coward that hath drunk so
    much sack as I to-day? Wilt thou tell a monstrous lie,
    being but half a fish and half a monster?

CALIBAN Lo, how he mocks me! Wilt thou let him, my   30
    lord?

TRINCULO "Lord," quoth he? That a monster should be
    such a natural!

CALIBAN Lo, lo again. Bite him to death, I prithee.

STEPHANO Trinculo, keep a good tongue in your head. If   35
    you prove a mutineer—the next tree! The poor monster's
    my subject, and he shall not suffer indignity.

CALIBAN I thank my noble lord. Wilt thou be pleas'd to
    hearken once again to the suit I made to thee?

STEPHANO Marry, will I; kneel, and repeat it. I will stand,   40
    and so shall Trinculo.

Enter ARIEL, *invisible.*

CALIBAN As I told thee before, I am subject to a tyrant,
    A sorcerer, that by his cunning hath
    Cheated me of the island.

ARIEL Thou liest.   45

CALIBAN   Thou liest, thou jesting monkey thou!
    I would my valiant master would destroy thee.
    I do not lie.

STEPHANO Trinculo, if you trouble him any more in's
    tale, by this hand, I will supplant some of your teeth.

TRINCULO Why, I said nothing.   50

---

17. list: (1) like; (2) lean (nautical term, supporting the joke of drunks not being
able to stand). (*Tiffany*) **no standard:** i.e., unable to stand.   **18. run:** i.e., run from
the enemy.   **19. go:** walk. **lie:** (1) lie down; (2) tell lies.   **26. case:** fit condition.
justle: jostle. (*Tiffany*) **debosh'd:** debauched.   **33. natural:** idiot. The point is that
a monster is by definition "unnatural."   **40. Marry:** indeed (originally the name
of the Virgin Mary used as an oath).

STEPHANO Mum then, and no more.—Proceed.

CALIBAN I say by sorcery he got this isle;
    From me he got it. If thy greatness will
    Revenge it on him—for I know thou dar'st,
    But this thing dare not—   55

STEPHANO That's most certain.

CALIBAN Thou shalt be lord of it, and I'll serve thee.

STEPHANO How now shall this be compass'd? Canst thou
    bring me to the party?

CALIBAN Yea, yea, my lord. I'll yield him thee asleep,   60
    Where thou mayst knock a nail into his head.

ARIEL Thou liest, thou canst not.

CALIBAN What a pied ninny's this! Thou scurvy patch!
    I do beseech thy greatness, give him blows,
    And take his bottle from him. When that's gone,   65
    He shall drink nought but brine, for I'll not show him
    Where the quick freshes are.

STEPHANO Trinculo, run into no further danger; interrupt
    the monster one word further, and by this hand,
    I'll turn my mercy out o' doors, and make a stock-fish   70
    of thee.

TRINCULO Why, what did I? I did nothing. I'll go
    farther off.

STEPHANO Didst thou not say he lied?

ARIEL Thou liest.   75

STEPHANO Do I so? Take thou that.   [*Beats Trinculo.*]
    As you like this, give me the lie another time.

TRINCULO I did not give the lie. Out o' your wits, and
    hearing too? A pox o' your bottle! this can sack
    and drinking do. A murrain on your monster, and the   80
    devil take your fingers!

CALIBAN Ha, ha, ha!

STEPHANO Now forward with your tale.—Prithee stand
    further off.

CALIBAN Beat him enough. After a little time   85
    I'll beat him too.

STEPHANO   Stand farther.—Come, proceed.

---

55. this thing: i.e., Trinculo.   **63. pied . . . patch:** foolish . . . fool (from the multicolored garb of the professional fool).   **67. quick freshes:** fresh-water springs.   **70. stock-fish:** dried cod, so stiff it had to be beaten before cooking.   **77. give me the lie:** accuse me of lying. (*Tiffany*)   **80. murrain:** a disease of cattle.

CALIBAN Why, as I told thee, 'tis a custom with him
　I' th' afternoon to sleep. There thou mayst brain him,
　Having first seiz'd his books; or with a log
　Batter his skull, or paunch him with a stake,　　　　　　90
　Or cut his wezand with thy knife. Remember
　First to possess his books; for without them
　He's but a sot, as I am; nor hath not
　One spirit to command: they all do hate him
　As rootedly as I. Burn but his books.　　　　　　　　　95
　He has brave utensils (for so he calls them)
　Which when he has a house, he'll deck withal.
　And that most deeply to consider is
　The beauty of his daughter. He himself
　Calls her a nonpareil. I never saw a woman　　　　　　100
　But only Sycorax my dam and she;
　But she as far surpasseth Sycorax
　As great'st does least.
STEPHANO　　　　　　Is it so brave a lass?
CALIBAN Ay, lord, she will become thy bed, I warrant,
　And bring thee forth brave brood.　　　　　　　　　　105
STEPHANO Monster, I will kill this man. His daughter
　and I will be king and queen—save our Graces! and
　Trinculo and thyself shall be viceroys. Dost thou like
　the plot, Trinculo?
TRINCULO Excellent.　　　　　　　　　　　　　　　110
STEPHANO Give me thy hand. I am sorry I beat thee; but
　while thou liv'st keep a good tongue in thy head.
CALIBAN Within this half hour will he be asleep.
　Wilt thou destroy him then?
STEPHANO　　　　　　　　Ay, on mine honor.
ARIEL This will I tell my master.　　　　　　　　　　115
CALIBAN Thou mak'st me merry; I am full of pleasure,
　Let us be jocund. Will you troll the catch
　You taught me but while-ere?
STEPHANO At thy request, monster, I will do reason, any
　reason. Come on, Trinculo, let us sing.　　　　　*Sings.*　120
　　"Flout 'em and [scout] 'em,
　　And scout 'em and flout 'em!
　　　Thought is free."

90. **paunch:** stab in the belly. 91. **wezand:** windpipe. 93. **sot:** fool.
96. **utensils:** furnishings. 97. **withal:** with. 117. **troll the catch:** sing the round.
118. **but while-ere:** a short time ago. 121. **scout:** jeer at.

CALIBAN That's not the tune.

Ariel plays the tune on a tabor and pipe.

STEPHANO What is this same?   125

TRINCULO This is the tune of our catch, play'd by the
picture of Nobody.

STEPHANO If thou beest a man, show thyself in thy like-
ness. If thou beest a devil, take't as thou list.

TRINCULO O, forgive me my sins!   130

STEPHANO He that dies pays all debts. I defy thee. Mercy upon us!

CALIBAN Art thou afeard?

STEPHANO No, monster, not I.

CALIBAN Be not afeard, the isle is full of noises,   135
Sounds, and sweet airs, that give delight and hurt not.
Sometimes a thousand twangling instruments
Will hum about mine ears; and sometime voices,
That if I then had wak'd after long sleep,
Will make me sleep again, and then in dreaming,   140
The clouds methought would open, and show riches
Ready to drop upon me, that when I wak'd
I cried to dream again.

STEPHANO This will prove a brave kingdom to me, where
I shall have my music for nothing.   145

CALIBAN When Prospero is destroy'd.

STEPHANO That shall be by and by. I remember the story.

TRINCULO The sound is going away. Let's follow it,
and after do our work.

STEPHANO Lead, monster, we'll follow. I would I could   150
see this taborer; he lays it on.

TRINCULO Wilt come? I'll follow Stephano.   *Exeunt.*

SCENE 3

Enter ALONSO, SEBASTIAN, ANTONIO, GONZALO,
ADRIAN, FRANCISCO, *etc.*

GONZALO By'r lakin, I can go no further, sir,
My old bones aches. Here's a maze trod indeed
Through forth-rights and meanders! By your patience,
I needs must rest me.

---

124. s.d. **tabor:** small drum. **127. picture of Nobody:** traditional image of a
man with arms and legs but no torso; but Trinculo means an invisible agency.
129. take't . . . list: do as you please (a challenge). 3.3. Location: Another part of
the island. **1. By'r lakin:** by our Ladykin, i.e., the Virgin Mary. **3. forth-rights:**
straight paths.

ALONSO   Old lord, I cannot blame thee,
  Who am myself attach'd with weariness   5
  To th' dulling of my spirits. Sit down, and rest.
  Even here I will put off my hope, and keep it
  No longer for my flatterer. He is drown'd
  Whom thus we stray to find, and the sea mocks
  Our frustrate search on land. Well, let him go.   10
ANTONIO [*Aside to Sebastian.*] I am right glad that he's so out of hope.
  Do not for one repulse forgo the purpose
  That you resolv'd t' effect.
SEBASTIAN   [*Aside to Antonio.*] The next advantage
  Will we take throughly.
ANTONIO   [*Aside to Sebastian.*] Let it be to-night,
  For now they are oppress'd with travail, they   15
  Will not, nor cannot, use such vigilance
  As when they are fresh.
SEBASTIAN   [*Aside to Antonio.*] I say to-night. No more.

    Solemn and strange music; and PROSPER *on the top, invisible.*

ALONSO What harmony is this? My good friends, hark!
GONZALO Marvellous sweet music!

       Enter several strange SHAPES, *bringing in a banket; and
       dance about it with gentle actions of salutations; and
       inviting the King, etc., to eat, they depart.*

ALONSO Give us kind keepers, heavens! what were these?   20
SEBASTIAN A living drollery. Now I will believe
  That there are unicorns; that in Arabia
  There is one tree, the phoenix' throne, one phoenix
  At this hour reigning there.
ANTONIO   I'll believe both;
  And what does else want credit, come to me,   25
  And I'll be sworn 'tis true. Travellers ne'er did lie,
  Though fools at home condemn 'em.
GONZALO   If in Naples
  I should report this now, would they believe me?
  If I should say I saw such [islanders]
  (For, certes, these are people of the island),   30

---

5. **attach'd:** seized. 8. **for:** as. 12. **for:** because of. 14. **throughly:** thoroughly. 17. s.d. **top.** Probably the third level of the tiring-house. 19. s.d. **banket:** banquet. 20. **kind keepers:** guardian angels. 21. **living drollery:** puppet show with live actors. 25. **want credit:** lack credence. 30. **certes:** certainly.

Who though they are of monstrous shape, yet note
Their manners are more gentle, kind, than of
Our human generation you shall find
Many, nay, almost any.

PROSPERO   [*Aside.*] Honest lord,
Thou hast said well; for some of you there present   35
Are worse than devils.

ALONSO   I cannot too much muse
Such shapes, such gesture, and such sound expressing
(Although they want the use of tongue) a kind
Of excellent dumb discourse.

PROSPERO   [*Aside.*] Praise in departing.

FRANCISCO They vanish'd strangely.

SEBASTIAN   No matter, since   40
They have left their viands behind; for we have stomachs.
Will't please you taste of what is here?

ALONSO   Not I.

GONZALO Faith, sir, you need not fear. When we were boys,
Who would believe that there were mountaineers,
Dew-lapp'd, like bulls, whose throats had hanging at 'em   45
Wallets of flesh? or that there were such men
Whose heads stood in their breasts? which now we find
Each putter-out of five for one will bring us
Good warrant of.

ALONSO   I will stand to, and feed,
Although my last, no matter, since I feel   50
The best is past. Brother, my lord the Duke,
Stand to, and do as we.

Thunder and lightning. Enter ARIEL, *like a harpy, claps his wings
upon the table, and with a quaint device the banquet vanishes.*

ARIEL You are three men of sin, whom Destiny,
That hath to instrument this lower world

31. **monstrous:** abnormal, unnatural.   36. **muse:** wonder at.   39. **Praise in departing:** i.e., don't judge until you see the conclusion (proverbial).   41. **viands:** foods. (*Tiffany*) **stomachs:** appetites.   45. **Dew-lapp'd:** with pouches of skin hanging from the neck (probably alluding to travellers' tales about goiter among Swiss mountaineers).   46–47. **men . . . breasts:** A common travellers' tale. See *Othello*, 1.3.144-45.   48. **Each . . . one:** Travellers deposited a sum of money at home to be repaid fivefold if they returned, forfeited if they did not.   49. **stand to:** take the risk.   51. **best:** i.e., best part of life.   52. s.d. **like a harpy:** in the shape of a harpy, a rapacious monster with the face of a woman and the wings and claws of a bird of prey. **with . . . device:** by means of an ingenious stage mechanism. 54. **to:** for.

And what is in't, the never-surfeited sea   55
Hath caus'd to belch up you; and on this island
Where man doth not inhabit—you 'mongst men
Being most unfit to live. I have made you mad;
And even with such-like valor men hang and drown
Their proper selves.
                              [*Alonso, Sebastian, etc. draw their swords.*]
                              You fools! I and my fellows 60
Are ministers of Fate. The elements,
Of whom your sword are temper'd, may as well
Wound the loud winds, or with bemock'd-at stabs
Kill the still-closing waters, as diminish
One dowle that's in my plume. My fellow ministers   65
Are like invulnerable. If you could hurt,
Your swords are now too massy for your strengths,
And will not be uplifted. But remember
(For that's my business to you) that you three
From Milan did supplant good Prospero,   70
Expos'd unto the sea (which hath requit it)
Him, and his innocent child; for which foul deed
The pow'rs, delaying (not forgetting), have
Incens'd the seas and shores—yea, all the creatures,
Against your peace. Thee of thy son, Alonso,   75
They have bereft; and do pronounce by me
Ling'ring perdition (worse than any death
Can be at once) shall step by step attend
You and your ways, whose wraths to guard you from—
Which here, in this most desolate isle, else falls   80
Upon your heads—is nothing but heart's sorrow,
And a clear life ensuing.

              He vanishes in thunder; then, to soft music, enter the SHAPES
              again, and dance, with mocks and mows, and carrying out the table.

PROSPERO Bravely the figure of this harpy hast thou
          Perform'd, my Ariel; a grace it had, devouring.

---

59. such-like valor: i.e., the valor of madness, very different from true courage. **60. proper:** own. **62. whom:** which. **63. bemock'd-at:** ridiculous.
(*Tiffany*) **64. still-closing:** always closing as soon as parted. **65. dowle:** small
feather. **66. like:** similarly. **71. requit it:** repaid the act (by casting you up
here). **77. Ling'ring perdition:** (1) long-lasting ruin; (2) eternal hellfire. (*Tiffany*) **79. whose:** i.e., those of the "pow'rs" of line 73. **81. is . . . sorrow:** there is
no means except repentance. **82. clear:** sinless. s.d. **mocks and mows:** mocking
gestures and grimaces. **84. devouring:** i.e., making the banquet disappear.

Of my instruction hast thou nothing bated   85
In what thou hadst to say; so with good life,
And observation strange, my meaner ministers
Their several kinds have done. My high charms work,
And these, mine enemies, are all knit up
In their distractions. They now are in my pow'r;   90
And in these fits I leave them, while I visit
Young Ferdinand, whom they suppose is drown'd,
And his and mine lov'd darling.   [Exit above.]
GONZALO I' th' name of something holy, sir, why stand you
In this strange stare?
ALONSO   O, it is monstrous! monstrous!   95
Methought the billows spoke, and told me of it;
The winds did sing it to me, and the thunder,
That deep and dreadful organ-pipe, pronounc'd
The name of Prosper; it did base my trespass.
Therefore my son i' th' ooze is bedded; and   100
I'll seek him deeper than e'er plummet sounded,
And with him there lie mudded.   Exit.
SEBASTIAN   But one fiend at a time,
I'll fight their legions o'er.
ANTONIO   I'll be thy second.
                        Exeunt [Sebastian and Antonio].
GONZALO All three of them are desperate: their great guilt
(Like poison given to work a great time after)   105
Now gins to bite the spirits. I do beseech you
(That are of suppler joints) follow them swiftly,
And hinder them from what this ecstasy
May now provoke them to.
ADRIAN   Follow, I pray you.   Exeunt omnes.

---

85. **bated:** omitted.   86. **life:** realism.   87. **observation strange:** exceptional care. **meaner:** i.e., inferior to Ariel.   88. **several kinds:** individual parts.   89–90. **knit ... distractions:** entangled in their confusion. (*Tiffany*)   94–95. **why ... stare:** Gonzalo has not heard Ariel's speech.   96. **it:** i.e., my sin.   99. **base:** (1) get to the base or bottom of; (*Tiffany*) (2) bass, i.e., utter in a deep voice.   100. **Therefore:** therefor, i.e., in consequence of his trespass.   101. **plummet:** a weight attached to a line, used by sailors to measure depth. (*Tiffany*)   103. **o'er:** one after another. 106. **gins:** begins.   108. **ecstasy:** fit of madness.

Act 4

SCENE I

Enter PROSPERO, FERDINAND, *and* MIRANDA.

PROSPERO If I have too austerely punish'd you,
  Your compensation makes amends, for I
  Have given you here a third of mine own life,
  Or that for which I live; who once again
  I tender to thy hand. All thy vexations   5
  Were but my trials of thy love, and thou
  Hast strangely stood the test. Here, afore heaven,
  I ratify this my rich gift. O Ferdinand,
  Do not smile at me that I boast her [off],
  For thou shalt find she will outstrip all praise   10
  And make it halt behind her.
FERDINAND   I do believe it
  Against an oracle.
PROSPERO Then, as my [gift], and thine own acquisition
  Worthily purchased, take my daughter. But
  If thou dost break her virgin-knot before   15
  All sanctimonious ceremonies may
  With full and holy rite be minist'red,
  No sweet aspersion shall the heavens let fall
  To make this contract grow; but barren hate,
  Sour-ey'd disdain, and discord shall bestrew   20

4.1. Location: Before Prospero's cell. **3. a third . . . life:** Various explanations have been put forward: for example, that the other two parts have been his dukedom and his books, or his late wife and his personal interests; or that Miranda represents his future, the other two parts being his past and his present; or that he has spent a third of his life on Miranda's education. **7. strangely:** wonderfully. **9. boast her off:** i.e., praise her so highly. **11. halt:** limp. **12. Against an oracle:** even if an oracle should declare otherwise. **16. sanctimonious:** sacred, holy. **18. aspersion:** i.e., blessing; literally, sprinkling, as of rain that promotes fertility and growth. **19. grow:** be fruitful.

The union of your bed with weeds so loathly
That you shall hate it both. Therefore take heed,
As Hymen's lamps shall light you.
FERDINAND   As I hope
For quiet days, fair issue, and long life,
With such love as 'tis now, the murkiest den,   25
The most opportune place, the strong'st suggestion
Our worser genius can, shall never melt
Mine honor into lust, to take away
The edge of that day's celebration,
When I shall think or Phoebus' steeds are founder'd   30
Or Night kept chain'd below.
PROSPERO   Fairly spoke.
Sit then and talk with her, she is thine own.
What, Ariel! my industrious servant, Ariel!

Enter ARIEL.

ARIEL What would my potent master? here I am.
PROSPERO Thou and thy meaner fellows your last service   35
Did worthily perform; and I must use you
In such another trick. Go bring the rabble
(O'er whom I give thee pow'r) here to this place.
Incite them to quick motion, for I must
Bestow upon the eyes of this young couple   40
Some vanity of mine art. It is my promise,
And they expect it from me.
ARIEL   Presently?
PROSPERO Ay, with a twink.
ARIEL Before you can say "come" and "go,"
And breathe twice, and cry "so, so,"   45
Each one, tripping on his toe,
Will be here with mop and mow.
Do you love me, master? no?
PROSPERO Dearly, my delicate Ariel. Do not approach

21. **weeds:** Instead of the flowers with which the marriage bed was customarily strewn.   23. **As ... you:** i.e., as you desire happiness in your marriage. The symbolic torch of Hymen, god of marriage, was supposed to promise happiness if it burned with a clear flame, the opposite if it smoked.   26. **suggestion:** temptation.   27. **Our ... can:** our bad angel is capable of.   30. **or ... founder'd:** either the sun-god's horses have gone lame (because the day is so long).   37. **trick:** ingenious device (technical term in pageantry). **rabble:** troop of inferior spirits.   41. **vanity:** show, delusive appearance.   42. **Presently:** immediately.   43. **with a twink:** in a twinkling.   47. **mop and mow:** gesture and grimace.

Till thou dost hear me call.

ARIEL　　　　　　　　　Well; I conceive.　　　　　*Exit.* 50
PROSPERO　Look thou be true; do not give dalliance
　Too much the rein. The strongest oaths are straw
　To th' fire i' th' blood. Be more abstenious,
　Or else good night your vow!
FERDINAND　　　　　　　I warrant you, sir,
　The white cold virgin snow upon my heart　　　55
　Abates the ardor of my liver.
PROSPERO　　　　　　Well.
　Now come, my Ariel, bring a corollary,
　Rather than want a spirit. Appear, and pertly!
　No tongue! all eyes! Be silent.　　　*Soft music.*

Enter IRIS.

IRIS　Ceres, most bounteous lady, thy rich leas　　60
　Of wheat, rye, barley, fetches, oats, and pease;
　Thy turfy mountains, where live nibbling sheep,
　And flat meads thatch'd with stover, them to keep;
　Thy banks with pioned and twilled brims,
　Which spungy April at thy hest betrims,　　　65
　To make cold nymphs chaste crowns; and thy broom-groves,
　Whose shadow the dismissed bachelor loves,
　Being lass-lorn; thy pole-clipt vineyard,
　And thy sea-marge, sterile and rocky-hard,
　Where thou thyself dost air—the Queen o' th' sky,　　70
　Whose wat'ry arch and messenger am I,
　Bids thee leave these, and with her sovereign Grace,
　Here on this grass-plot, in this very place,
　To come and sport. [Her] peacocks fly amain.

50. **conceive:** understand.　53. **abstenious:** abstemious.　56. **liver.** Supposed seat of the passions.　57. **corollary:** extra.　58. **want:** lack. **pertly:** briskly.　59. **No tongue:** Any speech from the spectators would make the spirits vanish. Cf. lines 126–27. s.d. **Iris:** goddess of the rainbow and Juno's messenger.　60. **Ceres:** goddess of agriculture. **leas:** meadows, cultivated land.　61. **fetches:** vetch, a fodder plant. **pease:** peas. (*Tiffany*)　63. **stover:** hay for winter use.　64. **pioned and twilled:** undercut by the stream and retained by interwoven branches.　65. **spungy:** spongy, i.e., wet.　66. **broom:** a kind of shrub bearing yellow flowers.　67. **dismissed bachelor:** rejected suitor.　68. **lass-lorn:** deprived of a sweetheart. (*Tiffany*) **pole-clipt:** poll-clipped, i.e., with top growth pruned back (?). If *clipt* means (as often) "embraced," the sense could be "enclosed by a fence of poles" or "with poles entwined by the vines."　69. **sea-marge:** sea-margin (shore). (*Tiffany*)　70. **air:** take air or fly. (*Tiffany*) **Queen . . . sky:** Juno.　74. **peacocks:** Juno's sacred birds, which drew her chariot. **amain:** swiftly.

124

Juno descends [slowly in her car].

Approach, rich Ceres, her to entertain.   75

Enter CERES.

CERES Hail, many-colored messenger, that ne'er
  Dost disobey the wife of Jupiter;
  Who with thy saffron wings upon my flow'rs
  Diffusest honey-drops, refreshing show'rs,
  And with each end of thy blue bow dost crown   80
  My bosky acres and my unshrubb'd down,
  Rich scarf to my proud earth—why hath thy Queen
  Summon'd me hither, to this short-grass'd green?
IRIS A contract of true love to celebrate,
  And some donation freely to estate   85
  On the bless'd lovers.
CERES   Tell me, heavenly bow,
  If Venus or her son, as thou dost know,
  Do now attend the Queen? Since they did plot
  The means that dusky Dis my daughter got,
  Her and her blind boy's scandall'd company   90
  I have forsworn.
IRIS   Of her society
  Be not afraid. I met her Deity
  Cutting the clouds towards Paphos; and her son
  Dove-drawn with her. Here thought they to have done
  Some wanton charm upon this man and maid,   95
  Whose vows are, that no bed-right shall be paid
  Till Hymen's torch be lighted; but in vain,
  Mars's hot minion is return'd again;
  Her waspish-headed son has broke his arrows,
  Swears he will shoot no more, but play with sparrows, 100
  And be a boy right out.
           [JUNO *alights.*]

CERES   Highest Queen of state,

75. entertain: receive. **81. bosky:** wooded. **down:** upland. **85. estate:** bestow. **87. son:** Cupid, the "blind boy" of line 90. **89. Dis:** Pluto, ruler of the underworld (hence *dusky*, or dark), who carried off Ceres' daughter Proserpine to be his queen. (*Tiffany*) **90. scandall'd:** scandalous. **93. Paphos:** place in Cyprus sacred to Venus. **94. Dove-drawn:** Venus' chariot was drawn by her sacred doves. **94–95. done . . . charm:** cast some unchaste spell. **98. hot minion:** lustful mistress. Venus and Mars were lovers. **return'd:** i.e., to Paphos. **99. waspish-headed:** peevish. **100. sparrows:** Like doves, sacred to Venus. Sparrows were proverbially lecherous. **101. right out:** outright. **Highest . . . state:** most majestic queen.

Great Juno, comes, I know her by her gait.
JUNO How does my bounteous sister? Go with me
  To bless this twain, that they may prosperous be,
  And honor'd in their issue. *They sing.* 105
JUNO   Honor, riches, marriage-blessing,
       Long continuance, and increasing,
       Hourly joys be still upon you!
       Juno sings her blessings on you.
[CERES]   Earth's increase, foison plenty, 110
       Barns and garners never empty;
       Vines with clust'ring bunches growing,
       Plants with goodly burthen bowing;
       Spring come to you at the farthest
       In the very end of harvest! 115
       Scarcity and want shall shun you,
       Ceres' blessing so is on you.
FERDINAND This is a most majestic vision, and
  Harmonious charmingly. May I be bold
  To think these spirits?
PROSPERO   Spirits, which by mine art 120
  I have from their confines call'd to enact
  My present fancies.
FERDINAND   Let me live here ever;
  So rare a wond'red father and a wise
  Makes this place Paradise.
       Juno and Ceres whisper, and send Iris on employment.
PROSPERO   Sweet now, silence!
  Juno and Ceres whisper seriously; 125
  There's something else to do. Hush and be mute,
  Or else our spell is marr'd.
IRIS You nymphs, call'd Naiades, of the windring brooks,
  With your sedg'd crowns and ever-harmless looks,
  Leave your crisp channels, and on this green land 130
  Answer your summons; Juno does command.
  Come, temperate nymphs, and help to celebrate

---

102. gait: walk. (*Tiffany*)   **108. still:** always.   **110. foison plenty:** plentiful abundance.   **111. garners:** granaries. (*Tiffany*)   **115. In . . . harvest:** i.e., without intervening winter.   **119. charmingly:** enchantingly, magically.   **123. wond'red:** (1) to be wondered at; (2) able to perform wonders; (3) possessed of that wonder, Miranda (see note to 3.1.37).   **124. Sweet now, silence:** Addressed to Miranda, who is about to speak.   **128. windring:** winding and wandering (apparently a coinage of Shakespeare's).   **129. sedg'd:** made of sedge, or marsh grass. (*Tiffany*) **ever-harmless:** ever-innocent.   **130. crisp:** rippling.   **132. temperate:** chaste.

A contract of true love; be not too late.

Enter CERTAIN NYMPHS.

You sunburn'd sicklemen, of August weary,
Come hither from the furrow and be merry.   135
Make holiday; your rye-straw hats put on,
And these fresh nymphs encounter every one
In country footing.

> *Enter* CERTAIN REAPERS, *properly habited: they join with the*
> *Nymphs in a graceful dance, towards the end whereof Prospero*
> *starts suddenly, and speaks; after which, to a strange, hollow, and*
> *confused noise, they heavily vanish.*

PROSPERO [*Aside.*] I had forgot that foul conspiracy
    Of the beast Caliban and his confederates   140
    Against my life. The minute of their plot
    Is almost come. [*To the Spirits.*] Well done, avoid; no more.
FERDINAND This is strange. Your father's in some passion
    That works him strongly.
MIRANDA   Never till this day
    Saw I him touch'd with anger, so distemper'd.   145
PROSPERO You do look, my son, in a mov'd sort,
    As if you were dismay'd; be cheerful, sir.
    Our revels now are ended. These our actors
    (As I foretold you) were all spirits, and
    Are melted into air, into thin air,   150
    And like the baseless fabric of this vision,
    The cloud-capp'd tow'rs, the gorgeous palaces,
    The solemn temples, the great globe itself,
    Yea, all which it inherit, shall dissolve,
    And like this insubstantial pageant faded   155
    Leave not a rack behind. We are such stuff
    As dreams are made on; and our little life
    Is rounded with a sleep. Sir, I am vex'd;
    Bear with my weakness, my old brain is troubled.
    Be not disturb'd with my infirmity.   160
    If you be pleas'd, retire into my cell,

---

137. fresh: young and beautiful. **encounter:** meet. **138. footing:** dance. s.d.
heavily: reluctantly. **142. avoid:** be gone. **144. works:** agitates. **146. mov'd
sort:** troubled state. **148. revels:** festivity, entertainment. **151. baseless fabric:**
structure without physical foundation. **154. which it inherit:** who occupy it.
155. insubstantial: without material substance. **156. rack:** wisp of cloud.
157. on: of. **158. rounded:** (1) surrounded; (2) made round, completed. (*Tiffany*)

And there repose. A turn or two I'll walk
To still my beating mind.
FERDINAND, MIRANDA.   We wish your peace.
PROSPERO [*To Ariel.*] Come with a thought. [*To Ferdinand and
  Miranda.*] I thank thee.

Exeunt [*Ferdinand and Miranda*].

Ariel! come.

Enter ARIEL.

ARIEL Thy thoughts I cleave to. What's thy pleasure?
PROSPERO   Spirit,   165
  We must prepare to meet with Caliban.
ARIEL Ay, my commander. When I presented Ceres,
  I thought to have told thee of it, but I fear'd
  Lest I might anger thee.
PROSPERO Say again, where didst thou leave these varlots?   170
ARIEL I told you, sir, they were red-hot with drinking,
  So full of valor that they smote the air
  For breathing in their faces; beat the ground
  For kissing of their feet; yet always bending
  Towards their project. Then I beat my tabor,   175
  At which like unback'd colts they prick'd their ears,
  Advanc'd their eyelids, lifted up their noses
  As they smelt music. So I charm'd their ears
  That calf-like they my lowing follow'd through
  Tooth'd briers, sharp furzes, pricking goss, and thorns,   180
  Which ent'red their frail shins. At last I left them
  I' th' filthy-mantled pool beyond your cell,
  There dancing up to th' chins, that the foul lake
  O'erstunk their feet.
PROSPERO   This was well done, my bird.
  Thy shape invisible retain thou still.   185
  The trumpery in my house, go bring it hither,
  For stale to catch these thieves.
ARIEL   I go, I go.   *Exit.*
PROSPERO A devil, a born devil, on whose nature

---

164. with: at the summons of.   **167. presented:** represented, took the part
of (?).   **170. varlots:** varlets, ruffians.   **174–75. bending . . . project:** pursuing
their purpose—the murder of Prospero.   **176. unback'd:** never ridden, unbroken.
177. Advanc'd: raised.   **178. As:** as if.   **180. furzes:** spiny shrubs. (*Tiffany*) **goss:**
gorse.   **182. filthy-mantled:** covered with dirty scum.   **186. trumpery:** showy
finery (the "glistering apparel" of line 193 s.d.).   **187. stale:** bait.

Nurture can never stick; on whom my pains,
Humanely taken, all, all lost, quite lost;   190
And as with age his body uglier grows,
So his mind cankers. I will plague them all,
Even to roaring.

Enter ARIEL, *loaden with glistering apparel, etc.*

Come, hang [them on] this line.

Enter CALIBAN, STEPHANO, *and* TRINCULO, *all wet.*
[*Prospero and Ariel remain, invisible.*]

CALIBAN Pray you tread softly, that the blind mole may not
Hear a foot fall; we now are near his cell.   195
STEPHANO Monster, your fairy, which you say is a harm-
less fairy, has done little better than play'd the Jack with us.
TRINCULO Monster, I do smell all horse-piss, at which
my nose is in great indignation.   200
STEPHANO So is mine. Do you hear, monster? If I should
take a displeasure against you, look you—
TRINCULO Thou wert but a lost monster.
CALIBAN Good my lord, give me thy favor still.
Be patient, for the prize I'll bring thee to   205
Shall hoodwink this mischance; therefore speak softly,
All's hush'd as midnight yet.
TRINCULO Ay, but to lose our bottles in the pool—
STEPHANO There is not only disgrace and dishonor in that,
monster, but an infinite loss.   210
TRINCULO That's more to me than my wetting; yet this
is your harmless fairy, monster!
STEPHANO I will fetch off my bottle, though I be o'er ears
for my labor.
CALIBAN Prithee, my king, be quiet. Seest thou here,   215
This is the mouth o' th' cell. No noise, and enter.
Do that good mischief which may make this island
Thine own for ever, and I, thy Caliban,
For aye thy foot-licker.
STEPHANO Give me thy hand. I do begin to have bloody   220
thoughts.

---

192. cankers: becomes malignant.   **193. line:** lime tree, linden.   **194. mole:**
Thought to have sensitive hearing.   **197. Jack:** (1) knave; (2) jack-o'-lantern, i.e.,
will-o'-the-wisp.   **206. hoodwink:** make you blind to.

TRINCULO O King Stephano! O peer! O worthy
    Stephano! look what a wardrobe here is for thee!
CALIBAN Let it alone, thou fool, it is but trash.
TRINCULO O, ho, monster! we know what belongs to a   225
    frippery. O King Stephano!
STEPHANO Put off that gown, Trinculo. By this hand,
    I'll have that gown.
TRINCULO Thy Grace shall have it.
CALIBAN The dropsy drown this fool! what do you mean   230
    To dote thus on such luggage? Let['t] alone
    And do the murther first. If he awake,
    From toe to crown he'll fill our skins with pinches,
    Make us strange stuff.
STEPHANO Be you quiet, monster. Mistress line, is not   235
    this my jerkin? Now is the jerkin under the line. Now,
    jerkin, you are like to lose your hair, and prove a bald
    jerkin.
TRINCULO Do, do; we steal by line and level, and't like
    your Grace.   240
STEPHANO I thank thee for that jest; here's a garment
    for't. Wit shall not go unrewarded while I am king of
    this country. "Steal by line and level" is an excellent
    pass of pate; there's another garment for't.
TRINCULO Monster, come put some lime upon your   245
    fingers, and away with the rest.
CALIBAN I will have none on't. We shall lose our time,
    And all be turn'd to barnacles, or to apes
    With foreheads villainous low.
STEPHANO Monster, lay-to your fingers. Help to bear this   250
    away where my hogshead of wine is, or I'll turn you
    out of my kingdom. Go to, carry this.

---

222. peer: Referring to the old ballad "King Stephen was a worthy peer," quoted in *Othello,* 2.3.89–96.   **226. frippery:** secondhand-clothes shop.   **230. dropsy:** disease which makes joints swell. (*Tiffany*) **drown:** suffocate.   **231. luggage:** encumbering baggage. (*Tiffany*)   **236. jerkin:** a kind of jacket. **under the line:** With pun on the sense "south of the equator." The joke involves the popular idea that travellers to tropical countries lost their hair through fevers, or from scurvy resulting from lack of fresh food on the long voyage.   **239. Do, do:** an expression of approval, equivalent to "bravo." **by . . . level:** with plumb-line and carpenter's level, i.e., with professional skill (continuing the puns on *line*). **and't like:** if it please.   **244. pass of pate:** thrust of wit ("thrust" is a fencing term, and "pate" = head or brain). (*Tiffany*)   **245. lime:** sticky substance; thieves were jokingly said to have lime on their fingers.   **248. barnacles:** a kind of geese traditionally supposed to develop from the shellfish so named.   **249. villainous:** wretchedly.

TRINCULO And this.

STEPHANO Ay, and this.

> *A noise of hunters heard. Enter divers* SPIRITS
> *in shape of dogs and hounds, hunting them about;*
> *Prospero and Ariel setting them on.*

PROSPERO Hey, Mountain, hey!   255

ARIEL Silver! there it goes, Silver!

PROSPERO Fury, Fury! there, Tyrant, there! hark, hark!

> [*Caliban, Stephano, and Trinculo are driven out.*]

Go, charge my goblins that they grind their joints
With dry convulsions, shorten up their sinews
With aged cramps, and more pinch-spotted make them   260
Than pard or cat o' mountain.

ARIEL   Hark, they roar!

PROSPERO Let them be hunted soundly. At this hour
Lies at my mercy all mine enemies.
Shortly shall all my labors end, and thou
Shalt have the air at freedom. For a little   265
Follow, and do me service.   *Exeunt.*

---

252. Go to: expression of exhortation or reproof, equivalent to "come, come!"
257. hark: "sic 'em!"   **259. dry convulsions:** Precisely what sort of painful seizure
is meant here is uncertain.   **260. aged:** such as old people have.   **261. pard:** leop-
ard. **cat o' mountain:** catamount, wildcat.

Act 5

SCENE I

Enter PROSPERO *in his magic robes, and* ARIEL.

PROSPERO Now does my project gather to a head:
　My charms crack not; my spirits obey; and Time
　Goes upright with his carriage. How's the day?
ARIEL On the sixt hour, at which time, my lord,
　You said our work should cease.
PROSPERO 　　　　　　　　　I did say so,　　　　5
　When first I rais'd the tempest. Say, my spirit,
　How fares the King and 's followers?
ARIEL 　　　　　　　　　　Confin'd together
　In the same fashion as you gave in charge,
　Just as you left them; all prisoners, sir,
　In the line-grove which weather-fends your cell;　　10
　They cannot boudge till your release. The King,
　His brother, and yours, abide all three distracted,
　And the remainder mourning over them,
　Brimful of sorrow and dismay; but chiefly
　Him that you term'd, sir, "the good old Lord Gonzalo,"　15
　His tears runs down his beard like winter's drops
　From eaves of reeds. Your charm so strongly works 'em
　That if you now beheld them, your affections
　Would become tender.
PROSPERO 　　　　　　Dost thou think so, spirit?
ARIEL Mine would, sir, were I human.
PROSPERO 　　　　　　　　　And mine shall.　　20
　Hast thou, which art but air, a touch, a feeling

5.1. Location: Before Prospero's cell.　**3. Goes . . . carriage:** walks upright under
what he is carrying (because his burden of coming events has been greatly
lightened).　**4. On:** approaching. **sixt:** sixth. On the time, see 1.2.240–41.　**10.
weather-fends:** serves as windbreak for.　**11. boudge:** budge, sir. **your release:**
i.e., their release by you.　**12. distracted:** out of their wits.　**17. eaves of reeds:**
thatched roofs.　**18. affections:** inclinations, bent of mind.　**21. touch:** Synonymous with *feeling.*

Of their afflictions, and shall not myself,
One of their kind, that relish all as sharply
Passion as they, be kindlier mov'd than thou art?
Though with their high wrongs I am strook to th'quick,   25
Yet, with my nobler reason, 'gainst my fury
Do I take part. The rarer action is
In virtue than in vengeance. They being penitent,
The sole drift of my purpose doth extend
Not a frown further. Go, release them, Ariel.   30
My charms I'll break, their senses I'll restore,
And they shall be themselves.
ARIEL   I'll fetch them, sir.
                    Exit. [Prospero traces a magic circle with his staff.]
PROSPERO Ye elves of hills, brooks, standing lakes, and groves,
And ye that on the sands with printless foot
Do chase the ebbing Neptune, and do fly him   35
When he comes back; you demi-puppets that
By moonshine do the green sour ringlets make,
Whereof the ewe not bites; and you whose pastime
Is to make midnight mushrumps, that rejoice
To hear the solemn curfew: by whose aid   40
(Weak masters though ye be) I have bedimm'd
The noontide sun, call'd forth the mutinous winds,
And 'twixt the green sea and the azur'd vault
Set roaring war; to the dread rattling thunder
Have I given fire, and rifted Jove's stout oak   45
With his own bolt; the strong-bas'd promontory
Have I made shake, and by the spurs pluck'd up
The pine and cedar. Graves at my command
Have wak'd their sleepers, op'd, and let 'em forth
By my so potent art. But this rough magic   50
I here abjure; and when I have requir'd
Some heavenly music (which even now I do)
To work mine end upon their senses that
This airy charm is for, I'll break my staff,

23. relish: experience. **all:** quite. **24. kindlier:** (1) more sympathetically; (2) more naturally (as "one of their kind"). **27. take part:** side. **rarer:** finer, nobler. **37. green sour ringlets:** so-called "fairy rings" in grass, actually caused by mushrooms. **39. mushrumps:** mushrooms, supposed because of their rapid growth to be made by elves during the night. **45. rifted:** split. **47. spurs:** roots. **51. requir'd:** requested. **53. their senses that:** the senses of those whom. **54. airy charm:** i.e., the music.

Bury it certain fadoms in the earth,   55
And deeper than did ever plummet sound
I'll drown my book.   *Solemn music.*

> *Here enters* ARIEL *before; then* ALONSO, *with a frantic gesture,*
> *attended by* GONZALO; SEBASTIAN *and* ANTONIO *in like manner,*
> *attended by* ADRIAN *and* FRANCISCO. *They all enter the circle*
> *which* PROSPERO *had made, and there stand charm'd;*
> *which* PROSPERO *observing, speaks.*

A solemn air, and the best comforter
To an unsettled fancy, cure thy brains,
Now useless, [boil'd] within thy skull! There stand,   60
For you are spell-stopp'd.
Holy Gonzalo, honorable man,
Mine eyes, ev'n sociable to the show of thine,
Fall fellowly drops. The charm dissolves apace,
And as the morning steals upon the night,   65
Melting the darkness, so their rising senses
Begin to chase the ignorant fumes that mantle
Their clearer reason. O good Gonzalo,
My true preserver, and a loyal sir
To him thou follow'st! I will pay thy graces   70
Home both in word and deed. Most cruelly
Didst thou, Alonso, use me and my daughter;
Thy brother was a furtherer in the act.
Thou art pinch'd for't now, Sebastian. Flesh and blood,
You, brother mine, that [entertain'd] ambition,   75
Expell'd remorse and nature, whom, with Sebastian
(Whose inward pinches therefore are most strong),
Would here have kill'd your king, I do forgive thee,
Unnatural though thou art.—Their understanding
Begins to swell, and the approaching tide   80
Will shortly fill the reasonable [shores]
That now lie foul and muddy. Not one of them
That yet looks on me, or would know me! Ariel,

---

58. and: i.e., which is. **59. thy brains:** The first sentence is addressed to Alonso, the next to all six now within the circle. **60. boil'd:** i.e., made useless by passion. **63. sociable:** sympathetic. **show:** appearance. **64. Fall:** let fall. **67. ignorant fumes:** fumes that make them uncomprehending. **mantle:** blanket. (*Tiffany*) **70–71. pay . . . Home:** reward your favors fully. **76. remorse:** pity. **nature:** natural feeling. **77. therefore:** therefor, to that end. **81. reasonable shores:** shores of reason, i.e., minds.

Fetch me the hat and rapier in my cell.

[*Exit Ariel, and returns immediately.*]

I will discase me, and myself present   85
As I was sometime Milan. Quickly, spirit,
Thou shalt ere long be free.

Ariel sings and helps to attire him.

ARIEL   Where the bee sucks, there suck I,
      In a cowslip's bell I lie;
      There I couch when owls do cry.   90
      On the bat's back I do fly
      After summer merrily.
      Merrily, merrily shall I live now,
      Under the blossom that hangs on the bough.

PROSPERO Why, that's my dainty Ariel! I shall miss thee,   95
But yet thou shalt have freedom. So, so, so.
To the King's ship, invisible as thou art;
There shalt thou find the mariners asleep
Under the hatches. The master and the boatswain
Being awake, enforce them to this place;   100
And presently, I prithee.

ARIEL I drink the air before me, and return
Or ere your pulse twice beat.   *Exit.*

GONZALO All torment, trouble, wonder, and amazement
Inhabits here. Some heavenly power guide us   105
Out of this fearful country!

PROSPERO   Behold, sir King,
The wronged Duke of Milan, Prospero.
For more assurance that a living prince
Does now speak to thee, I embrace thy body,
And to thee and thy company I bid   110
A hearty welcome.

ALONSO   Whe'er thou beest he or no,
Or some enchanted trifle to abuse me
(As late I have been), I not know. Thy pulse
Beats as of flesh and blood; and since I saw thee,
Th' affliction of my mind amends, with which   115
I fear a madness held me. This must crave
(And if this be at all) a most strange story.

---

85. discase me: take off my magician's robe. **86. As . . . Milan:** dressed as I formerly was as Duke of Milan. **96. So, so, so:** Probably an expression of approval as Ariel finishes attiring him. **101. presently:** at once. **112. enchanted trifle:** trick of magic. **abuse:** deceive. **116–17. This . . . story:** this demands, if it is really taking place, an extraordinary explanation.

Thy dukedom I resign, and do entreat
Thou pardon me my wrongs. But how should Prospero
Be living, and be here?

PROSPERO   [*To Gonzalo.*] First, noble friend,   120
Let me embrace thine age, whose honor cannot
Be measur'd or confin'd.

GONZALO   Whether this be,
Or be not, I'll not swear.

PROSPERO   You do yet taste
Some subtleties o' th' isle, that will [not] let you
Believe things certain. Welcome, my friends all!   125
[*Aside to Sebastian and Antonio.*] But you, my brace of lords,
    were I so minded,
I here could pluck his Highness' frown upon you
And justify you traitors. At this time
I will tell no tales.

SEBASTIAN   [*Aside.*] The devil speaks in him.

PROSPERO   No.
For you, most wicked sir, whom to call brother   130
Would even infect my mouth, I do forgive
Thy rankest fault—all of them; and require
My dukedom of thee, which perforce, I know
Thou must restore.

ALONSO   If thou beest Prospero,
Give us particulars of thy preservation,   135
How thou hast met us here, whom three hours since
Were wrack'd upon this shore; where I have lost
(How sharp the point of this remembrance is!)
My dear son Ferdinand.

PROSPERO   I am woe for't, sir.

ALONSO Irreparable is the loss, and patience   140
Says, it is past her cure.

PROSPERO   I rather think
You have not sought her help, of whose soft grace
For the like loss I have her sovereign aid,
And rest myself content.

ALONSO   You the like loss?

---

121. thine age: i.e., thy reverend self.   **121–22. cannot . . . confin'd:** i.e., is immeasurable and boundless.   **124. subtleties:** illusions, with play (as *taste* suggests) on the word as applied to fancy confections representing actual objects or allegorical figures.   **126. brace:** pair. (*Tiffany*)   **128. justify:** prove.   **141. her:** patience's. (*Tiffany*)   **142. of . . . grace:** by whose mercy.

PROSPERO As great to me as late, and supportable   145
  To make the dear loss, have I means much weaker
  Than you may call to comfort you; for I
  Have lost my daughter.
ALONSO   A daughter?
  O heavens, that they were living both in Naples,
  The King and Queen there! That they were, I wish   150
  Myself were mudded in that oozy bed
  Where my son lies. When did you lose your daughter?
PROSPERO In this last tempest. I perceive these lords
  At this encounter do so much admire
  That they devour their reason, and scarce think   155
  Their eyes do offices of truth, their words
  Are natural breath; but howsoev'r you have
  Been justled from your senses, know for certain
  That I am Prospero, and that very duke
  Which was thrust forth of Milan, who most strangely   160
  Upon this shore (where you were wrack'd) was landed,
  To be the lord on't. No more yet of this,
  For 'tis a chronicle of day by day,
  Not a relation for a breakfast, nor
  Befitting this first meeting. Welcome, sir;   165
  This cell's my court. Here have I few attendants,
  And subjects none abroad. Pray you look in.
  My dukedom since you have given me again,
  I will requite you with as good a thing,
  At least bring forth a wonder, to content ye   170
  As much as me my dukedom.

Here PROSPERO *discovers* FERDINAND *and* MIRANDA
playing at chess.

MIRANDA Sweet lord, you play me false.
FERDINAND   No, my dearest love,
  I would not for the world.
MIRANDA Yes, for a score of kingdoms you should wrangle,
  And I would call it fair play.
ALONSO   If this prove   175

145. **late:** recent. 146. **dear:** deeply felt. 150. **That:** provided that. 154. **admire:** marvel. 155. **devour their reason:** Presumably referring to the open-mouthed astonishment in which their rational powers are lost. 156. **do . . . truth:** function accurately. 160. **of:** from. 171. s.d. **discovers:** discloses (by pulling aside a curtain). 174. **Yes . . . wrangle:** i.e., certainly you should do so for the world; in fact, for less than the world—for twenty kingdoms you ought to do your utmost against me.

A vision of the island, one dear son
Shall I twice lose.

SEBASTIAN   A most high miracle!

FERDINAND Though the seas threaten, they are merciful;
I have curs'd them without cause.   [*Kneels.*]

ALONSO   Now all the blessings
Of a glad father compass thee about!   180
Arise, and say how thou cam'st here.

MIRANDA   O wonder!
How many goodly creatures are there here!
How beauteous mankind is! O brave new world
That has such people in't!

PROSPERO   'Tis new to thee.

ALONSO What is this maid with whom thou wast at play?   185
Your eld'st acquaintance cannot be three hours.
Is she the goddess that hath sever'd us,
And brought us thus together?

FERDINAND   Sir, she is mortal;
But by immortal Providence she's mine.
I chose her when I could not ask my father   190
For his advice, nor thought I had one. She
Is daughter to this famous Duke of Milan,
Of whom so often I have heard renown,
But never saw before; of whom I have
Receiv'd a second life; and second father   195
This lady makes him to me.

ALONSO   I am hers.
But O, how oddly will it sound that I
Must ask my child forgiveness!

PROSPERO   There, sir, stop.
Let us not burthen our remembrances with
A heaviness that's gone.

GONZALO   I have inly wept,   200
Or should have spoke ere this. Look down, you gods,
And on this couple drop a blessed crown!
For it is you that have chalk'd forth the way
Which brought us hither.

ALONSO   I say amen, Gonzalo!

GONZALO Was Milan thrust from Milan, that his issue   205
Should become kings of Naples? O, rejoice

---

176. vision: i.e., illusion. **180. compass:** surround. (*Tiffany*) **186. eld'st:** longest
possible. **200. heaviness:** grief. **205. Milan ... Milan:** the Duke ... the city.

Beyond a common joy, and set it down
With gold on lasting pillars: in one voyage
Did Claribel her husband find at Tunis,
And Ferdinand, her brother, found a wife   210
Where he himself was lost; Prospero, his dukedom
In a poor isle; and all of us, ourselves,
When no man was his own.

ALONSO   [*To Ferdinand and Miranda.*] Give
    me your hands.
Let grief and sorrow still embrace his heart
That doth not wish you joy!

GONZALO   Be it so, amen!   215

Enter ARIEL, *with the* MASTER *and* BOATSWAIN *amazedly following.*

O, look, sir, look, sir, here is more of us.
I prophesied, if a gallows were on land,
This fellow could not drown. Now, blasphemy,
That swear'st grace o'erboard, not an oath on shore?
Hast thou no mouth by land? What is the news?   220

BOATSWAIN The best news is, that we have safely found
    Our king and company; the next, our ship—
    Which, but three glasses since, we gave out split—
    Is tight and yare, and bravely rigg'd as when
    We first put out to sea.   225

ARIEL   [*Aside to Prospero.*] Sir, all this service
    Have I done since I went.

PROSPERO   [*Aside to Ariel.*] My tricksy spirit!

ALONSO These are not natural events, they strengthen
    From strange to stranger. Say, how came you hither?

BOATSWAIN If I did think, sir, I were well awake,
    I'ld strive to tell you. We were dead of sleep,   230
    And (how we know not) all clapp'd under hatches,
    Where, but even now, with strange and several noises
    Of roaring, shrieking, howling, jingling chains,
    And moe diversity of sounds, all horrible,
    We were awak'd; straightway, at liberty;   235

---

214. still: ever.   **214–15. his heart. That:** the heart of anyone who.   **218. blas-**
phemy: blasphemous fellow. Cf. *diligence* (= diligent creature) in line 241.
219. That . . . o'erboard: who are profane enough to make heavenly grace for-
sake the ship.   **223. glasses:** i.e., hours. **gave out:** reported.   **224. yare:** shipshape.
226. tricksy: ingenious, adroit.   **227–28. strengthen . . . stranger:** increase in
strangeness.   **230. of sleep:** asleep.   **234. moe:** more.   **235. at liberty:** i.e., no
longer under hatches.

Where we, in all our trim, freshly beheld
Our royal, good, and gallant ship; our master
Cap'ring to eye her. On a trice, so please you,
Even in a dream, were we divided from them,
And were brought moping hither.

ARIEL   [*Aside to Prospero.*] Was't well done?   240

PROSPERO [*Aside to Ariel.*] Bravely, my diligence. Thou shalt be free.

ALONSO This is as strange a maze as e'er men trod,
    And there is in this business more than nature
    Was ever conduct of. Some oracle
    Must rectify our knowledge.

PROSPERO   Sir, my liege,   245
    Do not infest your mind with beating on
    The strangeness of this business. At pick'd leisure,
    Which shall be shortly, single I'll resolve you
    (which to you shall seem probable) of every
    These happen'd accidents; till when, be cheerful   250
    And think of each thing well. [*Aside to Ariel.*] Come hither, spirit.
    Set Caliban and his companions free;
    Untie the spell. [*Exit Ariel.*] How fares my gracious sir?
    There are yet missing of your company
    Some few odd lads that you remember not.   255

        Enter ARIEL, *driving in* CALIBAN, STEPHANO, *and*
            TRINCULO *in their stol'n apparel.*

STEPHANO Every man shift for all the rest, and let no man
    take care for himself; for all is but fortune. *Coraggio,*
    bully-monster, *coraggio!*

TRINCULO If these be true spies which I wear in my
    head, here's a goodly sight.   260

CALIBAN O Setebos, these be brave spirits indeed!
    How fine my master is! I am afraid
    He will chastise me.

SEBASTIAN   Ha, ha!
    What things are these, my Lord Antonio?
    Will money buy 'em?

---

238. On: in.   **240. moping:** in a daze.   **244. conduct:** conductor.   **245. liege:** sovereign.   **246. infest:** annoy.   **247. pick'd:** i.e., convenient.   **248. single:** by myself (without an oracle).   **249. probable:** satisfactory.   **250. accidents:** occurrences.   **255. odd:** unaccounted for.   **256. Every . . . rest:** Stephano drunkenly inverts the proverbial "Every man for himself."   **257. Coraggio:** courage (Italian).   **259. true spies:** reliable observers (eyes).   **262. fine:** splendidly dressed (in his ducal robes).

ANTONIO   Very like; one of them   265
  Is a plain fish, and no doubt marketable.
PROSPERO Mark but the badges of these men, my lords,
  Then say if they be true. This misshapen knave—
  His mother was a witch, and one so strong
  That could control the moon, make flows and ebbs,   270
  And deal in her command without her power.
  These three have robb'd me, and this demi-devil
  (For he's a bastard one) had plotted with them
  To take my life. Two of these fellows you
  Must know and own, this thing of darkness I   275
  Acknowledge mine.
CALIBAN   I shall be pinch'd to death.
ALONSO Is not this Stephano, my drunken butler?
SEBASTIAN He is drunk now. Where had he wine?
ALONSO And Trinculo is reeling ripe. Where should they
  Find this grand liquor that hath gilded 'em?   280
  How cam'st thou in this pickle?
TRINCULO I have been in such a pickle since I saw you
  last that I fear me will never out of my bones. I shall
  not fear fly-blowing.
SEBASTIAN Why, how now, Stephano?   285
STEPHANO O, touch me not, I am not Stephano, but a
  cramp.
PROSPERO You'ld be king o' the isle, sirrah?
STEPHANO I should have been a sore one then.
ALONSO This is a strange thing as e'er I look'd on.   290
                [Pointing to Caliban.]
PROSPERO He is as disproportion'd in his manners
  As in his shape. Go, sirrah, to my cell;
  Take with you your companions. As you look
  To have my pardon, trim it handsomely.
CALIBAN Ay, that I will; and I'll be wise hereafter,   295
  And seek for grace. What a thrice-double ass

---

267. badges: insignia for servants, indicating what master they served. Stephano and Trinculo are of course dressed in stolen garments. **268. true:** honest. **271. her command:** i.e., the moon's authority. **without her power:** beyond the moon's influence. **280. gilded 'em:** flushed their faces (a common connection between blood and gold). Possibly *grand liquor* contains an alchemical allusion to the long-sought elixir that could transform base substances to gold. **282. pickle:** preservative (the horse urine of the pool being equivalent to vinegar). **284. fly-blowing:** infestation by maggots (to which unpickled meat would be subject). **288. sirrah:** form of address to an inferior. **289. sore:** (1) harsh; (2) pain-wracked. **294. trim it handsomely:** make the cell look fine. (*Tiffany*)

Was I to take this drunkard for a god,
And worship this dull fool!

PROSPERO   Go to, away!

ALONSO Hence, and bestow your luggage where you found it.

SEBASTIAN Or stole it, rather.   300

[Exeunt Caliban, Stephano, and Trinculo.]

PROSPERO Sir, I invite your Highness and your train
To my poor cell, where you shall take your rest
For this one night; which, part of it, I'll waste
With such discourse as, I not doubt, shall make it
Go quick away—the story of my life,   305
And the particular accidents gone by
Since I came to this isle. And in the morn
I'll bring you to your ship, and so to Naples,
Where I have hope to see the nuptial
Of these our dear-belov'd solemnized,   310
And thence retire me to my Milan, where
Every third thought shall be my grave.

ALONSO   I long
To hear the story of your life, which must
take the ear strangely.

PROSPERO   I'll deliver all,
And promise you calm seas, auspicious gales,   315
And sail so expeditious, that shall catch
Your royal fleet far off. *[Aside to Ariel.]* My Ariel, chick,
That is thy charge. Then to the elements
Be free, and fare thou well!—Please you draw near.

Exeunt omnes.

EPILOGUE

Spoken by PROSPERO.

Now my charms are all o'erthrown,
And what strength I have's mine own,
Which is most faint. Now 'tis true,
I must be here confin'd by you,
Or sent to Naples. Let me not,   5
Since I have my dukedom got,
And pardon'd the deceiver, dwell

---

303. waste: use up.   **314. Take:** enchant. **deliver:** report.   **316. sail:** voyage.
319. draw near: i.e., enter the cell.

In this bare island by your spell,
But release me from my bands
With the help of your good hands.   10
Gentle breath of yours my sails
Must fill, or else my project fails,
Which was to please. Now I want
Spirits to enforce, art to enchant,
And my ending is despair,   15
Unless I be reliev'd by prayer,
Which pierces so, that it assaults
Mercy itself, and frees all faults.
As you from crimes would pardon'd be,
Let your indulgence set me free.   *Exit.* 20

Epi. 9. bands: bonds. **10. hands:** (1) prayer; (*Tiffany*) (2) applause. **11. Gentle breath:** a favorable breeze produced by hands clapping or voices cheering (*Tiffany*). **13. want:** lack. **17. assaults:** storms the ear of. **18. frees:** remits.

NOTE ON THE TEXT

The First Folio (1623) is the only authority for *The Tempest;* all later texts are derived from that source. As was first demonstrated by Dover Wilson, following a suggestion of F.P. Wilson's, the manuscript underlying the F1 text was a transcript made from some form of Shakespeare's autograph (either "foul papers" or possibly slightly revised "fair copy") by Ralph Crane, a scrivener known to have been employed by the King's Men. It also seems likely that this transcript was prepared at the request of William or Isaac Jaggard expressly as copy for F1. Whether Shakespeare's manuscript had ever been used as a prompt-book is uncertain; no unambiguous evidence of playhouse association occurs in the F1 text. The text is unusually clean and offers few serious problems to the editor.

Since it is now believed that not only *The Tempest* but also *The Two Gentlemen of Verona, The Merry Wives of Windsor, The Winter's Tale,* probably *Measure for Measure* and *Cymbeline,* and possibly parts of *2 Henry IV* and *Timon of Athens* were printed from transcripts by Ralph Crane, his distinguishing characteristics as a scribe are worth noticing here. These are: (1) Regular and intelligent division of the play into acts and scenes. (2) A list of dramatis personae at the end of each play, except *Measure for Measure* and *Cymbeline.* For *Measure for Measure* such a list would have required a separate page in F1 and may have been omitted by the compositor for that reason; lack of space may also explain the absence of one for

Cymbeline, which ends halfway down the final page of F1 and had to be followed by a colophon and, for appearance's sake, a printer's ornament. (3) Use of the "massed entry" technique, found only in *The Two Gentlemen of Verona, The Merry Wives of Windsor,* and *The Winter's Tale.* (4) Heavy use of parentheses for parenthetical and appositive phrases, single words of address, and exclamations. (5) Frequent use of hyphenated forms, many of unusual pattern, perhaps the most distinctive being verb plus pronoun (in *The Tempest,* for example, *wide-chopt-rascall, sty-me, dark-backward, peg-thee, red-plague, flat-long, bemockt-at-Stabs, like-vulnerable, hearts-sorrow, Tur-phie-Mountaines, greene-Land, borne-Deuille, oo-zie*). (6) Generally careful and heavy punctuation (colons and semicolons) and fairly consistent use of the apostrophe to mark elided syllables or shortened forms (*'bove* for *above, 'Pray* for *I pray, 'pox* for *a pox, 'Save* for *God save*). There is also an occasional use of what W.W. Greg has called "Jonsonian elision" in such forms as *I'am, I'prethee,* and (in *Cymbeline*) *to' th'.* (7) A preference for *o'th'* over *a th',* and an occasional use of *you'r* or *you're* for *y'are.* Although singly some of these characteristics can be found here and there in other F1 texts, the combined appearance of four or five of them in any text may fairly be taken as strong evidence of Crane's hand in the manuscript copy. For a more detailed and inclusive study of Crane's scribal characteristics, see Howard-Hill.

As the Textual Notes indicate, the F1 text shows some apparent confusion in the printing of prose as verse in a number of the speeches of Trinculo and Stephano (2.2, 3.2, and the last parts of 4.1and 5.1) and of verse as prose in two or three of Caliban's speeches. Kermode suggests that the prose-as-verse anomaly in the speeches of Trinculo and Stephano may best be laid at the door of the compositors (B and D [or F?] for quire A, sigs. A4, A5; and C and D [or F] for quire B, sigs. B2 and B3ᵛ), who, having cast off their copy inaccurately, found it necessary to stretch it by breaking single prose lines into two shorter lines in order to fill out the page. So far as the problem in quire A is concerned, this is an appealing explanation, because, as Hinman shows, the six formes of quire A were not composed and printed off in the order usually employed by the F1 printers. But the theory encounters difficulties when it is applied to quire B, which, unlike quire A, employed the regular F1 composing and printing-off order (i.e., beginning with the third inner forme of the quire, B3ᵛ and B4ʳ), since the speeches in question do not fall on pages where the compositors might be expected to have found themselves with too much space on their hands. The few instances where Caliban's verse appears as prose do not pose a comparable problem and may most easily be explained as the result of revision in Shakespeare's manuscript, the intention of which was misinterpreted by Crane.

Shakespeare's authorship of the somewhat flat and plodding masque in 4.1 has often been questioned (and suggested authors are Francis Beaumont, George Chapman, or Thomas Heywood), but more recent opinion (Chambers, Kermode, Jowett, and Orgel) tends to accept it as by Shakespeare, arguing that it is an integral part of the play from the first, thus rejecting Lawrence's suggestion that the masque had been added for the second Court performance (perhaps 27 December 1612 or early 1613) as part of the festivities arranged for the espousal and marriage of Princess Elizabeth to Frederick V, Elector Palatine. One stage direction in the masque, (*"Iuno descends."*), which F1 places in the left margin opposite lines 72–3, has troubled editors. Based on the argument that a descent beginning at this point distracts the audience from attending to the speeches of Iris and Ceres (76–101) which immediately follow, Theobald moved Juno's descent to follow line 101, while some editors (e.g., Capell, Dyce, Globe, Kittredge) dispense with her descent altogether, simply entering her after line 101. Most recently, however, Jowett/Wells and Orgel postpone the actual descent, but show Juno appearing *"in the air"* following line 72 (Orgel, line 74), where she "floats" until alighting from her "machine" after line 101 (Orgel, after 102). Since there is little difference, so far as distraction is concerned, between slowly descending and dangling uneasily in midair, the present text preserves F1's *"Iuno descends."* following line 72, adding *"slowly in her car"* (after Collier) and lets her "alight" after the first half of line 101.

Among Shakespeare's plays, generally, except for *Henry VIII,* the stage directions in *The Tempest* are the most detailed and directive/prescriptive of action and reaction. This may be in part a result of the play's close relation to the Court masque (which contained elaborate stage directions) and in part Shakespeare's attempt to "direct" after his retirement to Stratford. It has also been shown, however, that to some small extent, as Greg suggested, the stage directions seem to reveal the hand of someone, other than the author, who has witnessed a performance of the play. That someone is almost certainly Crane, who, from the evidence of other Crane transcripts, is known to have "improved" the original stage directions in the course of transcribing. See Roberts and Jowett and such examples as: 3.3.52 s.d. *"with a quaint device"* and 82 s.d. *"with mocks and mows";* 4.1.138 s.d. *"to a strange, hollow, and confused noise, they heavily vanish";* 5.1.57 s.d. *"with a frantic gesture."*

For further information, see W. J. Lawrence, "The Masque in *The Tempest,*" *The Fortnightly Review,* n.s. CVII (1920), 941–6; F. P. Wilson, "Ralph Crane, Scrivener to the King's Players," *The Library,* 4th sec., VII (1926–27), 194–215; J. D. Wilson, ed., New Shakespeare *The Tempest* and *The Winter's Tale* (Cambridge, 1921 and 1931); E. K. Chambers, *Shakespearean Gleanings* (Oxford, 1944); W. W. Greg, *The Shakespeare First Folio* (Oxford, 1955, repr. 1999) and *The Editorial Problem in Shakespeare* (Oxford, 1967, repr. 1999); Frank Kermode, ed., New Arden *The Tempest* (London, rev. ed., 1958); Charlton Hinman, *The Printing and Proof-Reading of the First Folio of Shakespeare,* 2 vols. (Oxford, 1963); T. H. Howard-Hill, *Ralph Crane and Some Shakespeare First Folio Comedies*

(Charlottesville, Va., 1972) and "The Compositors of Shakespeare's Folio Comedies," *SB,* XXVI (1973), 61–106; J. A. Roberts, "Ralph Crane and the Text of *The Tempest,*" *S St,* XIII (1980), 213–33; John Jowett, "New Created Creatures: Ralph Crane and the Stage Directions in *The Tempest,*" *S Sur,* XXXVI (1983), 107–20; Stephen Orgel, ed., New Oxford *The Tempest* (Oxford, 1987); Stanley Wells, Gary Taylor, John Jowett, and William Montgomery, *William Shakespeare: A Textual Companion* (Oxford, 1987); Peter W. M. Blayney, *The First Folio of Shakespeare* (Washington, D.C.: Folger Shakespeare Library, 1991) and "Introduction to the Second Edition," *The Norton Facsimile [of] The First Folio of Shakespeare*, prepared by Charlton Hinman and Peter W. M. Blayney, 2nd ed. (NY: Norton, 1996, pp. xxvii-1); and Virginia Mason Vaughan and Alden T. Vaughan, eds., The Arden Shakespeare *The Tempest,* Third Series (London: Thomas Nelson, 1999), especially pp. 124-38. An elaboration of the thematic reading which supports the emendation "So rare a wond'red father and a wife" at 4.1.123 can be found in Ian McAdam, *Magic and Masculinity in Early Modern Drama* (Duquesne: Pittsburgh U P, 2009), pp. 339-41.

TEXTUAL NOTES

Dramatis personae: *as given in F1, following the play, with slight additions by later editors*
Act-scene division: *from F1*

I.1
Location: *Pope*
5 **hearts! cheerly**] *Capell* (hearts; cheerly); hearts, cheerely *F1* (*F4 and eds. until Capell om.* cheerely)
4 **cheerly, my**] *F2* (*comma, Theobald*); cheerely my *F1*
8 **s.d. Antonio**] *Theobald;* Anthonio *F1* (*throughout*)
21 **councillor**] *Wilson;* Counsellor *F1*
26 **Cheerly**] *F4;* Cheerely *F1*
33 **s.d. Exeunt.**] *Theobald;* Exit. *F1*
35 **s.d. A cry within.**] *placed as in Johnson; in F1 follows* plague (*see next note*)
36 **plague**] *Pope;* plague—— *F1*
37 **s.d. Enter . . . Gonzalo.**] *placed as in Capell; in F1 follows* A cry within. (*see note to l. 35 s.d.*)
52 **s.p. Mariners.**] *Dyce;* Mari. *F1*
52 **s.d. Exeunt.**] *Theobald*
54–5 **The . . . theirs.**] *as verse, Pope; as prose, F1*

54 **Prince**] *F4;* Prince, *F1*
55 **I am**] *Steevens;* I'am *F1*
57–8 **This . . . tides!**] *as verse, Pope; as prose, F1*
57 **wide-chopp'd rascal**] *F4;* wide-chopt-rascall *F1*
60–2 **"Mercy . . . split!"**] *first marked as part of the* confused noise within *by Capell; apparently part of Gonzalo's speech, F1*
62 **s.d. Exit Boatswain.**] *Dyce*
63 **wi' th'**] *White;* with' *F1*
64 **s.d. with Antonio**] *Cambridge (subs.)*
66 **furze**] *Rowe;* firrs *F1*

I.2
Location: *Pope, Theobald*
15 **woe**] *Pope;* woe, *F1*
24 **s.d. Lays . . . mantle.**] *Pope*
29 **soul—**] *Steevens;* soule *F1;* soul, *F3*
50 **dark backward**] *F3;* dark-backward *F1*
54 **Milan**] *Rowe* (Millan); Millaine *F1* (*throughout*)
59 **princess**] *Knight;* Princesse; *F1*
62 **foul play**] *F3;* fowle-play *F1*
77 **studies.**] *F4 (subs.);* studies, *F1*

91 **that which, . . . retir'd,**] *Pope;* that, which . . . retir'd *F1*

99 **exact—**] *Capell;* exact. *F1*

107 **screen**] *F4;* Schreene *F1*

109 **Milan—me**] *Wilson;* Millaine, Me *F1*

110 **royalties**] *F2;* roalties *F1*

112 **wi' th'**] *Rowe;* with *F1*

113–4 **homage, . . . crown,**] *F3* (Crowne, *F2*); homage/Subject his Coronet, to his Crowne *F1*

159 **divine.**] *F4 (subs.);* diuine, *F1*

169 **arise.**] *Pope (subs.);* arise, *F1*

169 **s.d. Puts . . . robe.**] *Collier MS (subs.)*

173 **princes**] *Rowe;* Princesse *F1*

181 **zenith**] *Capell;* Zenith *F1 (in italics)*

186 **s.d. Miranda sleeps.**] *Theobald*

203 **sight-outrunning**] *Capell;* sight out-running *F1*

265, 284, 346 **human**] *F4;* humane *F1*

282 **she**] *Rowe;* he *F1*

286 **service.**] *F2 (subs.);* seruice, *F1*

295 **peg thee**] *F2;* peg-thee *F1*

304 **s.d. Ariel**] *Rowe*

305 **Awake**] *Rowe;* Pro. Awake *F1* (*repeated s.p.*)

327 **Shall, . . . work,**] *Rowe;* Shall . . . night, . . . worke *F1*

342 **sty me**] *Rowe;* sty-me *F1*

372 **s.d. Aside.**] *Johnson*

375, 397 song headings **Ariel's**] *F3;* Ariel *F1*

377 **kiss'd,**] *Rowe;* kist *F1*

380 **the burthen bear**] *Pope (after Davenant-Dryden);* beare the burthen *F1*

381–7 **Hark . . . Cock-a-diddle-dow.**] *arranged as by Capell (and Daniel, l. 387); Burthen dispersedly./Harke, harke, bowgh wawgh: the watch-Dogges barke,/bowgh-wawgh./Ar. Hark, hark, I heare, the straine of strutting Chanticlere/cry cockadidle-dowe. F1*

382, 384, 404 **s.dd. within**] *Bullen*

390–1 **island. . . . wrack,**] *Pope;* Iland, . . . wracke. *F1*

410 **What,**] *ed. (after Daniel);* What *F1*

420 **s.d. Aside.**] *Pope*

439 **s.d. Aside.**] *Collier MS*

451 **s.d. Aside.**] *Capell*

459 **ill spirit**] *F4;* ill-spirit *F1*

484 **s.d. To Ferdinand.**] *Wilson*

494 **s.d. Aside.**] *Capell*

494, 495 **s.dd. To Ferdinand.**] *Cambridge*

496 **s.d. To Ariel.**] *Theobald*

502 **s.d. To Ferdinand.**] *Craig*

502 **s.d. To Miranda.**] *Munro*

2.1

Location: *Pope*

16 **entertain'd**] *Rowe;* entertaind, *F1*

16 **offer'd,**] *Capell;* offer'd *F1*

18 **dollar**] *Capell;* dollor *F1*

28–9 **Which . . . crow?**] *as prose, Pope; as verse, F1*

53–4 **How lush . . . green!**] *as prose, Pope; as verse, F1*

95 **Ay**] *Rowe;* I *F1*

106 **marriage?**] *Capell;* marriage. *F1*

153 **Bourn**] *Rowe;* Borne *F1*

170 **And—**] *Cambridge;* And *F1*

182 **mettle**] *Capell;* mettal *F1*

184 **s.d. invisible**] *Malone*

190 **s.d. All . . . Antonio.**] *Capell (subs., after Rowe)*

198 **s.d. Alonso sleeps.**] *Capell*

198 **s.d. Exit Ariel.**] *Malone*

203 **consent;**] *Capell;* consent *F1*

231 **throes**] *Pope;* throwes *F1*

278 **Twenty**] *F3;* 'Twentie *F1*

296 **s.d. They talk apart.**] *Capell*

296 **s.d. invisible**] *Capell*

306 **s.d. Waking.**] *Dyce*

307 **s.d. Wakes Alonso.**] *Neilson*

2.2

Location: *Pope*

14 **s.d. Enter Trinculo.**] *placed as in Rowe; in margin opposite ll. 14, 15, F1*

29 **holiday fool**] *F3 (subs.);* holiday-foole *F1*

37 **s.d. Thunder.**] *Capell*

41 **s.d. a . . . hand**] *Capell*

44–5 **This . . . comfort.**] *as prose, Pope; as verse, F1*

55 **This . . . comfort.**] *as prose, Pope; as verse, F1*

57 **What's . . . here?**] *as prose, Pope; as verse, F1*

86 **s.d. Caliban drinks.**] *Collier MS*

87 **I . . . be—**] *as prose, Pope; as verse, F1*

87 **be—**] *F2;* be, *F1*

93–4 **s.d. Caliban drinks again.**] *Wilson*

116 **s.d. Aside.**] *Dyce*

116–8 **These . . . him.**] *as verse, Johnson; as prose, F1*

119–20 **How didst . . . hither?**] *as prose, Pope; as verse, F1*

124 **ashore**] *F3;* a'-/shroe *F1*

130 **s.d. Passing the bottle.**] *Neilson-Hill (after Craig)*

135–6 **How . . . ague?**] *as prose, Pope; as verse, F1*

143 **s.d. Caliban drinks.**] *Collier*

146 **7 The . . . sooth!**] *as prose, Pope; as verse, F1*

148–9 **I'll . . . god.**] *as verse, Johnson; as prose, F1*

156 **him—**] *Pope;* him. *F1*

158–9 **But . . . monster!**] *as prose, Pope; as verse, F1*

159 **abominable**] *F4;* abhominable *F1*

160–1 **I'll . . . enough.**] *as verse, Pope; as prose, F1*

163–4 **I'll . . . man.**] *as verse, Pope; as prose, F1*

167–72 **I . . . me?**] *as verse, Pope; as prose, F1*

178 **s.p. Cal. (Sings drunkenly.)**] *given as* Caliban Sings drunkenly. *above l. 178, F1*

3.1

Location: *Theobald (after Pope)*

2 **sets**] *Rowe;* set *F1*

15 **busil'est**] *Kermode* (busilest, *after Bulloch conj.* busiliest); busie lest, *F1*

15 **s.d. at . . . unseen**] *Rowe*

25 **No,**] *Rowe;* No *F1*

31 **s.d. Aside.**] *Capell*

34–5 **you—Chiefly**] *Pope (subs., after Rowe);* you/Cheefely, *F1*

61 **would,**] *Theobald;* would *F1*

62 **wooden**] *F2* (woodden); wodden *F1*

74 **s.d. Aside.**] *Capell*

91 **s.d. Ferdinand . . . severally**] *Capell*

93 **withal**] *Theobald;* with all *F1*

3.2

Location: *Pope*

15 **on.**] *Cambridge;* on, *F1*

15–6 **lieutenant, monster**] *Rowe;* Lieutenant Monster *F1*

40–1 **Marry . . . Trinculo.**] *as prose, Pope; as verse, F1*

48–9 **Trinculo . . . teeth.**] *as prose, Pope; as verse, F1*

52 **isle;**] *Theobald;* Isle *F1*

54–5 **him—for . . . not—**] *Theobald (subs.);* him, (for . . . dar'st) . . . not. *F1*

58–9 **How . . . party?**] *as prose, Pope; as verse, F1*

68 **Trinculo . . . danger.**] *as prose, Pope; as verse, F1*

72–3 **Why . . . off.**] *as prose, Pope; as verse, F1*

76–7 **Do . . . time.**] *probably means as prose, Pope; as verse, F1*

76 **s.d. Beats Trinculo.**] *Rowe (subs.)*

78–81 **I . . . fingers**] *as prose, Pope; as verse, F1*

80 **murrain**] *F3;* murren *F1*

108–9 **Dost . . . Trinculo?**] *as prose, Pope; as verse, F1*

111–2 **Give . . . head.**] *as prose, Pope; as verse, F1*

119–20 **At . . . sing.**] *as prose, Pope; as verse, F1*

121 **scout**] *Rowe;* cout *F1*

128–9 **If . . . list.**] *as prose, Pope; as verse, F1*

144–52 **This . . . Stephano.**] *as prose, Pope; as verse, F1*

3.3

Location: *Theobald (after Pope)*

2 **aches**] *Sisson;* akes *F1;* ake *F2*

11 **s.d. Aside to Sebastian.**] *Hanmer*

13, 17 **s.dd. Aside to Antonio.**] *Capell*

14 **s.d. Aside to Sebastian.**] *Capell*

17 **s.d. Solemn . . . invisible.**] *placed as in Pope; after* fresh. *l. 17, F1*

19 **s.d. Enter . . . depart.**] *placed as in Wilson; part of s.d. at l. 17, F1*

29 **islanders**] *F2;* Islands *F1*

33 **human**] *Rowe;* humaine *F1*

34, 39 **s.dd. Aside.**] *Capell*

35 **present**] *Rowe;* present; *F1;* present, *F2*

42 **Will't**] *Pope;* Wilt *F1*

48 **putter-out**] *hyphen, Capell*

52 **to**] *F4;* too *F1*

60 **s.d. Alonso . . . swords.**] *Cambridge (after Hanmer)*

63 **bemock'd-at stabs**] *Rowe;* bemockt-at-Stabs *F1*

64 **still-closing**] *hyphen, Pope*

65 **plume**] *Rowe;* plumbe *F1*

66 **like invulnerable**] *Rowe;* like-invulnerable *F1*

81 **heart's sorrow**] *Pope (after Rowe);* hearts-sorrow *F1*

82 **s.d. to . . . enter**] *Rowe;* (to soft Musicke.) Enter *F1*

93 **s.d. Exit above.**] *Theobald*

103 **s.d. Sebastian and Antonio**] *Malone*

4.1

Location: *Capell (after Pope)*

9 **off**] *F2;* of *F1*

13 **gift**] *Rowe;* guest *F1*

17 **rite**] *Rowe;* right *F1*

25 **love . . . now,**] *Rowe;* loue, . . . now *F1*

52 **rein**] *F4;* raigne *F1*

59 **s.d. Soft music.**] *placed as in Pope; after l. 58, F1*

62 **turfy mountains**] *F2;* Turphie-Mountaines *F1*

63 **thatch'd**] *Rowe;* thetchd *F1*

74 **Her**] *Rowe;* here *F1*

74 **s.d. slowly . . . car**] *ed. (after Collier MS and Wilson); s.d. in margin opposite ll. 72, 73, F1*

83 **short-grass'd**] *F3* (hyphen, *Rowe*);
short gras'd *F1*

90 **blind boy's**] *F3* (subs.); blind-Boyes *F1*

101 **s.d. Juno alights.**] *Wilson*

106 **marriage-blessing**] *Theobald;*
marriage, blessing *F1*

110 **s.p. Cer.**] *Theobald; lines continued to
Juno, F1*

123 **wise**] *some copies of F1 may read
wife*

124 **s.d. Juno . . . employment.**] *placed
as in Capell; after l. 127, F1*

125 **seriously;**] *F4;* seriously, *F1*

130 **green land**] *Warburton;* Greene-
Land *F1*

134 **sicklemen,**] *F4;* Sicklemen *F1*

136 **holiday**] *Capell;* holly day *F1*

139 **s.d. Aside.**] *Johnson*

142 **s.d. To the Spirits.**] *Johnson*

147 **sir.**] *Pope* (subs.); Sir, *F1*

160 **infirmity.**] *F4* (subs.); infirmitie, *F1*

162 **repose.**] *F3* (subs.); repose, *F1*

164 **s.d. To Ariel.**] *ed.*

164 **s.d. To . . . Miranda.**] *ed.*

164 **thee. Ariel! come.**] *ed. (after
Kermode);* thee Ariel: come. *F1*

164 **s.d. Exeunt . . . Miranda.**] *ed.;* Exit.
F1 (after l. 163)

173 **princes**] *Rowe;* Princesse *F1 (a Crane
spelling of* Princes)

180 **furzes**] *Rowe;* firzes *F1*

182 **filthy-mantled**] *hyphen, Cambridge*

188 **born devil**] *F4* (born *F3*); borne-
Deuill *F1*

193 **s.d. Enter . . . etc.**] *placed as in Dyce;
after l. 193, F1*

193 **them on**] *Rowe;* on them *F1*

193 **s.d. Prospero . . . invisible.**] *Capell
(after Theobald)*

193 **s.d. Enter . . . wet.**] *placed as in Capell;
in F1 follows etc. in preceding s.d.*

194–5 **Pray . . . cell.**] *as verse, Rowe; as
prose, F1*

196–202 **monster . . . you—**] *as prose,
Pope; as verse, F1*

206 **hoodwink**] *F3;* hudwinke *F1*

211–4 **That's . . . labor.**] *as prose, Pope; as
verse, F1*

220–1 **Give . . . thoughts.**] *as prose, Pope;
as verse, F1*

222–3 **O . . . thee!**] *probably meant as prose,
Pope; as verse, F1*

226 **frippery.**] *Theobald* (subs.);
frippery, *F1*

231 **Let't**] *Rann;* let's *F1*

250 **lay-to**] *hyphen, Steevens*

257 **s.d. Caliban . . . out.**] *Theobald* (subs.)

5.1

Location: *Theobald*

10 **line-grove**] *Collier;* Line-groue *F1 (in
italics)*

14 **Brimful**] *F4* (subs.); Brim full *F1*

20 **human**] *Rowe;* humane *F1*

32 **s.d. Prospero . . . staff.**] *Wilson*

35 **ebbing Neptune**] *F3;* ebbing-
Neptune *F1*

39 **midnight mushrumps**] *ed.;*
midnight-Mushrumps *F1;* hyphen om.
*F4 (*midnight Mushromes)

46 **strong-bas'd**] *hyphen, Pope*

54 **airy charm**] *F3;* Ayrie-charme *F1*

60 **boil'd**] *Rowe;* boile *F1*

72 **Didst**] *F1 catchword;* Did *F1*

75 **entertain'd**] *F2;* entertaine *F1*

81 **shores**] *Malone;* shore *F1*

84 **s.d. Exit . . . immediately.**] *Theobald
(after l. 85); placed as in Capell*

88 **s.p. Ari.**] *Craig*

111 **Whe'er**] *Capell;* Where *F1*

120 **s.d. To Gonzalo.**] *Wilson*

124 **not**] *F3;* nor *F1*

126 **s.d. Aside . . . Antonio**] *Johnson*

129 **s.d. Aside.**] *Johnson*

151 **oozy**] *Rowe;* oo-zie *F1*

179 **s.d. Kneels.**] *Theobald*

191 **advice**] *F4;* aduise *F1*

213 **s.d. To . . . Miranda.**] *Hanmer*

219 **shore?**] *Pope;* shore, *F1*

224 **tight**] *Rowe;* tyte *F1*

225, 240 **s.dd. Aside to Prospero.**] *Capell*

226, 241, 251 **s.dd. Aside to Ariel.**] *Capell*

241 **my diligence. Thou**] *F4* (subs.); (my
diligence) thou *F1*

248 **Which . . . shortly, single**] *Pope;*
(Which . . . shortly single) *F1*

253 **s.d. Exit Ariel.**] *Capell*

256–8 **Every . . . coraggio!**] *as prose,
Pope; as verse, F1*

258 **coraggio**] *F2;* Corasio *F1*

272 **robb'd**] *F3;* robd *F1*

282–4 **I . . . fly-blowing.**] *as prose, Pope;
as verse, F1*

290 **s.d. Pointing to Caliban.**] *Steevens*

296 **thrice-double**] *hyphen, Theobald*

300 **s.d. Exeunt . . . Trinculo.**] *Capell*

314 **strangely**] *F2;* strangely *F1*

317 **s.d. Aside to Ariel.**] *Capell*

Epilogue

2 **own,**] *F2;* owne. *F1*

14 **enforce, art**] *Rowe;* enforce: Art *F1*

20 **s.d. Exit.**] Exit. [*list of actors*]
FINIS. *F1*

SOURCES AND CONTEXTS

FROM A DISCOVERY
OF THE BARMUDAS

By Sylvester Jourdain (1610)

. . . All our men, being utterly spent, tired, and disabled for longer labor, were even resolved, without any hope of their lives, to shut up the hatches and to have committed themselves to the mercy of the sea (which is said to be merciless) or rather to the mercy of their mighty God and redeemer. . . . So that some of them, having some good and comfortable waters in the ship, fetched them and drunk the one to the other, taking their last leave one of the other, until their more joyful and happy meeting in a more blessed world; when it pleased God out of his most gracious and merciful providence, so to direct and guide our ship (being left to the mercy of the sea) for her most advantage; that Sir George Somers . . . most wishedly happily descried land; whereupon he most comfortably encouraged the company to follow their pumping, and by no means to cease bailing out of the water. . . . Through which weak means it pleased God to work so strongly as the water was stayed for that little time (which, as we all much feared, was the last period of our breathing) and the ship kept from present sinking, when it pleased God to send her within half an English mile of that land that Sir George Somers had not long before descried— which were the islands of the Barmudas. And there neither did our ship sink, but more fortunately in so great a misfortune fell in between two rocks, where she was fast lodged and locked for further budging.

[*The men come to the island*]

But our delivery was not more strange in falling so opportunely and happily upon the land, as our feeding and preservation was beyond our hopes and all men's expectations most admirable. . . . Yet did we find there the air so temperate and the country so abundantly fruitful of all fit necessaries for the sustenation and preservation of man's life, that most in a manner of all our provisions of bread, beer, and victual being quite spoiled in lying long drowned in salt water, notwithstanding we were there for the space of nine months (few days over or under) not only well refreshed, comforted, and with good satiety contented but, out of the abundance thereof, provided us some reasonable quantity and proportion of provision to carry us for Virginia and to maintain ourselves and that company we found there, to the great relief of them, as it fell out in their so great extremities . . . until it pleased God . . . that their store was better supplied. And greater and better provisions we might have had, if we had had better means for the storing and transportation thereof. Wherefore my opinion sincerely of this island is, that whereas it hath been and is full accounted the most dangerous, unfortunate, and most forlorn place of the world, it is in truth the richest, healthfulest, and pleasing land (the quantity and bigness thereof considered) and merely natural, as ever man set foot upon.

From Sylvester Jourdain, *A Discovery of the Barmudas,* 1610. Facsimile edition. Ed. J. Q. Adams. NY: Scholars' Facsimiles and Reprints, 1940.

From
A TRUE REPORTORY
OF THE WRACKE AND REDEMPTION
OF SIR THOMAS GATES, KNIGHT

By William Strachey (1610)[1]

ATRUE REPORTORY of the wracke, and redemption of Sir Thomas Gates Knight; upon, and from the Ilands of the Bermudas: his comming to Virginia, and the estate of that Colonie then, and after, under the government of the Lord La Warre, July 15. 1610. written by William Strachy, Esquire.

I

A most dreadfull Tempest (the manifold deaths whereof, are here to the life described) their wracke on Bermuda, and the description of those Ilands.

Excellent Lady, know that upon Friday late in the evening, we brake ground out of the Sound of Plymouth, our whole Fleete then consisting of seven good Ships, and two Pinnaces, all which from the said second of June, unto the twenty three of July, kept in friendly consort together, not a whole watch at any time losing the sight each of other . . . We were within seven or eight dayes at the most, by Cap. Newports reckoning of making Cape Henry upon the coast of Virginia. When on S. James his day, July 24. being Monday (preparing for no lesse all the blacke night before) the cloudes gathering thicke upon us, and the windes singing, and whistling most unusually which made us to cast off our Pinnace towing the same until then asterne, a dreadfull storme and hideous began to blow from out the North-east, which swelling, and roaring as it were by fits, some houres with more violence then others, at length did beate all light from heaven; which like an hell of darkenesse turned blacke upon us; so much the more fuller of horror, as in such cases horror and feare

1. From *Purchas his Pilgrimes,* Pt II, Bk X, 1625. Marginal notes are omitted.

use to overrunne the troubled, and overmastered sences of all which (taken up with amazement) the eares lay so sensible to the terrible cries, and murmurs of the windes, and distraction of our Company, as who was most armed, and best prepared, was not a little shaken. For surely (Noble Lady) as death comes not so sodaine nor apparant, so he comes not so elvish and painfull (to men especially even then in health and perfect habitudes of body) as at Sea; who comes at no time so welcome, but our frailty (so weake is the hold of hope in misrable demonstrations of danger) it makes guilty of many contrary changes, and conflicts: For indeede death is accompanied at no time, nor place with circumstances every way so uncapable of particularities of goodness and inward comforts, as at Sea…

During all this time, the heavens look'd so blacke upon us, that it was not possible the elevation of the Pole might be observed: nor a Starre by night, nor Sunne beame by day was to be seene. Onely upon the Thursday night Sir George Summers being upon the watch, had an apparition of a little round light, like a faint Starre, trembling, and streaming along with a sparkeling blaze, halfe the height upon the Maine Mast, and shooting sometimes from Shroud to Shroud, tempting to settle as it were upon any of the foure Shrouds: and for three or foure hours together, or rather more, halfe the night it kept with us; running sometimes along the Maine-yard to the very end, and then returning. At which, Sir George Summers called divers about him, and shewed them the same, who observed it with much wonder, and carefulnesse: but upon a sodaine, towards the morning watch, they lost the sight of it, and knew not what way it made. The superstitious Sea-men make many constructions of this Sea-fire, which neverthelesse is usuall in stormes: the same (it may be) which the Graecians were wont in the Mediterranean to call Castor and Pollux, of which, if one onely appeared without the other, they tooke it for an evill signe of great tempest. The Italians, and such, who lye open to the Adriatique and Tyrrene Sea, call it (a sacred Body) Corpo sancto: the Spaniards call it Saint Elmo, and have an authentique and miraculous Legend for it. Be it what it will, we laid other foundations of safety or ruine, then in the rising or falling of it, but could it have served us now miraculously to have taken our height by, it might have strucken amazement, and a reverence in our devotions, according to the due of a miracle. But it did not light us any whit the more to our knowne way, who ran now (as doe hoodwinked men) at all adventures, sometimes North, and North-east, then North and by West, and in an instant againe varying two or three points, and sometimes halfe the Compasse. East and by South we steered away as much as we could to beare upright, which was no small carefulnesse nor paine to

doe, albeit we much unrigged our Ship, threw over-boord much luggage, many a Trunke and Chest (in which I suffered no meane losse)
and staved many a Butt of Beere, Hogsheads of Oyle, Syder, Wine,
and Vinegar, and heaved away all our Ordnance on the Starboord
side, and had now purposed to have cut downe the Maine Mast, the
more to lighten her, for we were much spent, and our men so weary,
as their strengths together failed them, with their hearts, having tra-
vailed now from Tuesday till Friday morning, day and night, without
either sleepe or foode; . . . and it being now Friday, the fourth morning, it wanted little, but that there had bin a generall determination,
to have shut up hatches, and commending our sinfull soules to God,
committed the Shippe to the mercy of the Sea: surely, that night we
must have done it, and that night had we then perished: but see the
goodnesse and sweet introduction of better hope, by our mercifull
God given unto us. Sir George Summers, when no man dreamed of
such happinesse, had discovered, and cried Land. Indeede the morning now three quarters spent, had wonne a little cleerenesse from the
dayes before, and it being better surveyed, the very trees were seene
to move with the winde upon the shoare side: whereupon our Gov-
ernour commanded the Helme-man to beare up, the Boate-swaine
sounding at the first, found it thirteene fathome, & when we stood
a little in seven fatham; and presently heaving his lead the third time,
had ground at foure fathome, and by this, we had got her within a
mile under the South-east point of the land, where we had somewhat
smooth water. But having no hope to save her by comming to an
anker in the same, we were inforced to runne her ashoare, as neere
the land as we could, which brought us within three quarters of a
mile of shoare, and by the mercy of God unto us, making out our
Boates, we had ere night brought all our men, women, and children,
about the number of one hundred and fifty, safe into the Ilands.

We found it to be the dangerous and dreaded Iland, or rather Ilands
of the Bermuda: whereof let mee give your Ladyship a briefe description, before I proceed to my narration. And that the rather, because
they be so terrible to all that ever touched on them, and such tempests,
thunders, and other fearefull objects are seene and heard about them,
that they be called commonly, The Devils Ilands, and are feared and
avoyded of all sea travellers alive, above any other place in the world.
Yet it pleased our mercifull God, to make even this hideous and hated
place, both the place of our safetie, and meanes of our deliverance.

And hereby also, I hope to deliver the world from a foule and generall errour: it being counted of most, that they can be no habitation
for Men, but rather given over to Devils and wicked Spirits; whereas
indeed wee find them now by experience, to bee as habitable and

commodious as most Countries of the same climate and situation: in-somuch as if the entrance into them were as easie as the place it selfe is contenting, it had long ere this beene inhabited, as well as other Ilands. Thus shall we make it appeare, That Truth is the daughter of Time, and that men ought not to deny every thing which is not subject to their owne sense.

From William Strachey, *A True Reportory of the Wracke and Redemption of Sir Thomas Gates, Knight.* In *Narrative and Dramatic Sources of Shakespeare.* Ed. Geoffrey Bullough. Vol. 8. NY: Columbia UP, 1975.

From Essayes

Michel De Montaigne

CHAPTER XI. OF CRUELTIE

Me thinks vertue is another manner of thing, and much more noble than the inclinations unto goodnesse, which in us are ingendered. Mindes well borne, and directed by themselves, follow one same path, and in their actions represent the same visage, that the vertuous doe. But vertue importeth, and soundeth somewhat I wot not what greater and more active, than by an happy complexion, gently and peaceably, to suffer it selfe to be led or drawne, to follow reason.

He that through a naturall facilitie, and genuine mildnesse, should neglect or contemne injuries received, should no doubt performe a rare action, and worthy commendation: But he who being toucht and stung to the quicke, with any wrong or offence received, should arme himselfe with reason against this furiously-blind desire of revenge, and in the end after a great conflict, yeeld himselfe master over-it, should doubtlesse doe much more. The first should doe well, the other vertuously: the one action might be termed goodnesse, the other vertue. For, *It seemeth, that the verie name of vertue presupposeth difficultie, and inferreth resistance, and cannot well exercise it self without an enemie.*

But to returne to my former discourse, I have a verie feeling and tender compassion of other mens afflictions, and should more easily weep for companie sake, if possiblie for any occasion whatsoever, I could shed teares. There is nothing sooner moveth teares in me, than to see others weepe, not onely fainedly, but howsoever, whether truly or forcedly. I do not greatly waile for the dead, but rather envie them. Yet doe I much waile and moane the dying. The Canibales and savage people do not so much offend me with roasting and eating of dead bodies, as those which torment and persecute the living.

From Michel De Montaigne, *The Essayes of Michael Lord of Montaigne*. Trans. John Florio. 1613 edition. NY: E. P. Dutton and Co., 1928.

From THE TEMPEST, OR,
THE ENCHANTED ISLAND
William Davenant and John Dryden

ACT 2, SCENE 2

Scene Cypress Trees and Cave.
Enter PROSPERO *alone.*

PROSPERO 'Tis not yet fit to let my Daughters know
    I kept the Infant Duke of *Mantua*
    So near them in this Isle, whose Father dying,
    Bequeath'd him to my care; Till my false Brother
    (When he design'd t'usurp my Dukedome from me)
    Expos'd him to that fate he meant for me.
    By calculation of his birth I saw
    Death threat'ning him, if, till some time were past,
    He should behold the face of any Woman:
    And now the danger's nigh: *Hippolito*!   10

Enter HIPPOLITO.

HIPPOLITO Sir, I attend your pleasure.
PROSPERO How I have lov'd thee from thy infancy,
    Heav'n knows, and thou thy self canst bear me witness,
    Therefore accuse not me for thy restraint.
HIPPOLITO Since I knew life, you've kept me in a Rock,
    And you this day have hurri'd me from thence,
    Onely to change my Prison, not to free me.
    I murmur not, but I may wonder at it.
PROSPERO O gentle Youth, Fate waits for thee abroad,
    A black Star threatens thee, and death unseen
    Stands ready to devour thee.   20
HIPPOLITO   You taught me
    Not to fear him in any of his shapes:
    Let me meet death rather then be a prisoner.
PROSPERO 'Tis pity he should seize thy tender youth.
HIPPOLITO Sir, I have often heard you say, no creature liv'd
    Within this Isle, but those which Man was Lord of;
    Why then should I fear?

PROSPERO But here are creatures which I nam'd not to thee,
  Who share Mans Sovereignty by Nature's Laws,
  And oft depose him from it.   30
HIPPOLITO What are those Creatures, Sir?
PROSPERO Those dangerous enemies of men call'd Women.
HIPPOLITO Women! I never heard of them before.
  What are Women like?
PROSPERO Imagine something between young Men and Angels:
  Fatally beauteous, and have killing Eyes,
  Their voices charm beyond the Nightingales,
  They are all enchantment, those who once behold 'em,
  Are made their slaves for ever.
HIPPOLITO Then I will wink and fight with 'em.   40
PROSPERO 'Tis but in vain,
  They'l haunt you in your very sleep.
HIPPOLITO Then I'l revenge it on 'em when I wake.
PROSPERO You are without all possibility of revenge,
  They are so beautiful, that you can ne'r attempt,
  Nor wish to hurt them.
HIPPOLITO   Are they so beautiful?
PROSPERO Calm sleep is not so soft, nor Winter Suns,
  Nor Summer shades so pleasant.
HIPPOLITO Can they be fairer then the Plumes of Swans?
  Or more delightful then the Peacocks Feathers?   50
  Or than the gloss upon the necks of Doves?
  Or have more various beauty then the Rainbow?
  These I have seen, and without danger wondred at.
PROSPERO All these are far below 'em: Nature made
  Nothing but Woman dangerous and fair:
  Therefore if you should chance to see 'em,
  Avoid 'em streight I charge you.
HIPPOLITO Well, since you say they are so dangerous,
  I'l so far shun' em as I may with safety
  Of the unblemish'd honour which you taught me.   60
  But let' em not provoke me, for I'm sure
  I shall not then forbear them.
PROSPERO Go in and read the Book I gave you last.
  Tomorrow I may bring you better news.
HIPPOLITO I shall obey you, Sir.   [*Exit* HIPPOLITO.
PROSPERO So, so; I hope this Lesson has secur'd him,
  For I have been constrain'd to change his lodging
  From yonder Rock where first I bred him up,
  And here have brought him home to my own Cell,

Because the Shipwrack happen'd near his Mansion.   70
I hope he will not stir beyond his limits,
For hitherto he hath been all obedience:
The Planets seem to smile on my designs,
And yet there is one sullen cloud behind,
I would it were disperst.

Enter MIRANDA *and* DORINDA.

How, my Daughters! I thought I had instructed
Them enough: Children! retire;
Why do you walk this way?
MIRANDA   It is within our bounds, Sir.
PROSPERO   But both take heed, that path is very dangerous.   80
Remember what I told you.
DORINDA   Is the man that way, Sir?
PROSPERO   All that you can imagine ill is there,
The curled Lion, and the rugged Bear,
Are not so dreadful as that man.
MIRANDA   Oh me, why stay we here then?
DORINDA   I'l keep far enough from his Den, I warrant him.
MIRANDA   But you have told me, Sir, you are a man;
And yet you are not dreadful.
PROSPERO   I Child! but I am a tame man;   90
Old men are tame by Nature, but all the danger
Lies in a wild young man.
DORINDA   Do they run wild about the Woods?
PROSPERO   No, they are wild within doors, in Chambers,
And in Closets.
DORINDA   But, Father, I would stroak'em,
And make 'em gentle, then sure they would not hurt me.
PROSPERO   You must not trust them, Child: no Woman can
Come near 'em, but she feels a pain, full nine moneths.
Well, I must in; for new affairs require
My presence: be you, *Miranda*, your Sisters Guardian.[*Exit* PROSPERO.
DORINDA   Come, Sister, shall we walk the other way?   101
The Man will catch us else: we have but two legs,
And he perhaps has four.
MIRANDA   Well, Sister, though he have; yet look about you,
And we shall spy him ere he comes too near us.
DORINDA   Come back, that way is towards his Den.
MIRANDA   Let me alone; I'l venture first, for sure
He can devour but one of us at once.
DORINDA   How dare you venture?

MIRANDA We'l find him sitting like a Hare in's Form,   110
    And he shall not see us.
DORINDA I, but you know my Father charg'd us both.
MIRANDA But who shall tell him on't? we'l keep each
    Others counsel.
DORINDA   I dare not for the world.
MIRANDA But how shall we hereafter shun him, if we do not
    Know him first?
DORINDA   Nay, I confess I would
    Fain see him too. I find it in my Nature,
    Because my Father has forbidden me.
MIRANDA I, there's it, Sister, if he had said nothing,
    I had been quiet. Go softly, and if you see him   120
    First, be quick, and becken me away.
DORINDA Well, if he does catch me, I'l humble my self to him,
    And ask him pardon, as I do my Father,
    When I have done a fault.
MIRANDA And if I can but scape with life, I had rather
    Be in pain nine moneths, as my Father threatn'd,
    Then lose my longing.   [*Exeunt.*

ACT 2, SCENE 3

The Scene continues.
Enter HIPPOLITO.

HIPPOLITO *Prospero* has often said, that Nature makes
    Nothing in vain: why then are women made?
    Are they to suck the poison of the Earth,
    As gaudy colour'd Serpents are? I'l ask
    That Question, when next I see him here.

Enter MIRANDA *and* DORINDA *peeping.*

DORINDA O Sister, there it is, it walks about like one of us.
MIRANDA I, just so, and has legs as we have too.
HIPPOLITO It strangely puzzles me: yet 'tis most likely
    Women are somewhat between men and spirits.
DORINDA Heark! it talks, sure this is not it my Father   10
    Meant, for this is just like one of us:
    Methinks I am not half so much afraid on't
    As I was; see, now it turns this way.
MIRANDA Heaven! What a goodly thing it is?
DORINDA I'l go nearer it.

MIRANDA O no 'tis dangerous, Sister! I'l go to it.
   I would not for the world that you should venture.
   My Father charg'd me to secure you from it.
DORINDA I warrant you this is a tame man, dear Sister,
   He'll not hurt me, I see it by his looks.   20
MIRANDA Indeed he will! but go back, and he shall eat
   Me first: Fie, are you not asham'd to be
   So much inquisitive?
DORINDA You chide me for't, and wou'd give your self.
MIRANDA Come back, or I will tell my Father.
   Observe how he begins to stare already.
   I'l meet the danger first, and then call you.
DORINDA Nay, Sister, you shall never vanquish me in kindness.
   I'l venture you no more then you will me.
PROSPERO within. *Miranda*, Child, where are you!   30
MIRANDA Do you not hear my Father call? go in.
DORINDA 'Twas you he nam'd, not me; I will but say
   My prayers, and follow you immediately.
MIRANDA Well, Sister, you'l repent it.   [*Exit* MIRANDA.
DORINDA Though I die for't, I must have th'other peep.
HIPPOLITO *seeing her.* What thing is that? sure' tis some Infant of
   The Sun, dress'd in his Fathers gayest Beams,
   And comes to play with Birds: my sight is dazl'd,
   And yet I find I'm loth to shut my Eyes.
   I must go nearer it—but stay a while;   40
   May it not be that beauteous Murderer, Woman,
   Which I was charg'd to shun? Speak, what art thou?
   Thou shining Vision!
DORINDA Alas, I know not; but I'm told I am a Woman;
   Do not hurt me, pray, fair thing.
HIPPOLITO I'd sooner tear my eyes out, then consent
   To do you any harm; though I was told
   A Woman was my Enemy.
DORINDA I never knew what 'twas to be an Enemy,
   Nor can I e'r prove so to that which looks   50
   Like you: for though I have been charg'd by him
   (Whom yet I never disobey'd) to shun
   Your presence, yet I'd rather die then lose it;
   Therefore I hope you will not have the heart
   To hurt me: though I fear you are a Man,
   That dangerous thing of which I have been warn'd.
   Pray tell me what you are?
HIPPOLITO I must confess, I was inform'd I am a Man,

But if I fright you, I shall wish I were
Some other Creature. I was bid to fear you too.   60
DORINDA Ay me! Heav'n grant we be not poison to each other!
Alas, can we not meet but we must die?
HIPPOLITO I hope not so! for when two poisonous Creatures,
Both of the same kind, meet, yet neither dies.
I've seen two Serpents harmless to each other,
Though they have twin'd into a mutual knot:
If we have any venome in us, sure, we cannot be
More poisonous, when we meet, then Serpents are.
You have a hand like mine, may I not gently touch it?
                                              [*Takes her hand.*
DORINDA I've touch'd my Father's and my Sister's hands,   70
And felt no pain; but now, alas! There's something,
When I touch yours, which makes me sigh: just so
I've seen two Turtles mourning when they met;
Yet mine's a pleasing grief; and so me thought
Was theirs: For still they mourn'd, and still they seem'd
To murmur too, and yet they often met.
HIPPOLITO Oh Heavens! I have the same sense too: your hand
Methink goes through me; I feel at my heart,
And find it pleases, though it pains me.
PROSPERO *within.*   *Dorinda!*
DORINDA My Father calls again; ah, I must leave you.   80
HIPPOLITO Alas, I'm subject to the same command.
DORINDA This is my first offence against my Father,
Which he, by severing us, too cruelly does punish.
HIPPOLITO And this is my first trespass too: but he
Hath more offended truth than we have him:
He said our meeting would destructive be,
But I no death but in our parting see.   [*Exeunt several ways.*]

From ACT 5, SCENE 2

Enter PROSPERO, ALONZO, ANTONIO, GONZALO.

ALONZO *to* PROSPERO Let it no more be thought of, your purpose,
Though it was severe, was just. In losing *Ferdinand*
I should have mourn'd, but could not have complain'd.
PROSPERO Sir, I am glad kind Heaven decreed it otherwise.
DORINDA O wonder! How many goodly Creatures   130
Are there here! How beauteous Mankind is!
HIPPOLITO O brave new world, that has such People in't!
ALONZO *to* FERDINAND Now all the blessings of a glad Father
Compass thee about, and make thee happy

In thy beauteous choice.

GONZALO I've inward wept, or should have spoken ere this.
Look down, sweet Heaven, and on this Couple drop
A blessed Crown, For it is you chalk'd out the
Way which brought us hither.

ANTONIO Though penitence forc'd by necessity can scarce   140
Seem real, yet, dearest Brother, I have hope
My bloud may plead for pardon with you; I resign
Dominion, which, 'tis true, I could not keep,
But Heaven knows too, I would not.

PROSPERO All past crimes I bury in the joy
Of this blessed day.

ALONZO And, that I may not be behind in Justice,
To this young Prince I render back his Dukedom,
And as the Duke of *Mantua* thus salute him.

HIPPOLITO What is it that you render back, methinks   150
You give me nothing.

PROSPERO You are to be Lord of a great People,
And o're Towns and Cities.

HIPPOLITO And shall these People be all Men and Women?

GONZALO Yes, and shall call you Lord.

HIPPOLITO Why then I'll live no longer in a Prison,
But have a whole Cave to my self hereafter.

PROSPERO And that your happiness may be compleat,
I give you my *Dorinda* for your Wife,
She shall be yours for ever, when the Priest   160
Has made you one.

HIPPOLITO How can he make us one? Shall I grow to her?

PROSPERO By saying holy words you shall be joyn'd
In Marriage to each other.

DORINDA I warrant you those holy words are charms.
My Father means to conjure us together.

PROSPERO *to his Daughters.* My *Ariel* told me, when last night you quarrell'd,
You said you would for ever part your beds;
But what you threaten'd in your anger, Heaven
Has turn'd to Prophecy.   170
For you, *Miranda*, must with *Ferdinand,*
And you, *Dorinda*, with *Hippolito*
Lie in one Bed hereafter.

ALONZO And Heaven make those Beds still fruitful in
Producing Children, to bless their Parents Youth,
And Grandsires age.

MIRANDA *to* DORINDA If Children come by lying in a Bed,
I wonder you and I had none between us.

163

DORINDA Sister, it was our fault, we meant like fools
 To look 'em in the fields, and they, it seems,   180
 Are onely found in Beds.
HIPPOLITO I am o'rjoy'd that I shall have *Dorinda*
 In a Bed, we'll lie all night and day
 Together there, and never rise again.
FERDINAND *aside to him.* *Hippolito!* you yet are ignorant
 Of your great Happiness, but there is somewhat,
 Which for your own and fair *Dorinda's* sake,
 I must instruct you in.
HIPPOLITO Pray teach me quickly how Men and Women
 In your World make love, I shall soon learn,   190
 I warrant you.

   Enter ARIEL, *driving in* STEPHANO, TRINCALO, MUSTACHO,
      VENTOSO, CALIBAN, SYCORAX.

PROSPERO Why that's my dainty *Ariel,* I shall miss thee,
 But yet thou shalt have freedom.
GONZALO O look, Sir, look the Master and the Saylors—
 The Bosen too—my Prophecy is out,
 That if a Gallows were on land, that man
 Could ne'r be drown'd.
ALONZO *to* TRINCALO Now, Blasphemy, what not one Oath ashore?
 Hast thou no mouth by Land? Why star'st thou so?
TRINCALO What, More Dukes yet? I must resign my Dukedom;   200
 But 'tis no matter, I was almost starv'd in't.
MUSTACHO Here's nothing but wild Sallads, without Oyl or Vinegar.
STEPHANO The Duke and Prince alive! would I had now
 Our gallant Ship agen, and were her Master,
 I'd willingly give all my Island for her.
VENTOSO And I my Vice-Roy-ship.
TRINCALO I shall need no Hangman, for I shall e'n hang
 My self, now my friend Butt has shed his last
 Drop of life. Poor Butt is quite departed.
ANTONIO They talk like mad-men.   210
PROSPERO No matter, time will bring 'em to themselves,
 And now their Wine is gone, they will not quarrel.
 Your Ship is safe and tight, and bravely rigg'd,
 As when you first set Sail.
ALONZO   This news is wonderful.
ARIEL Was it well done, my Lord?
PROSPERO   Rarely, my Diligence.
GONZALO But pray, Sir, what are those mishapen Creatures?

PROSPERO Their Mother was a Witch, and one so strong,
    She would controul the Moon, make Flows and Ebbs,
    And deal in her command without her power.
SYCORAX O *Setebos!* these be brave Sprights indeed. 220
PROSPERO *to* CALIBAN Go, Sirrah, to my Cell, and as you hope
    For Pardon, trim it up.
CALIBAN Most carefully. I will be wise hereafter.
    What a dull Fool was I, to take those Drunkards
    For Gods, when such as these were in the world?
PROSPERO Sir, I invite your Highness and your Train
    To my poor Cave this night; a part of which
    I will employ, in telling you my story.
ALONZO No doubt it must be strangely taking, Sir.
PROSPERO When the morn draws, I'l bring you to your Ship, 230
    And promise you calm Seas, and happy Gales.
    My *Ariel*, that's thy charge: then to the Elements
    Be free, and fare thee well.
ARIEL   I'll do it, Master.
PROSPERO Now to make amends
    For the rough treatment you have found to day,
    I'll entertain you with my Magick Art:
    I'll, by my power, transform this place, and call
    Up those that shall make good my promise to you.
                [Scene changes to the Rocks, with the Arch of Rocks,
                  and calm Sea. Musick playing on the Rocks.
PROSPERO *Neptune*, and your fair *Amphitrite*, rise;
    Oceanus, with your *Tethys* too, appear; 240
    All ye Sea-Gods, and Goddesses, Appear!
    Come, all ye *Trytons;* all ye *Nereides,* come,
    And teach your sawcy Element to obey:
    For you have Princes now to entertain,
    And unsoil'd Beauties, with fresh youthful Lovers.
                [Neptune, Amphitrite, Oceanus and Tethys *appear in a*
                Chariot drawn with Sea-horses; on each side of the
                Chariot, Sea-gods and Goddesses, Tritons and Nereides.
ALONZO This is prodigious.
ANTONIO Ah! What amazing Objects do we see?
GONZALO This Art doth much exceed all humane skill.

SONG

AMPHITRITE   *My Lord: Great* Neptune, *for my sake,*
                Of these bright Beauties pity take: 250

And to the rest allow
Your mercy too.
Let this inraged Element be still,
Let Æolous obey my will:
Let him his boystrous Prisoners safely keep
In their dark Caverns, and no more
Let 'em disturb the bosome of the Deep,
Till these arrive upon their wish'd-for Shore.

NEPTUNE *So much my* Amphitrite's *love I prize,*
That no commands of hers I can despise.   260
Tethys no furrows now shall wear,
Oceanus *no wrinkles on his brow,*
Let your serenest looks appear!
Be calm and gentle now.

NEPTUNE & ⎫ *Be calm, ye great Parents of the Flouds and the Springs,*
AMPHITRITE ⎭ *While each* Nereide *and* Triton *Plays, Revels, and Sings.*

OCEANUS *Confine the roaring Winds, and we*
Will soon obey you cheerfully.

CHORUS OF ⎫ *Tie up the Winds, and we'll obey,*   ⎧*Here the Dancers*
TRITONS ⎬ *Upon the Flouds we'll sing and play,* ⎨ *mingle with*
AND NEREIDE ⎭ *And celebrate a* Halcyon *day.*   ⎩ *the Singers.*
                                                  [*Dance.*

NEPTUNE *Great Nephew* Æolus *make no noise,*   272
Muzle your roaring Boys,   [Æolus *appears.*

AMPHITRITE *Let 'em not bluster to disturb our ears,*
Or strike these Noble Passengers with fears.

NEPTUNE *Afford 'em onely such an easie Gale,*
As pleasantly may swell each Sail.

AMPHITRITE *While fell Sea-monsters cause intestine jars,*
This Empire you invade with foreign Wars.

NEPTUNE *But you shall now be still,*   280
And shall obey my Amphitrites *will.*

AEOLUS *descends.* You I'll obey, who at one stroke can make,
With your dread Trident, the whole Earth to quake.
Come down, my Blusterers, swell no more,
Your stormy rage give o'r.   ⎧*Winds from the*
Let all black Tempests cease—   ⎨ *four corners*
And let the troubled Ocean rest: ⎩ *appear.*
Let all the Sea enjoy as calm a peace,
As where the Halcyon *builds her quiet Nest.*
To your Prisons below,   290
Down, down you must go:
You in the Earths Entrals your Revels may keep;

	But no more till I call shall you trouble the Deep.
	[*Winds fly down.*
	Now they are gone, all stormy Wars shall cease:
	Then let your Trumpeters proclaim a Peace.
AMPHITRITE	*Tritons, my Sons, your Trumpets sound,*
	And let the noise from Neighbouring Shores rebound.

CHORUS {
Sound a Calm.
Sound a Calm.
Sound a Calm.   300
[*Sound*] *a Calm.*
Sound a Calm.
[*Here the* Trytons, *at every repeat of* Sound a Calm,
*changing their Figure and Postures, seem to sound
their wreathed Trumpets made of Shells.*
}

A Symphony of Musick, like Trumpets, to which
four *Trytons* Dance.

NEPTUNE	*See, see, the Heavens smile, all your troubles are past,*
	Your joys by black Clouds shall no more be o'rcast.
AMPHITRITE	*On this barren Isle ye shall lose all your fears*
	Leave behind all your sorrows, and banish your cares.
BOTH	*And your Loves and your Lives shall in safety enjoy;*
	No influence of Stars shall your quiet destroy.
CHORUS OF ALL	*And your Loves, & c.*
	No influence, & c. [*Here the Dancers mingle* 310
	with the Singers.
OCEANUS	*We'll safely convey you to your own happy Shore,*
	And yours and your Countrey's soft peace we'll
	restore.
TETHYS	*To treat you blest Lovers, as you sail on the Deep,*
	The Trytons *and* Sea-Nymphs *their Revels*
	shall keep.
BOTH	*On the swift Dolphins backs they shall sing and*
	shall play;
	They shall guard you by night, and delight you
	by day.
CHORUS OF ALL	*On the swift, & c.*
	And shall guard, & c.
	[*Here the Dancers mingle with the Singers.*
	[*A Dance of twelve Tritons.*

MIRANDA What charming things are these?
DORINDA What heavenly power is this?   320
PROSPERO Now, my *Ariel*, be visible
And let the rest of your Aerial Train

Appear, and entertain 'em with a Song;

[*Scene changes to the Rising Sun, and a number of Aerial*
Spirits in the Air, Ariel *flying from the Sun, advances*
towards the Pit.

And then farewell my long lov'd *Ariel.*

ALONZO Heav'n! what are these we see?

PROSPERO They are Spirits, with which the Air abounds
In swarms, but that they are not subject to
Poor feeble mortal Eyes.

ANTONIO O wondrous skill!

GONZALO   O power Divine!

Ariel *and the rest sing the following Song.*

ARIEL   *Where the Bee sucks, there suck I,*   330
In a Cowslips Bed I lie;
There I couch when Owls do cry.
On the Swallows wings I fly
After Summer merrily.
Merrily, merrily shall I live now,
Under the Blossom that hangs on the Bow.

[*Song ended,* Ariel *speaks, hovering in the Air.*

ARIEL My Noble Master!
May theirs and your blest Joys never impair.
And for the freedom I enjoy in Air,
I will be still your *Ariel,* and wait   340
On Aiery accidents that work for Fate.
What ever shall your happiness concern,
From your still faithful *Ariel* you shall learn.

PROSPERO Thou hast been always diligent and kind!
Farewell, my long lov'd *Ariel,* thou shalt find,
I will preserve thee ever in my mind.
Henceforth this Isle to the afflicted be
A place of Refuge, as it was to me:
The promises of blooming Spring live here,
And all the blessings of the ripening Year.   350
On my retreat, let Heav'n and Nature smile,
And ever flourish the *Enchanted Isle.*   [*Exeunt.*

EPILOGUE

Gallants, by all good signs it does appear,
That Sixty seven's a very damning year,
For Knaves abroad, and for ill Poets here.

Among the Muses there's a gen'ral rot,
The Rhyming Monsieur, and the Spanish Plot:
Defie or Court, all's one, they go to Pot.

The Ghosts of Poets walk within this place,
And haunt us Actors wheresoe'r we pass,
In Visions bloudier then King Richard's *was.*

For this poor Wretch, he has not much to say   10
But quietly brings in his part o' th' Play,
And begs the favour to be damn'd to day.

He sends me onely like a Sh'riff's man here,
To let you know the Malefactor's near,
And that he means to die, en Cavalier.

For if you shou'd be gracious to his Pen,
Th' Example will prove ill to other men,
And you'll be troubl'd with 'em all agen.

From William Davenant and John Dryden, *The Tempest, or, The Enchanted Island.*
In *Five Restoration Adaptations of Shakespeare.* Ed. and intro. Christopher Spencer.
Urbana: U of Illinois P, 1965.

From *UNE TEMPÊTE*

Aimé Césaire

From ACT I SCENE 2

ARIEL Master, I must beg you to spare me this kind of labour.

PROSPERO *(shouting)* Listen, and listen good! There's a task to be performed, and I don't care how it gets done!

ARIEL You've promised me my freedom a thousand times, and I'm still waiting.

PROSPERO Ingrate! And who freed you from Sycorax, may I ask? Who rent the pine in which you had been imprisoned and brought you forth?

ARIEL Sometimes I almost regret it... After all, I might have turned into a real tree in the end... Tree: that's a word that really gives me a thrill! It often springs to mind: palm tree—springing into the sky like a fountain ending in nonchalant, squid-like elegance. The baobab—twisted like the soft entrails of some monster. Ask the calao bird that lives a cloistered season in its branches. Or the Ceiba tree—spread out beneath the proud sun. O bird, o green mansions set in the living earth!

PROSPERO Stuff it! I don't like talking trees. As for your freedom, you'll have it when I'm good and ready. In the meanwhile, see to the ship. I'm going to have a few words with Master Caliban. I've been keeping my eye on him, and he's getting a little too emancipated. *(Calling)* Caliban! Caliban! *(He sighs.)*

Enter CALIBAN.

CALIBAN Uhuru!

PROSPERO What did you say?

CALIBAN I said, Uhuru!

PROSPERO Mumbling your native language again! I've already told you, I don't like it. You could be polite, at least; a simple "hello" wouldn't kill you.

CALIBAN Oh, I forgot... But make that as froggy, waspish, pustular and dung-filled a "hello" as possible. May today hasten by a decade the day when all the birds of the sky and beasts of the earth will feast upon your corpse!

PROSPERO Gracious as always, you ugly ape! How can anyone be so ugly?

CALIBAN You think I'm ugly...well, I don't think you're so handsome yourself. With that big hooked nose, you look just like some old vulture. *(Laughing)* An old vulture with a scrawny neck!

PROSPERO Since you're so fond of invective, you could at least thank me for having taught you to speak at all. You, a savage...a dumb animal, a beast I educated, trained, dragged up from the bestiality that still clings to you.

CALIBAN In the first place, that's not true. You didn't teach me a thing! Except to jabber in your own language so that I could understand your orders: chop the wood, wash the dishes, fish for food, plant vegetables, all because you're too lazy to do it yourself. And as for your learning, did you ever impart any of *that* to me? No, you took care not to. All your science you keep for yourself alone, shut up in those big books.

PROSPERO What would you be without me?

CALIBAN Without you? I'd be the king, that's what I'd be, the King of the Island. The king of the island given me by my mother, Sycorax.

PROSPERO There are some family trees it's better not to climb! She's a ghoul! A witch from whom—and may God be praised—death has delivered us.

CALIBAN Dead or alive, she was my mother, and I won't deny her! Anyhow, you only think she's dead because you think the earth

itself is dead... It's so much simpler that way! Dead, you can walk
on it, pollute it, you can tread upon it with the steps of a con-
queror. I respect the earth, because I know that it is alive, and I
know that Sycorax is alive.
Sycorax. Mother.
Serpent, rain, lightning.
And I see thee everywhere!
In the eye of the stagnant pool which stares back at me,
through the rushes,
in the gesture made by twisted root and its awaiting thrust.
In the night, the all-seeing blinded night,
the nostril-less all-smelling night!
... Often, in my dreams, she speaks to me and warns me ...
Yesterday, even, when I was lying by the stream on my belly
lapping at the muddy water, when the Beast was about to spring
upon me with that huge stone in his hand ...

PROSPERO If you keep on like that even your magic won't save you
from punishment!

CALIBAN That's right, that's right! In the beginning, the gentleman
was all sweet talk: dear Caliban here, my little Caliban there! And
what do you think you'd have done without me in this strange
land? Ingrate! I taught you the trees, fruits, birds, the seasons, and
now you don't give a damn... Caliban the animal, Caliban the
slave! I know that story! Once you've squeezed the juice from the
orange, you toss the rind away!

PROSPERO Oh!

CALIBAN Do I lie? Isn't it true that you threw me out of your house
and made me live in a filthy cave. The ghetto!

PROSPERO It's easy to say "ghetto"! It wouldn't be such a ghetto if
you took the trouble to keep it clean! And there's something you
forgot, which is that what forced me to get rid of you was your
lust. Good God, you tried to rape my daughter!

CALIBAN Rape! Rape! Listen, you old goat, you're the one that
put those dirty thoughts in my head. Let me tell you something:
I couldn't care less about your daughter, or about your cave, for
that matter. If I gripe, it's on principle, because I didn't like
living with you at all, as a matter of fact. Your feet stink!

PROSPERO I did not summon you here to argue. Out! Back to work!
Wood, water, and lots of both! I'm expecting company today.

CALIBAN I've had just about enough. There's already a pile of wood
that high...

PROSPERO Enough! Careful, Caliban! If you keep grumbling you'll
be whipped. And if you don't step lively, if you keep dragging
your feet or try to strike or sabotage things, I'll beat you. Beating
is the only language you really understand. So much the worse for
you: I'll speak it, loud and clear. Get a move on!

CALIBAN All right, I'm going...but this is the last time. It's the last
time, do you hear me? Oh...I forgot: I've got something important
to tell you.

PROSPERO Important? Well, out with it.

CALIBAN It's this: I've decided I don't want to be called Caliban any
longer.

PROSPERO What kind of rot is that? I don't understand.

CALIBAN Put it this way: I'm *telling* you that from now on I won't
answer to the name Caliban.

PROSPERO Where did you get that idea?

CALIBAN Well, because Caliban *isn't* my name. It's as simple as that.

PROSPERO Oh, I suppose it's mine!

CALIBAN It's the name given me by your hatred, and every time it's
spoken it's an insult.

PROSPERO My, aren't we getting sensitive! All right, suggest something else... I've got to call you something. What will it be?
Cannibal would suit you, but I'm sure you wouldn't like that,
would you? Let's see...what about Hannibal? That fits. And why
not...they all seem to like historical names.

CALIBAN Call me X. That would be best. Like a man without a name.
Or, to be more precise, a man whose name has been stolen. You talk

about history…well, that's history, and everyone knows it! Every time you summon me it reminds me of a basic fact, the fact that you've stolen everything from me, even my identity! Uhuru! *(He exits.)*

Enter ARIEL *as a sea-nymph.*

PROSPERO My dear Ariel, did you see how he looked at me, that glint in his eye? That's something new. Well, let me tell you, Caliban is the enemy. As for those people on the boat, I've changed my mind about them. Give them a scare, but for God's sake don't touch a hair of their heads! You'll answer to me if you do.

ARIEL I've suffered too much myself for having made them suffer not to be pleased at your mercy. You can count on me, Master.

PROSPERO Yes, however great their crimes, if they repent you can assure them of my forgiveness. They are men of my race, and of high rank. As for me, at my age one must rise above disputes and quarrels and think about the future. I have a daughter. Alonso has a son. If they were to fall in love, I would give my consent. Let Ferdinand marry Miranda, and may their marriage bring us harmony and peace. That is my plan. I want it executed. As for Caliban, does it matter what that villain plots against me? All the nobility of Italy, Naples and Milan henceforth combined, will protect me bodily. Go!

ARIEL Yes, Master. Your orders will be fully carried out.

Ariel sings:

> *Sandy seashore, deep blue sky,*
> *Surf is rising, sea birds fly*
> *Here the lover finds delight,*
> *Sun at noontime, moon at night.*
> *Join hands lovers, join the dance,*
> *Find contentment, find romance.*
>
> *Sandy seashore, deep blue sky,*
> *Cares will vanish…so can I…*

FERDINAND What is this music? It has led me here and now it stops… No, there it is again…

ARIEL *(singing)*

> *Waters move, the ocean flows,*
> *Nothing comes and nothing goes…*
> *Strange days are upon us…*

Oysters stare through pearly eyes
Heart-shaped corals gently beat
In the crystal undersea

Waters move and ocean flows,
Nothing comes and nothing goes...
Strange days are upon us...

FERDINAND What is this that I see before me? A goddess? A mortal?

MIRANDA I know what *I'm* seeing: a flatterer. Young man, your ability to pay compliments in the situation in which you find yourself at least proves your courage. Who are you?

FERDINAND As you see, a poor shipwrecked soul.

MIRANDA But one of high degree!

FERDINAND In other surroundings I might be called "Prince," "son of the King"... But, no, I was forgetting:...not "Prince" but "King," alas... "King" because my father has just perished in the shipwreck.

MIRANDA Poor young man! Here, you'll be received with hospitality and we'll support you in your misfortune.

FERDINAND Alas, my father...Can it be that I am an unnatural son? Your pity would make the greatest of sorrows seem sweet.

MIRANDA I hope you'll like it here with us. The island is pretty. I'll show you the beaches and the forests, I'll tell you the names of fruits and flowers, I'll introduce you to a whole world of insects, of lizards of every hue, of birds... Oh, you cannot imagine! The birds!...

PROSPERO That's enough, daughter! I find your chatter irritating... and let me assure you, it's not at all fitting. You are doing too much honor to an impostor. Young man, you are a traitor, a spy, and a woman-chaser to boot! No sooner has he escaped the perils of the sea than he's sweet-talking the first girl he meets! You won't get round me that way. Your arrival is convenient, because I need more manpower: you shall be my house servant.

FERDINAND Seeing the young lady, more beautiful than any wood-nymph, I might have been Ulysses on Nausicaa's isle. But hearing you, Sir, I now understand my fate a little better...I see I have come ashore on the Barbary Coast and am in the hands of a cruel pirate. *(Drawing his sword)* However, a gentleman prefers death to dishonor! I shall defend my life with my freedom!

PROSPERO Poor fool: your arm is growing weak, your knees are trembling! Traitor! I could kill you now...but I need the manpower. Follow me.

ARIEL It's no use trying to resist, young man. My master is a sorcerer: neither your passion nor your youth can prevail against him. Your best course would be to follow and obey him.

FERDINAND Oh God! What sorcery is this? Vanquished, a captive— yet far from rebelling against my fate, I am finding my servitude sweet. Oh, I would be imprisoned for life if only heaven will grant me a glimpse of my sun each day, the face of my own sun. Farewell, Nausicaa.

They exit.

ACT 2 SCENE I

Caliban's cave. CALIBAN *is singing as he works when* ARIEL *enters. He listens to him for a moment.*

CALIBAN *(singing)*

> *May he who eats his corn heedless of Shango*
> *Be accursed! May Shango creep beneath*
> *His nails and eat into his flesh!*
> *Shango, Shango ho!*
> *Forget to give him room if you dare!*
> *He will make himself at home on your nose!*
>
> *Refuse to have him under your roof at your own risk!*
> *He'll tear off your roof and wear it as a hat!*
> *Whoever tries to mislead Shango*
> *Will suffer for it!*
> *Shango, Shango ho!*

ARIEL Greetings, Caliban. I know you don't think much of me, but after all we *are* brothers, brothers in suffering and slavery, but brothers in hope as well. We both want our freedom. We just have different methods.

CALIBAN Greetings to you. But you didn't come to see me just to make that profession of faith. Come on, Alastor! The old man sent you, didn't he? A great job: carrying out the Master's fine ideas, his great plans.

ARIEL No, I've come on my own. I came to warn you. Prospero is planning horrible acts of revenge against you. I thought it my duty to alert you.

CALIBAN I'm ready for him.

ARIEL Poor Caliban, you're doomed. You know that you aren't the stronger, you'll never be the stronger. What good will it do you to struggle?

CALIBAN And what about you? What good has your obedience done you, your Uncle Tom patience and your sucking up to him. The man's just getting more demanding and despotic day by day.

ARIEL Well, I've at least achieved one thing: he's promised me my freedom. In the distant future, of course, but it's the first time he's actually committed himself.

CALIBAN Talk's cheap! He'll promise you a thousand times and take it back a thousand times. Anyway, tomorrow doesn't interest me. What I want is *(shouting)* "Freedom now!"

ARIEL Okay. But you know you're not going to get it out of him "now," and that he's stronger than you are. I'm in a good position to know just what he's got in his arsenal.

CALIBAN The stronger? How do you know that? Weakness always has a thousand means and cowardice is all that keeps us from listing them.

ARIEL I don't believe in violence.

CALIBAN What *do* you believe in, then? In cowardice? In giving up? In kneeling and groveling? That's it, someone strikes you on the right cheek and you offer the left. Someone kicks you on the left buttock and you turn the right...that way there's no jealousy. Well, that's not Caliban's way...

ARIEL You know very well that that's not what I mean. No violence, no submission either. Listen to me: Prospero is the one we've got to change. Destroy his serenity so that he's finally forced to acknowledge his own injustice and put an end to it.

CALIBAN Oh sure...that's a good one! Prospero's conscience! Prospero is an old scoundrel who has no conscience.

ARIEL Exactly—that's why it's up to us to give him one. I'm not fighting just for *my* freedom, for *our* freedom, but for Prospero too, so that Prospero can acquire a conscience. Help me, Caliban.

CALIBAN Listen, kid, sometimes I wonder if you aren't a little bit nuts. So that Prospero can acquire a conscience? You might as well ask a stone to grow flowers.

ARIEL I don't know what to do with you. I've often had this inspiring, uplifting dream that one day Prospero, you, me, we would all three set out, like brothers, to build a wonderful world, each one contributing his own special thing: patience, vitality, love, will-power too, and rigor, not to mention the dreams without which mankind would perish.

CALIBAN You don't understand a thing about Prospero. He's not the collaborating type. He's a guy who only feels something when he's wiped someone out. A crusher, a pulveriser, that's what he is! And you talk about brotherhood!

ARIEL So then what's left? War? And you know that when it comes to that, Prospero is invincible.

CALIBAN Better death than humiliation and injustice. Anyhow, I'm going to have the last word. Unless nothingness has it. The day when I begin to feel that everything's lost, just let me get hold of a few barrels of your infernal powder and as you fly around up there in your blue skies you'll see this island, my inheritance, my work, all blown to smithereens...and, I trust, Prospero and me with it. I hope you'll like the fireworks display—it'll be signed Caliban.

ARIEL Each of us marches to his own drum. You follow yours. I follow the beat of mine. I wish you courage, brother.

CALIBAN Farewell, Ariel, my brother, and good luck.

From Aimé Césaire, *Une Tempête*. Trans. Richard Miller. NY: Editions du Seuil, 1992.

THE TEMPEST

Hilda Doolittle (H.D.)

I

Come as you will, but I came home
Driven by *The Tempest;* you may come,

With banner or the beat of drum;
You may come with laughing friends,

Or tired, alone; you may come
In triumph, many kings have come

And queens and ladies with their lords,
To lay their lilies in this place,

Where others, known for wit and song,
Have left their laurel; you may come,

Remembering how your young love wept
With Montague long ago and Capulet.

I I

I came home driven by *The Tempest;*
That was after the wedding-feast;
'Twas a sweet marriage, we are told;
And she *a paragon . . . who is now queen,*
And the rarest that e'er came there;

We know little of *the king's fair daughter*
Claribel; her father was Alonso,
King of Naples, her brother, Ferdinand,
And we read later, *in one voyage*
Did Claribel her husband find at Tunis:
Claribel was outside all of this,
The Tempest came after they left her;
Read for yourself, *Dramatis Personae.*

III

Read for yourself, *Dramatis Personae,*
Alonso, Sebastian, Prospero,
Antonio, Ferdinand, Gonzalo,
Adrian, Francisco, Caliban
(Whom some call Pan),
Trinculo, Stephano, Miranda,
Ariel, Iris, Ceres, Juno;

These are the players, chiefly,
Caliban, a savage and deformed slave,
Ariel, an airy Spirit, Miranda,
The magician's lovely daughter,
The magician—ah indeed, I had forgot
Boatswain, Mariners, Nymphs and Reapers,

And among these, are other
Spirits attending on Prospero.

IV

Read through again, *Dramatis Personae;*
She is not there at all, but Claribel,
Claribel, the birds shrill, Claribel,
Claribel echoes from this rainbow-shell,
I stooped just now to gather from the sand;

Where? From an island somewhere . . .
Some say the *Sea-Adventure* set out,
(In May, 1609, to be exact)
For the new colony, Virginia;

Some say the *Sea-Adventure* ran aground
On the Bermudas; but all on board
Were saved, built new ships
And sailed on, a year later;

It is all written in an old pamphlet,
Did he read of her there, Claribel?

V

The flagship, the *Sea-Adventure*
Was one of nine ships; it bore
Sir Thomas Gates and Sir George Somers;
So the poet read, some say
Of the five hundred colonists;
(O the wind, the spray,
The birds wheeling out of the mist,
The strange birds, whistling from strange trees,
Bermuda); there was more than one pamphlet,
(The newspaper of his day),
He searched them all;
Gates, Somers—who were they?

Englishmen like himself, who felt the lure
Of the sea-ways—here we are in London—
A new court festival, a masque?
Elizabeth, our princess, is to wed
The Elector Palatine—who's that?
Frederick, I think. And where's the place—
Bohemia? I don't think so,
But anyhow it doesn't matter,
A foreign fellow is to wed our princess,
The grand-daughter of Scotland's Mary;
Occasion—compliment—another play!

VI

That was yesterday or day before yesterday;
To-day (April 23, 1945, to be exact),
We stand together; it always rains
On Shakespeare's Day, the townsfolk say,
But to-day, there is soft mist only . . .

Slowly, there are so many of us,
We pass through the churchyard gate,
And pausing wait and read old names
On the stones under our feet;
Look—there's a Lucy—O, the hunter's heart,
The hunter's stealth,

But listen to this,
He's caught at last—who?
John Shakespeare's lad—up to no good—
Sir Thomas Lucy caught him at it—
Poaching—(O feet of wind,
O soul of fire, so Lucy caught you
Stalking deer?)—poaching?

VII

He stole everything,
There isn't an original plot
In the whole lot of his plays;
They're scattered everywhere, hotchpotch;
A little success with the old Queen?

Well, yes—by patching up
Other men's plots and filling in
With odds and ends he called his own,
But now—he's gone back home,

And time he went;
He couldn't compete with the new wits,
New fashions—that last, he called *The Tempest,*
Was taken out of the news-sheet,
Stale news at that and best forgot,

The *Sea-Adventure* and that lot,
Gates, Somers—who are they anyway?
Or who *were* they? They'll come to no good,
(No one ever did) in that colony,
What d'you call it? Virginia?
Look at Drake, Raleigh.

VIII

Awkwardly, tenderly,
We stand with our flowers,
Separate, self-consciously,
Shyly or in child-like
Delicate simplicity;
Each one waits patiently,
Now we are near the door;

Till sudden, wondrously,
All shyness drops away,
Awkwardness, complacency;

Ring, ring and ring again,
'Twas a sweet marriage,
So they say, *my beloved is mine*
And I am his; Claribel
The chimes peel;

Claribel, the chimes say,
The king's fair daughter
Marries Tunis; O spikenard,
Myrrh and myrtle-spray,
'Twas a sweet marriage;

Tenderly, tenderly,
We stand with our flowers,
Our belovèd is ours,
Our belovèd is ours,
To-day? Yesterday?

H. D., "The Tempest." From *By Avon River*. NY: The Macmillan Company, 1949.

From ARIEL

Grace Tiffany

CHAPTER 4

THE CURSE

When Sycorax cried out again, Ariel waved her hand, and Acrazia, Nous, and Fantasia vanished into thin air. She had no patience for their chatter now. She listened, fascinated, to the loud yells coming from the hut.

But she did not answer them. Instead she flew up to the top branch of the gumbo-limbo tree and crouched there in the form of a small, winged dragon, only two feet high and waving a vermilion tail.

"*Ariel!*" The cry was anguished, and after it came another wordless howl. Then: "Your promise!"

Sycorax's voice was closer. Ariel could tell she had risen from her mat and come to the door of the hut.

The moon was full and white, and it lit the fine sands almost as though it were day. Every ridged leaf on the gumbo-limbo tree was clearly visible. Ariel blew on the leaves with fiery breath. They rustled but did not burn.

Limping, Sycorax came slowly forth onto the beach, grabbing the thin trunks of the high palms with one hand as she passed them, to steady herself. With the other hand she held her belly. "Ariel," she sobbed.

Her mind was open to Ariel, but Ariel saw in it things she did not recognize: urgency, and red pain, and through the pain a determined and practical plan to find banana leaves on which to place the coming babe. She felt herself shrink to the size of a cat.

"*ARIEL!*" screamed Sycorax, and let fly a string of Saxon curses that Ariel thought delightfully colorful. Her wings grew half an inch. "*Your promise!*" Sycorax stopped at the edge of the forest, gripping the trunk of a palm tree so hard that her knuckles grew white.

Ariel flew down to a lower branch of the gumbo-limbo tree. She was still shaped like a dragon, but was now only the size of a kitten. "I am here." She sighed in a silvery whisper. "But I cannot help you."

"Oh... *oh* ... it hurts!" cried Sycorax. "I feel him coming!"

"Don't," said Ariel quickly. "Don't—don't speak of it. I can do nothing for your pain, and the more you speak of it, the smaller I grow!" She was as little as a lizard now.

"It's not the pain," panted Sycorax. "For that I can bite on a rag, an old shred of sail, if you bring me one. I *know*—uh!—you cannot stop the pain. But the child! You must come here by me. The child needs hands to help it into the world."

"Do not speak of it!" hissed Ariel. "I have no hands; I am too delicate for your task; I can do nothing for you!"

Again Ariel sensed the wall in her own mind, the one that had risen inside her two centuries before, when she'd tried and failed to sail through the barrier that divided the island in two.

What Sycorax did not know was that Ariel could not have helped her bring her son into the world, any more than the simple Saxon girl could have erupted into a shower of golden sparks, or blown harp songs into the air, or blinked twelve flying purple fish into being. Ariel could no more be a midwife to a baby than she could have fetched Sycorax a stick of firewood, or wiped sweat from the girl's brow, or cried.

"I will sing to you," she suggested brightly.

Sycorax staggered toward her with a look of rage. "*SETEBOS!*" she yelled.

A dim murmur of thunder troubled the air.

Ariel shrank to the size of a hermit crab. But she still glowed faintly with the brightness of the dragon whose form she wore.

"*SETEBOS!*" Sycorax yelled again.

As Ariel looked at the woman's mottled, grubby face, now contorted with rage, she saw in it a great power. It seemed to flow from Sycorax's body, and from the body of the child inside her, which Ariel could not see.

That power smote her, and she shrank to the size of a ladybug. She lifted herself from the branch to flee, but to her horror she felt leaden and fell back, and as she struggled to lift her tiny wings again, the third prayer of Sycorax landed heavy on her back.

"*SETEBOS!*" Sycorax bellowed. *"Curse this worthless sprite who lies! Give her a body so she knows the feel of it!"*

And Setebos answered.

When the thunderclap split the air, Ariel was blinded. The lightning lit the island like the midday sun, a hundred times brighter than moonlight, and she felt the branch give way beneath her as the gumbo-limbo tree split asunder. She was thrown into the air, but she felt herself falling, felt with agony her new heaviness pushing her down toward earth. She tried to move her wings, but they had vanished. She tried to dissolve into air but felt herself trapped in the body of a bug. She was a wingless thing, an ant with six legs and a heavy head, and she fell on her back onto the split wood of the cloven tree's base.

It hurt—hurt!—and she tried to cry out but could make no words, only an ugly grunt. Even as she tried painfully to right herself, to scurry away with her five legs (one had broken), to crawl like the insect she now was, the wood of the gumbo-limbo tree closed around her and trapped her inside.

She could not move.

To have the body of an ant thrust upon her was agony. To be heavy, embodied, and flightless was torment. But this wooden entrapment was a thousand times more painful. Now the bulk of the tree pushed in on her, squeezed her, so she could not budge at all. She was paralyzed. She tried again to scream, but what emerged from the tree bark was a whisper. In the back of her tiny brain she heard the faint, panicked shrieks of Acrazia, Nous, and Fantasia, and their cries tortured her further. Her minions were trapped as well.

One thing was left to her: she could still see. But what Ariel now saw she regarded with horror.

Right in front of her, Sycorax birthed her child. Crouched at the edge of the forest, with two hands gripping the palm tree, she pushed the boy into the world.

Perhaps she was helped by the Saxon goddess Setebos. Perhaps she did it alone. But the child came, as Sycorax cried with rage and cursed Ariel for her false friendship. Ariel did not recognize her bravery or understand her curses. She was made for beauty and fancy, and she did not know what courage or friendship was. What *she* saw was a mat-haired girl spattered with mud and yelling in agony. Hours later—for now, at last, trapped in her ant's body, she knew minutes and hours—she saw the infant in Sycorax's arms, a thing not haloed like the baby of her vision, but a dark, howling moppet.

He was not a shimmering vision or a spirit. He was a plain human boy, and he was twisted.

Helping hands could have guided his passage from the womb into the world, but his mother had had no helping hands, and so on the way out his leg had caught and now was bent in a way it should not have been. That had made Sycorax's labor prolonged and much more painful, and what it had been like for the boy his mother did not like to wonder. But now he was here, in the fresh air, and the seabirds were calling, and both mother and child had survived.

"You are here, little one." She spoke in tired victory. "Caliban, I call you, after my brother, whom the Vikings slew as he plowed his wheat field. But there are no Vikings here, my brave boy, and all may yet be well with us."

She was exhausted and wanted only to lie on the beach, but she made herself cut his cord with her teeth, and found water to wash him. She wrapped him in the torn shred of sail, and put him to her breast. As she nursed him, the sun came up over the ocean to the east, casting its pink light on the sand, and the mother and little boy slept.

Ariel did not sleep. The sun smote her eyes, and she could not close them or even blink. Trapped in the gumbo-limbo tree, she looked with rage at the smiling Sycorax, who dozed with her back against the broad base of a palm, waking now and then to croon tunelessly over her ugly child. Sycorax, whom she had meant one day to take her across the barrier, so that those humans who dwelled on the other side might see Ariel's glory! Sycorax, who had dashed Ariel's hope to draw from men's minds the strength to birth a hundred new spirits, to grow a thousandfold in size and spread her wings over all of the island, not to mention the islands beyond! *Sycorax,* who had foiled that grand plan with her garden of tubers and her yowling baby boy, who had cursed Ariel into silence, whose god had thrust her into a tight wooden jail.

Sycorax, who hated her.

From Grace Tiffany, *Ariel.* NY: HarperCollins, 2005.

From SEVEN LECTURES

Samuel Taylor Coleridge

THE NINTH LECTURE

Among the ideal plays, I will take "The Tempest," by way of example. ...

In this play Shakespeare has especially appealed to the imagination, and he has constructed a plot well adapted to the purpose. According to his scheme, he did not appeal to any sensuous impression (the word "sensuous" is authorised by Milton) of time and place, but to the imagination, and it is to be borne in mind, that of old, and as regards mere scenery, his works may be said to have been recited rather than acted—that is to say, description and narration supplied the place of visual exhibition: the audience was told to fancy that they saw what they only heard described; the painting was not in colours, but in words.

This is particularly to be noted in the first scene—a storm and its confusion on board the king's ship. The highest and the lowest characters are brought together, and with what excellence! Much of the genius of Shakespeare is displayed in these happy combinations—the highest and the lowest, the gayest and the saddest; he is not droll in one scene and melancholy in another, but often both the one and the other in the same scene. Laughter is made to swell the tear of sorrow, and to throw, as it were, a poetic light upon it, while the tear mingles tenderness with the laughter. Shakespeare has evinced the power, which above all other men he possessed, that of introducing the profoundest sentiments of wisdom, where they would be least expected, yet where they are most truly natural. One admirable secret of his art is, that separate speeches frequently do not appear to have been occasioned by those which preceded, and which are consequent upon each other, but to have arisen out of the peculiar character of the speaker.

Before I go further, I may take the opportunity of explaining what is meant by mechanic and organic regularity. In the former the copy must appear as if it had come out of the same mould with the original; in the latter there is a law which all the parts obey, conforming themselves to the outward symbols and manifestations of the essential principle. If we look to the growth of trees, for instance, we shall observe that trees of the same kind vary considerably, according to the circumstances of soil, air, or position; yet we are able to decide at once whether they are oaks, elms, or poplars.

So with Shakespeare's characters: he shows us the life and principle of each being with organic regularity. The Boatswain, in the first scene of "The Tempest," when the bonds of reverence are thrown off as a sense of danger impresses all, gives a loose to his feelings, and thus pours forth his vulgar mind to the old Counsellor:—

"Hence! What care these roarers for the name of King? To cabin: silence! trouble us not."

Gonzalo replies—"Good; yet remember whom thou hast aboard." To which the Boatswain answers—"None that I more love than myself. You are a counsellor: if you can command these elements to silence, and work the peace of the present, we will not hand a rope more; use your authority: if you cannot, give thanks that you have lived so long, and make yourself ready in your cabin for the mischance of the hour, if it so hap.—Cheerly, good hearts!—Out of our way, I say."

An ordinary dramatist would, after this speech, have represented Gonzalo as moralising, or saying something connected with the Boatswain's language; for ordinary dramatists are not men of genius: they combine their ideas by association, or by logical affinity; but the vital writer, who makes men on the stage what they are in nature, in a moment transports himself into the very being of each personage, and, instead of cutting out artificial puppets, he brings before us the men themselves. Therefore, Gonzalo soliloquises,—"I have great comfort from this fellow: methinks, he hath no drowning mark upon him; his complexion is perfect gallows. Stand fast, good fate, to his hanging! make the rope of his destiny our cable, for our own doth little advantage. If he be not born to be hanged, our case is miserable."

In this part of the scene we see the true sailor with his contempt of danger, and the old counsellor with his high feeling, who, instead of condescending to notice the words just addressed to him, turns off, meditating with himself, and drawing some comfort to his own mind, by trifling with the ill expression of the boatswain's face, founding upon it a hope of safety.

Shakespeare had pre-determined to make the plot of this play such as to involve a certain number of low characters, and at the beginning he pitched the note of the whole. The first scene was meant as a lively commencement of the story; the reader is prepared for something that is to be developed, and in the next scene he brings forward Prospero and Miranda. How is this done? By giving to his favourite character, Miranda, a sentence which at once expresses the violence and fury of the storm, such as it might appear to a witness on the land, and at the same time displays the tenderness of her feelings—the exquisite feelings of a female brought up in a desert, but with all the advantages of education, all that could be communicated by a wise and affectionate father. She possesses all the delicacy of innocence, yet with all the powers of her mind unweakened by the combats of life, Miranda exclaims:—

> "O! I have suffered
> With those that I saw suffer: a brave vessel,
> Who had, no doubt, some noble creatures in her,
> Dash'd all to pieces."

The doubt here intimated could have occurred to no mind but to that of Miranda, who had been bred up in the island with her father and a monster only: she did not know, as others do, what sort of creatures were in a ship; others never would have introduced it as a conjecture. This shows, that while Shakespeare is displaying his vast excellence, he never fails to insert some touch or other, which is not merely characteristic of the particular person, but combines two things—the person, and the circumstances acting upon the person. She proceeds:—

> "O! the cry did knock
> Against my very heart. Poor souls! they perish'd.
> Had I been any god of power, I would
> Have sunk the sea within the earth, or e'er
> It should the good ship so have swallow'd, and
> The fraughting souls within her."

She still dwells upon that which was most wanting to the completeness of her nature—these fellow creatures from whom she appeared banished, with only one relict to keep them alive, not in her memory, but in her imagination.

Another proof of excellent judgment in the poet, for I am now principally adverting to that point, is to be found in the preparation of the reader for what is to follow. Prospero is introduced, first in his magic robe, which, with the assistance of his daughter, he lays aside, and we then know him to be a being possessed of supernatural powers. He then instructs Miranda in the story of their arrival in the island, and this is conducted in such a manner, that the reader never conjectures the technical use the poet has made of the relation, by informing the auditor of what it is necessary for him to know.

The next step is the warning by Prospero, that he means, for particular purposes, to lull his daughter to sleep; and here he exhibits the earliest and mildest proof of magical power. In ordinary and vulgar plays we should have had some person brought upon the stage, whom nobody knows or cares anything about, to let the audience into the secret. Prospero having cast a sleep upon his daughter, by that sleep stops the narrative at the very moment when it was necessary to break it off, in order to excite curiosity, and yet to give the memory and understanding sufficient to carry on the progress of the history uninterruptedly.

Here I cannot help noticing a fine touch of Shakespeare's knowledge of human nature, and generally of the great laws of the human mind: I mean Miranda's infant remembrance. Prospero asks her—

> "Canst thou remember
> A time before we came unto this cell?
> I do not think thou canst, for then thou wast not
> Out three years old.

Miranda answers,

> "Certainly, sir, I can."

Prospero inquires,

> "By what? by any other house or person?
> Of any thing the image tell me, that
> Hath kept with thy remembrance."

To which Miranda returns,

> "'Tis far off;
> And rather like a dream than an assurance
> That my remembrance warrants. Had I not
> Four or five women once, that tended me?"
>
> *Act 1., Scene 2.*

This is exquisite! In general, our remembrances of early life arise from vivid colours, especially if we have seen them in motion: for instance, persons when grown up will remember a bright green door, seen when they were quite young; but Miranda, who was somewhat older, recollected four or five women who tended her. She might know men from her father, and her remembrance of the past might be worn out by the present object, but women she only knew by herself, by the contemplation of her own figure in the fountain, and she recalled to her mind what had been. It was not, that she had seen such and such grandees, or such and such peeresses, but she remembered to have seen something like the reflection of herself: it was not herself, and it brought back to her mind what she had seen most like herself.

In my opinion the picturesque power displayed by Shakespeare, of all the poets that ever lived, is only equalled, if equalled, by Milton and

Dante. The presence of genius is not shown in elaborating a picture: we have had many specimens of this sort of work in modern poems, where all is so dutchified, if I may use the word, by the most minute touches, that the reader naturally asks why words, and not painting, are used? I know a young lady of much taste, who observed, that in reading recent versified accounts of voyages and travels, she, by a sort of instinct, cast her eyes on the opposite page, for coloured prints of what was so patiently and punctually described.

The power of poetry is, by a single word perhaps, to instil that energy into the mind, which compels the imagination to produce the picture. Prospero tells Miranda,

> "One midnight,
> Fated to the purpose, did Antonio open
> The gates of Milan; and i' the dead of darkness,
> The ministers for the purpose hurried thence
> Me, and thy crying self."

Here, by introducing a single happy epithet, "crying," in the last line, a complete picture is presented to the mind, and in the production of such pictures the power of genius consists.

In reference to preparation, it will be observed that the storm, and all that precedes the tale, as well as the tale itself, serve to develope completely the main character of the drama, as well as the design of Prospero. The manner in which the heroine is charmed asleep fits us for what follows, goes beyond our ordinary belief, and gradually leads us to the appearance and disclosure of a being of the most fanciful and delicate texture, like Prospero, preternaturally gifted.

In this way the entrance of Ariel, if not absolutely forethought by the reader, was foreshewn by the writer: in addition, we may remark, that the moral feeling called forth by the sweet words of Miranda,

> "Alack, what trouble
> Was I then to you!"

in which she considered only the sufferings and sorrows of her father, puts the reader in a frame of mind to exert his imagination in favour of an object so innocent and interesting. The poet makes him wish that, if supernatural agency were to be employed, it should be used for a being so young and lovely. "The wish is father to the thought," and Ariel is introduced. Here, what is called poetic faith is required and created, and our common notions of philosophy give way before it: this feeling may be said to be much stronger than historic faith, since for the exercise of poetic faith the mind is previously prepared. I make this remark, though somewhat digressive, in order to lead to a future subject of these lectures—the poems of Milton. When adverting to those, I shall have to explain farther the distinction between the two.

Many Scriptural poems have been written with so much of Scripture in them, that what is not Scripture appears to be not true, and like mingling lies with the most sacred revelations. Now Milton, on the other hand, has taken for his subject that one point of Scripture of which we have the mere fact recorded, and upon this he has most judiciously constructed his whole fable. So of Shakespeare's "King Lear:" we have little historic evidence to guide or confine us, and the few facts handed down to us, and admirably employed by the poet, are sufficient, while we read, to put an end to all doubt as to the credibility of the story. It is idle to say that this or that incident is improbable, because history, as far as it goes, tells us that the fact was so and so. Four or five lines in the Bible include the whole that is said of Milton's story, and the Poet has called up that poetic faith, that conviction of the mind, which is necessary to make that seem true, which otherwise might have been deemed almost fabulous.

But to return to "The Tempest," and to the wondrous creation of Ariel. If a doubt could ever be entertained whether Shakespeare was a great poet, acting upon laws arising out of his own nature, and not without law, as has sometimes been idly asserted, that doubt must be removed by the character of Ariel. The very first words uttered by this being introduce the spirit, not as an angel, above man; not a gnome, or a fiend, below man; but while the poet gives him the faculties and the advantages of reason, he divests him of all mortal character, not positively, it is true, but negatively. In air he lives, from air he derives his being, in air he acts; and all his colours and properties seem to have been obtained from the rainbow and the skies. There is nothing about Ariel that cannot be conceived to exist either at sun-rise or at sun-set: hence all that belongs to Ariel belongs to the delight the mind is capable of receiving from the most lovely external appearances. His answers to Prospero are directly to the question, and nothing beyond; or where he expatiates, which is not unfrequently, it is to himself and upon his own delights, or upon the unnatural situation in which he is placed, though under a kindly power and to good ends.

Shakespeare has properly made Ariel's very first speech characteristic of him. After he has described the manner in which he had raised the storm and produced its harmless consequences, we find that Ariel is discontented—that he has been freed, it is true, from a cruel confinement, but still that he is bound to obey Prospero, and to execute any commands imposed upon him. We feel that such a state of bondage is almost unnatural to him, yet we see that it is delightful for him to be so employed.—It is as if we were to command one of the winds in a different direction to that which nature dictates, or one of the waves, now rising and now sinking, to recede before it bursts upon the shore: such is the feeling we experience, when we learn that a being like Ariel is commanded to fulfil any mortal behest.

When, however, Shakespeare contrasts the treatment of Ariel by Prospero with that of Sycorax, we are sensible that the liberated spirit ought to be grateful, and Ariel does feel and acknowledge the obligation; he immediately assumes the airy being, with a mind so elastically correspondent, that when once a feeling has passed from it, not a trace is left behind.

Is there anything in nature from which Shakespeare caught the idea of this delicate and delightful being, with such child-like simplicity, yet with such preternatural powers? He is neither born of heaven, nor of earth; but, as it were, between both, like a May-blossom kept suspended in air by the fanning breeze, which prevents it from falling to the ground, and only finally, and by compulsion, touching earth. This reluctance of the Sylph to be under the command even of Prospero is kept up through the whole play, and in the exercise of his admirable judgment Shakespeare has availed himself of it, in order to give Ariel an interest in the event, looking forward to that moment when he was to gain his last and only reward—simple and eternal liberty.

Another instance of admirable judgment and excellent preparation is to be found in the creature contrasted with Ariel—Caliban; who is described in such a manner by Prospero, as to lead us to expect the appearance of a foul, unnatural monster. He is not seen at once: his voice is heard; this is the preparation; he was too offensive to be seen first in all his deformity, and in nature we do not receive so much disgust from sound as from sight. After we have heard Caliban's voice he does not enter, until Ariel has entered like a water-nymph. All the strength of contrast is thus acquired without any of the shock of abruptness, or of that unpleasant sensation, which we experience when the object presented is in any way hateful to our vision.

The character of Caliban is wonderfully conceived: he is a sort of creature of the earth, as Ariel is a sort of creature of the air. He partakes of the qualities of the brute, but is distinguished from brutes in two ways:—by having mere understanding without moral reason; and by not possessing the instincts which pertain to absolute animals. Still, Caliban is in some respects a noble being: the poet has raised him far above contempt: he is a man in the sense of the imagination: all the images he uses are drawn from nature, and are highly poetical; they fit in with the images of Ariel. Caliban gives us images from the earth, Ariel images from the air. Caliban talks of the difficulty of finding fresh water, of the situation of morasses, and of other circumstances which even brute instinct, without reason, could comprehend. No mean figure is employed, no mean passion displayed, beyond animal passion, and repugnance to command.

The manner in which the lovers are introduced is equally wonderful, and it is the last point I shall now mention in reference to this, almost miraculous, drama. The same judgment is observable in every scene, still preparing, still inviting, and still gratifying, like a finished piece of music. I have omitted to notice one thing, and you must give me leave to advert to it before I proceed: I mean the conspiracy against the life of Alonzo. I want to shew you how well the poet prepares the feelings of the reader for this plot, which was to execute the most detestable of all crimes, and which, in another play, Shakespeare has called "the murder of sleep."

Antonio and Sebastian at first had no such intention: it was suggested by the magical sleep cast on Alonzo and Gonzalo; but they are previously introduced scoffing and scorning at what was said by others, without regard to age or situation—without any sense of admiration for the excellent truths they heard delivered, but giving themselves up entirely to the malignant and unsocial feeling, which induced them to listen to everything that was said, not for the sake of profiting by the learning and experience of others, but of hearing something that might gratify vanity and self-love, by making them believe that the person speaking was inferior to themselves.

This, let me remark, is one of the grand characteristics of a villain; and it would not be so much a presentiment, as an anticipation of hell, for men to suppose that all mankind were as wicked as themselves, or might be so, if they were not too great fools. Pope, you are perhaps aware, objected to this conspiracy; but in my mind, if it could be omitted, the play would lose a charm which nothing could supply.

Many, indeed innumerable, beautiful passages might be quoted from this play, independently of the astonishing scheme of its construction. Every body will call to mind the grandeur of the language of Prospero in that divine speech, where he takes leave of his magic art; and were I to indulge myself by repetitions of the kind, I should descend from the character of a lecturer to that of a mere reciter. Before I terminate, I may particularly recall one short passage, which has fallen under the very severe, but inconsiderate, censure of Pope and Arbuthnot, who pronounce it a piece of the grossest bombast. Prospero thus addresses his daughter, directing her attention to Ferdinand:

> "The fringed curtains of thine eye advance,
> And say what thou seest yond."
> *Act 1., Scene 2.*

Taking these words as a periphrase of—"Look what is coming yonder," it certainly may to some appear to border on the ridiculous, and to fall under the rule I formerly laid down,—that whatever, without injury, can be translated into a foreign language in simple terms, ought to be in simple terms in the original language; but it is to be borne in mind, that different modes of expression frequently arise from difference of situation and education: a blackguard would use very different words, to express the same thing, to those a gentleman would employ, yet both would be natural and proper; difference of feeling gives rise to difference of language: a gentleman speaks in polished terms, with due regard to his own rank and position, while a blackguard, a person little better than half a brute, speaks like half a brute, showing no respect for himself, nor for others.

But I am content to try the lines I have just quoted by the introduction to them; and then, I think, you will admit, that nothing could be more fit and appropriate than such language. How does Prospero introduce them? He has just told Miranda a wonderful story, which deeply affected her, and filled her with surprise and astonishment, and for his own purposes he afterwards lulls her to sleep. When she awakes, Shakespeare has made her wholly inattentive to the present, but wrapped up in the past. An actress, who understands the character of Miranda, would have her eyes cast down, and her eyelids almost covering them, while she was, as it were, living in her dream. At this moment Prospero sees Ferdinand, and wishes to point him out to his daughter, not only with great, but with scenic solemnity, he standing before her, and before the spectator, in the dignified character of a great magician. Something was to appear to Miranda on the sudden, and as unexpectedly as if the hero of a drama were to be on the stage at the instant when the curtain is elevated. It is under such circumstances that Prospero says, in a tone calculated at once to arouse his daughter's attention,

> "The fringed curtains of thine eye advance,
> And say what thou seest yond."

Turning from the sight of Ferdinand to his thoughtful daughter, his attention was first struck by the downcast appearance of her eyes and eyelids; and, in my humble opinion, the solemnity of the phraseology assigned to Prospero is completely in character, recollecting his preternatural capacity, in which the most familiar objects in nature present themselves in a mysterious point of view. It is much easier to find fault with a writer by reference to former notions and experience, than to sit down and read him, recollecting his purpose, connecting one feeling with another, and judging of his words and phrases, in proportion as they convey the sentiments of the persons represented.

Of Miranda we may say, that she possesses in herself all the ideal beauties that could be imagined by the greatest poet of any age or country; but it is not my purpose now, so much to point out the high poetic powers of Shakespeare, as to illustrate his exquisite judgment, and it is solely with this design that I have noticed a passage with which, it seems to me, some critics, and those among the best, have been unreasonably dissatisfied. If Shakespeare be the wonder of the ignorant, he is, and ought to be, much more the wonder of the learned: not only from profundity of thought, but from his astonishing and intuitive knowledge of what man must be at all times, and under all circumstances, he is rather to be looked upon as a prophet than as a poet. Yet, with all these unbounded powers, with all this might and majesty of genius, he makes us feel as if he were unconscious of himself, and of his high destiny, disguising the half god in the simplicity of a child.

End of the ninth lecture.

From S. T. Coleridge, *Seven Lectures on Shakespeare and Milton,* London, 1856. NY: Burt Franklin, 1968.

From CHARACTERS OF SHAKESPEAR'S PLAYS

William Hazlitt

THE TEMPEST

The 'Tempest' is one of the most original and perfect of Shakespear's productions, and he has shown in it all the variety of his powers. It is full of grace and grandeur. The human and imaginary characters, the dramatic and the grotesque, are blended together with the greatest art, and without any appearance of it. Though he has here given "to airy nothing a local habitation and a name," yet that part which is only the fantastic creation of his mind has the same palpable texture, and coheres "semblably" with the rest. As the preternatural part has the air of reality, and almost haunts the imagination with a sense of truth, the real characters and events partake of the wildness of a dream. The stately magician, Prospero, driven from his dukedom, but around whom (so potent is his art) airy spirits throng numberless to do his bidding; his daughter Miranda ("worthy of that name"), to whom all the power of his art points, and who seems the goddess of the isle; the princely Ferdinand, cast, by fate upon the haven of his happiness in this idol of his love; the delicate Ariel; the savage Caliban, half brute, half demon; the drunken ship's crew—are all connected parts of the story, and can hardly be spared from the place they fill. Even the local scenery is of a piece and character with the subject. Prospero's enchanted island seems to have risen up out of the sea; the airy music, the tempest-tossed vessel, the turbulent waves, all have the effect of the landscape back-ground of some fine picture. Shakespear's pencil is (to use an allusion of his own) "like the dyer's hand, subdued to what it works in." Everything in him, though it partakes of "the liberty of wit," is also subjected to "the law" of the understanding. For instance, even the drunken sailors, who are made reeling-ripe, share, in the disorder of their minds and bodies, in the tumult of the elements, and seem on shore to be as much at the mercy of chance as they were before at the mercy of the winds and waves. These fellows with their sea-wit are the least to our taste of any part of the play: but they are as like drunken sailors as they can be, and are an indirect foil to Caliban, whose figure acquires a classical dignity in the comparison.

The character of Caliban is generally thought (and justly so) to be one of the author's masterpieces. It is not indeed pleasant to see this character on the stage any more than it is to see the god Pan personated there. But in itself it is one of the wildest and most abstracted of all Shakespeare's characters, whose deformity whether of body or mind is redeemed by the power and truth of the imagination displayed in it. It is the essence of grossness, but there is not a particle of vulgarity in it. Shakespear has described the brutal mind of Caliban in contact with the pure and original forms of nature; the character grows out of the soil where it is rooted, uncontrolled, uncouth, and wild, uncramped by any of the meannesses of custom. It is "of the earth, earthy." It seems almost to have been dug out of the ground, with a soul instinctively superadded to it answering to its wants and origin. Vulgarity is not natural coarseness, but conventional coarseness, learned from others, contrary to, or without an entire conformity of natural power and disposition; as fashion is the common-place affectation of what is elegant and refined without any feeling of the essence of it. Schlegel, the admirable German critic on Shakespear, observes that Caliban is a poetical character, and "always speaks in blank verse." He first comes in thus:

> "*Caliban.* As wicked dew as e'er my mother brush'd
> With raven's feather from unwholesome fen,
> Drop on you both! a south-west blow on ye,
> And blister you all o'er!
>   *Prospero.* For this, be sure, to-night thou shalt have cramps,
> Side-stitches that shall pen thy breath up; urchins
> Shall for that vast of night that they may work,
> All exercise on thee: thou shalt be pinch'd
> As thick as honey-comb, each pinch more stinging
> Than bees that made 'em.
>   *Caliban.*   I must eat my dinner.
> This island's mine, by Sycorax my mother,
> Which thou tak'st from me. When thou cam'st first,
> Thou strok'dst me, and mad'st much of me; would'st give me
> Water with berries in't; and teach me how
> To name the bigger light, and how the less,
> That burn by day and night; and then I lov'd thee,
> And show'd thee all the qualities o' th' isle,
> The fresh springs, brine-pits, barren place and fertile:
> Curs'd be I that did so! All the charms
> Of Sycorax, toads, beetles, bats, light on you!
> For I am all the subjects that you have,

Which first was mine own king; and here you sty me
In this hard rock, whiles you do keep from me
The rest o' th' island."[1]

. . .

And again, he promises Trinculo his services thus, if he will free him
from his drudgery:

"I'll show thee the best springs; I'll pluck thee berries,
I'll fish for thee, and get thee wood enough. . . .
I prithee, let me bring thee where crabs grow;
And I with my long nails will dig thee pig-nuts,
Show thee a jay's nest, and instruct thee how
To snare the nimble marmozet: I'll bring thee
To clust'ring filberds; and sometimes I'll get thee
Young scamels from the rock." [2]

In conducting Stephano and Trinculo to Prospero's cell, Caliban
shows the superiority of natural capacity over greater knowledge and
greater folly; and in a former scene, when Ariel frightens them with
his music, Caliban to encourage them accounts for it in the eloquent
poetry of the senses:

"Be not afeard; the isle is full of noises,
Sounds, and sweet airs, that give delight and hurt not.
Sometime a thousand twangling instruments
Will hum about mine ears, and sometime voices,
That if I then had waked after long sleep,
Would make me sleep again; and then, in dreaming,
The clouds methought would open, and show riches
Ready to drop upon me; that, when I wak'd,
I cried to dream again." [3]

This is not more beautiful than it is true. The poet here shows us the savage with the simplicity of a child, and makes the strange monster amia-
ble. Shakespear had to paint the human animal rude and without choice
in its pleasures, but not without the sense of pleasure or some germ of
the affections. Master Barnardine in 'Measure for Measure,' the savage of
civilised life, is an admirable philosophical counterpart to Caliban.

Shakespear has, as it were by design, drawn off from Caliban the elements of whatever is ethereal and refined, to compound them in the
unearthly mould of Ariel. Nothing was ever more finely conceived than
this contrast between the material and the spiritual, the gross and delicate.

1. Act I., sc. 2. 2. Act 2., sc. 2. 3. Act 3., sc. 2.

Ariel is imaginary power, the swiftness of thought personified. When told to make good speed by Prospero, he says, "I drink the air before me." This is something like Puck's boast on a similar occasion, "I'd put a girdle round about the earth in forty minutes." But Ariel differs from Puck in having a fellow-feeling in the interests of those he is employed about. How exquisite is the following dialogue between him and Prospero!

> "ARIEL   Your charm so strongly works 'em,
> That if you now beheld them, your affections
> Would become tender.
>   PROSPERO   Dost thou think so, spirit?
>   ARIEL Mine would, sir, were I human.
>   PROSPERO   And mine shall.
> Hast thou, which art but air, a touch, a feeling
> Of their afflictions, and shall not myself,
> One of their kind, that relish all as sharply
> Passion as they, be kindlier moved than thou art?"[1]

It has been observed that there is a peculiar charm in the songs introduced in Shakespear, which, without conveying any distinct images, seem to recall all the feelings connected with them, like snatches of half-forgotten music heard indistinctly and at intervals. There is this effect produced by Ariel's songs, which (as we are told) seem to sound in the air, and as if the person playing them were invisible. We shall give one instance out of many of this general power:

> "*Enter* FERDINAND; *and* ARIEL, *invisible, playing and singing:*
>   FERDINAND *following.*
>
>   ARIEL'S SONG.
>   Come unto these yellow sands,
>   And then take hands;
>   Court'sied when you have, and kiss'd,—
>   The wild waves whist:—
>   Foot it featly here and there;
>   And sweet sprites the burden bear.
>   Hark, Hark!
>   [*Burden dispersedly within*: Bow, wow;]
>   The watch-dogs bark:
>   [*Burden dispersedly within*: Bow, wow.]
>   Hark, hark! I hear
>   The strain of strutting chanticleer
>   Cry, Cock-a-doodle-doo.

1. Act 5., sc. 1.

FERDINAND Where should this music be? i' the air or
   th' earth?
It sounds no more: and sure it waits upon
Some god o' th' island. Sitting on a bank
Weeping again the king my father's wreck,
This music crept by me upon the waters,
Allaying both their fury and my passion
With its sweet air; thence I have follow'd it,
Or it hath drawn me rather:—but 'tis gone.—
No, it begins again.
          ARIEL *sings:*
Full fathom five thy father lies,
   Of his bones are coral made:
Those are pearls that were his eyes,
   Nothing of him that doth fade,
But doth suffer a sea change
Into something rich and strange
Sea-nymphs hourly ring his knell—
   [*Burden within*: Ding, dong:]
Hark! now I hear them, Ding-dong, bell.
FERDINAND The ditty does remember my drown'd father.
   This is no mortal business, nor no sound
   That the earth owes: I hear it now above me."—[1]

The courtship between Ferdinand and Miranda is one of the chief
beauties of this play. It is the very purity of love. The pretended inter-
ference of Prospero with it heightens its interest, and is in character
with the magician, whose sense of preternatural power makes him
arbitrary, tetchy, and impatient of opposition.

The 'Tempest' is a finer play than the 'Midsummer Night's Dream,'
which has sometimes been compared with it; but it is not so fine a
poem. There are a greater number of beautiful passages in the latter.
Two of the most striking in the 'Tempest' are spoken by Prospero. The
one is that admirable one when the vision which he has conjured up
disappears, beginning "The cloud-capp'd towers, the gorgeous palaces,"
&c., which has been so often quoted, that every school-boy knows it
by heart; the other is that which Prospero makes in abjuring his art:

   "Ye elves of hills, brooks, standing lakes, and groves,
   And ye that on the sands with printless foot
   Do chase the ebbing Neptune, and do fly him
   When he comes back; you demi-puppets that

1. Act I., sc. 2.

By moonshine do the green sour ringlets make,
Whereof the ewe not bites; and you whose pastime
Is to make midnight mushrooms, that rejoice
To hear the solemn curfew, by whose aid—
Weak masters though ye be—I have be-dimm'd
The noon-tide sun, call'd forth the mutinous winds,
And 'twixt the green sea and the azur'd vault
Set roaring war: to the dread rattling thunder
Have I given fire, and rifted Jove's stout oak
With his own bolt; the strong-bas'd promontory
Have I made shake, and by the spurs pluck'd up
The pine and cedar: graves at my command
Have wak'd their sleepers, oped, and let them forth
By my so potent art. But this rough magic
I here abjure; and when I have requir'd
Some heavenly music—which even now I do—
To work mine end upon their senses that
This airy charm is for, I'll break my staff,
Bury it certain fadoms in the earth,
And deeper than did ever plummet sound,
I'll drown my book."[1]

We must not forget to mention among other things in this play, that
Shakespear has anticipated nearly all the arguments on the Utopian
schemes of modern philosophy:

"GONZALO Had I plantation of this isle, my lord—
ANTONIO He'd sow't with nettle-seed.
SEBASTIAN   Or docks, or mallows.
GONZALO And were the king on't, what would I do?
SEBASTIAN 'Scape being drunk, for want of wine.
GONZALO I' the commonwealth I would by contraries
    Execute all things: for no kind of traffic
    Would I admit; no name of magistrate;
    Letters should not be known; riches, poverty,
    And use of service, none; contract, succession,
    Bourn, bound of land, tilth, vineyard, none;
    No use of metal, corn, or wine, or oil;
    No occupation, all men idle, all,
    And women too—but innocent and pure:
    No sovereignty.
SEBASTIAN   Yet he would be king on't.

1. Act 5., sc. 1.

ANTONIO The latter end of his commonwealth forgets the
   beginning.
GONZALO All things in common nature should produce
   Without sweat or endeavour; treason, felony,
   Sword, pike, knife, gun, or need of any engine
   Would I not have; but nature should bring forth,
   Of its own kind, all foison, all abundance
   To feed my innocent people!
SEBASTIAN No marrying 'mong his subjects?
ANTONIO None, man; all idle:—whores and knaves.
GONZALO I would with such perfection govern, sir,
   T' excel the golden age.
SEBASTIAN   Save his majesty!"[1]

1. Act 2., sc. 1.

From William Hazlitt, *Lectures on the Literature of the Age of Elizabeth and Characters of Shakespear's Plays,* 1820. London: George Bell and Sons, 1909.

From *SHAKSPEARE'S HEROINES*

Anna Jameson

From MIRANDA

We might have deemed it impossible to go beyond Viola, Perdita, and Ophelia, as pictures of feminine beauty—to exceed the one in tender delicacy, the other in ideal grace, and the last in simplicity—if Shakspeare had not done this; and he alone could have done it. Had he never created a Miranda, we should never have been made to feel how completely the purely natural and the purely ideal can blend into each other.

The character of Miranda resolves itself into the very elements of womanhood. She is beautiful, modest, and tender, and she is these only; they comprise her whole being, external and internal. She is so perfectly unsophisticated, so delicately refined, that she is all but ethereal. Let us imagine any other woman placed beside Miranda—even one of Shakspeare's own loveliest and sweetest creations—there is not one of them that could sustain the comparison for a moment; not one that would not appear somewhat coarse or artificial when brought into immediate contact with this pure child of nature, this "Eve of an enchanted Paradise."

What, then, has Shakspeare done?—"O wondrous skill and sweet wit of the man!"—he has removed Miranda far from all comparison with her own sex; he has placed her between the demi-demon of earth and the delicate spirit of air. The next step is into the ideal and supernatural; and the only being who approaches Miranda, with whom she can be contrasted, is Ariel. Beside the subtile essence of this ethereal sprite, this creature of elemental light and air, that "ran upon the winds, rode the curl'd clouds, and in the colours of the rainbow lived," Miranda herself appears a palpable reality, a woman, "breathing thoughtful breath," a woman, walking the earth in her mortal loveliness, with a heart as frail-strung, as passion-touched, as ever fluttered in a female bosom.

I have said that Miranda possesses merely the elementary attributes of womanhood; but each of these stand in her with a distinct and peculiar grace. She resembles nothing upon earth: but do we therefore compare her, in our own minds, with any of those fabled beings with which the fancy of ancient poets peopled the forest depths, the fountain, or the ocean?—oread or dryad fleet, sea-maid or naiad of the stream? We cannot think of them together. Miranda is a consistent, natural, human being. Our impression of her nymph-like beauty, her peerless grace and purity of soul, has a distinct and individual character. Not only is she exquisitely lovely, being what she is, but we are made to feel that she *could not* possibly be otherwise than as she is portrayed. She has never beheld one of her own sex; she has never caught from society one imitated or artificial grace. The impulses which have come to her, in her enchanted solitude, are of heaven and nature, not of the world and its vanities. She has sprung up into beauty beneath the eye of her father, the princely magician; her companions have been the rocks and woods, the many-shaped, many-tinted clouds, and the silent stars; her playmates the ocean billows, that stooped their foamy crests and ran rippling to kiss her feet. Ariel and his attendant sprites hovered over her head, ministered duteous to her every wish, and presented before her pageants of beauty and grandeur. The very air, made vocal by her father's art, floated in music around her. If we can pre-suppose such a situation with all its circumstances, do we not behold in the character of Miranda not only the credible, but the natural, the necessary results of such a situation? She retains her woman's heart, for that is unalterable and inalienable, as a part of her being; but her deportment, her looks, her language, her thoughts—all these, from the supernatural and poeti-cal circumstances around her, assume a cast of the pure ideal; and to us, who are in the secret of her human and pitying nature, nothing can be more charming and consistent than the effect which she produces upon others, who never having beheld anything resembling her, approach her as "a wonder," as something celestial:

> Be sure! the goddess on whom these airs attend!

And again—

> What is this maid?
> Is she the goddess who hath sever'd us,
> And brought us thus together?

And Ferdinand exclaims, while gazing on her,

> My spirits as in a dream are all bound up!
> My father's loss, the weakness which I feel,
> The wreck of all my friends, or this man's threats,
> To whom I am subdued, are but light to me,
> Might I but through my prison once a day
> Behold this maid: all corners else o' the earth
> Let liberty make use of, space enough
> Have I in such a prison.

Contrasted with the impression of her refined and dignified beauty, and its effect on all beholders, is Miranda's own soft simplicity, her virgin innocence, her total ignorance of the conventional forms and language of society. It is most natural that, in a being thus constituted, the first tears should spring from compassion, "suffering with those that she saw suffer"—

> O the cry did knock
> Against my very heart. Poor souls! they perish'd.
> Had I been any god of power, I would
> Have sunk the sea within the earth, or e'er
> It should the good ship so have swallow'd,
> And the freighting souls within her;

and that her first sigh should be offered to a love at once fearless and submissive, delicate and fond. She has no taught scruples of honour like Juliet; no coy concealments like Viola; no assumed dignity standing in its own defence. Her bashfulness is less a quality than an instinct; it is like the self-folding of a flower, spontaneous and unconscious. I suppose there is nothing of the kind in poetry equal to the scene between Ferdinand and Miranda. In Ferdinand, who is a noble creature, we have all the chivalrous magnanimity with which man, in a high state of civilization, disguises his real superiority, and does humble homage to the being of whose destiny he disposes; while Miranda, the mere child of nature, is struck with wonder at her own new emotions. Only conscious of her own weakness as a woman, and ignorant of those usages of society which teach us to dissemble the real passion, and assume (and sometimes abuse) an unreal and transient power, she is equally ready to place her life, her love, her service beneath his feet.

> MIRANDA
> Alas, now! pray you,
> Work not so hard. I would the lightning had
> Burnt up those logs that you are enjoin'd to pile!
> Pray set it down and rest you. When this burns,
> 'Twill weep for having wearied you. My father
> Is hard at study; pray now, rest yourself:
> He's safe for these three hours.

> FERDINAND
> O most dear mistress,
> The sun will set before I shall discharge
> What I must strive to do.

MIRANDA
          If you'll sit down,
I'll bear your logs the while. Pray give me that,
I'll carry it to the pile.

FERDINAND
               No, precious creature;
I'd rather crack my sinews, break my back,
Than you should such dishonour undergo
While I sit lazy by.

MIRANDA
          It would become me,
As well as it does you; and I should do it
With much more ease; for my good will is to it,
And yours it is against.

. . . . As Miranda, being what she is, could only have had a Ferdinand
for her lover, and an Ariel for an attendant, so she could have had with
propriety no other father than the majestic and gifted being who
fondly claims her as "a thread of his own life—nay, that for which he
lives." Prospero, with his magical powers, his superhuman wisdom,
his moral worth and grandeur, and his kingly dignity, is one of the
most sublime visions that ever swept with ample robes, pale brow, and
sceptred hand before the eye of fancy. He controls the invisible world,
and works through the agency of spirits; not by any evil and forbidden
compact, but solely by superior might of intellect—by potent spells
gathered from the lore of ages, and abjured when he mingles again as
a man with his fellow-men. He is as distinct a being from the nec-
romancers and astrologers celebrated in Shakspeare's age as can well
be imagined:★ and all the wizards of poetry and fiction, even Faust
and St. Leon, sink into common-places before the princely, the philo-
sophic, the benevolent Prospero.

★ Such as Cornelius Agrippa, Michael Scott, Dr. Dee. The last was the contemporary of Shakspeare.

From Anna Jameson, *Shakspeare's Heroines: Characteristics of Women, Moral, Poetical,
and Historical.* London: George Bell and Sons, 1889. Reprinted NY: AMS Press, 1967.

The Tempest and The Concept of The Machiavellian Playwright

Richard Abrams

> From jigging veins of rhyming mother wits,
> And such conceits as clownage keeps in pay,
> We'll lead you to the stately tents of war,
> Where you shall hear the Scythian Tamburlaine
> Threat'ning the world with high astounding terms.[1]

I T IS difficult to specify where, in the first line of Christopher Marlowe's first independent play, the poet's vaunt leaves off and Tamburlaine's begins. Marlowe, with his "mighty line" reminiscent of epic verse, challenges the kept rhymers who have gone soft in office much as, on the greater stage of the world, the former shepherd Tamburlaine defies the hereditary rulers with his high astounding terms. Among his other virtues, Tamburlaine is a master rhetorician, an unparalleled leader of men, able to stir his companions' imaginations to a dream of world conquest. His "words are swords," as is wrongly maintained of another character in the play; he is verbally irresistible. It is no accident that the first of Tamburlaine's victims will be a feeble aesthete, a poet-king, who yields his throne because he lacks the oratory of command. The "thund'ring speech" required for successful rule will be heard in the *Tamburlaine* plays only from Tamburlaine himself. Yet, extending the implied comparison of the Prologue, one might say that Tamburlaine owes his success to his speech-writer, the poet Marlowe—and this Marlowe himself understands in casting his lot with Tamburlaine by choosing to write a play about him. With the victories of his champion, the poet will be carried in triumph to the forefront of the dramatic profession.

Marlowe's self-appointment to a destiny of power through the conqueror Tamburlaine was an unrepeatable performance, a *tour de force* of poetic authority. In a slightly different key, however, a similar author-protagonist "collaboration" occurs throughout the Shakespearean canon. Tamburlaine in his valor embodies what Machiavelli called the *virtù* of

1. Christopher Marlowe, *Tamburlaine The Great, Parts I and II*, ed. John Jump (Lincoln, Nebr., 1967), Part I, Prol. 1–5.

the lion; there is no comparable Shakespearean hero. But Shakespearean drama abounds in Machiavels of another mold, what the Florentine called the style of the fox; and if Tamburlaine with his high astounding terms recalls the epic poet, then the illusion-contriving Machiavellian fox suggests the dramatist. In this essay I will try to show that, of various character-types on the Shakespearean stage, it is the Machiavel who most faithfully gives back to the playwright the image of his own powers and aspirations, his privilege to do nearly whatever he pleases within his artistic creation.[2] After surveying the grounds of the villain-playwright analogy in the first section of this essay, I will discuss the analogy as it is focused in a single drama, *The Tempest*, in connection with Shakespeare's most widely-accepted exemplar of the art of playwriting, the conjurer Prospero.

To show that tyrants and villains (and temporary "justified" Machiavels, avengers like Hamlet and Prospero) are regularly regarded by Shakespeare as the "playwrights" of human history would not, of course, imply as a necessary converse the villainy or immorality of dramaturgy. Yet as I intend to argue in the final section of this essay, Shakespeare's use of the villain-playwright analogy is indeed reciprocal. There exists at the core of the playwright's art an irreducible element of aggression which Shakespeare seems to have been keenly aware of throughout his career, and which he treats directly in *The Tempest* in terms of the reluctant fraternity of the magician Prospero and his evil brother Antonio. When Prospero abjures his "rough magic" which has allowed him to control the action of the play, he is impelled by qualms that, arising in connection with the betrothal masque, afford him a new perspective on his motives as an avenger. By Act 5 a moral contagion has spread from metaphorical playwriting (the art of the Machiavel, epitomized in Prospero's revenge-plot) to literal playwriting (Shakespeare's own artistry in *The Tempest*, conceived on analogy with Prospero's art of the masque); and in the epilogue Prospero offers on Shakespeare's behalf a facetious apology in reversal of the moment on Marlowe's stage a generation earlier when fire leapt from the audacious young poet to his juggernaut hero Tamburlaine.

I. THE ART OF THE MACHIAVELLIAN PLAYWRIGHT

The roots of the villain-playwright analogy lie in the concept of plotting. Plotting, the forging of linked chains of causality, is recommended in different ways both by Machiavelli, who writes of the necessity of

2. Other studies of the Machiavellian playwright include Bernard Spivack, *Shakespeare and the Allegory of Evil* (New York, 1958), ch. 2; Sigurd Burckhardt, *Shakespearean Meanings* (Princeton, N.J., 1968), chs. 1, 9; Sidney Homan, "Iago's Aesthetics: Othello and Shakespeare's Portrait of an Artist," *Shakespeare Survey*, 5 (1969), 141–48.

controlling fortune, and by Aristotle, who prescribes for tragedy sequences of probable action. The dual meaning of "plot"—the plotting of a historical action and the plotting of a story—is common in the Renaissance and in Shakespeare.[3] Humphrey, Duke of Gloucester, speaks of a "plotted tragedy," meaning a bloodbath plotted like a stageplay (*2H6* 3.1.153).[4] In *Twelfth Night* the "plot" against Malvolio is literally Shakespeare's subplot, an "interlude" devised by a group of "authors" or plotting collaborators (2.5.70; 5.1.362, 343). In *Richard III,* to take an extended example, Richard's plot is, until the final act, virtually congruent with Shakespeare's own. In his opening soliloquy Richard as prologue rules out the comic sports of peace and sets the stage for a tragedy which Richard himself, as surrogate playwright, has contrived. Closing his soliloquy, he initiates the action of the play with a double theatrical metaphor, "Plots have I laid, inductions dangerous"—and pat on cue Enter Clarence, the announced first victim of Richard's plot, as though Richard himself had written him into the opening scene, which in a sense he has.

As well as satisfying internal criteria of coherence, a plot must catch the imagination of an audience, whether the general populace or a theatre public on whose box-office support a production stands or falls. The plotter, in a word, must achieve significance through his plotting. Richard III consummates his climb to power by staging an interlude for the Lord Mayor. Richard propped between two stage-prop bishops "play[s] the maid's part" (*R3* 3.7.51) while his henchman Buckingham as protagonist ("counterfeit[ing] the deep tragedian," 3.5.5) seduces him to accept the crown. But Richard falls through unpopularity. He loses sight of his wider audience, which the Machiavel must never do. "I love the people," says the Duke in *Measure for Measure,* "But do not like to stage me to their eyes;/Though it do well" (1.1.67–69). Coriolanus will learn the cost at which this luxury is maintained. Like Bolingbroke in *Richard II,* the ambitious politician must be a demagogue: now "a well-graced actor" playing to the gallery (5.2.24), now an invisible impresario staging smoothly efficient abdication-scenes.[5]

---

3. The basic metaphor in "laying a plot" appears to be from landscaping; cf. *Oxford English Dictionary,* "plot," *sb. 2,* 4, 6; 3, 7; also "plat," *sb. 2,* 3–5.   **4.** All Shakespearean citations are from the Pelican edition of *The Complete Works,* gen. ed. Alfred Harbage (Baltimore, 1969).   **5.** For the state-stage analogy in *Richard II,* see Leonard Dean, "From *Richard II* to *Henry V*: A Closer View," in *Shakespeare: Modern Essays in Criticism,* ed. Leonard Dean (New York, 1967), pp. 188–205; also Maynard Mack Jr., *Killing the King* (New Haven, Conn. 1973), In *Richard III,* the groundswell of rebellion begins with the Scrivener, who may be regarded as a disgruntled groundling rejecting Richard's "palpable device" (3.6.11). A discussion of the citizenry as audience may be found in Burckhardt, ch. 1. Anne Righter, *Shakespeare and the Idea of the Play* (Baltimore, 1967), pp. 31–40, discusses the casting of the audience in the role of Mankind in the morality plays.

The plotter's special expertise is motivational psychology. A Machiavel allows only such confrontations to occur as advance his plot; a playwright "edits out" (by simply not writing) interaction that distracts from the tenor of his story. Similarly, a Machiavel must carefully judge character, delegating responsibilities to the proper agents; a playwright (or director) must cast the roles he has conceived on the likeliest performers. In *The Tempest* this process of rolecasting, called "new-creating," places the Machiavel and the dramatist in diabolic competition with divinity. God creates by releasing new creatures into the world *ex nihilo*; man, by corrupting or transforming an existing creation, by leading souls to "wander in an unknown field" where they stray from the "pure truth" of their idenities (*Err.* 3.2.37–38). Thus Iago (adapting Lodovico's phrase, *Oth.* 4.1. 269) "new-creates a fault" in Othello. In imagination he conceives a cold-blooded murderer Othello whom he proceeds to mold from the inchoate matter of Othello the lover and warrior. Godlike, he creates him new, as Antipholus of Syracuse whimsically accuses Luciana of doing:

> Against my soul's pure truth why labor you
> To make it wander in an unknown field?
> Are you a god? Would you create me new?
> Transform me then, and to your power I'll yield. (*Err.* 3.2.37–40)

The metaphor of rolecasting as "creating" has an interesting background. In a common derived usage of the word, "create" assumes a political orientation. Creating is dubbing, a verbal act paralleling the divine fiat of Genesis, through which a king invests his subjects with titles and offices ("Richard, I will create thee Duke of Gloucester," *3H6* 2.6. 103); God's special verb is applicable to the king presumably because, in raising a subject politically, a king acts in his capacity of God's deputy on earth; the creating is performed as though by an extension of divine power. Shakespeare frequently uses the word in this sense or with slight variations as when Ross tells Malcolm, "Your eye in Scotland/Would create soldiers" (*Mac.* 4.3.186–87). Here the creating proceeds from the consciences of the Scottish people rather than from an official act of conscription. Malcolm is rightful pretender; his glance is as good as a royal seal. And yet he is not king. A shade beyond this usage lies a revolution in the meaning of the word, for if rightful pretenders can create, so too may wrongful usurpers. A climbing tyrant creates proleptically. He deals out promises of titles, and the more bad vouchers accepted the better their chances of validation. Prospero alludes to this paradoxical inflationary politics when he complains of his brother who, "Being once perfected how to grant suits, / ... new created / The creatures that were mine" (1.2.79–82). This account of

Antonio's transformation of the creatures of state through the assignment of alien political roles is of exceptional interest as a metaphor for the dramatist's relation to his actors who are transformed to "new creatures" by their assumption of fictional roles.

In addition to their arts of "new-creating," the Machiavel and the playwright rival divinity by assuming a providential relationship to the passage of time. This relationship may be demonstrated through the technical meaning of "plot" as an Elizabethan stage term. A plot was a scene-by-scene outline of a play, apparently drawn up from a prompt-copy and posted backstage, listing the characters appearing in each scene together with the necessary props and sound effects. Thus, as in the root metaphor of a plot of land, the plot offered a "groundplan" or survey of the dramatic action. Although action unfolds temporally, an actor or prompter scanning the plot could conceive it visually and simultaneously. In a similar way the Machiavel takes an overview of past, present, and future; he learns to see history not as currents of events, unalterable currents, but as patterns of causality, static patterns, susceptible to manipulation. "Be a child o' th' time," exclaims a drunken Antony at Pompey's feast in *Antony and Cleopatra*; "Possess it, I'll make answer," answers Caesar deliberately (2.7.99–100). Possessing the time—seizing the moment or taking the tide at its flood (Brutus), transcending the "ignorant present" (Lady Macbeth)—was a keynote of Machiavelli's message to the Renaissance. Machiavelli recommends a god's-eye view of, or detachment from, the flow of history; he suggests the occupation of an observer's post outside the normal sentimental sphere of human relations which, if attained, confers on the politician an almost superhuman power in the determination of events. Hence the uncanny quality of Lady Macbeth "beguil[ing] the time" with her guest Duncan, or of Richard III engaging in cat-and-mouse play with his prospective victims. Whatever mask the Machiavellian actor dons, we sense that he has just come from "behind the scenes," that he comes onstage fresh from having "read the plot." He has access to a divine or forbidden knowledge in the mind of his creator, the dramatist, which exempts him from the ebb and flow of circumstance that engulfs the innocents in the drama.

The Machiavel, then, is a god of the play-world, a solipsist thrilling to his own sheer control. "I am myself alone," says Richard, Duke of Gloucester, parodying the divine tautology (*3H6* 5.6.83); and more diabolically, Iago: "I am not what I am" (*Oth.* 1.1.65). Because of his extraordinary power, however, the Machiavel often transcends his own villainy and partakes of an exultation otherwise reserved for God and the artist. We catch the mood in Lady Macbeth's gloating over her license to violate the king's person lodged in her chambers. When the chamberlains are drowned in swinish sleep, she hints obscenely to Macbeth:

> What cannot you and I perform upon
> Th' unguarded Duncan? what not put upon
> His spongy officers, who shall bear the guilt
> Of our great quell? (1.7.69–72)

Lady Macbeth's giddiness as she contemplates the infinity of forms her act of murder may assume momentarily overshadows her mercenary ends; she approaches a state of aesthetic disinterestedness. Her use of rhetorical questions betokens, not so much the guilt that will later develop, as an artistic reticence, a refusal to specify prematurely lest naming bind conception to the hackneyed forms of nature and society which must serve merely as a springboard for her and Macbeth's "creation." She conceives an act so cosmic in its possibilities that it can be defined only by negatives. Rather than emphasizing her cruelty, the theatrical allusions (if that is what they are: "perform"; "put upon," as in rolecasting) serve euphemistically to dilute the horror of "our great quell."

A similar instance of the villain's exuberant creativity occurs as Iago incites Othello to the murder of Desdemona:

OTHELLO   Get me some poison, Iago, this night. I'll not
          expostulate with her, lest her body and beauty
          unprovide my mind again. This night, Iago!
IAGO   Do it not with poison. Strangle her in her bed, even
          the bed she hath contaminated.
OTHELLO   Good, good! The justice of it pleases. Very good!
          (4.1.200–05)

The villain-playwright analogy is crucial to an understanding of Iago's motivation in the absence of conventional drives.[6] Why mustn't Othello kill Desdemona impersonally by poison? If all Iago wanted were to see the deed discharged, his suggestion would introduce a needless risk, since Othello confesses his fear of faltering in a direct confrontation. But Iago knows Othello's fortitude better than Othello does, and he is out for bigger game than mere practical results. His interests at the moment are identified with the playwright's; he is

---

6. Bernard Spivack, pp. 30–31, describes an Iago "with a purpose that has nothing to do with either revenge or ambition.... Iago is an artist eager to demonstrate his skill by achieving a masterpiece of craft.... He is outside the play in another sense. He is the show-man who produces it and the chorus who interprets it, and his essential relationship is with the audience."

motivated purely by a sense of theatre. As though on Shakespeare's behalf he assures that the murder will be as flagrant, as excruciatingly intimate as possible. To guarantee a moving tragedy, he tightens the screws and wrings from Othello his intensest passions, even affording him an ultimate dignity that Othello could never have recovered had he been allowed to poison Desdemona.

In summary, the villain-playwright analogy rests on the following points of comparison. Both villain and playwright plot or devise an action that is causally coherent and conformable, at least in appearances, with the standards of a judging community, whether the *res publica* or the theatre public. Second, both types of plotters are obliged to cast their mental scenarios on intermediary performers (agents or actors), effecting a temporary transformation of identity ("new-creating"). Third, in the psychological control that the Machiavel and the playwright exercise over their victims and agents, characters and actors, respectively, and in their various means of transcending temporality, both encroach on the prerogatives of a creative and providential divinity. Finally, in the supremacy of his power which frees him from practical considerations, the Machiavel is sometimes able to perform gratuitous actions in keeping with a sense of ideal form, meeting the playwright on his own ground of ideal imitation or aesthetic expression.

2. MACHIAVELLIAN PLAYWRIGHT IN *THE TEMPEST*

The recent critical tendency to view Prospero as a type of the playwright—a "god o' th' island" or force of providence in control of the action of *The Tempest*—is to an extent reactionary, going back to nineteenth-century readings of the play, though always with the New Critical stipulation that to identify the conjurer's art with the playwright's need not imply a biographical association with Shakespeare himself on his eve of retirement from the Jacobean stage.[7] From

7. Among recent discussions of Prospero as dramatist, see Norman Rabkin, *Shakespeare and the Common Understanding* (New York, 1967), pp. 224–26; Philip Edwards, *Shakespeare and the Confines of Art* (London, 1968), pp. 151–52; David Young, *The Heart's Forest* (New Haven, Conn., 1972), pp. 154–59, 166–67; Robert Egan, "This Rough Magic: Perspectives of Art and Morality in *The Tempest*," *Shakespeare Quarterly*, 23 (1972), 171–82; Harriet Hawkins, "Fabulous Counterfeits: Dramatic Construction and Dramatic Perspectives in *The Spanish Tragedy, A Midsummer Night's Dream* and *The Tempest*," *Shakespeare Survey*, 6 (1972), 58–59; Sidney Homan, "*The Tempest* and Shakespeare's Last Plays: The Aesthetic Dimensions," *Shakespeare Quarterly*, 24 (1973), 69–76; Robert Egan, *Drama within Drama* (New York, 1975), pp. 90–119.

his raising of the sea-storm in the opening scene to his claiming of the entire *Tempest* as his "project" in the epilogue, Prospero not only dominates the action of the play as its powerful protagonist, but also curiously stands behind the action as a supernatural source or prime mover. Dramaturgical metaphor is introduced in Prospero's first exchange with Ariel:"Hast thou, spirit, / Performed to point the tempest that I bade thee?" (1.2. 193–94). As a type of dramatist (distinct from, say, the epic poet), Prospero works his spellbinding effects through intermediaries. The metaphor of "performance" recurs in reference to Ariel's impersonation of a harpy (3.3.84) and in anticipation of the betrothal masque (4.1.36), linking the staging of the storm which gives the play its name to a specifically theatrical enterprise within the play.

More important than particular instances of theatrical metaphor, however, is the overall shape and pacing of the play. As is quickly apparent with the subjugation of Caliban and Ferdinand in Act 1, Prospero's "art" exempts him from direct confrontations with the other characters. When a threat of sorts presents itself, it comes not from the treacherous Antonio but from the ineffectual comic plotters led by Caliban and generates little anxiety as to the outcome. Prospero's omnipotence gives *The Tempest* a unique structure among Shakespeare's plays (putting it, in fact, in a class with the *Tamburlaine* plays).The story lacks plot complication; its structure is one of continual dénouement. It traces, simply, the working out of Prospero's design, beginning as a project of vengeance and shifting to one of mercy and reconciliation. The central conflict occurs not on the level of action as a struggle of antagonists, but in Prospero's conscience as a *psychomachia* of "virtue" versus presumption. In effect, the action of the play is presented as through the eyes of the author who similarly transcends all quarrel with the characters, and in whose mind the story exists prior to composition in an eternal state without differentiation of rising and falling movements, awaiting only its "unravelling" onto the page. Like Shakespeare preparing to tell his story, Prospero has only to decide which of his motives are worthy of expression, whether those of a revenge-tragedy or of a comedy of forgiveness.

Despite the conspicuous use of Prospero as an interior-playwright, the greatest concentration of theatrical imagery in the play rests with Antonio. This fact is usually interpreted blandly as suggesting that Antonio is a parody of his brother, a failed artist operating within a political sphere. But a survey of Shakespeare's use of the villain-playwright analogy in other plays indicates that theatrical metaphor is one legacy, at least, that Antonio comes by honorably, and indeed that Prospero becomes a type of the dramatist only by emulating his evil brother.

> I have bedimmed
> The noontide sun, called forth the mutinous winds,
> And 'twixt the green sea and the azured vault
> Set roaring war; to the dread rattling thunder
> Have I given fire and rifted Jove's stout oak
> With his own bolt. (5.1.41–46)

Here is Prospero as Prometheus, Prospero against the gods, plying his art in a political vacuum. Though elsewhere the conjuring of the storm offers a paradigm of dramatic art, it is evident from this passage that Prospero's conjuring is insufficient in itself to provoke comparison with playwriting. The theatrical metaphor enters the play only with his revenge-plot, his "project" of taking back his dukedom from Antonio. Prospero the dramatist is pre-eminently a Machiavel using magical rather than political science: pre-empting fortune (1.2. 178–84), commanding his spirit-armies (4.1.166–67), synchronizing strategies (5.1.1–3), a "prince of power" (1.2.55) or Machiavellian lion as never in Milan.

As Prospero becomes a political realist, his old post of academic dreamer devolves upon Antonio. Counseling Sebastian to seize the moment and murder the sleeping Alonso, Antonio fancies himself a wide-awake pragmatist; yet, disdaining to learn the laws of his new island setting, he still plots pedantically by the book as though he were back in Machiavelli's Italy. But if Antonio merely sleepwalks through his accustomed role of villain, his art as the shadow of his brother's provides an interesting commentary. The figure of a tempest is present from the beginning. Antonio remarks how Gonzalo, Alonso, and the rest have "dropped as by a thunder-stroke" (2.1.198). The "thunder-stroke," of course, is Prospero's doing, a further instance of his magic that raised the tempest in the opening scene. He plans to test Antonio to see if his brother has changed; and Antonio responds on cue by slipping into his old role of Machiavellian playwright. Like Prospero, Antonio begins to conjure his own tempest—a tempest of ambition in the "standing water" of Sebastian's brain (l. 215). "I'll teach you how to flow," he promises (l. 216), and through magic of rhetoric animates "ev'ry cubit" of water between Naples and Tunis to "cry out" his theme of murder with impunity (ll. 251–52; cf. 3.3.96–99). As a meta-phorical dramatist, he offers to "cast" Sebastian in "an act/Whereof what's past is prologue, what to come/In yours and my discharge" (ll. 245–48). At the same time he disguises his own hand; he pretends that the storm or "destiny" has recast Sebastian and himself in their new roles, as Prospero similarly lays his work of raising the tempest at the door of "Fate" or "The pow'rs" of justice (3.3.61, 73–75).

Besides designing a play around Sebastian, Antonio rehearses his pro-
tégé in the act he must perform: "Here lies your brother,/No better than
the earth he lies upon/If he were that which now he's like—that's dead"
(2.1.274—76). The directorial evocation of a climate of make-believe is
essential. Sebastian could hardly perform the act of murdering a brother
in propria persona; he must do it as in the "discharge" of a dramatic role.
Murder requires a somnambulistic detachment such as that observed in
Antonio speaking passionately out of character about Sebastian's vocation
to be king. Sebastian comments: "This is a strange repose, to be asleep/
With eyes wide open; standing, speaking, moving,/And yet so fast asleep"
(ll. 207–09). A similar "strange repose" descends in the central dream section of *A Midsummer Night's Dream* as the four lovers rise out of sleep
and bemusedly exchange roles of suitor and pursued. In *The Tempest*,
however, the main metaphors for the agent-actor's somnambulism are
magical possession and "new-creating," both emphasizing the agency
of the villain-playwright in the actor's identity-loss or transformation.
Through rhetorical persuasion Antonio "wake[s]" (l. 254) in his companion an ambition foreign to Sebastian's "Hereditary sloth." "O, that you
bore/The mind that I do!" (ll. 217, 260–61), he declares insidiously, and
proceeds to effect the transfer, instilling a portion of his own mind, his
murderous will, into Sebastian's body. The result is a new double-natured
being, an ontological chimera, part actor and part dramatic role.

Antonio's imposition upon Sebastian is further defined in a veiled
self disclosure. He proposes to kill Alonso and Gonzalo, making Sebastian king and replacing Gonzalo in his role of councilor with another
lord of his own choosing:

> There be that can rule Naples
> As well as he that sleeps; lords that can prate
> As amply and unnecessarily
> As this Gonzalo; I myself could make
> A chough of as deep chat. (ll. 256–60)

Antonio is a mimetic extremist who believes optimistically that art
can permanently replace nature. With a new lord performing Gonzalo's
nebulous functions and Sebastian himself to stand in for Alonso,
there will be no further need for the original models; and imitation
Gonzalos are as easily come by as birds to mimic human speech. He
presents himself as a case of an actor who has successfully lived a lie by
replacing his original:

SEBASTIAN   I remember
      You did supplant your brother Prospero.
ANTONIO   True.

And look how well my garments sit upon me,
Much feater than before. (ll. 264–67)

But Prospero, discussing Antonio's histrionic ambition "To have no
screen between this part he played/And him he played it for" (1.2.
107–08), indicates that there have been subtle problems of which Antonio is unaware. When Antonio usurped Prospero, he estranged himself from his identity as an actor lost in a dramatic role and entered a
state of mad delusion:

> like one ...
> Who having unto truth, by telling of it,
> Made such a sinner of his memory
> To credit his own lie, he did believe
> He was indeed the Duke (1.2.99–103)

Thus when Antonio corrupts Sebastian he proposes a double crime:
the murders of Alonso and Gonzalo, and a subtler crime against the
actors who will impersonate them, a crime of putting words—a script
or speech—into the chough's mouth. Sebastian, although he doesn't
realize it, is the chough. Prepared to discharge a role invented by
Antonio, he is in danger of becoming a puppet or chimera, a mixed
creation of God and man. Though Antonio flatters him, his case is
identical to the other members of the court party who, Antonio
boasts, will "take suggestion as a cat laps milk" and "tell the clock to
any business that/We say befits the hour" (2.1.282–84).

Antonio's art of transforming character hypnotically is described
as "new-creating," a term which suggests a parody of divine art.
Prospero's brother, as regent,

> new-created ...
> The creatures that were mine ... or changed 'em,
> Or else new-formed 'em; having both the key
> Of officer and office, set all hearts i' th' state
> To what tune pleased his ear, that now he was
> The ivy which had hid my princely trunk
> And sucked my verdure out on't. (1.2.81–87)

More than royal deputizing, "new-creating" alters the structure of
personality Antonio's followers, their hearts "set" and spirits leaping
"To that tune pleased his ear" (music, as elsewhere in the play, causes
fascination), are possessed as by a sorcerer: "They'll take suggestion
as a cat laps milk." But Antonio, so to speak, has *men* lapping milk.
The talking chough, the yes-men telling the hours of Antonio's clock,
are transformed into "new creatures" through the incorporation of

an alien will. Though they may grow into or excel in their roles as Antonio himself has done, they do so at the cost of what Antipholus of Syracuse called their souls' pure truths.

Ironically, the chief creator of chimeras in the play is Prospero, who recounts how he "Awaked an evil nature" in Antonio (as Antonio in turn will "wake" ambition in Sebastian) by "cast[ing]" on his brother's shoulders the responsibilities of government (1.2.93, 75). The figure of the oak and ivy cuts two ways. It is meant to emphasize Antonio's greed: Prospero's ducal strength was sapped by his parasitic brother. But also the oak and ivy may be seen as a composite or symbiotic life-form, the genetic model of the subsequent chimeras in the play. Antonio battening on Prospero's authority new-created the creatures of state with his powers derived as regent; but Antonio's own self-divided parasitic nature owes his corruption by Prospero who selfishly created his brother in the royal image in order to retire to the "dukedom" of his library.[8] Thus, the chimerical oak-and-ivy team of himself and his brother nurtured by Prospero affords both occasion and model for Antonio's villainy of new creating his fellow creatures. When Antonio manipulates Sebastian, pretending to adorn his friend in a plan of action while secretly feeding on his will, he is merely reviving a role taught him by his accuser.

As the play opens, Prospero's social conscience has awakened considerably, and though still unprepared to acknowledge his guilt in corrupting Antonio, he has abandoned his cloistered vocation of student to become a "schoolmaster" on the island (1.2.172)—not only to Miranda. His profession is the cure of souls, the nurturing of nature. Ferdinand will honor him as a "second father" from whom he has received a "second life" (5.1.195). Prospero's regenerative art is new-creating with a difference, a sublime transformation of the careless art which led him once to spoil his brother as a parent, after the initial procreative act, "beget[s]" corruption in a child through permissive rearing (1.2.94). Where Antonio is a puppet-master, anaesthetizing the soul and possessing the body, Prospero wakens consciences, giving back "all of us ourselves," as Gonzalo says, "When no man was his own" (5.1.212-13). Particularly with Alonso, his most successful patient, Prospero attempts to rouse the soul from its torpor of empty roleplay by jogging the actor's "sinful" memory: "remember," proclaims Ariel the harpy on Prospero's instructions, "(For that's my business to you)" (3.3.68-69). He creates the soul anew by reminding it of

8. Prospero's guilt is stressed by Harry Berger Jr., "Miraculous Harp: A Reading of Shakespeare's *Tempest*," *Shakespeare Survey*, 5 (1969), 253–83.

what is divine in itself, the "deity in [the] bosom" that Antonio seeks to deny (2.1.272).[9]

On the basis of their different styles of new-creating, an ethical distinction may be drawn between Prospero's and Antonio's Machiavellian arts. Prospero as an avenger imitates his plotting brother by exerting an absolute control over actions and events, but he draws the line at new-creating in Antonio's sense; in respect for the integrity of his subjects' wills, he indulges in only the most restrained rolecasting. He brings Miranda and Ferdinand together hoping they will fall in love, but as he must he lets a natural magic breed between them.[10] He punishes Caliban, threatens Ariel, leaves Alonso to his regenerative suffering; he tests, cajoles devises therapeutic ordeals—but he disdains to operate by "suggestion" as Antonio does; refuses to make chimeras of his fellow creatures by subliminally imposing roles upon them. The first principle of Prospero's political art, derived in reaction to his unscrupulous brother, is simply, "they shall be themselves" (5.1.32): they shall be as God created them and not made mechanical travesties of human beings. The transfiguration of nature effected by Antonio trenches perilously on the divine power of creation and must be forsworn. Indeed, so strong an article of faith is this with Prospero that, reclaiming his dukedom, he neglects to guarantee his own safety by imposing a lasting virtue on Antonio by magical means, because grace at a brother's hands would be a supererogation.

The difference in Prospero's and Antonio's politics corresponds to two distinct views of the purposes and limitations of dramatic art. Antonio is an extremist who audaciously assumes he can make a permanent "sinner" of his own and other's memories, supplanting nature by substituting a theatrical counterfeit for the rightful government of Milan. Consonant with his deception of the people (analogous to a theatre audience) is Antonio's high-handed treatment of his agents like Sebastian whom he seduces to the performance of self-alienating

9. The association of conscience with a moral dimension of memory is broadly based in the Renaissance with roots in the Platonic doctrine of *anamnesis* and the meditative tradition of *memento mori*. In the *Consolation of Philosophy*, Lady Philosophy repeatedly instructs Boethius to remember his way back to spiritual health (prose *2, 5, 6, et passim*). In Sidney's *The New Arcadia*, Book 1, ch. 12, Musidorus offers similar advice to his afflicted friend Pyrocles. In *Christian Morals*, sec. 12, Sir Thomas Browne designates conscience "the punctual Memorist within us."
10. Because Miranda and Ferdinand are "both in either's pow'rs" (1.2.451), Prospero's role in the love-plot is reduced from playwright to prompter (l. 421). Each lover is at first awestruck spectator to the *tableau vivant* of the beloved's beauty (ll. 409-10). But Prospero resumes his dramaturgical function by devising a hostile "entertainment" for Ferdinand (l. 466). Impersonating an irascible *senex*, he casts their romance in the traditional mold of New Comedy.

roles. Prospero's own politics is both higher-minded in its ends and more modest in its means. He might be described as a mimetic idealist seeking to reveal the divine perfection in nature from which it has fallen; thus, as a casting director, he attempts the liberation, rather than exploitation, of his actors through the vehicle of his dramatic plot. Yet it is hard to imagine a practical dramatic enterprise going forward under Prospero's commitment to absolute truth and the free expression of his performers' personalities. Every script involves a selective distortion of reality and every dramatic performance requires the subordination of a group of players willing to sacrifice their personal preoccupations to the fulfillment of a group ideal. Art and morality in the play are antinomian interests, and Prospero's high moral instincts lead not to drama like *The Tempest* but to the palinode of the epilogue.

3. AESTHETIC CRIME IN *THE TEMPEST*

Rarely is it possible to glean from a Shakespearean epilogue a metaphor defining the transaction that takes place between the author and the audience. The epilogue's normal function is to establish, in terms of the thematics of a given play, a relationship between the audience and the actors; the spectator is asked to justify an individual performer who steps forward as spokesman for the whole cast (e.g., Puck as representative of "we shadows"). In *The Tempest,* however, the audience is invited to make a leap of imagination and sympathy on the playwright's behalf. As Prospero throughout the play plotted the action and supervised the other actors' movements, so in the epilogue the actor playing Prospero identifies himself not with the acting troupe but with the dramatist, taking full responsibility for the play (referred to as "*my* project") in both its conception and execution. This identification affords a unique critical opportunity to "get outside" the drama (as the epilogue is outside the play) while still within the precincts of its five acts and, by interpreting metaphorically the unfolding theme of Prospero's conversion from a project of vengeance to one of virtue (a theme that gives rise to the judgment-mercy motif in the epilogue), to survey the entire theatrical enterprise from an authorial standpoint.

The epilogue fulfills Prospero's promise to Alonso in his final speech of Act 5 to provide "calm seas, auspicious gales,/And sails so expeditious that shall catch/Your royal fleet far off." Though the former magician disarmingly protests that he comes before the audience with "charms . . . o'erthrown," he still possesses a single rhetorical trick through which he conjures us to make good his promise: "Gentle breath of yours my sails/Must fill, or else my project fails,/Which was to please." The spectator is able to write a happy ending to the story by sending the "confined" Prospero back to Naples in imagination. As the new playwrights or apprentice magicians to whom he turns over his powers, we are induced to perform the magical trick of making Prospero vanish from the stage with a clap of the hands. According to the conventions of the Shakespearean epilogue, Prospero conjures applause by insisting on the worthiness of his intentions. If his "project" of producing the play failed in its objective "Which was to please," yet it is deserving of applause, and he of "pardon," by the same standard that the spectator, appearing someday before a court of judgment as he stands now, would hope to see applied to himself. As we would desire a judgment tempered with mercy, so we must excuse the shortcomings of the play, rewarding good faith, at least, if not good works. As we "from crimes would pardoned be," we must pardon, or pray for Prospero's pardon, by bringing hands together in a gesture that is at once the classical attitude of prayer and the traditional sign of critical approval.

The crime confessed by Prospero on the author's behalf may be detected analogically. In the story Prospero's "project" of providing fair winds for the homeward journey supersedes his initial project of revenge inaugurated, symmetrically, by his raising of the ill winds that shipwrecked his enemies. On another level, however, Prospero's project as sponsor of the dramatic action has been to please the audience; his main commitment is not to fictional characters like Antonio, but to his fellow beings whom the actor, half out of character in the epilogue, addresses directly. Now, as the fictional Prospero's project has been, at different times, both vengeful and benign, so the playwright's project is ambivalent—and indeed, the use of the word "project," hitherto reserved for political intrigues (2.1.293; 4.1.175; 5.1.1), suggests a hidden crime confessed in the eleventh hour lest judgment fall too heavily after the play is over.

Prospero's crime in the story is clearly defined. As if faultless, he righteously sought to punish his enemies, usurping the divine prerogative of vengeance. But Prospero, too, has been a sinner, as he discovers, and is obliged to leave vengeance to the Lord. His sin was a self-indulgent evasion of royal responsibilities; creating Antonio regent, he awoke an evil nature in his brother which precipitated a wave of corruption in the state. Therefore, as Prospero is in a weak moral position to extract revenge, he must forgive his enemies. And similarly as we have sinned in our private lives—"As you from crimes would pardoned be"—we are bid to follow his example and forgive the playwright. An explicit proportion is set up:

> Let me not,
> Since I have my dukedom got,
> And pardoned the deceiver, dwell
> In this bare island by your spell ...

As Prospero pardoned "the deceiver" Antonio, so the audience may pardon a deceiving magician who now lacks "art to enchant." But the epithet "deceiver" continues to resonate in ways that implicate the dramatist. Antonio the deceiver is to Prospero the deceived duke who managed to regain his power and sit in judgment on his enemies as the deceiving playwright is to a deceived audience who, at the end of the play, will likewise pass judgment and could conceivably wreak vengeance by refusing to applaud. For two hours Shakespeare has unseated our collective reason with the spell of his enchantments, but in the epilogue we are like Prospero's "spell-stopped" antagonists (5.1.61), of whom the magician says:

> Their understanding
> Begins to swell, and the approaching tide
> Will shortly fill the reasonable shore,
> That now lies foul and muddy. (5.1.79-82)

As *The Tempest* subsides at last in the epilogue, the spectator is restored to an awareness of his own being which, from a point of the "soul's pure truth," has been in sorry state since it began to be played upon by the dramatist. Therefore, as if admitting an agressive act, the author throws himself on our mercy, recalling that his deception has been in the service of a benign plot, a pious fraud, perpetrated solely "to please."

The concept of aesthetic crime occurs in another of Shakespeare's romances, *The Winter's Tale,* where Hermione's revival may be regarded as a hoax or conspiracy which the actors, the playwright, the director have all been "in on" from the beginning. Though we participate delightedly in the "notable passion of wonder" advertised throughout the final act, we realize too that the ending is fanciful and that, in a deeper sense, we have been "mocked with art" (5.3.68). Shakespeare gives the game away in the opening scene in the dialogue between the courtiers Camillo and Archidamus. Speaking of an "entertainment" to come, Archidamus delivers a speech that would have been recognizable moments earlier as a standard presenter's apology: "Wherein our entertainment shall shame us, we will be justified in our loves" (1.1.8-9). Camillo protests; no excuses are necessary. And Archidamus rallies from his embarrassment with a facetious warning: "We cannot with such magnificence—in so rare—I know not what to say.

We will give you sleepy drinks, that your senses, unintelligent of our insufficience, may, though they cannot praise us, as little accuse us" (1.1.12-15). Archidamus' proposed sabotage of Camillo's critical faculties constitutes an aggression, and thus his jest takes the rhetorical form of a threat. In a darker vein Leontes will bid Camillo "bespice a cup/To give mine enemy a lasting wink" (1.2.315-16). But Shakespeare's assault on the audience through the plot of *The Winter's Tale* is benevolent, like Archidamus' proposed assault or entertainment. The play's tactic too will be one of drugging our drinks, of inducing a "lethargy" (as Autolycus says, 4.4.605), so that finally we will relish the warmed-over fairytale ending.[11]

It is possible, then, to view Shakespeare's derangement of our senses through a dramatic illusion as a "plot" to please his audience. This paradoxical view of comic entertainment is reflected in the betrothal masque where Prospero's purpose is similarly to please, to "Bestow upon the eyes" of the young lovers "Some vanity of mine art" (4.1.40-41). As discussed earlier, Prospero's esteem as a type of the playwright owes not to his conjuring *per se,* but to his emulation of Antonio whereby he enters the mainstream of a tradition of Machiavellian playwrights in Shakespearean theatre. But if the avenger Prospero is metaphorically a dramatist, then the dramatist Prospero—the producer of the betrothal masque—is metaphorically a Machiavellian tyrant. In his art of the masque he tyrannizes over his spirit-actors in the same way that Antonio, through his unprincipled art of new-creating, possesses and controls his lackeys like Sebastian. The crucial text is the brief exchange in which Ferdinand asks Prospero to explain his artistry:

FERDINAND This is a most majestic vision, and
    Harmonious charmingly. May I be bold
    To think these spirits?
PROSPERO   Spirits, which by mine art
    I have from their confines called to enact
    My present fancies.
FERDINAND   Let me live here ever!
    So rare a wond'red father and a wise
    Makes this place Paradise. (4.1.118-24)

11. Covert aggressions are similarly disclosed by the vaudeville rhetoric of "knock 'em dead" and "lay them in the aisles," where the audience is "slain" by being put to the torment of uncontrollable laughter. However spontaneous a joke may be in its conception, however dedicated to the audience's ultimate pleasure, its deliberate rehearsal suggests, from the teller's standpoint, a delicately timed plot against the listener, culminating in a "punch line" (another hostility metaphor).

Prospero's dramaturgy scarcely resembles his handling of the human characters in the story whom he immobilizes or moves strategically about the island, but never obliges to enact his commands; but his account—the second part at least—applies perfectly to Antonio, whose followers "take suggestion" automatically, rather like the pawns on Ferdinand's and Miranda's chessboard. In ruling his actors, Prospero is absolute, dictatorial; as a "potent" tyrant, he bids his henchman Ariel "bring the rabble" and "Incite them to quick motion" (4.1.34, 37, 39). If one wished to confound the realms of art and nature, it would be difficult to distinguish out of context between Prospero's iron-handed rule of spirits "to enact/My present fancies" (4.1.120-21) and Antonio's policy of setting "all hearts i' th' state/To what tune pleased his ear" (1.2.84-85).

Nevertheless, a distinction is necessary and explicit. The phrase "called from their confines" indicates an enlargement of the spirits' condition rather than a narrow exploitation. What and where their pneumatological confines are is left a mystery, but the concept is a recurrent one and evidently of some importance. Ariel, we recall, was found confined in a cloven pine and released to the relative liberty of indentureship (1.2.274-77). Prospero in the epilogue will speak of his confinement to his "bare island," the stage, unless sent back to Naples by the audience's mercy. Prospero is confined because the script has run out; the masquers, because their play has not yet begun. Confinement, then, is a metaphor describing the futility of the unemployed actor and, measured against this condition, Prospero's use of the spirits to enact his fancies is not a tyranny but an emancipation. Thus the spirits display a consternation or heavy confusion on being set free—or rather, sent back to their "confines" of being left alone. Their ostensible liberty on dismissal from the stage is, in a larger sense, the bondage spoken of in Donne's "The Ecstasy," where the soul as "a great Prince in prison lies" so long as it is locked out of its kingdom, the body. "[W]hoever gives, takes liberty," as Donne writes elsewhere, in the "Hymn to Christ, at the Author's Last Going into Germany." It is a fact of our human existence that, with Ferdinand, the freedom we seek, far short of the freedom of "mountain winds" aspired to by Ariel, is a protected freedom, a freedom-in-confinement, its locus a "Paradise" or enclosed garden. The freedom envisaged by Caliban is simply service to a kinder master; that of Ferdinand and Miranda, a lifetime of service to one another. And the freedom that actors aspire to, which playwrights grant, lies in the discharge of a given role. The appropriate political analogy is that of the benevolent despot; Prospero "uses" the spirits, true, but to their own advantage and diversion. The playwright confers on his actors a relative freedom: not the pure state envisaged by Prospero in the last word of the play—the freedom of being defunct, discharged of *all* roles—but a temporary reprieve from the confines of personality, a respite from the thralldom of forever enacting oneself in the world.

Involving both the possession and liberation of his spirit-actors, Prospero's art of the masque represents a compromise between his own and Antonio's arts of new-creating. But the compromise of art breaks down in two related ways. First, Prospero's aesthetic power is morally corruptive, leading him to play God in the real world as blithely as he controls his actors on the stage. Second, his entertainment is debilitating in its effects, as seen in Ferdinand's desire to live forever in the world of art and his "dismayed" reaction as the masque dissolves. Because Prospero is unable to sustain or bring to fruition the tantalizing dream-world he discloses (a failure which wrings from him his first admission of human "infirmity"), he incurs an obscure guilt—a guilt which, existing independent of ill intents, must be defined, as in the epilogue, precisely in terms of his will "to please." As I hope to show, a complementary relationship obtains between Prospero's moral and aesthetic crimes, the one regarded as a presumption to the divine right of judgment or vengeance, the other—the playwright's crime—regarded, curiously, as the usurpation of a divine right of mercy.

The masque occurs in a structural position corresponding to the tempest, and these two magical illusions have more in common than first meets the eye. In Act 1 the violence of Prospero's art is apparent in his attempt to mete out divine justice with his sea-storm. But self-mastery and aesthetic control quickly become evident, and in Act 4, immediately following the interval, a new paradigm of Prospero's art is unveiled. If the tempest was typically theatrical, or identified with the entire play through its title, then the masque is also typical as a fulfillment of the meaning of Prospero's name. The word "prosperous," along with "bounteous," "foison," and a host of allusions to harvest in abundance conjure a harmony antithetical to the chaos of the opening scene. Through his chief mouthpiece the goddess Ceres (played by Ariel[12]), Prospero blesses the contract of the young lovers, as the earlier wrathful Prospero (again through Ariel) "Incensed the seas and shores . . . /Against [the] peace" of his enemies (3.3.74-75). But the calm of the masque is deceptive; the tempest is soon to erupt again because of internal and external stresses. Before Ceres will agree to answer Juno's summons and pronounce blessing, she must be assured of the exclusion from the festivities of Venus and her son Cupid "Since

12. Irwin Smith, "Ariel and the Masque in *The Tempest*," *Shakespeare Quarterly*, 21 (1970), 213-22.

they did plot / The means that dusky Dis my daughter got" (4.1. 88–89). Similarly Prospero extracted from Ferdinand a vow of premarital abstinence as the condition of his prothalamic blessing conferred through the masque. But if lust and the devil may be excluded from a utopian play-world, they continue to thrive in fallen nature. They assert themselves in the person of Caliban who, like Dis, has attempted the rape of a maiden, Miranda, and whom Prospero now remembers as "A devil, a born devil, on whose nature/Nurture can never stick" (ll.188–89). Caliban's plot destroys what is left of the masque. What is repugnant to Prospero's imagination, hence suppressed in his dramatic plot, furnishes material for a "plot" against him (l. 141), Caliban's conspiracy recalling Venus' "plot" in collaboration with Dis. The sentimental idealism of the masque is a precarious tyranny that must bow in judgment to the world it has excluded.

Like Prospero, Caliban is a dealer in illusions, a dream merchant; his "project" (l. 175) of murder has been presented as a fictive "plot" or "story" from the outset (3.2.106, 145). As a villain-playwright, he casts Stephano in a role corresponding to Sebastian's and sets him on Prospero, whom he hopes to take sleeping in his cell, as Antonio plans to kill the sleeping Alonso. But if the folly of an idealizing imagination is revealed in Caliban's easy defeat, then by the same token Caliban's defeat points back to Prospero's own folly of exposing himself to conspiracy by concentrating too heavily on the masque. Moreover, the moral is reinforced insofar as Prospero's vain contentment to rule his stage recalls his ancient error of retirement to the "dukedom large enough" of his library (1.2.110), which left him easy prey to the plotting Antonio.

Thus, the pendulum swinging far in the opposite direction, Prospero returns to his vengeance with a new ferocity. His reformer's zeal enflamed by his power to create a perfect world in art, he brutally scourges the comic villains and threatens to turn his magic against his "enemies" Antonio and Alonso (4.1.262). But in this sense, subordinating his "nobler reason" to the role of avenger, he has begun to resemble what he despises. To the same degree as Antonio he has "Made such a sinner of his memory/To credit his own lie" (1.2.101–02); like Antonio he has wished away "a screen between this part he played/And him he played it for" (ll.107–08)—in Prospero's case, the God of Judgment himself. His righteous anger implicitly denies an involvement in the sinful humanity he undertakes to punish. Yet as he is forced to admit when confronted with the gentle Ariel's compassion for his former enemies, he is precisely "One of their kind" (5.1.23), most transparently so when he forgets himself in a role of power. In newfound humility Prospero realizes that his alternatives are not vengeance versus mercy as he proudly assumed, but vengeance versus the "virtue" of his own soul which he has mislaid in presuming to waver between two divine prerogatives.

As noted earlier, Prospero's decision to relent in judgment expresses itself in his relinquishing of the complementary divine power of creativity. Renouncing judgment he resolves, "My charms I'll break, their senses I'll restore,/And they shall be themselves" (5.1.31-32). This decision no longer to impose upon his antagonists recalls Prospero's freeing of the spirits and beholders from the "spell" of the masque (4.1.127) and anticipates his release of the theatre audience in the epilogue. But by Act 5 the once-clear distinction between Prospero's dramatic project to please, to improve the world in art, and his political project to revenge has been blurred. While the providential and judgmental, creative and destructive aspects of divinity are in accord, in Prospero's imperfect human nature they are hopelessly confused, so that for the artist in his mercy to deliver a reformed golden world is to presume to a godlike power of judgment insidiously reminiscent of man's aspiration to the knowledge of good and evil which caused the Fall. Thus, as Prospero at the end of Act 4 and the beginning of Act 5 prepares to mete out divine justice, Ferdinand's hyperbolic, seemingly innocuous comparison of his father-in-law with God the Father creating a new Paradise is tinged with retrospective irony.

The express purpose of the masque, which, leaving out the Caliban side of nature, reveals a dangerous presumption in its creator, is to make amends for having "too austerely punished" (4.1.1) Ferdinand by blessing his union with Miranda. In effect Prospero extends to Ferdinand the same storm-pacifying sympathy which (in his first words of the play) stilled Miranda's turbulence caused by the spectacle of the sinking ship: "Be collected./No more amazement. Tell your piteous heart/There's no harm done". (1.2.13-15). Eventually, as he is able to broaden his definition of "kind" by discovering his own human frailty, Prospero will show the same compassion to his former enemies, guaranteeing calm waters for the return voyage to Naples. Finally, in a larger framework, the actor-Prospero's (or Shakespeare's) purpose is similarly to "please" or soothe the Spectator who, in flight from the turbulence of daily life, enters the theatre to partake of the serenity of art: to see the tempest of life made orderly on the stage; and of course *The Tempest* has achieved this effect for generations of viewers; it is our adult fairytale. But in a sense Shakespeare has no more right to make such affirmations on his stage than Prospero has a right to keep Miranda forever sheltered on his island. Discord is the ground of human existence: Prospero is certified alive by Alonso on the evidence that his "pulse/ *Beats*" (5.1.113-14; italics added), a word first associated with Miranda's turmoil caused by the fright of the storm (1.2. 176). In place of a tempestuous heterogeneous reality, the playwright grants a fragile static illusion, like the improved nature of the masque where Prospero's vision of the magical harmony of the seasons depends on the elimination of the season of winter (4.1.114-15). As Bacon asserts in his *De augmentis scientiarum* (2.13), the poet offers "a more ample greatness, a more perfect order, and a more beautiful variety than it ["the spirit of man"] can anywhere (since the Fall) find in nature." Yet as Bacon well knows and reflects in his program to improve the natural sciences, although poetry "conduces . . . to magnanimity and morality," it enfeebles man in his practical struggle to survive in the material world. The "dream of learning . . . that would be thought to have in it something of the divine" *(De aug.* 3.1) confers a premature grace, a benediction of mercy that is the Lord's to bestow as properly as vengeance is his. In the epilogue of *The Tempest,* then, the moment has arrived when Shakespeare must renounce his paternalistic deception of the audience and must apologize for his aesthetic crime of presenting a pacifying illusion as substitute for a fallen world.

The issue between playwright and author is foreshadowed in Ferdinand's sad desire to remain forever sheltered in the "majestic vision" (4.1.118) of the betrothal masque. He fancies an easy escape from the stresses of fallen nature. But the world of the masque, as an insular microcosm, is contingent on the maintenance of political order on the island itself, much as Prospero's cloistered happiness in the "dukedom" of his library was dependent on his maintenance of political order in Milan. Insofar as the spectator Ferdinand retreats with the dramatist Prospero into a world of dream, they put themselves at the mercy of a hostile world, for without reference to a "present business," as Prospero tells Miranda in his lengthy narrative at the beginning of the play, "this story/Were most impertinent" (1.2.136-38).

Yet what finally mitigates Shakespeare's aesthetic crime is not his intent to please but rather his repeated efforts to induce a self-awareness in the audience to prevent a rude awakening at the end of the play. Despite its celebrated adherence to the classical unities, the action of *The Tempest* is remarkably discontinuous, lending an air of palpable fiction to the whole. Instead of evolving organically through internal laws and assumptions, the story is established precariously event by event, making constant use of "stop-action" techniques (e.g., the freezing of an armed Ferdinand, the abrupt foiling of Antonio's plot). One sudden disorientation which serves to disabuse us of the art of the theatre is the dissolution of the masque. Though Prospero has "foretold" that "These our actors . . . were all spirits," neither we nor Ferdinand were prepared for them to vanish suddenly "into thin air." But the event, when it takes place, constitutes sufficient warning to expect a similar melting of the "baseless fabric" of *The Tempest* itself (4.1.148-51). A like admonition not to put faith in a fallible artifact which, collapsing, must strand us in waking reality is the destruction of the ship—a sort of man-made floating island—in the opening scene. The *"confused"* mariners (the adjective in *s.d.* 1.1.57 recurs in the stage direction for the dissolution of the masque, *s.d.* 4.1.138) are like the spirit-actors at the moment when Prospero's lapse in concentration cuts the ground from under them. Finally, the very transition from ship to shore between the first two scenes is an exercise in disenchantment, rehearsing the spectator in the crossing he must eventually negotiate, like Ferdinand with "lusty stroke," from the concluded *Tempest* to the shore of his own identity. The viewer who sits down to a performance of the play for a first time, not knowing what to expect beyond the clue in the title, makes the usual sporting attempt to lose himself in the excitement of the opening scene; but for once the investment of imagination is misplaced. The tempest is precisely the contrived illusion it appeared to be in the first place before we consented to forget its unreality. If then, in spite of Miranda's allusion to Prospero's "art" (1.2.1) which takes us behind the scenes of the drama, we choose to immerse ourselves in a second illusion—one that will gather verisimilitude throughout the drama—at least we have been hoodwinked with eyes wide open. If there is finally a crime to repent, the audience too, as forewarned collaborators, are culpable of accepting a known fraud. Thus in the epilogue Prospero frames his prayer for playwright and audience alike:

> As you from crimes would pardoned be,
> Let your indulgence set me free.

"*The Tempest* and the Concept of the Machiavellian Playwright" first appeared in *English Literary Renaissance* 8.1 (1978): 43–66.

Caribbean and African
Appropriations of *The Tempest*

Rob Nixon

> Remember
> First to possess his books.
> —*The Tempest*

The era from the late fifties to the early seventies was marked in Africa and the Caribbean by a rush of newly articulated anticolonial sentiment that was associated with the burgeoning of both international black consciousness and more localized nationalist movements. Between 1957 and 1973 the vast majority of African and the larger Caribbean colonies won their independence; the same period witnessed the Cuban and Algerian revolutions, the latter phase of the Kenyan "Mau Mau" revolt, the Katanga crisis in the Congo, the Trinidadian Black Power uprising and, equally important for the atmosphere of militant defiance, the civil rights movement in the United States, the student revolts of 1968, and the humbling of the United States during the Vietnam War. This period was distinguished, among Caribbean and African intellectuals, by a pervasive mood of optimistic outrage. Frequently graduates of British or French universities, they were the first generation from their regions self-assured and numerous enough to call collectively for a renunciation of Western standards as the political revolts found their cultural counterparts in insurrections against the bequeathed values of the colonial powers.

In the context of such challenges to an increasingly discredited European colonialism, a series of dissenting intellectuals chose to utilize a European text as a strategy for (in George Lamming's words) getting "out from under this ancient mausoleum of [Western] historic achievement."[1] They seized upon *The Tempest* as a way of amplifying their calls for decolonization within the bounds of the dominant cultures. But at the same time these Caribbeans and Afri-

---

1. George Lamming, *The Pleasures of Exile* (New York, 1984), p. 27; all further references to this work, abbreviated *PE*, will be included in the text.

cans adopted the play as a founding text in an oppositional lineage which issued from a geopolitically and historically specific set of cultural ambitions. They perceived that the play could contribute to their self-definition during a period of great flux. So, through repeated, reinforcing, transgressive appropriations of *The Tempest,* a once silenced group generated its own tradition of "error" which in turn served as one component of the grander counterhegemonic nationalist and black internationalist endeavors of the period. Because that era of Caribbean and African history was marked by such extensive, open contestation of cultural values, the destiny of *The Tempest* at that time throws into uncommonly stark relief the status of value as an unstable social process rather than a static and, in literary terms, merely textual attribute.

Some Caribbean and African intellectuals anticipated that their efforts to unearth from *The Tempest* a suppressed narrative of their historical abuse and to extend that narrative in the direction of liberation would be interpreted as philistine. But Lamming, for one, wryly resisted being intimidated by any dominant consensus: "I shall reply that my mistake, lived and deeply felt by millions of men like me—proves the positive value of error" (*PE,* p. 13). Lamming's assertion that his unorthodoxy is collectively grounded is crucial: those who defend a text's universal value can easily discount a solitary dissenting voice as uncultured or quirky, but it is more difficult to ignore entirely a cluster of allied counterjudgments, even if the group can still be stigmatized. Either way, the notion of universal value is paradoxically predicated on a limited inclusiveness, on the assumption that certain people will fail to appreciate absolute worth. As Pierre Bourdieu, Barbara Herrnstein Smith, and Tony Bennett have all shown, a dominant class or culture's power to declare certain objects or activities self-evidently valuable is an essential measure for reproducing social differentiation.[2] But resistance to the hegemony of such hierarchies is still possible. In this context, Lamming's statement exudes the fresh confidence of the high era of decolonization, in which a "philistinism" arose that was sufficiently powerful and broadly based to generate an alternative orthodoxy responsive to indigenous interests and needs.

2. See Pierre Bourdieu and Jean-Claude Passeron, *La Reproduction: Eléments pour une théorie du système d'enseignement* (Paris, 1970), and Bourdieu, *La Distinction: Critique Sociale du jugement* (Paris, 1979); Barbara Herrnstein Smith, "Contingencies of Value," *Critical Inquiry* 10 (Sept. 1983): 1–35; Tony Bennett, *Formalism and Marxism* (London, 1979), "*Formalism and Marxism* Revisited," *Southern Review* 16 (1982): 3–21, and "Really Useless 'Knowledge': A Political Critique of Aesthetics," *Thesis* 11 12 (1985): 28–52.

For Frantz Fanon, decolonization was the period when the peoples of the oppressed regions, force-fed for so long on foreign values, could stomach them no longer: "In the colonial context the settler only ends his work of breaking in the native when the latter admits loudly and intelligibly the supremacy of the white man's values. In the period of decolonization, the colonized masses mock at these very values, insult them, and vomit them up."[3] From the late fifties onward, there was a growing resistance in African and Caribbean colonies to remote-controlled anything, from administrative structures to school curricula, and the phase of "nauseating mimicry" (in Fanon's phrase) gave way to a phase in which colonized cultures sought to define their own cultures reactively and aggressively from within.[4] In short, decolonization was the period when "the machine [went] into reverse."[5] This about-face entailed that indigenous cultural forms be substituted for alien ones—inevitably a hybrid process of retrieving suppressed traditions and inventing new ones. Both approaches were present in the newfound preoccupation with *The Tempest*: hints of New World culture arid history were dragged to the surface, while at other moments the play was unabashedly refashioned to meet contemporary political and cultural needs.[6]

Given the forcefulness of the reaction against the values of the colonial powers, it may appear incongruous that Caribbean and African intellectuals should have integrated a canonical European text like *The Tempest* into their struggle; it made for, in Roberto Fernández

3. Frantz Fanon, *The Wretched of the Earth,* trans. Constance Farrington (New York, 1968), p. 43.   4. Jean-Paul Sartre, preface, ibid., p. 9.   5. Ibid., p. 16.
6. Shakespeare's debt to the Bermuda pamphlets and other Elizabethan accounts of the New World has been extensively analyzed, often in relation to the evolution of British colonial discourse in the seventeenth century. See especially Frank Kenmode, introduction to *The Tempest* (New York, 1954), pp. xxv-xxxiv; Stephen J. Greenblatt, "Learning to Curse: Aspects of Linguistic Colonialism in the Sixteenth Century," in *First Images of America: The Impact of the New World on the Old,* ed. Fredi Chiappelli, 2 vols. (Berkeley and Los Angeles, 1976), 2:561-80; Leslie A. Fiedler, "The New World Savage as Stranger: Or, 'Tis new to thee,'" *The Stranger in Shakespeare* (New. York, 1972), pp. 199-253; Peter Hulme, "Hurricanes in the Caribbees: The Constitution of the Discourse of English Colonialism," in *1642: Literature and Power in the Seventeenth Century: Proceedings of the Essex Conference on the Sociology of Literature, July 1980,* ed. Francis Barker et al. (Colchester, 1981), pp. 55-83; Barker and Hulme, "Nymphs and Reapers Heavily Vanish: The Discursive Con-texts of *The Tempest,*" in *Alternative Shakespeares,* ed. John Drakakis (London, 1985), pp. 191-205; and Paul Brown, " 'This thing of darkness I acknowledge mine': *The Tempest* and the Discourse of Colonialism," in *Political Shakespeare: New Essays in Cultural Materialism,* ed. Jonathan Dollimore and Alan Sinfield (Ithaca, N.Y., 1985), pp. 48-71.

Retamar's words, "an alien elaboration."[7] And this response may seem doubly incongruous given Shakespeare's distinctive position as a measure of the relative achievements of European and non-European civilizations. In discussions of value, Shakespeare is, of course, invariably treated as a special case, having come to serve as something like the gold standard of literature. For the English he is as much an institution and an industry as a corpus of texts: a touchstone of national identity, a lure for tourists, an exportable commodity, and one of the securest forms of cultural capital around. But the weight of Shakespeare's ascribed authority was felt differently in the colonies. What for the English and, more generally, Europeans, could be a source of pride and a confirmation of their civilization, for colonial subjects often became a chastening yardstick of their "backwardness." The exhortation to master Shakespeare was instrumental in showing up non-European "inferiority," for theirs would be the flawed mastery of those culturally remote from Shakespeare's stock. A schooled resemblance could become the basis for a more precise discrimination, for, to recall Homi Bhabha's analysis of mimicry in colonial discourse, "to be Anglicized is *emphatically* not to be English."[8] And so, in colonial circumstances, the bard could become symptomatic and symbolic of the education of Africans and Caribbeans into a passive, subservient relationship to dominant colonial culture.

One aspect of this passive orientation toward Europe is touched on by Lamming, the Barbadian novelist who was to appropriate *The Tempest* so actively for his own ends. Discussing his schooling during the early 1940s, Lamming recalls how the teacher "followed the curriculum as it was. He did what he had to do: Jane Austen, some Shakespeare, Wells's novel *Kipps,* and so on. What happened was that they were teaching exactly whatever the Cambridge Syndicate demanded. That was the point of it. These things were directly connected. Papers were set in Cambridge and our answers were sent back there to be corrected. We had to wait three to four months. Nobody knew what was happening till they were returned."[9] Given

7. Roberto Fernández Retamar, "Caliban: Notes Toward a Discussion of Culture in Our America," trans. Lynn Garafola, David Arthur McMurray, and Robert Marquez, *Massachusetts Review* 15 (Winter/Spring 1974): 27; all further references to this work, abbreviated "C," will be included in the text. 8. Homi Bhabha, "Of Mimicry and Man: The Ambivalence of Colonial Discourse," *October* 28 (Spring 1984): 128. 9. Ian Munro and Reinhard Sander, eds., *Kas-Kas: Interviews with Three Caribbean Writers in Texas: George Lamming, C. L. R. James, Wilson Harris* (Austin, Tex., 1972), p. 6. For kindred treatments of the way British-centered curricula generated mimicry and cultural dependency in the former British West Indies, see Austin Clarke, *Growing Up Stupid Under the Union Jack: A Memoir* (Toronto, 1980), and Chris Searle, *The Forsaken Lover: White Words and Black People* (London, 1972).

the resistance during decolonization to this kind of cultural dependency, those writers who took up *The Tempest* from the standpoint of the colonial subject did so in a manner that was fraught with complexity. On the one hand, they hailed Caliban and identified themselves with him; on the other, they were intolerant of received colonial definitions of Shakespeare's value. They found the European play compelling but insisted on engaging with it on their own terms.

The newfound interest in *The Tempest* during decolonization was, in items of the play's history, unprecedentedly sudden and concentrated. However, in the late nineteenth and early twentieth century, *The Tempest's* value had been augmented by a prevalent perception of it as a likely vehicle first for Social Darwinian and later for imperial ideas. This tendency, which Trevor Griffiths has thoroughly documented, was evident in both performances and critical responses to the play.[10] A notable instance was *Caliban: The Missing Link* (1873), wherein Daniel Wilson contended that Shakespeare had preempted some of Darwin's best insights by creating "a novel anthropoid of a high type."[11] Amassing evidence from the play, Wilson deduced that Caliban would have been black, had prognathous jaws, and manifested a low stage of cultural advancement. Wilson's text shuttles between *The Tempest,* Darwin, and Linnaeus and is interlarded with detailed brain measurements of gibbons, baboons, chimpanzees, and a range of ethnic groupings.

Ironically, it was Beerbohm Tree's unabashedly jingoistic production of *The Tempest* in 1904 that elicited the first recorded response to the play in anti-imperial terms, as one member of the audience assimilated the action to events surrounding the Matabele uprising in Rhodesia:

> When the man-monster, brutalised by long continued torture, begins, 'This island's mine, by Sycorax my mother, which thou takest from me', we have the whole case of the aboriginal against

---

10. Trevor R. Griffiths, " 'This Island's Mine': Caliban and Colonialism," *Yearbook of English Studies* 13 (1983): 159–80. Although Griffiths does not tackle the question of value directly, his essay complements mine insofar as it focuses on how *The Tempest* was appropriated not in the colonies but in Britain. Griffiths' analysis treats both the heyday of imperialism and the subsequent retreat from empire. For discussion of how *The Tempest* was taken up from the seventeenth century onward, see Ruby Cohn, *Modern Shakespeare Offshoots* (Princeton, N.J., 1976), pp. 267–309. Cohn's account of the two adaptations of the play by the nineteenth-century French historian and philosopher Ernest Renan is especially comprehensive. 11. Daniel Wilson, *Caliban: The Missing Link* (London, 1873), p. 79.

aggressive civilisation dramatised before us. I confess I felt a sting of conscience—vicariously suffered for my Rhodesian friends, notably Dr. Jameson—when Caliban proceeded to unfold a similar case to that of the Matebele. It might have been the double of old King Lobengula rehearsing the blandishments which led to his doom: "When thou camest first/Thou strok'dst me, and mad'st much of me; would'st give me"—all that was promised by the Chartered Company to secure the charter.[12]

Just as the Matabele uprising was a distant, premonitory sign of the anticolonial struggles to come, so, too, W. T. Stead's unorthodox response to *The Tempest* anticipated a time when the play would be widely mobilized and esteemed as an expression of "the whole case of the 'aboriginal' against aggressive civilisation."

But it was another forty-four years before any text provided a sustained reassessment of *The Tempest* in light of the immediate circumstances leading up to decolonization. That text was *Psychologie de la colonisation,* written by the French social scientist, Octave Mannoni. However much Third World intellectuals have subsequently quarreled with his manner of mobilizing the play, Mannoni's inaugural gesture helped to shape the trajectory of those associated appropriations which lay ahead and, concomitantly, to bring about the reestimation of *The Tempest* in Africa and the Caribbean. Mannoni's novel response enabled him to evolve a theory of colonialism with Prospero and Caliban as prototypes; conversely, his hypotheses about colonial relations, arising from his experiences in Madagascar, made it possible for him to rethink the play. This reciprocal process was not gratuitous but prompted by an early stirring of African nationalism: Mannoni is insistent that his theory only fell into place through his exposure to one of the twilight moments of French colonialism—the Madagascan uprising of 1947-48 in which sixty thousand Madagascans, one thousand colonial soldiers, and several hundred settlers were killed. In 1947 his ideas began to take shape, and, by the time the revolt had been suppressed a year later, the manuscript was complete. The occasional character of *Psychologie de la colonisation* is foregrounded in the introduction, which Mannoni closes by marking the coincidence of his ideas with "a certain moment in history, a crisis in the evolution of politics when many things that had been hidden were brought into the light of day; but it was only a moment, and time will soon have

---

12. W. T. Stead, "First Impressions of the Theatre," *Review of Reviews* 30 (Oct. 1904); quoted in Griffiths, " 'This Island's Mine,'" p. 170.

passed it by."[13] The pressing horrors of the Madagascan crisis prompted Mannoni to find a new significance for *The Tempest,* encouraging him to weave a reading of Shakespeare's poetic drama through his reading of the incipient drama of decolonization.

Mannoni's account of the psychological climate of colonialism is advanced through an opposition between the Prospero (or inferiority) complex and the Caliban (or dependence) complex. On this view, Europeans in Madagascar typically displayed the need, common among people from a competitive society, to feel highly regarded by others. However, the Prospero-type is not just any white man, but specifically the sort whose "grave lack of sociability combined with a pathological urge to dominate" drives him to seek out uncompetitive situations where, among a subservient people, his power is amplified and his least skills assume the aspect of superior magic (*PC,* p. 102). Whether a French settler in Africa or Shakespeare's duke, he is loath to depart his adopted island, knowing full well that back home his standing will shrink to mundane dimensions. Mannoni found the Madagascans, on the other hand, to be marked by a Caliban complex, a dependence on authority purportedly characteristic of a people forced out of a secure "tribal" society and into the less stable, competitively edged hierarchies of a semi-Westernized existence. According to this theory, colonialism introduced a situation where the Madagascan was exposed for the first time to the notion and possibility of abandonment. Crucially, the colonist failed to comprehend the Madagascan's capacity to feel "neither inferior nor superior but yet wholly dependent," an unthinkable state of mind for someone from a competitive society (*PC,* p. 157). So, in Mannoni's terms, the Madagascan revolt was fueled less by a desire to sunder an oppressive master-servant bond than by the people's resentment of the colonizers' failure to uphold that bond more rigorously and provide them with the security they craved. What the colonial subjects sought was the paradoxical freedom of secure dependence rather than any autonomous, self-determining freedom. This assumption clearly shaped Mannoni's skepticism about the Madagascans' desire, let alone their capacity, to achieve national independence.

Mannoni values *The Tempest* most highly for what he takes to be Shakespeare's dramatization of two cultures' mutual sense of a trust betrayed: Prospero is a fickle dissembler, Caliban an ingrate. The nodal

13. [Dominique] O. Mannoni, *Prospero and Caliban: The Psychology of Colonization,* trans. Pamela Powesland (New York, 1964), p. 34; all further references to this work, abbreviated *PC,* will be included in the text. The centrality of *The Tempest* to Mannoni's theory was given added emphasis by the extended title of the English translation.

lines here, and those that draw Mannoni's densest commentary, are spoken by Caliban in the play's second scene. They should be quoted at length; for they are taken up repeatedly by subsequent Caribbean and African appropriators of *The Tempest*.

> When thou cam'st first,
> Thou strok'st me, and made much of me, wouldst give me
> Water with berries in't, and teach me how
> To name the bigger light, and how the less,
> That burn by day and night, and then I lov'd thee
> And show'd thee all the qualities o' th' isle,
> The fresh springs, brine-pits, barren place and fertile:
> Curs'd be I that did so! All the charms
> Of Sycorax, toads, beetles, bats, light on you!
> For I am all the subjects that you have,
> Which first was mine own king; and here you sty me
> In this hard rock, whiles you do keep from me
> The rest o' th' island.[14]

To Mannoni, it appears evident that "Caliban does not complain of being exploited; he complains of being betrayed." He "has fallen prey to the resentment which succeeds the breakdown of dependence" (*PC*, p. 106). This view is buttressed by an analogous interpretation of Caliban's revolt in league with Trinculo as an action launched "not to win his freedom, for he could not support freedom, but to have a new master whose 'foot-licker' he can become. He is delighted at the prospect. It would be hard to find a better example of the dependence complex in its pure state" (*PC*, pp. 106-7).

Such statements rankled badly with Caribbean and African intellectuals who, in the fifties, for the first time sensed the imminence of large-scale decolonization in their regions. In such circumstances, the insinuation that Caliban was incapable of surviving on his own and did not even aspire to such independence in the first place caused considerable affront and helped spur Third Worlders to mount adversarial interpretations of the play which rehabilitated Caliban into a heroic figure, inspired by noble rage to oust the interloping Prospero from his island. Fanon and Aimé Césaire, two of Mannoni's most vehement critics, found the "ethnopsychologist's" disregard for economic exploitation especially jarring and accused him of reducing colonialism to an encounter between two psychological types with complementary predispositions who, for a time

---

14. William Shakespeare, *The Tempest,* act 1, sc. 2, ll. 332-44; all further references to the play will be included in the text.

at least, find their needs dovetailing tidily.[15] *Psychologie de la colonisa-tion,* these critics charged, made Caliban out to be an eager partner in his own colonization. Mannoni, in a statement like "wherever Europeans have founded colonies of the type we are considering, it can safely be said that their coming was unconsciously expected—even desired—by the future subject peoples," seemed to discount any possibility of Europe being culpable for the exploitation of the colonies (*PC,* p. 86). Mannoni's critics foresaw, moreover, just how readily his paradigm could be harnessed by Europeans seeking to thwart the efforts for self-determination that were gathering impetus in the fifties.

Fanon and Césaire's fears about the implications of Mannoni's thesis were vindicated by the appearance in 1962 of *Prospero's Magic: Some Thoughts on Class and Race* by Philip Mason, an English colonial who sought to give credence to Mannoni's ideas by using them to rationalize resistance to colonialism in Kenya ("Mau Mau"), India, and Southern Rhodesia. The upshot of this effort was Mason's conclusion that "a colonial rebellion may be a protest not against repression but against progress, not against the firm hand but against its withdrawal" and that (for such is every "tribal" society's craving for firm authority) "countries newly released from colonialism... [will experience] a reduction of personal freedom."[16]

Prospero's Magic is an intensely autobiographical and occasional work. Its author, in siding with Mannoni, was also seeking to counteract the first fully fledged Caribbean appropriation of *The Tempest,* Lamming's recently published *Pleasures of Exile* (1960). The lectures comprising *Prospero's Magic* were delivered at the University College of the West Indies on the eve of Jamaica's independence and are based on Mason's more than twenty years as a colonial employee in India, Nigeria, and Rhodesia, where he witnessed the death throes—or as he terms it, the fulfillment—of British imperialism. Rereading *The Tempest* in the political atmosphere of 1962, he was discomfited by his recognition of the Prospero in himself. Circumstances had altered: "While many of us today find we dislike in Prospero things we dislike in ourselves, our fathers admired him without question and so indeed

15. See Fanon, *Peau noire, masques blancs* (Paris, 1952), and Aimé Césaire, *Discours sur le colonialisme,* 3d ed. (Paris, 1955). See also the section, "Caliban on the Couch," in O. Onoge, "Revolutionary Imperatives in African Sociology," in *African Social Studies: A Radical Reader,* ed. Peter C. W. Gutkind and Peter Waterman (New York, 1977), pp. 32–43. **16.** Philip Mason, *Prospero's Magic: Some Thoughts on Class and Race* (London, 1962), p. 80; all further references to this work, abbreviated *PM,* will be included in the text.

did my generation until lately" (*PM*, p. 92).[17] Mason tried to square his awareness that colonialism was becoming increasingly discredited with his personal need to salvage some value and self-respect from his decades of colonial "service." So he was at once a member of the first generation to acknowledge distaste for Prospero and personally taken aback by his own sudden redundancy: "With what deep reluctance does the true Prospero put aside his book and staff, the magic of power and office, and go to live in Cheltenham!" (*PM*, p. 96). Mason, for one, conceived of himself as writing at the very moment when the colonial master was called upon to break and bury his staff.

By the time Caribbeans and Africans took up *The Tempest*, that is, from 1959 onward, widespread national liberation seemed not only feasible but imminent, and the play was mobilized in defense of Caliban's right to the land and to cultural autonomy. "This island's mine by Sycorax my mother/Which thou tak'st from me" (1.2.333-34) are the lines that underlie much of the work that was produced by African and Caribbean intellectuals in the 1960s and early 1970s.[18] Those same two lines introduce Caliban's extended complaint (quoted at length above), the nodal speech Mannoni had cited as evidence that Shakespeare was dramatizing a relation of dependence, not one of exploitation. But, significantly, and in keeping with his very different motives for engaging with the play, Mannoni had lopped off those two lines when working the passage into his argument. On this score, Third World responses consistently broke with Mannoni Caliban, the decolonizer, was enraged not at being orphaned by colonial paternalism but at being insufficiently abandoned by it.

The first Caribbean writer to champion Caliban was Lamming. His nonfictional *Pleasures of Exile* can be read as an effort to redeem from the past, as well as to stimulate, an indigenous Antillean line of creativity to rival the European traditions which seemed bent on arrogating to themselves all notions of culture. Lamming's melange of a text—part essay on the cultural politics of relations between colonizer and colonized part autobiography, and part textual criticism of, in particular, *The Tempest* and C. L. R. James' *The Black Jacobins* (1938)—was sparked by two events, one personal, the other more

---

17. Though it is underscored by a different politics, Sartre makes a related remark in his preface to *The Wretched of the Earth:* "We in Europe too are being decolonized: that is to say that the settler which is in every one of us is being savagely rooted out" (Sartre, preface, p. 24).   **18.** For a thematic rather than a historical survey of the figure of Caliban in Third World writing, see Charlotte H. Bruner, "The Meaning of Caliban in Black Literature Today," *Comparative Literature Studies* 13 (Sept. 1976): 240-53.

broadly historical.[19] Lamming began his text in 1959, shortly after disembarking in Southampton as part of the great wave of West Indian immigrants settling in Britain in the fifties. But his circumstances differed from those of most of his compatriots, for he was immigrating as an aspirant writer. As such he was keenly aware of taking up residence in the headquarters of the English language and culture and, concomitantly, of being only ambiguously party to that language and culture, even though a dialect of English was his native tongue and even though—for such was his colonial schooling—he was more intimate with Shakespeare and the English Revolution than with the writings and history of his own region.

Lamming's reflections on the personal circumstances which occasioned *The Pleasures of Exile* are suffused with his sense of the book's historical moment. Writing on the brink of the sixties, he was highly conscious that colonial Africa and the Caribbean were entering a new phase. The political mood of the book is expectant ("Caliban's history...belongs entirely to the future" [*PE*, p. 107]), most evidently in his account of an envious visit to Ghana, the first of the newly independent African states. That trip sharpened his anguished sense of the British West Indies' failure as yet to achieve comparable autonomy. He recalls the intensity of that feeling in his introduction to the 1984 edition: "There were no independent countries in the English-speaking Caribbean when I started to write *The Pleasures of Exile* in 1959. With the old exceptions of Ethiopia and Liberia, there was only one in Black Africa, and that was Ghana. Twenty years later almost every rock and pebble in the Caribbean had acquired this status" (*PE*, p. 7). While looking ahead to Caribbean self-determination, Lamming was also writing self-consciously in the aftermath of an action one year back that had quickened nationalist ambitions throughout the area: "Fidel Castro and the Cuban revolution reordered our history...The Cuban revolution was a Caribbean response to that imperial menace which Prospero conceived as a civilising mission" (*PE*, p. 7).

Lamming's relationship to decolonization is markedly distinct from Mannoni's. The Frenchman was in Madagascar as a social scientist observing and systematizing the psychological impulses behind an incipient struggle for national autonomy, while the Barbadian's reflections on decolonization are less distanced and more personal, as he declares himself to be Caliban's heir. Lamming's and Mannoni's different tacks are most conspicuous in their treatment of Caliban's pronouncement: "You taught me language; and my profit on't/Is,

---

19. See C. L. R. James, *The Black Jacobins: Toussaint Louverture and the San Domingo Revolution* (New York, 1963).

I know how to curse" (1.2.363-64). From that quotation Mannoni launches an analysis of the role in 1947-48 of the westernized Malagasies, some of whom had become so acculturated during study abroad that they could no longer engage with their countryfellows. The cross-cultural status of yet others who were less thoroughly assimilated but had become fluent in acrimony facilitated their rise to positions of leadership in the national resistance. Lamming, by contrast, takes up Caliban's remarks on language as one who is himself a substantially Europeanized Third Worlder, a West Indian nationalist living in England, and someone reluctant to segregate his theoretical from his autobiographical insights.[20] Much of the personal urgency of Lamming's text stems from his assimilation of Caliban's linguistic predicament to his own. As a writer by vocation, he is especially alert to the way colonialism has generated linguistic discrimination, to how, as a West Indian born into English, he is branded a second-class speaker of his first language.

Though Lamming addresses the question of the unlanded Caliban who declares "This island's mine," he dwells most obsessively on the educational inheritance which he finds enunciated in the speech "You taught me language." While the nationalist struggle provides a shaping context for *The Pleasures of Exile,* Lamming's Caliban is not just any colonial subject but specifically the colonized writer-intellectual, the marginal person of letters. Lamming's root frustration is the ostensible lack of parity between the possibilities for political and for cultural freedom. Come formal independence, the people may establish their own laws and governments, but won't Caribbean writers still lag behind, permanently shackled to the colonizer's language—whether English, French, or Spanish—since it is the only one they have? "Prospero lives in the absolute certainty that Language which is his gift to Caliban is the very prison in which Caliban's achievements will be realised and restricted. Caliban can never reach perfection, not even the perfection implicit in Miranda's

---

20. Given the antipathy between Trinidadian-born V. S. Naipaul and the more radical Lamming, and given Lamming's identification with Caliban, it is probable that Naipaul had the Barbadian in mind in his fictional *A Flag on the Island,* where the narrator parodies Caribbean celebrations of Caliban by citing a local autobiography, *I Hate You: One Man's Search for Identity,* which opens: "'I am a man without identity. Hate has consumed my identity. My personality has been distorted by hate. My hymns have not been hymns of praise, but of hate. How terrible to be Caliban, you say. But I say, how tremendous. Tremendousness is therefore my unlikely subject'" (Naipaul, *A Flag on the Island* [London, 1967], p.154).

privileged ignorance" (*PE*, p. 110).[21] That is, as long as Caliban is still bound to his former master's language, he is still partly condemned to live the life of a servant.

What holds for language holds equally for culture in general. If Caliban's accent sounds sour and deformed to the British ear, so too his knowledge of British traditions—no matter how relentlessly they have been drummed into him in Barbados—will be shown up as flawed and fragmentary. Yet on this score Lamming is unevenly pessimistic, for his very appropriation of *The Tempest* testifies to his faith in the Caribbean intellectual's capacity to scale the conventional heights of British culture. Instead of deferring slavishly to a British norm, Lamming manages—with Caliban's lines at the ready—to treat that norm as a pretext for and object of abuse. To write about Shakespeare is a strategy for commanding a hearing in the West, but he values this audibility primarily because it enables him to draw attention to his ostracism. He is only too aware of the implications of quoting Shakespeare to legitimate his "illegitimate" treatment of that same hallowed author:

> It is my intention to make use of *The Tempest* as a way of presenting a certain state of feeling which is the heritage of the exiled and colonial writer from the British Caribbean.
>
> Naturally, I anticipate from various quarters the obvious charge of blasphemy; yet there are occasions when blasphemy must be seen as one privilege of the excluded Caliban. [*PE*, p. 9]

Lamming seizes the outcast's prerogative to impiety in part to shake the insiders' monopoly of a text that draws and bears on Caribbean history. But this destructive impulse feeds a more positive one: the desire to mount an indigenous countertradition, with a reinterpreted Caliban from 1611 and the contemporary, about-to-be-liberated Antillean of 1959 flanking that tradition. So for all its dense, original analogies between *The Tempest* and the Caribbean of the late fifties, what is at stake in *The Pleasures of Exile* is something larger than the immediate, local value of a Shakespearean play: it is the very possibility of decolonizing the area's cultural history by replacing an imposed with an endemic line of thought and action. Within the context of this grand design, the initial gesture of annexing Shakespeare was pivotal, as it generated a Caliban who could stand as a prototype for

---

21. Cf. the remark by Chris Searle, another writer who reads Caribbean culture through the Prospero—Caliban dichotomy: "The ex-master's language ... is still the currency of communication which buys out the identity of the child as soon as he begins to acquire it (Searle, *The Forsaken Lover,* p. 29).

successive Caribbean figures in whom cultural and political activism were to cohere. Lamming's reconstructed tradition runs through Toussaint Louverture, C. L. R. James, and Fidel Castro to the author himself who, like many of his generation of West Indian writers, immigrated to England to embark on a literary career but while there also pressed for his region's independence. That these particular figures should have been selected to brace the countertradition points to Lamming's conviction that—linguistic dilemmas notwithstanding—Caribbean culture and politics had been and should ideally continue to be allies in each other's decolonization.

In spirit, Lamming's dissident reassessment of one of the high texts of European culture had been matched by the Trinidadian James' reverse angle in *The Black Jacobins* on one of the most celebrated periods of European history, the French Revolution. *The Pleasures of Exile* is designed to make these two unorthodox gestures seem of a piece, through remarks such as "[there] C. L. R. James shows us Caliban as Prospero had never known him" (*PE*, p. 119). James' Caliban is Toussaint Louverture, leader of the first successful Caribbean struggle for independence, the Haitian slave revolt of 1791-1803. As the title of his book might suggest, James was concerned to dredge up a counternarrative, from a Caribbean perspective, of events which had been submerged beneath the freight of Eurocentric history. For Lamming, James' action and others like it were essential to the establishment of a Calibanic lineage; but once established, that lineage had still to be sustained, which would require one salvaging operation after another. This apprehension was borne out when, at the time of writing *The Pleasures of Exile,* Lamming discovered that James' book, out of print for twenty years, was in danger of sinking into neglect. So he set himself the task of doing in turn for James what James had done for Louverture: keeping afloat a vital, remedial tradition that was threatening to disappear.

During the era of decolonization, negritude proved to be one of the strongest components of this remedial tradition, and it was the negritudist from Martinique, Césaire, who came to renovate *The Tempest* theatrically for black cultural ends in a manner indebted to Lamming if fiercer in its defiance. These two writers' approaches coincided most explicitly in their determination to unearth an endemic lineage of cultural-cum-political activists; it is telling that within the space of two years, each man published a book resuscitating Toussaint Louverture and celebrating his example.[22]

22. See Lamming, *The Pleasures of Exile,* and Césaire, *Toussaint Louverture: la révolution française et le problème colonial* (Paris, 1961).

Césaire's *Une Tempête* (1969) exemplifies the porous boundaries bettween European and Afro-Caribbean cultures even within the anticolonial endeavors of the period. As an influence on Césaire's response to Shakespeare, Lamming keeps company with Mannoni and the German critic, Janheinz Jahn. Mannoni had experience of French island colonies in both Africa and the Caribbean for, prior to his stint in Madagascar, he had served as an instructor in a Martinican school where Césaire had been his precocious student. More than twenty years later, in *Discours sur le colonialisme,* Césaire upbraided his former schoolmaster for not thinking through the implications of his colonial paradigm. And Césaire's subsequent, inevitably reactive adaptation of Shakespeare further demonstrated just how far he had diverged from Mannoni's motives for valuing *The Tempest.* More in keeping with the spirit of *Une Tempête* was Jahn's *Geschichte der neo-afrikanischen Literatur,* which appeared a few years before Césaire wrote his play. Jahn's pioneering study gave prominence to the Calibanesque in Mannoni and Lamming and, by designating the negritude writers (Césaire, Leopold Senghor, and Ousmane Diop) black cultural liberators à la Caliban, hinted at ideas that Césaire was to develop more amply. Notable among these was Jahn's attempt to counteract Lamming's dejected pronouncements about the confining character of Prospero's language by exhorting Caliban to free himself through cultural bilingualism—by recovering long-lost African strains and using them to offset the derivative, European components of his cultural identity. Jahn urged further that suitable elements of European culture be transformed into vehicles for black cultural values. Along these lines, negritude could be defined as "the successful revolt in which Caliban broke out of the prison of Prospero's language, by converting that language to his own needs of self-expression."[23]

Césaire has been quite explicit about his motives for reworking *The Tempest:*

> I was trying to 'de-mythify' the tale. To me Prospero is the complete totalitarian. I am always surprised when others consider him the wise man who 'forgives.' What is most obvious, even in Shakespeare's version, is the man's absolute will to power. Prospero is the man of cold reason, the man of methodical conquest—in other words, a portrait of the 'enlightened' European. And I see the whole play in such terms: the 'civilized' European world coming face to face for the first time with the world of primitivism and

23. Janheinz Jahn, *Neo-African Literature: A History of Black Writing,* trans. Oliver Coburn and Ursula Lehrburger (New York, 1969), p. 242.

magic. Let's not hide the fact that in Europe the world of reason has inevitably led to various kinds of totalitarianism...Caliban is the man who is still close to his beginnings, whose link with the natural world has not yet been broken. Caliban can still *participate* in a world of marvels, whereas his master can merely 'create' them through his acquired knowledge. At the same time, Caliban is also a rebel—the positive hero, in a Hegelian sense. The slave is always more important than his master—for it is the slave who makes history.[24]

Césaire's perception of Prospero as "the man of methodical conquest" and his insistence on the slave as the preeminent historical agent become the touchstones for his radically polarized adaptation of Shakespeare. Forgiveness and reconciliation give way to irreconcilable differences; the roles of Ferdinand and Miranda are whittled down to a minimum; and the play's colonial dimensions are writ large. Antonio and Alonso vie with Prospero for control over newly charted lands abroad, and Shakepeare's rightful Duke of Milan is delivered to the island not by the providence of a "happy storm" but through a confederacy rooted in imperial ambitions. Prospero is demythologized and rendered contemporary by making him altogether less white magical and a master of the technology of oppression; his far from inscrutable power is embodied in antiriot control gear and an arsenal. Violating rather than communing with life on the island, he is, in Caliban's phrase, the *"anti-Natur."*

Une Tempête self-consciously counterpoises the materialist Prospero with an animistic slave empowered by a culture that coexists empathetically with nature. Indeed, Caliban's culture of resistance is his sole weaponry, but it is more formidable than the shallow culture Shakespeare permits him; as Césaire plumbs the depths of the slave's African past to make him a more equal adversary.[25] Caliban's defiance is expressed most strongly through the celebration of the Yoruba gods Shango and Eshu; two of his four songs of liberation fete Shango, an African figure who has survived in Caribbean voodoo and Brazilian macumba. And in a critical irruption, Eshu scatters Prospero's carefully ordered classical masque, making the imported divinities seem precious, effete, and incongruous.

24. Césaire, quoted in S. Belhassen, "Aimé Césaire's *A Tempest*," in *Radical Perspectives in the Arts*, ed. Lee Baxandall (Harmondsworth, 1972), p. 176.   **25.** For the fullest discussion concerning Césaire's Africanizing of Shakespeare, see Thomas A. Hale, "Aimé Césaire: His Literary and Political Writings with a Bio bibliography" (Ph.D. diss., University of Rochester, 1974), and "Sur *Une tempête* d'Aimé Césaire," *Etudes Littéraires* 6 (1973): 21–34.

Césaire's Caliban also goes beyond Shakespeare's in his refusal to subscribe to the etiquette of subjugation:

CALIBAN Uhuru!
PROSPERO Qu'est-ce que tu dis?
CALIBAN Je dis Uhuru!
PROSPERO Encore une remontée de ton langage barbare.
          Je t'ai déjà dit que n'arrive pas ça. D'ailleurs, tu pourrais
          être poli, un bonjour ne te tuerait pas![26]

This opening exchange between Caliban and his colonial overlord sets the stage for Césaire's conviction that the culture of slaves need not be an enslaved culture. Here he is more optimistic than Lamming, who saw Caribbean cultures of resistance as ineluctably circumscribed by the colonizer's language; one thinks particularly of Lamming in Ghana, casting an envious eye over children chatting in their indigenous tongue, a language that "owed Prospero no debt of vocabulary" (*PE*, p. 162). Even if Césaire's Caliban cannot throw off European influences entirely, his recuperation of a residual past is sufficient to secure his relative cultural autonomy. Crucially, his first utterance is "Uhuru," the Swahili term for freedom which gained international currency through the struggles for decolonization in the late fifties and sixties. And Caliban retorts to Prospero's demand for a *bonjour* by charging that he has only been instructed in the colonial tongue so he can submit to the magisterial imperatives, and by declaring that he will no longer respond to the name Caliban, a colonial invention bound anagramatically to the degrading "cannibal. Instead, the island's captive king christens himself "X" in a Black Muslim gesture that commemorates his lost name, buried beneath layers of colonial culture. The play supposes, in sum, that Caribbean colonial subjects can best fortify their revolt by reviving, wherever possible, cultural forms dating back to before that wracking sea-change which was the Middle Passage.

Césaire's remark that the slave, as maker of history, "is always more important than his master" has both a retrospective and an anticipatory force, pointing back to Louverture, Haiti, and the only triumphant slave revolt, and forward through the present to colonialism's demise. Césaire steeps his play most explicitly in the contemporary Afro-Caribbean struggles for self-determination when he stages, via Ariel and Caliban, the debate, ubiquitous in the late fifties and sixties, between the rival strategies for liberation advanced by proponents of

---

26. Césaire, *Une Tempête: D'après "la Tempête" de Shakespeare—Adaptation pour un théâtre nègre* (Paris, 1969), p. 24.

evolutionary and revolutionary change. The mulatto Ariel shuns violence and holds that, faced with Prospero's stockpiled arsenal, they are more likely to win freedom through conciliation than refractoriness. But from Caliban's perspective Ariel is a colonial collaborator, a political and cultural sellout who, aspiring both to rid himself nonviolently of Prospero and to emulate his values, is reduced to negotiating for liberty from a position of powerlessness. The success of Caliban's uncompromising strategies is imminent at the end of the drama. When the other Europeans return to Italy, Prospero is unable to accompany them, for he is in the thrall of a psychological battle with his slave (shades of Mannoni here), shouting "Je défendrai la civilisation!" but intuiting that "le climat a changé." At the close, Caliban is chanting ecstatically, "La Liberté Ohé, La Liberté," and defying the orders of a master whose authority and sanity are teetering.[27]

Césaire, then, radically reassessed *The Tempest* in terms of the circumstances of his region, taking the action to the brink of colonialism's demise. He valued the play because he saw its potential as a vehicle for dramatizing the evolution of colonialism in his region and for sharpening the contemporary ideological alternatives open to would-be-liberated Antilleans. Césaire sought, from an openly interested standpoint, to amend the political acoustics of Shakespeare's play, to make the action resonate with the dangers of supine cultural assimilation, a concern since his student days that was accentuated during the high period of decolonization. This renovation of the play for black cultural ends was doubly impertinent: besides treating a classic sacrilegiously, it implicitly lampooned the educational practice, so pervasive in the colonies, of distributing only bowdlerized versions of Shakespeare, of watering him down "for the natives." *Une Tempête* can thus be read as parodying this habit by indicating how the bard might have looked were he indeed made fit reading for a subject people.

Césaire's play was published in 1969. The years 1968 through 1971 saw the cresting of Caribbean and African interest in *The Tempest* as a succession of essayists, novelists, poets, and dramatists sought to integrate the play into the cultural forces pitted against colonialism. During those four years, *The Tempest* was appropriated among the Caribbeans by Césaire, Fernández Retamar (twice), Lamming (in a novelistic reworking of some of the ideas first formulated in *The Pleasures of Exile*), and the Barbadian poet Edward Braithwaite. In Africa, the play was taken up during the same period by John Pepper

27. Ibid., p. 92.

Clark in Nigeria, Ngugi wa Thiong'o in Kenya, and David Wallace in Zambia.[28] Among these, Braithwaite and Fernández Retamar followed Lamming's lead, finding a topical, regional urgency for the play through articulating the Cuban revolution to Caliban's revolt. Braithwaite's poem, "Caliban," salutes the Cuban revolution against a backdrop of lamentation over the wrecked state of the Caribbean. The body of the poem, with its clipped calypso phrasing, knits together allusions to Caliban's song, "'Ban, 'Ban, Ca-Caliban," Ferdinand's speech, "Where should this music be?" and Ariel's response, "Full fadom five." But it is Caliban the slave, not the royal Alonso, who suffers a sea-change, falling "through the water's / cries / down / down / down / where the music hides / him / down / down / down / where the si- / lence lies." And he is revived not by Ariel's ethereal strains and, behind them, Prospero's white magic, but by the earthy music of the carnival and the intercession of black gods.[29]

But it was Fernández Retamar, a prominent figure in the cultural renovation of postrevolutionary Cuba, whose interest in the play was most specifically sparked by that nation's experience of decolonization. He first brought *The Tempest* glancingly to bear on the circumstances of his region in "Cuba Hasta Fidel" (1969); two years later he elaborated more fully on this correspondence. The second essay, "Caliban: Notes Towards a Discussion of Culture in Our America," at

---

28. See Fernández Retamar, "Cuba Hasta Fidel," *Bohemia* 61 (19 September 1969): 84–97, and "Caliban: Notes Toward a Discussion of Culture in Our America;" Lamming, *Water with Berries* (London, 1971); Edward Braithwaite, *Islands* (London, 1969), pp. 34–38; John Pepper Clark, "The Legacy of Caliban," *Black Orpheus* 2 (Feb. 1968): 16–39; Ngugi Wa Thiong'o, "Towards a National Culture," *Homecoming: Essays on African and Caribbean Literature, Culture, and Politics* (Westport, Conn., 1983); David Wallace, *Do You Love Me Master?* (Lusaka, 1977). In Lamming's allegorical novel, Caliban resurfaces in the form of three West Indian artists who reside in London and collectively play out the dilemmas of colonizer-colonized entanglements during the era of decolonization. Clark's reflections turn on the relation between "the colonial flag and a cosmopolitan languages. Clark both follows and reroutes Lamming's insights on this subject as, unlike his Caribbean predecessor, he approaches English from an African perspective, that is, as a second language. Ngugi's essay, published in 1972, was originally delivered at a conference in 1969. In it he assails Prospero for first dismantling Caliban's heritage and then denying that such a culture ever existed. Ngugi proceeds to sketch strategies for reaffirming the value of that damaged inheritance, notably by decolonizing language and education. Wallace's play was first performed in 1971. Regional nuances aside, *Do You Love Me Master?* is much of a piece with trends already discussed: aided by rioting prisoners, Caliban, a cursing Zambian "houseboy," drives the "bossman," Prospero, out of the country. In the final scene. Prospero's stick, more truncheon than wand, is broken, and the crowd encircles the masters shouting "Out, out!" and waves banners proclaiming freedom. The play incorporates songs in three African languages.
29. Braithwaite, "Caliban," *Islands*, p. 36.

once passionately chronicles the accumulative symbolic significance of Caliban and commemorates those whose deeds and utterances bodied forth the author's conception of the Calibanesque. This sixty-five-page exhortative history draws together many of the issues deliberated by earlier writers:

> Our symbol then is not Ariel...but rather Caliban. This is something that we, the *mestizo* inhabitants of these same isles where Caliban lived, see with particular clarity: Prospero invaded the islands, killed our ancestors, enslaved Caliban, and taught him his language to make himself understood. What else can Caliban do but use that same language—today he has no other—to curse him, to wish that the "red plague" would fall on him? I know no other metaphor more expressive of our cultural situation, of our reality. ["C," p. 24]

Fernández Retamar proceeds to list thirty-five exemplary Calibans, among, them Louverture, Castro, Césaire, and Fanon. And just as Lamming had singled out Louverture for special treatment, here José Martí, the late nineteenth-century Cuban intellectual and political activist who died in the struggle for Cuban independence, is commended at length for his fidelity to the spirit of Caliban.[30]

Fernández Retamar, as flagrantly as Lamming, makes it apparent how little interest he has in affecting any "scholarly distance" from *The Tempest*. Far from striving to efface his personality, affiliations, and the circumstances of his reading of *The Tempest,* he steeps his essay in occasion and function and speaks consistently in the first-person plural, a voice that inflects his words with a sense of collective autobiography. His interest is in the advantage to be derived from the play by a community who, from a European perspective, could possess at best an ancillary understanding of Shakespeare and, at worst, would be likely perpetrators of barbarous error.[31] Yet that very exclusion conferred on them a coherent identity: "For it is the coloniser who brings us together, who reveals the profound similarities existing above and beyond our secondary differences" ("C," p. 14). Oppositional appropriations of *The Tempest* could be enabling because "to

---

30. The strong historical presence of Martí in the essay is redoubled by Fernández Retamar's invocation, from the same era, of José Enrique Rodó's *Ariel*. Published in 1900, this Uruguayan novel was written in direct response to the 1898 American intervention in Cuba. Rodó identifies Latin America with Ariel, not Caliban.
31. The European suspicion that colonized people would treat Shakespeare with, to invoke Fernández Retamar's phrase, "presumed barbarism" was starkly evident when the Parisian critics dismissed Césaire's *Une Tempête* as a "Betrayal" of the Bard. See Hale, "Sur *Une Tempête* d'Aimé Césaire," p. 21.

assume our condition as Caliban implies rethinking our history from the *other* side, from the viewpoint of the *other* protagonist" ("C," p. 28). Put differently, having the nerve to push the play against the Western critical grain, marginalized Caribbeans were relieved of the struggle, unwinnable in Western terms, to gain admission to the *right* side. Their brazen unorthodoxy thus became instrumental in redefining the *wrong* as the *other* side, in opening up a space for themselves where their own cultural values need no longer be derided as savage and deformed.

Fernández Retamar's essay is synoptic yet retains a distinctively Cuban bent, illustrative of the diversity among the consistently adversarial readings of the play. For one thing, Cuba straddles the Caribbean and Latin America geographically and culturally, and Fernández Retamar's arguments are marked by this double affinity. His focus is hemispheric, and his Caliban, originally the victim of European conquistadors, now labors more directly under North American imperialism. And coming from a society where mulattos predominate, he instinctively defines "our America" as *mestizaje,* as culturally and ethnically mixed; the conflict between Prospero and Caliban is consequently seen in class rather than racial terms.[32] Where for the negritudist Césaire Caliban had most emphatically to be black and Ariel, the favored servant and counterrevolutionary, to be mulatto (a correspondence between race and privilege native to Martinique and much of the formerly French and British Caribbean), for Fernández Retamar, the Ariel-Caliban split is predominantly one of class. The lofty Ariel is representative of the intellectual who must choose between collaborating with Prospero and deliberately allying himself with Caliban, the exploited proletarian who is to advance revolutionary change.

Lemuel Johnson's volume of poems, *highlife for caliban* (1973), marks the decline of *The Tempest*'s value as an oppositional force in decolonizing cultures. Johnson writes out of the historical experience of Freetown, Sierra Leone's capital, a forlorn city of slaves who had been liberated by Britain and had resettled there. Their freedom is announced but scarcely felt as such. The backdrop to the poems is neocolonial: Caliban is now head of state, but his nationalist ideals have become corrupted and enfeebled by power. By the same token, he has experienced the gulf between formal independence and authentic autonomy, as his nation remains in Prospero's cultural and economic thrall and the final exorcism of the master seems improbable. This condition is psychologically dissipating, for "it is the neocolonial

32. See Marta E. Sánchez, "Caliban: The New Latin-American Protagonist of *The Tempest,*" *Diacritics* 6 (Spring 1976): 54-61.

event that finally divests Caliban of that which had kept him whole—a dream of revenge against Prospero. But how shall he now revenge himself upon himself?"[33]

The Tempest's value for African and Caribbean intellectuals faded once the plot ran out. The play lacks a sixth act which might have been enlisted for representing relations among Caliban, Ariel, and Prospero once they entered a postcolonial era, or rather (in Harry Magdoff's phrase), an era of "imperialism without colonies."[34] Over time, Caliban's recovery of his island has proved a qualified triumph, with the autonomy of his emergent nation far more compromised than was imagined by the generation of more optimistic nationalists—politicians and writers alike—who saw independence in. Third Worlders have found it difficult to coax from the play analogies with these new circumstances wherein Prospero, having officially relinquished authority over the island, so often continues to manage it from afar.

With the achievement of formal independence, the anticolonial spirit of insurrection has been dampened and the assertive calls to reconstruct endemic cultures attenuated. By the early seventies the generation of more idealistic (and often more literary) leaders who bridged the periods pre- and postindependence was being replaced by a cohort of Third World leaders who in power have become preoccupied, as Edward Said has noted, primarily with technocratic concerns and defense.[35] Issues of national or racial identity have largely been superseded by issues of survival. In this climate, Shakespeare's play has been drained of the immediate, urgent value it was once found to have, and the moment has passed when a man like Lamming could assert so sanguinely that *"The Tempest* was also prophetic of a political future which is our present. Moreover, the circumstances of my life, both as a colonial and exiled descendant of Caliban in the twentieth century, is an example of that prophecy" (*PE,* p. 13). The play's declining pertinence to contemporary Africa and the Caribbean has been exacerbated by the difficulty of wresting from it any role for female defiance or leadership in a period when protest is coming increasingly from that quarter. Given that Caliban is without a female counterpart in his oppression and rebellion, and given the largely autobiographical cast of African and Caribbean appropriations of the play, it follows

33. Sylvia Wyriter, "Afterword," in Lemuel Johnson, *highlife for caliban* (Ann Arbor, Mich., 1973), p.137. **34.** Harry Magdoff, "Imperialism without Colonies," in *Studies in the Theory of Imperialism,* ed. Roger. Owen and Bob Sutcliffe (New York, 1972), pp. 144-70. **35.** See Edward Said, "In the Shadow of the West," *Wedge* 7/8 (Winter/Spring 1985), p. 10.

that all the writers who quarried from *The Tempest* an expression of their lot should have been men. This assumption of heroic revolt as a preeminently male province is most palpable in Fernández Retamar's inclusion of only one woman in his list of thirty-five activists and intellectuals who exemplify the Calibanesque.

Between the late fifties and early seventies *The Tempest* was valued and competed for both by those (in the "master"-culture's terms) traditionally possessed of discrimination and those traditionally discriminated against. On the one hand, a broad evaluative agreement existed between the two sets of feuding cultures, the colonizers and the colonized both regarding the play highly. On the other hand, the two groups brought utterly different social ambitions to bear on the play. Writers and intellectuals from the colonies appropriated *The Tempest* in a way that was outlandish in the original sense of the word. They reaffirmed the play's importance from outside its central tradition not passively or obsequiously, but through what may best be described as a series of insurrectional endorsements. For in that turbulent and intensely reactive phase of Caribbean and African history, *The Tempest* came to serve as a Trojan horse, whereby cultures barred from the citadel of "universal" Western values could win entry and assail those global pretensions from within.

"Caribbean and African Appropriations of *The Tempest*" first appeared in *Critical Inquiry* 13:3 (Spring, 1987): 557–78.

RAPE AND THE ROMANTICIZATION OF SHAKESPEARE'S MIRANDA

Jessica Slights

I N 1981, Jean Elshtain issued a plea that political philosophy recognize female agency as a valid focus of study: "The feminist political thinker aims to transform her discipline as well as her social
world in important ways. This necessitates locating the woman as subject of political and social inquiry, moving away from the abstracted,
disembodied 'product' of social forces featured in much contemporary
social science. This female subject, as the object of inquiry, must be
approached as an active agent of a life-world of intense personaliza-
tion and immediacy."[1] Twenty years later, I am taking up Elshtain's
call in a literary context in order to suggest that the history of *Tempest*
criticism stands as powerful proof that political criticism of Shakespearean drama has yet to devise a solid theoretical basis from which
to approach female characters as dynamic participants in the fictional
worlds of which they are constitutive members. Specifically, this paper
seeks to account for, and to challenge, Miranda's exclusion from critical
discourse. By exploring what happens when Miranda is treated merely
as an emblem of a colonialist ruling class rather than understood as
an active agent in the life-world of the play, my paper participates in
a recent dialogue concerned with evaluating the role a rehabilitated
notion of character might play in the development of an ethical—and
also historically aware—criticism of Shakespearean drama.

These days, "character criticism," an approach initiated in the eighteenth century and popularized in the early twentieth century by
A. C. Bradley, is most often considered synonymous with the twin sins
of essentialism and ahistoricity. I want to join here with a growing
number of challenges to this dismissive account and to argue instead
that this now-unfashionable approach has much to offer contemporary readers of Shakespeare. Christy Desmet has argued persuasively
that it is time for Shakespeareans to stop emphasizing the distinctions
between their own interest in the playwright's language and the "naive
explorations" of his characters by earlier critics.[2] Rather than insisting
on difference, Desmet's work proposes a critical model that depends
on layering—in her words "heaping up"—poststructuralist accounts

of the relationship between the self and the literary text with early character criticism's interest in exploring the mechanics of a reader's imaginative engagement with fictional characters in an explicitly ethical context.[3] Michael D. Bristol is also concerned with resemblances, and he offers the work of Harry Berger Jr. as an antidote to a post-modern tendency to differentiate too emphatically between an "aggressively historicist" materialism and an older tradition of ethically based criticism.[4] Berger, in turn, challenges materialist criticism's tendency to efface individual human agency by reading *dramatis personae* as figures for the depersonalized movements of ideological forces, and he proposes a return to a "modified character-and-action approach" as a means of reviving a notion of individual agency.[5] Even the influential cultural materialist Alan Sinfield has been preoccupied, of late, with the issue of character. Identifying character as "one of the major discursive formations" at work in Shakespeare's plays, Sinfield argues in *Faultlines* that character "needs to be addressed if we are to explore how subjectivities are constituted."[6] Although wary of returning to a character criticism originally based in essentialist humanist values, Sinfield is also unwilling to dismiss character as an "altogether inappropriate" category of analysis.[7] Instead, like Desmet, Bristol, and Berger, Sinfield wants to mediate between "subjectivity and character, between traditional and poststructuralist criticism."[8]

That such a diverse group of critics should be returning to character as an analytical category suggests that a new synthesis between "traditional" and poststructuralist modes of criticism is emerging in Shakespeare studies. None of these critics proposes a wholesale return to the essentialism of Bradley; rather, each insists in a different way on the importance of developing an approach to reading Shakespeare that acknowledges that fictional characters can effectively model human actions, but that accounts too for the influential role that historical and cultural forces play in the formation of individual identity. My reading of *The Tempest* contributes to this new synthesis by arguing that employing character as an analytical category can enable a feminist reading of the play that identifies Miranda's agency and at the same time insists on her embeddedness in a formative social and political community. Using the work of the late Romantic critic Anna Jameson as a springboard for a re-evaluation of Miranda, I contend that past and present readings of *The Tempest* alike have misread the play by emphasizing the nature of Prospero's relationship with the island of his exile without considering the alternative models of selfhood, moral agency, and community life posited by the magician's daughter. An ethically based reading of the play can, I argue, provide an antidote both to a nineteenth-century tradition that understood Miranda merely as a trope for a feminized conception of nature, and to a more recent materialist tradition that conceives of her merely as an unwitting object of exchange in a matrix of colonial and nuptial economies.

I

Sentimental readings of *The Tempest* reigned throughout the eighteenth and well into the nineteenth century. Most critics seemed to agree that the play was a complex allegory in which a series of archetypal binary opposites—nature/culture, instinct/reason, savage/civilized man—vie for supremacy. From Nicholas Rowe's 1709 pronouncement that Prospero's magic had "something in it very Solemn and very Poetical" to William Hazlitt's 1817 characterization of him as a "stately magician," critics emphasized Prospero's dignity and intellect, discovering in Shakespeare's princely necromancer a model of patriarchal wisdom and refined authority.[9] In contrast, Caliban—the island's original inhabitant—appears most often in the readings of nineteenth-century critics as an unregenerate brute, naturally resistant to his master's attempts to educate and to civilize him. In accordance with an earlier tradition of primitivism that idealized the figure of the noble savage, critics did periodically attempt to recuperate Shakespeare's "salvage and deformed slave" by depicting him as an uncorrupted innocent destined to follow his own uncontrollable instinctual urges.[10] Hazlitt, for instance, associates Caliban with the "earthy" elements of nature: "Shakespear has described the brutal mind of Caliban in contact with the pure and original forms of nature: the character grows out of the soil where it is rooted, uncontrouled [sic], uncouth and wild, uncramped by any of the meannesses of custom. It is 'of the earth, earthy.' It seems almost to have been dug out of the ground, with a soul instinctively superadded to it answering to its wants and origin."[11] While in Hazlitt's account, Caliban's connectedness to the "original forms of nature" lends him a kind of wild purity, this is hardly an association to be envied. Although free of the "meannesses of custom," Hazlitt's "natural" Caliban is barely human; his soul is apparently tacked on to an earthy body and a brutal mind merely as a sort of divine afterthought. Such recuperative readings may have understood Prospero's attempts to acculturate Caliban as in some respects destructive, but they continued to cast Prospero as a civilized creative genius and Caliban as a savage beast.

On the subject of Miranda, these critics are notably silent. When she is mentioned at all, Miranda appears either as an archetype of pliant womanliness or as an allegorical, sentimentalized figure for the tender and fecund aspects of untamed nature.[12] The Victorian actor Fanny

259

Kemble, for example, characterizes Caliban as a "gross and uncouth but powerful savage" and associates him with "the more ponderous and unwieldy natural elements," while arguing that the play's young lovers are symbols of nature's undomesticated bounty.[13] Like many of her contemporaries, Kemble emblematizes Miranda while reserving in her account of *The Tempest* a more central authoritative role for Prospero. Constructing the magician as the physical and moral center of *The Tempest*, Kemble both celebrates and naturalizes his centrality by figuring him as the "middle link" in a "wonderful chain of being."[14]

Reacting, in part, to such characterizations of Prospero's autocratic rule as essentially benign, much recent criticism has sought means to critique what it reads as a glorification of *The Tempest's* exploitative colonialism.[15] Rereading Caliban against traditional views of his savagery and ineducability, these critics have queried the play's relation to British imperialism in both the seventeenth and the nineteenth centuries. Like the nineteenth-century readers they seek to challenge, however, these contemporary scholars dispense with discussions of Miranda in favor of analyses of the politically and culturally charged confrontation between Prospero and Caliban. While such commentators as Francis Barker, Peter Hulme, Paul Brown, Stephen Orgel, and Eric Cheyfitz define their political and interpretative projects against the sentimentalized readings of their eighteenth- and nineteenth-century predecessors, their treatments of Miranda bear some important similarities to this earlier tradition. Not unlike the nineteenth century's habit of allegorizing Miranda, postcolonial readings of *The Tempest* that seek to emphasize the exploitative nature of Prospero's relationship to his island home have a tendency to exclude Miranda by focusing on the enslavement of Caliban. This new critical orthodoxy often presents Miranda not as emblematic of the natural world, but as a cipher, a figure important only for her unwitting role in helping to realize her father's political aspirations.

Miranda has not fared much better at the hands of many recent feminist critics. Although occasionally more sympathetic to her situation, contemporary feminist readers of *The Tempest* also appear reluctant to focus attention on Prospero's daughter, often preferring instead to discuss female characters who are either marginal to the action or absent entirely from the narrative. Caliban's dead mother Sycorax, Alonso's daughter Claribel, and the various female spirits who dance attendance on Prospero have all figured prominently in a variety of recent articles about the play.[16] When feminist critics do elect to discuss the play's only human female presence, Miranda appears in their commentaries most often as a prototype of that unlikely invention of Puritan conduct book authors and late-twentieth-century scholars:

the woman who is chaste, silent, and obedient. Small wonder then that Ann Thompson's female students find Miranda "an extremely feeble heroine and scorn to identify with her."[17]

Turning now to Jameson, I want to argue that her reading of *The Tempest*—which appears in her 1832 study, *Shakspeare's Heroines*—creates an avenue for challenging interpretations of Miranda as a disempowered subject whose actions are merely reactions to the various male agential forces with whom she shares an island.[18] Rather than either ignoring her completely or reading Miranda through traditional Romanticism's figuring of nature as a source of divine creative power, Jameson associates Miranda with nature as a means of showing up the destructiveness of misguided social pressures on women.[19] For Jameson, it is Miranda's "total ignorance of the conventional forms and language of society" that makes her capable of both independence and love.[20] Arguing that she is "ignorant of those usages of society which teach us to dissemble the real passion," Jameson contends that Miranda's sympathetic nature results from her lack of contact with a coercive notion of propriety generated by a society seldom kind to women, especially those who find strength in passion.[21] On Jameson's account, Miranda's "naturalness" is constructed not as an alternative to reason or refinement, but as a model of compassionate independence.

Miranda first appears in Jameson's critical narrative as an emblem for an almost impossibly immaculate vision of celestial perfection—in an early passage Jameson calls her "all but ethereal"—but Miranda gains both shape and substance as the account continues.[22] Noting that Shakespeare has elected to remove her "far from all comparison with her own sex," Jameson points out that Miranda's humanity is deliberately juxtaposed with the magical nature of the island's other inhabitants.[23] When she is compared with the "subtile essence" of the "ethereal sprite" Ariel, "Miranda herself appears a palpable reality, a woman, 'breathing thoughtful breath,' a woman, walking the earth in her mortal loveliness, with a heart as frail-strung, as passion-touched, as ever fluttered in a female bosom."[24] Bracketing for a moment its dated prose, I want to point to this passage's clear attempt to move us away from an account of Miranda as an incorporeal being and toward an understanding of her as a material girl. As the repetition of the word "woman" insists, the rhetorical emphasis here is on Miranda's humanity, her physicality, and her sexuality—in short, on what Jameson would call her womanliness.

Jameson's insistence on Miranda's gendered corporeality should not be dismissed as naïve effusion. She is in no danger of confusing the character of Prospero's daughter with the milliner's assistant in her local hat shop. Rather, her treatment of Miranda as a "real" person signals a deliberate decision to invoke lived experience as an interpretative context appropriate—even integral—to the study of *The Tempest*. Jameson makes this theoretical move explicit when, in the introduction to *Shakespeare's Heroines*, Alda—the author's fictional alter ego—argues that Shakespeare's characters "combine history and real life; they are complete individuals, whose hearts and souls are laid open before us." She continues: "We hear Shakspeare's men and women discussed, praised and dispraised, liked, disliked, as real human beings: and in forming our opinions of them we are influenced by our own characters, habits of thought, prejudices, feelings, impulses, just as we are influenced with regard to our acquaintances and associates."[25] Such an understanding of the vital role that a reader's ordinary knowledge of people, places, and things plays in the practice of literary criticism is at once distinctive and distinctly Romantic.

Like Jameson, Samuel Taylor Coleridge constructs the experience of reading or watching a play as an interaction between reader or audience member and dramatic character. For Coleridge, however, this experience of encountering unfamiliar characters in new and different situations is associated with the unconscious acquisition of a universalizable self-knowledge. In Shakespeare's plays, he argues, "[e]ach speech is what every man feels to be latent in his nature; what he would have said in that situation if he had had the ability and readiness to do it."[26] Elsewhere, Coleridge's universalizing impetus is even more pronounced: in Shakespeare's plays, he declares, "every man sees himself, without knowing that he does so."[27] Jameson, on the other hand, describes the process of engaging with Shakespearean drama as a meeting between reader and character, but is eager to particularize what she describes as an inherently moral interpretative encounter.[28] That is, lived experience for Jameson consists in specific "habits of thought," "prejudices," "feelings," and "impulses"—the ethically weighted means by which people evaluate each other and the larger world and thereby assert their personhood. Criticism, she seems to suggest, ought also to partake of this moral realm.

What I am proposing in essence—following Jameson's comments on the ethics of reading—is a literary critical model of what philosopher Charles Taylor has described as an orientation within the space of moral questions. According to Taylor, being oriented in moral space is constitutive of human agency; that is, knowing oneself as a person requires situating oneself in a space within which questions can be formulated about what is good and what is bad, what is valuable and what is worthless.[29] By locating criticism within this moral space, I want to lay the theoretical ground-work for an ethically oriented reading of *The Tempest* that refuses to dismiss its characters as allegorized ciphers.

Miranda's humanity and gendered physicality are confirmed for Jameson by a discrete identity that sets her apart from the more generic creatures of fable with whom she shares an island. "Miranda is," Jameson argues, "a consistent, natural, human being. Our impression of her nymph-like beauty, her peerless grace and purity of soul, has a distinct and individual character. Not only is she exquisitely lovely, being what she is, but we are made to feel that she *could not* possibly be otherwise than as she is portrayed."[30] Jameson recognizes Miranda's particular qualities not as unimportant variations within the same basic human nature, but as fundamental differences that set her apart from those around her. In Jameson's account, Miranda is more than simply her father's daughter; she has an immutably "distinct and individual character"[31] all her own. Finally, it is not her ethereality, then, but Miranda's identity as an independent moral agent that Jameson celebrates.

If Jameson acclaims Miranda as an independent young woman, she also, nevertheless, acknowledges Miranda's embeddedness in a complex array of familial relationships, and much of her analysis of *The Tempest* is devoted to a discussion of Miranda's roles as daughter and wife. Rather than grounding her account of the play, as her male counterparts so often do, in a celebration of Prospero as autonomous master of the cosmos, Jameson foregrounds Miranda's more collaborative model of social interaction. By locating identity within a larger social matrix of family and community, Jameson focuses attention on Miranda's filial duties and romantic desires as a means of better understanding her as a fully developed self. This reading of the self as a relational construct—as a creation shaped by the nexus of relationships that give meaning to its existence—in turn allows us to read Miranda as at once daughter, wife, and independent human agent.

2

Moving now to a fuller discussion of Miranda as both independent and embedded self, I want to argue that her romance with, and marriage to, Ferdinand is best understood not merely as a political affiliation effected for Prospero's pleasure, but also as a crucial opportunity for Miranda to derive a sense of herself as an agent in the world. Many critics have assumed that Prospero maintains an iron grip over his strange little family throughout *The Tempest*. Marilyn Williamson, for instance, argues that the "absolute power of the ruler to control the lives of others is unquestioned" in all four of Shakespeare's late romances, and she sketches a picture of Prospero as a manipulative father and governor who exerts a rough and self-serving authority over his daughter.[32] Political and personal ambitions are certainly prime motives for Prospero's actions throughout the play. As rightful duke of Milan, he is anxious to regain his home and to consolidate his power by arranging a marriage between his daughter and the heir to the Neapolitan throne. As a betrayed brother, he is eager to avenge his exile and to confront Antonio with his treachery. At the same time, however, love for his daughter and concern for her future also prompt Prospero to action. He tells Miranda: "I have done nothing, but in care of thee/(Of thee my dear one, thee my daughter)."[33]

Williamson is doubtless right to remind us that Prospero's displays of affection for his daughter should not blind us to his manipulation of her, but I am unconvinced by the claim that Miranda remains merely "an object of exchange between Prospero and Ferdinand."[34] Such a reading grants too much control to the play's male characters and too little agency to the quick witted Miranda. While she is certainly influenced by her powerful father and by the expectations imposed upon her as the daughter of a duke, Miranda proves to be strong-willed and independent minded in her dealings with both Prospero and Ferdinand. Her moments of domestic defiance are brief, but they constitute a repeated challenge to the dynastic preoccupations of the men who rule her world.

Consider, for instance, the moment in which Miranda and Ferdinand first catch sight of one another. Rather than depicting a sterile meeting between two heirs destined to marry purely for reasons of political expedience, this scene presents a moving and comic portrait of romantic attraction and sexual awakening. Miranda, awed by Ferdinand's arrival on the island, believes, at first, that she has come upon a specter of some kind. Curious rather than afraid, and eager to share her find with her father, she discusses the apparition with Prospero:

MIRANDA   What, is't a spirit?
   Lord, how it looks about! Believe me, Sir.
   It carries a brave form. But 'tis a spirit.
PROSPERO No, wench, it eats, and sleeps, and hath such senses
   As we have—such. This gallant which thou seest
   Was in the wrack; and but he's something stain'd
   With grief (that's beauty's canker), thou mightst call him
   A goodly person. He hath lost his fellows,
   And strays about to find 'em.
MIRANDA   I might call him
   A thing divine, for nothing natural
   I ever saw so noble.
                   (1.2.410–20)

Despite her father's assurance that Ferdinand is indeed a man, Miranda seems captivated by the notion that she has discovered a spirit, and even Prospero's gruffness cannot succeed in dampening her enthusiasm for her handsome new discovery. Ferdinand, too, appears convinced that he has discovered some supernatural creature when he first catches sight of Miranda and he assumes that she must be "the goddess/On whom these airs attend!" (1.2.422–3).

While these confusions of the real with the magical, the natural with the celestial, underscore the mysterious essence of the powers which have brought the lovers together, they also insist on a genuine magnetism between Miranda and Ferdinand. Prospero may have contrived their meeting, but, as his reaction to their flirtation testifies, even he is surprised by the intensity of the impetuous lovers' attraction to one another. He observes to Ariel:

> At the first sight
> They have chang'd eyes. Delicate Ariel.
> I'll set thee free for this . . .
> ....
> They are both in either's pow'rs: but this swift business
> I must uneasy make, lest too light winning
> Make the prize light.
>
> (1.2.441–53)

Prospero's account of the mutual infatuation between Miranda and Ferdinand acknowledges Ariel's role in bringing the lovers together, but it also constructs love as a potent force and implies that the magician is well aware that they are in thrall not to him but to each other. Nevertheless, fearing that an overly brief courtship will lead his daughter and her suitor to take the serious business of marriage lightly, Prospero exerts his parental authority in an attempt to slow their wooing.

Miranda, however, immediately subverts her father's attempts to meddle in her love life. Rather than obeying his instruction that she refrain from speaking with Ferdinand, Miranda instead seeks out the handsome shipwreck victim and announces her attraction to him. Her defiant passion for the prince of Naples is ardent, and bears none of the hesitancy of a woman about to embark on a marriage of convenience. She tells him:

> How features are abroad
> I am skilless of: but by my modesty
> (The jewel in my dower), I would not wish
> Any companion in the world but you:
> Nor can imagination form a shape.

Besides yourself, to like of. But I prattle
Something too wildly, and my father's precepts
I therein do forget.

(3.1.52–9)

Though mindful of Prospero's "precepts," Miranda is willing to risk her father's wrath in order to spend more time investigating a man whose "shape" she clearly finds irresistible. While this scene presents a funny and touching image of Miranda's love for the Neapolitan heir, it also emphasizes her willingness to defy her father in search of her own destiny since, for Prospero's daughter, heterosexual desire and marriage entail a measure of resistance rather than simple capitulation to patriarchy.

The politically subversive potential of Miranda's deliberate disobedience of her father should not be exaggerated. Like a teenager who breaks her curfew and defies her parents in order to date the boy of her choosing, Miranda resents her father's attempt to intrude in her social life and resists his efforts to constrain her. Her defiance is localized, and she clearly risks little more than her father's displeasure by her rebellious behavior; although powerful and easily angered, Prospero is never presented as a physical threat to his daughter. Nevertheless, Miranda's decision to marry Ferdinand should not be dismissed as the inevitable consequence of Prospero's political ambitions. Miranda's choices are admittedly few, but she is presented as an imaginative and headstrong young woman who shows no signs of acquiescing unthinkingly to her father's wishes.

While Prospero is outwardly acknowledged as the legislator of his island, Miranda proves to be a subtle and consistent challenger to his autocratic ways. Indeed, even before Ferdinand's arrival on the island, Miranda is unwilling to let her father manipulate her world. Guessing that her father has been responsible for creating the storm, which has destroyed a ship before her eyes, Miranda demands that Prospero calm the seas: "If by your art, my dearest father, you have/Put the wild waters in this roar, allay them" (1.2. 1–2). Miranda's command underscores the extent of Prospero's remarkable abilities, but as her speech continues she grants herself an equal or even superior power to control the cosmos:

Had I been any God of power, I would
Have sunk the sea within the earth or ere
It should the good ship so have swallow'd, and
The fraughting souls within her.

(1.2.10–3)

Prospero at one point describes himself as a "prince of power" (1.2.55). Here his daughter goes him one better, as she imagines herself a "God of power" and claims the ability to command nature and to save lives.

If Miranda proves she is aware of the operation of magical power on the island and ambitious for a compassionate power of her own, she also demonstrates that she is conscious of the more mundane workings of political power. Although Prospero's repeated admonitions that she listen to his story—"ope thine ear./Obey, and be attentive" (1.2.37–8); "Dost thou attend me?" (line 78); Thou attend'st not!" (line 87); "Dost thou hear?" (line 106)—imply that Miranda may be a less than attentive listener; her responses to his tale indicate quite the opposite. Miranda appears not only alert, but also attuned to the political nuances of Prospero's description of their past as she punctuates her father's narrative with perceptive questions. "What foul play had we, that we came from thence?" she asks upon hearing of her illustrious Milanese ancestry (1.2.60). And later, when Prospero has described Antonio's treachery with the Neapolitan king and recounted their removal from the city, Miranda asks: "Wherefore did they not/That hour destroy us?" (1.2.138–9). Such questions reveal that she is listening intently and quickly grasps the import of the situation in which Prospero finds himself. Miranda's persistent questioning might also be read as a subtle form of challenge to Prospero's authority; as John Robinson notes in his 1625 *Observations Divine and Morall:* "it is a kind of impeachment of Authoritie, to examine the Reasons of Things."[35]

Miranda's assertiveness also extends to her dealings with Ferdinand. Although smitten with him, she retains a strong sense of her own worth and an earnest faith in her own abilities. Indeed, it is Miranda who must teach Ferdinand a thing or two about effective wooing. Having defied her father and sought out Ferdinand, Miranda is met not with words of tenderness, but with grumbling as he complains about the laborious task Prospero has assigned him: "O most dear mistress,/The sun will set before I shall discharge/What I must strive to do" (3.1.21–3). Only when Miranda offers to carry the logs herself—"If you'll sit down./I'll bear your logs the while. Pray give me that,/ I'll carry it to the pile" (3.1.23–5)—does her prince awaken to his role as courtly lover. Invoking the terms of Petrarchan discourse, Ferdinand then claims to have been in "bondage" to "full many a lady" and he declares that his heart is now in "service" to the "perfect and . . . peerless" Miranda (3.1.39–48). As the scene continues, Miranda pushes his generic flirtation toward a more personal commitment to love and marriage by adopting for herself the role of courtly lover and domesticating Ferdinand's extravagant conceits. "Do you love me?" she asks her "patient log-man" (3.1.67). Ferdinand responds with a strangely inverted affirmative:

O heaven, O earth, bear witness to this sound,
And crown what I profess with kind event
If I speak true! If hollowly, invert

What best is boded me to mischief! I,
Beyond all limit of what else i' th' world,
Do love, prize, honor you.

(3.1.68–73)

The backward shape of Ferdinand's vow belies the apparent certainty
of its hyperbolic imagery. Indeed, by postponing his declaration of
love until after he has raised the possibility that he may not "speak
true," Ferdinand appears almost uncertain about his feelings for Miranda. This rhetorical inversion provides an effective parallel to the
social inversion of this unconventional courtship.

Apparently unaware of the ambiguity implicit in his speech. Miranda
claims that the gladness inspired by her lover's words has moved her to
tears. Her commentary on her inner turmoil suggests, however, that
sexual arousal, rather than chaste gladness, is prompting her. "Wherefore weep you?" asks a bemused Ferdinand. "At mine unworthiness,"
responds Miranda.

                    that dare not offer
What I desire to give: and much less take
What I shall die to want. But this is trifling.
And all the more it seeks to hide itself.
The bigger bulk it shows. Hence, bashful cunning,
And prompt me, plain and holy innocence!
I am your wife, if you will marry me;
If not, I'll die your maid. To be your fellow
You may deny me, but I'll be your servant.
Whether you will or no.

(3. 1.76–86)

With its conventional pun on orgasm as a "little death," Miranda's
speech reveals her as both engagingly self-aware and forthrightly honest about her erotic desires. Labeling her own attempts at self-discipline
as "trifling," and vowing instead to validate the growing "bulk" of her
passion for Ferdinand by banishing "bashful cunning," Miranda borrows
from his masculinist Petrarchan tradition by apostrophizing "plain and
holy innocence" to spur herself to the decidedly anti-Petrarchan action
of proposing marriage to her male lover. Reversing the conventional
pattern of courtship. Miranda offers herself to Ferdinand in unequivo-
cal terms that recognize the submission that marriage entails—"I'll be
your servant"—but that insist, too, on her right to self-determination—
"Whether you will or no." Ferdinand's reply picks up on Miranda's
terminology, the language of domestic hierarchy, and offers her an alternative to the roles of wife, maid, fellow, and servant that she has proposed
for herself: "My mistress, dearest,/And I thus humble ever" (3.1.86–7).

According to the OED, a "mistress" is "a woman who rules, or has control . . . the female head of a household or family."[36] By offering her a domestic title that claims some measure of control for its holder, Ferdinand acknowledges the sacrifice that marriage necessitates for Miranda. The two lovers then conclude their betrothal with a metaphoric exchange of hearts and hands, another moment of intimacy initiated by Miranda's emphasis on the specific domestic roles that await them:

MIRANDA   My husband then?
FERDINAND Ay, with a heart as willing
    As bondage e'er of freedom. Here's my hand.
MIRANDA And mine, with my heart in't. And now farewell
                        (3.1.87–90)

Miranda's marriage to Ferdinand is often read as a manifestation—even a consolidation—of Prospero's irresistible regulatory force. For instance, Peter Greenaway's 1991 cinematic adaptation of the play, *Prospero's Books*, presents a powerful visual image of the exiled duke as author of his daughter's nuptial fate. Such readings ignore, however, the extent to which Miranda involves herself in the process of selecting a husband. Prospero certainly engineers and closely supervises the initial encounter between his daughter and the man he hopes she will marry, but Miranda quickly takes the matter of falling in love and becoming betrothed into her own capable hands. As Natalie Zemon Davis's work on marriage practices in sixteenth-century France has demonstrated, occasionally early modern women responded to restrictive cultural practices in enterprising ways. Davis argues, indeed, that "a thread of female autonomy may have been built precisely around [a] sense of being given away, that women sometimes turned the cultural formulation around, and gave themselves away."[37] Miranda's clandestine flirtation with Ferdinand, her decision to marry, and the inverted courtship that follows present, I would argue, a convincing fictional analogue to this real world strategy for achieving self-expression and even, perhaps, a sense of agency through marriage.

While Miranda and Ferdinand seem to have reached a meeting of hearts and minds upon their engagement, some good-natured tension develops between them not long after the wedding masque. In the final scene of the play, Prospero and Alonso witness an odd exchange in which Miranda calls Ferdinand on an attempt to cheat her at chess:

MIRANDA Sweet lord, you play me false.
FERDINAND   No, my dearest love,
    I would not for the world.
MIRANDA Yes, for a score of kingdoms you should wrangle.
    And I would call it fair play.
                        (5.1.172–5)

A political realist, Miranda is aware that "wrangling" over kingdoms sometimes entails "false plays," but her accusation also reminds Ferdinand of the value of loyalty in matters of the heart as well as in matters of state. Her public challenge to his authority consolidates her own domestic power by demonstrating that she will not let herself be manipulated by her new husband any more than she will by her father.

3

I have argued thus far that *The Tempest* encourages us to recognize Miranda's interactions with both her father and her husband as the defiant actions of a self-fashioning woman rather than the programmatic reactions of a dehumanized cipher. Such a reading, I have suggested, puts the dynastic preoccupations of Prospero and Ferdinand into stark relief. I want now to turn to a consideration of Caliban's obsession with lineage and to the direct threat that his fixation with dynasty poses to Miranda.

It is Prospero who first refers to Caliban's attempted rape of Miranda. He tells Caliban:

> I have us'd thee
> . . . with human care, and lodgd thee
> In mine own cell, till thou didst seek to violate
> The honor of my child.
>
> (1.2. 345–8)

"O ho, O ho," retorts Caliban, "would't had been done!/Thou didst prevent me: I had peopled else/This isle with Calibans" (lines 349–51). "Abhorred slave," replies Miranda in her turn.

> Which any print of goodness wilt not take,
> Being capable of all ill! I pitied thee,
> Took pains to make thee speak, taught thee each hour
> One thing or other. When thou didst not, savage,
> Know thine own meaning, but wouldst gabble like
> A thing most brutish. I endow'd thy purposes
> With words that made them known. But thy vild race
> (Though thou didst learn) had that in't which good natures
> Could not abide to be with; therefore wast thou
> Deservedly confin'd into this rock,
> Who hadst deserv'd more than a prison.
>
> (1.2.351–62)

For the editors of the 1999 Arden edition of the play, this "stinging rebuke" confirms both Miranda's assertiveness and a "timely and appropriate anger" at Caliban.[38] However, the nature of the attack that provokes Miranda's furious response and the implications of Caliban's highly politicized desire to impregnate her have received little attention from most commentators. Dismissing Miranda's fury at Caliban's posturing as part of a colonialist powerplay, many critics either ignore the attempted rape or imply that Miranda is responsible for it.

Although Caliban clearly admits to his attack on Miranda, there has been considerable reluctance among many critics to acknowledge it.[39] Others seem aware of Miranda's vulnerability, but resist holding Caliban responsible for his acts. Lorie Jerrell Leininger, for example, comes close to excusing Caliban's violence when she argues that "anyone who is forced into servitude, confined to a rock, kept under constant surveillance, and punished by supernatural means would wish his enslavers ill."[40] If Leininger blames Miranda and her father for Caliban's attack, Paul Brown's influential account of the play transforms the attempted rape into an issue of colonialist interpellation and interpretation.[41] Suggesting that Prospero's principal aim in recounting his history is to authenticate his role as master, Brown reads the narrative of Prospero's arrival on the island as his attempt to interpolate Ariel, Miranda, and Caliban as both subjects of his discourse and legatees of his civil philanthropy. For Brown, then, it is not the effects of rape itself, but rather the effects of the charge of rape that are of interest. Its first effect, he says, "is to circumvent Caliban's version of events by reencoding his boundlessness as rapacity: his inability to discern a concept of private, bounded property concerning his own dominions is reinterpreted as a desire to violate the chaste virgin, who epitomises courtly property."[42] Although her victimization is the ostensible subject of Brown's account, Miranda is abruptly sidelined as Prospero's concern for his daughter becomes an attempt to "reencode" Caliban; rape becomes a process of "reinterpretation," and Miranda herself becomes "courtly property."

Kim F. Hall tackles the issue of Caliban's culpability when she acknowledges that "it may seem ... possibly offensive to seem to 'explain' Caliban's behavior."[43] Nevertheless, she reads Caliban's attack as the "ultimate threat" to Prospero's "quest for social and political integrity" without discussing the threat that it poses to Miranda's bodily integrity.[44] Calling Miranda the "emblem of purity ... whose person is the grounds of [the] struggle" between Caliban and Prospero, Hall exposes the need for control over women that underpins the territorial claims of the play's male characters; Miranda is relevant to this discussion only insofar as she represents her father's economic interests.[45] Like Hall, Jyotsna Singh reads Prospero as an omnipotent ruler interested in controlling his subjects' sexuality as a means of perpetuating an exclusionary colonialist project.[46] Finding an analogy for this sexual economy in the models of gift exchange developed by such social anthropologists as Claude Lévi-Strauss and Marcel Mauss, Singh presents Caliban's attempt to rape Miranda as an effort to challenge Prospero's right to control the gift of sexual access to his daughter. On this account, Miranda's narrow escape functions not as an assertion of individual identity, or even as a symbol of the vulnerability of women within patriarchy, but rather as a denial of Caliban's rights as political rapist. "Neither Prospero nor Miranda," Singh argues, allow Caliban an identity as a desiring subject who wishes to gain sexual access to Miranda for the legitimate aim of "'peopl[ing] . . . This isle with Calibans.'"[47]

Clearly, Singh does not mean to propose rape as an acceptable means of asserting national identity in the face of oppression. Nevertheless, like so many of her predecessors in both the distant and the more recent past of *Tempest* criticism, she understands Miranda as a counter in a power game dominated by the male characters in the play. It is this objectification of Miranda that, in turn, legitimates Caliban's attempted rape as the self-actualizing act of a "desiring subject." As Caliban's gleeful politicization of his violent assault on Miranda emphasizes—and as horrifying recent events in Bosnia, Algeria, and Kosovo have demonstrated—rape can be deployed as a powerful tool of war. By generating terror, by violating social and ethical standards, and by hijacking the reproductive cycle of entire communities, political rapists' attacks on individual women become a means to ethnic cleansing. Singh recognizes sexism in the failure of both Shakespeare and the mostly male revisionists who have recast, revised, and rewritten his play to provide an aboriginal mate for Caliban, but she never questions Caliban's right to force a woman—any woman—to "people his isle" for him.[48]

Such accounts of *The Tempest* substitute an acknowledgment of Caliban as "desiring subject" for a humane reading of Miranda. They assume that Miranda is merely an unwitting pawn in a game of political intrigue being acted out by the men in the play, and accept that her chastity can have value only as a symbol of her father's power and his political aspirations. As a result, they blind themselves to the possibility that Miranda refuses to allow her victimization to silence her and actively chooses to be Ferdinand's wife so that she may play an active role in her own self-definition. Eager to present Caliban as a victim of colonial usurpation, such critics tend to understand his attack on Miranda as either the inevitable act of an unregenerate savage at the mercy of his "intrinsically evil nature," or as the emancipatory apex of a colonized subject's bumbling attempts at self-fashioning.[49] Rather than problematizing nineteenth-century readings of the play that present Caliban as a monster who is either incapable of understanding the immorality of his attack on Miranda or unable to restrain his violent impulses, many critics of *The Tempest* either follow their forefathers in the paternalist claim that Caliban is unable to control his own behavior—Marilyn Williamson, for instance, refers obliquely to Caliban's "rampant" sexuality—or they imply that his attempt to rape Miranda should be understood as some kind of a revolutionary accomplishment rather than as a morally repugnant act.[50] Ironically, even as they attempt to reclaim Caliban as an oppressed revolutionary, these contemporary critics repeat the primitivization of Caliban initiated by their predecessors and thereby deny him the moral agency upon which the political rights they are rightly so eager to grant him must necessarily be predicated.

Understanding Caliban as a moral agent, which entails acknowledging that he is wrong to try to rape Miranda, does not logically (and certainly not ethically) require either that we justify his enslavement or that we deny Miranda the right to freedom from violence. The assumption that both Miranda and Caliban cannot act simultaneously as moral agents in the life-world of *The Tempest* is the product, I suspect, of the epidemic of binary thinking that swept through academe as postcolonial criticism was gaining a hold in both North America and Britain. The political issues raised by the interpretative minefield of Caliban's attempted rape of Miranda are only problematic, however, if Caliban's and Miranda's claims to freedom (and to our sympathy) are understood as mutually exclusive. This case offers a particularly vivid illustration of the limitations of a critical binarism that has been unable to reconcile feminist theory's insistence that women be read as active agents of discourse and postcolonial theory's insistence that ethnic and racial others be recognized as legitimate subjects within that same discourse. I have argued that a feminism that cannot deplore Miranda's attempted rape is no meaningful kind of feminism at all. I have also combined Jameson's model of ethical criticism with postcolonial theory's insistence that the institutions and practices of Western literary criticism recognize and remedy their tendency to read past an ignoble imperialist history in an effort to grant Caliban the moral agency too often denied him. An agent at the mercy of either uncontrollable social forces or irrepressible psychological yearnings is surely not a moral agent in any meaningful sense of that term.

I want to make clear that I am not arguing that Miranda is a completely unencumbered self, free to behave exactly as she pleases. Her world is dominated by powerful men whose overwhelming preoccupations with questions of lineage necessarily limit her choices. Rather, I am proposing a reading of *The Tempest* that accepts Miranda as a moral agent in her own right. This reading, and the understanding of selfhood on which it is predicated, acknowledges that there are limitations on her behavior and at the same time allows us to recognize the importance of the choices she is able to make. An emphasis on Miranda as a bravely independent but always embedded self reminds us that *The Tempest* does offer some alternative to the paternalist order with which the play opens. The play's emphasis on Miranda's fierce protection of her chastity and her desire to marry Ferdinand combine to present her as a desiring self who gains a sense of moral agency not by seeking complete autonomy, but instead by recognizing the importance of her domestic ties.

NOTES

I wish to thank Michael D. Bristol and Camille Wells Slights for their invaluable comments on earlier versions of this paper; members of the SAA 2000 seminar on Shakespeare and Character for stimulating discussions about the possibilities and pitfalls of "character criticism"; and the anonymous reader at *SEL* for encouraging me to sharpen my argument about Miranda.

1. Jean Bethke Elshtain, *Public Man, Private Woman: Women in Social and Political Thought* (Princeton: Princeton Univ. Press, 1981), p. 304.
2. Christy Desmet, *Reading Shakespeare's Characters: Rhetoric, Ethics, and Identity* (Amherst: Univ. of Massachusetts Press, 1992), p. 4.
3. Desmet, *Reading Shakespeare's Characters,* p. 9.
4. Michael D. Bristol, "Recent Studies in Tudor and Stuart Drama," *SEL* 38, 2 (Spring 1998): 363–409, 403.
5. Harry Berger Jr., *Making Trifles of Terrors: Redistributing Complicities in Shakespeare,* ed. Peter Erickson (Stanford: Stanford Univ. Press, 1997), p. 25.
6. Alan Sinfield, *Faultlines: Cultural Materialism and the Politics of Dissident Reading* (Berkeley: Univ. of California Press, 1992), p. 63.
7. Sinfield, p. 58.
8. Sinfield, p. 61.
9. Nicholas Rowe, *The Works of Mr. William Shakespear,* 6 vols. (New York: AMS Press, 1967), 1:24. William Hazlitt, *Characters of Shakespear's Plays* (London: Dent, 1905), p. 89.
10. This phrase stands as Caliban's descriptor in the First Folio of 1623, although there is no evidence to indicate whether it is Shakespeare's own or whether it was inserted by later editors.
11. Hazlitt, p. 90. See Samuel Taylor Coleridge's claim that although Caliban is "a sort of creature of the earth" he is "in some respects a noble being" (*Shakespearean Criticism,* ed. Thomas Middleton Raysor, 2 vols. [London: Dent. 1960], 2:137–8).
12. I am thinking here of Mary Shelley's use of Miranda as a model for Ethel in *Lodore* ([1835]. ed. Lisa Vargo [Peterborough ON: Broadview

Press, 1997], pp. 79, 155). The Folger Shakespeare Library's art files contain numerous engravings depicting windblown Mirandas inspired by this critical tradition. Sentimental romanticizations of Miranda were also popular on stage throughout the nineteenth century. One contemporary photograph, reproduced as an illustration in the 1900 George Bell and Sons edition of Anna Jameson's *Shakspeare's Heroines*, shows Mrs. F. R. Rensen as a typically pensive Miranda, draped in a flowing white gown and posed at the intersection of forest and sea (facing p. 148).

13. Frances Anne Kemble, *Notes upon Some of Shakespeare's Plays* (London: R. Bentley, 1882), pp. 132–3.

14. Kemble, p. 132.

15. Readings of *The Tempest* in "the discourse of colonialism" began in earnest in North America with the publication of Stephen Greenblatt's influential 1976 essay "Learning to Curse: Aspects of Linguistic Colonialism in the Sixteenth Century" (in *First images of America. The Impact of the New World on the Old*, ed. Fredi Chiappelli, 2 vols. [Berkeley: Univ. of California Press, 1976], 2:561 30). Since then Greenblatt's postcolonial project has been adopted and adapted in articles by numerous critics. For an account of the most notable of these see Ben Ross Schneider Jr. "'Are We Being Historical Yet?': Colonialist Interpretations of Shakespeare's *Tempest*," *ShakS* 23 (1995): 120–45. For an early challenge to this approach, see Meredith Anne Skura's "Discourse and the Individual: The Case of Colonialism in *The Tempest*," *SQ* 40, 1 (Spring 1989): 42–69.

16. See, for example, Marjorie Raley's thought-provoking article about Claribel's Tunisian marriage. While Raley is most interested in locating the king of Tunis at the center of a dynastic European regime which must suppress the claims to racial difference upon which its own claims to authority are based, she also investigates the commodification of Claribel by reading her marriage as a form of transnational trade ("Claribel's Husband," in *Race, Ethnicity, and Power in the Renaissance*, ed. Joyce Green MacDonald [Madison NJ: Fairleigh Dickinson Univ. Press, 1997], pp. 95-119). See also Sylvia Wynter's discussion of what she calls the play's "most significant absence of all, that of Caliban's Woman, of Caliban's physiognomically complementary mate . . . the ontologically absent, potential genetrix" ("Beyond Miranda's Meanings: Un/silencing the 'Demonic Ground' of Caliban's 'Woman,'" in *Out of the Kumbla: Caribbean Women and Literature*, ed. Carole Boyce Davies and Elaine Savory Fido [Trenton NJ: Africa World Press. 1990], pp. 355–72, 360).

17. Ann Thompson, "'Miranda, Where's Your Sister?': Reading Shakespeare's *The Tempest*," in *Feminist Criticism: Theory and Practice*, ed. Susan Sellers (Toronto: Univ. of Toronto Press, 1991), pp. 45–55, 47.

18. Jameson, *Shakspeare's Heroines*, originally published as *Characteristics of Women, Moral, Poetical, and Historical*, Jameson's study takes as its

subject twenty-five of Shakespeare's female protagonists and is the first substantial and systematic discussion of these characters on record. The book's impressive publication record (it was reprinted at least eighteen times before 1925) testifies to its early popularity, but currently Jameson's work is most often dismissed as hopelessly sentimental. For an account of Jameson's reception, see Desmet, "'Intercepting the Dew-Drop': Female Readers and Readings in Anna Jameson's Shakespearean Criticism," in *Women's Re-Visions of Shakespeare: On the Responses of Dickinson, Woolf, Rich, H.D., George Eliot, and Others,* ed. Marianne Novy (Urbana: Univ. of Illinois Press, 1990), pp. 41–57. See also Judith Johnston, Anna Jameson, *Victorian Feminist, Woman of Letters* (Hants UK: Scholar Press, 1997), pp. 73–6.

19. For a discussion of this conventional trope, see Anne K. Mellor, *Romanticism and Gender* (New York: Routledge, 1993), p. 209.

20. Jameson, p. 151.

21. Jameson, pp. 151–2. Jameson argues throughout *Shakspeare's Heroines* that intelligent, passionate women are particularly vulnerable to the restrictions and attacks of a narrow-minded society. See especially her discussions of Portia of Belmont and Lady Macbeth (pp. 31–54 and 318–41).

22. Jameson, p. 149.

23. Ibid.

24. Ibid.

25. Jameson, p. 10.

26. Coleridge, 2:252.

27. Coleridge, 2:125.

28. For a more extensive comparison of Jameson and Coleridge see Desmet. "'Intercepting the Dew-Drop,'" pp. 42–3, 52. Desmet observes that identification is central to the process of reading character for both critics, and goes on to argue that for Jameson the "advocacy" produced by her identification with Shakespeare's heroines is "temper[ed] . . . with cool judgment" (p. 43).

29. Charles Taylor, *Sources of the Self: The Making of the Modern Identity* (Cambridge MA: Harvard Univ. Press, 1989), pp. 25–52.

30. Jameson, pp. 149–50.

31. Ibid.

32. Marilyn L. Williamson, *The Patriarchy of Shakespeare's Comedies* (Detroit: Wayne State Univ. Press. 1986), pp. 112, 155–6.

33. William Shakespeare, "The Tempest." in The *Riverside Shakespeare,* ed. G. Blakemore Evans, 2d edn. (Boston: Houghton Mifflin, 1997), pp. 1656–88, 1.2.16–7. All subsequent quotations are from this edition and will be cited parenthetically in the text by act, scene, and line number.

34. Williamson, p. 156.

35. John Robinson, *Observations Divine and Morall, for the furthering of knowledge and virtue* (London, 1625), p. 65.

36. OED, 2d edn., s.v. "mistress," I, 2a.

37. Natalie Zemon Davis, "Boundaries and the Sense of Self in Sixteenth-Century France," in *Reconstructing Individualism: Autonomy, Individuality, and the Self in Western Thought,* ed. Thomas C. Heller, Morton Sosna, and David E. Wellbery (Stanford: Stanford Univ. Press, 1986), pp. 53–63, 61.

38. Virginia Mason Vaughan and Alden T. Vaughan, eds. *The Tempest, by William Shakespeare,* Arden Shakespeare, Third Series (Surrey UK: Thomas Nelson and Sons, 1999), pp. 27, 135. While they argue here that Miranda is not as "meek and submissive as she is often portrayed," Vaughan and Vaughan finally characterize her as "the chaste ideal of early modern womanhood" (p. 27).

39. In their 1991 cultural history of Caliban, for instance, Vaughan and Vaughan raise the possibility that the attack on Miranda is a fabrication by arguing that "it is a matter of textual interpretation to accept or reject the characters' accuracy in reporting events, as in Prospero's charge that Caliban tried to rape Miranda" (*Shakespeare's Caliban: A Cultural History* [Cambridge. Cambridge Univ. Press. 1991], p. 1). Although in a later synopsis of the play Vaughan and Vaughan seem to assume that the attempted rape has taken place, no explanation of their earlier hesitation is offered (p. 17).

40. Lorie Jerrell Leininger, "The Miranda Trap: Sexism and Racism in Shakespeare's *Tempest,*" in *The Woman's Part: Feminist Criticism of Shakespeare,* ed. Carolyn Ruth Swift Lenz, Gayle Greene, and Carol Thomas Neely (Urbana: Univ. of Illinois Press, 1983), pp. 285–94, 288.

41. Paul Brown, "'This thing of darkness I acknowledge mine': *The Tempest* and the Discourse of Colonialism, in *Political Shakespeare: New Essays in Cultural Materialism,* ed. Jonathan Dollimore and Alan Sinfield (1985: rprt. Manchester. Manchester Univ. Press, 1994), pp. 40–71.

42. Brown, p. 62.

43. Kim E. Hall, Things of Darkness: Economics of Race and Gender in *Early Modern England* (Ithaca: Cornell Univ. Press, 1995), p. 143.

44. Hall, p. 151.

45. Hall, pp. 142, 151.

46. Jyotsna G. Singh, "Caliban versus Miranda: Race and Gender Conflicts in Postcolonial Rewritings of *The Tempest,*" in *Feminist Readings of Early Modern Culture: Emerging Subjects,* ed. Valerie Traub, M. Lindsay Kaplan, and Dympna Callaghan (Cambridge: Cambridge Univ. Press, 1996), pp. 191–209.

47. Singh, p. 196.

48. See Singh, p. 207.

49. Leininger, p. 288.

50. Williamson, p. 163.

"Rape and the Romanticization of Shakespeare's Miranda" was first published in *Studies in English Literature* 41:2 (2001): 357–79.

VIRTUE, VICE, AND COMPASSION IN MONTAIGNE AND *THE TEMPEST*

Arthur Kirsch

I T HAS long been recognized that Shakespeare borrowed from Montaigne. Gonzalo's Utopian vision in *The Tempest* (2.1.142–76)[1] is indebted to a passage in Florio's translation of Montaigne's essay. "Of the Cannibals,"[2] and Prospero's speech affirming that "The rarer action is/In virtue than in vengeance" (5.1.20–32) is derived from the opening of Florio's translation of the essay, "Of Cruelty" (2:108). The king's speech in *All's Well That Ends Well* on the distinction between virtue and nobility (2.3.117–44) appears to be a similarly direct, if less well-known, borrowing from "Upon Some Verses of Virgil" (3:72–3), an essay whose treatment of the polarization of sensuality and affection also has bearing upon *Othello*.[3] Leo Salingar has perspicuously shown that a number of the major themes of *King Lear*, as well as much of its distinctive vocabulary, are drawn from "An Apology of Raymond Sebond" and "Of the Affection of Fathers to their Children" as well as other essays;[4] and D. J. Gordon brilliantly demonstrated analogies between the critical stress upon names in *Coriolanus* and Montaigne's essay, "Of Glory."[5] Finally, as Robert Ellrodt has argued, the inward characterizations of Hamlet as well as of many of Shakespeare's other tragic heroes show clear affinities with the dynamics of self-consciousness, "a simultaneous awareness of experience and the experiencing self,"[6] that is fundamental to Montaigne's quest in all his essays to represent what he called "le passage" (3:23), the "minute to minute" movement of his mind.

The Tempest, however, remains the work in which Shakespeare's relation to Montaigne is most palpable and most illuminating. Shakespeare's play, of course, is exceptionally elusive. A variety of models and analogues have been proposed for it—Roman comedy, the Jacobean masque, and voyage literature among them—but it has no single, governing source to offer a scaffold for interpretation, and it remains in many ways as ineffable as Ariel's songs. Confronted with such suggestiveness, and in revolt against the apparent sentimentality of traditional readings, the disposition of most critics of the last two decades has been to follow W. H. Auden's lead in *The Sea and the*

ARTHUR KIRSCH

Mirror (1942–44)[7] and stress ironic and subversive ambiguities in the play as well as its apparently patriarchal and colonialist assumptions.[8]

Shakespeare's demonstrable borrowings from Montaigne in *The Tempest*, which are among the very few verifiable sources for the play, can provide a complementary, and I think more spacious, way of understanding *The Tempest*'s ambiguities. In the absence of a narrative source, Shakespeare's organization of the action, as well as Prospero's, seems unusually informed by the kind of working out of ideas that suggests the tenor of Montaigne's thinking: inclusive; interrogative rather than programmatic; anti-sentimental but humane; tragicomic rather than only tragic or comic, incorporating adversities rather than italicizing them as subversive ironies. The particular constellation of ideas in the play, moreover—the mutual dependence of virtue and vice, forgiveness, compassion, imagination—is habitual in Montaigne.

Of the two clear borrowings from Montaigne in *The Tempest*, Gonzalo's vision of Utopia is by far the most well-known and most discussed, but it is the play's more neglected relation to "Of Cruelty" as well as several associated essays that is more fundamental and that I wish mainly to focus upon in this essay. Montaigne remarks in "Of Cruelty" that "If vertue cannot shine but by resisting contrarie appetites, shall we then say, it cannot passe without the assistance of vice, and oweth him this, that by his meanes it attaineth to honour and credit" (2:110). He elaborates on the same theme in "Of Experience": "Even as the Stoickes say, *that Vices were profitably brought in; to give esteeme and make head unto vertue;* So may we with better reason and bold conjecture, affirme, that Nature hath lent us griefe and paine, for the honour of pleasure and service of indolency" (3:357). He also writes in "Of Experience," in a passage drawn from Plutarch: "Our life is composed, as is the harmony of the World, of contrary things; so of divers tunes, some pleasant, some harsh, some sharpe, some flat, some low and some high: What would that Musition say, that should love but some one of them? He ought to know how to use them severally and how to entermingle them. So should we both of goods and evils, which are consubstantiall to our life. Our being cannot subsist without this commixture, whereto one side is no lesse necessary than the other" (3:352–3).

Such a view of virtue's dependence on vice—paradoxical rather than invidiously binary—is clearly relevant to both the structure and texture of *The Tempest*. Antonio and Sebastian's unregenerate rapaciousness and desperation are contrasted throughout to Gonzalo's beneficence and hopefulness, quite directly during the very speech in which Gonzalo paraphrases Montaigne. Venus is counterpointed with

279

Ceres within the wedding masque, and the conspiracy of Caliban, Stephano, and Trinculo complements as well as disrupts the performance of the masque itself, whose high artifice and graciousness remain in our memory as much as the drunken malice of the conspiracy does in Prospero's. Caliban's own earthiness is constantly in counterpoint to Ariel's spirit—they are conceived in terms of each other.

Similarly, Miranda's celebrated verse, "O brave new world/That has such people in't," is not denied by, but co-exists with, Prospero's answer, "'Tis new to thee" (5.1.183–4). Neither response is privileged: youth and age are as consubstantial in the play as good and evil. Prospero's skepticism is directed toward the court party Miranda admires, not toward her and Ferdinand, whose marriage he himself speaks of with reverence and hope:

> Fair encounter
> Of two most rare affections! Heavens rain grace
> On that which breeds between 'em.
>
> (3.1.72–4)

The marriage, indeed, is at the heart of Prospero's "project" within the play and is finally associated with the "project" of the play itself, "Which was to please," that the actor playing Prospero refers to in the Epilogue.

Both projects depend upon a union of opposites, of goods and evils, that ultimately suggests transformation as well as symbiosis. At the outset of the action Prospero tells Miranda, when she sees the shipwreck, that there is "no harm done ... No harm," and that he has "done nothing but in care" of her (1.2.15–7). His care culminates in Miranda's betrothal, but evolves through her suffering as well as his own, and he associates that suffering with the blessing as well as pain of their exile from Milan. They were driven from the city, he tells her, "By foul play," but "blessedly holp hither" (1.2.62–3):

> There they hoist us
> To cry to th' sea that roared to us, to sigh
> To th' winds, whose pity, sighing back again,
> Did us but loving wrong.
>
> (1.2. 148–51)

The same motif is expressed by Ferdinand as he submits to Prospero's rule and works as a "patient log-man" (3.1.68), a ritual ordeal that Prospero contrives to make him earn and value the love of Miranda:

> There be some sports are painful, and their labour
> Delight in them set off; some kinds of baseness

Are nobly undergone; and my most poor matters
Point to rich ends. This my mean task
Would be as heavy to me, as odious, but
The mistress which I serve quickens what's dead,
And makes my labours pleasures. O, she is
Ten times more gentle than her father's crabbed,
And he's composed of harshness. I must remove
Some thousands of these logs and pile them up,
Upon a sore injunction. My sweet mistress
Weeps when she sees me work, and says such baseness
Had never like executor. I forget.
But these sweet thoughts do even refresh my labours,
Most busil'est when I do it.

(3.1.1–15)

This paradoxical combination of opposites—delight and pain, gentleness and harshness, the quickening of the dead—is analogous to the Christian idea of *felix culpa* that nourished Guarini's conception of the genre of tragicomedy to which *The Tempest* belongs and that is also to be found in the voyage literature frequently associated with *The Tempest*.[9] In "A true reportory of the wreck" off the islands of Bermuda, for example, William Strachey exalted the marvelous beneficence of the shipwreck at the same time that he delineated the vicious dissension among the voyagers that developed in Bermuda and later in Virginia, the result, he wrote, of "the permissive providence of God."[10]

The manner in which the possibility of fortunate suffering informs the moral consubstantiality of the action of *The Tempest,* however, suggests the particular force of the process of Montaigne's thought in the play, a process that reaches its climax in Prospero's forgiveness of his enemies, the speech that Shakespeare derived directly from "Of Cruelty." In the ostensibly digressive manner that is typical of him, Montaigne opens the essay with a discussion of virtue, the passage Shakespeare paraphrases in the play. "Me thinks vertue is another manner of thing," Montaigne writes,

and much more noble than the inclinations unto goodnesse,
which in us are ingendered. Mindes well borne, and directed
by themselves, follow one same path, and in their actions represent
the same visage, that the vertuous doe. But vertue importeth, and
soundeth somewhat I wot not what greater and more active, than
by an happy complexion, gently and peaceably, to suffer it selfe
to be led or drawne, to follow reason. He that through a naturall
facilitie, and genuine mildnesse, should neglect or contemne
injuries received, should no doubt performe a rare action, and

281

worthy commendation: But he who being toucht and stung to
the quicke, with any wrong or offence received, should arme
himselfe with reason against this furiously-blind desire of revenge,
and in the end after a great conflict, yeeld himselfe master over-it,
should doubtlesse doe much more. The first should doe well, the
other vertuously: the one action might be termed goodnesse, the
other vertue. For, *It seemeth that the verie name of vertue presupposeth
difficultie, and inferreth resistance, and cannot well exercise it selfe without
an enemie.* It is peradventure the reason we call God good, mightie,
liberall, and just, but we terme him not vertuous.

(2:108)[11]

Shakespeare's version of this passage occurs in the last act of *The
Tempest*, after Ariel tells Prospero of the sufferings of the court party.

ARIEL Your charm so strongly works 'em
 That if you now beheld them, your affections
 Would become tender.
PROSPERO Dost thou think so, spirit?
ARIEL Mine would, sir, were I human.
PROSPERO And mine shall.
 Hast thou, which art but air, a touch, a feeling
 Of their afflictions, and shall not myself,
 One of their kind, that relish all as sharply
 Passions as they, be kindlier moved than thou art?
 Though with their high wrongs I am struck to th' quick,
 Yet with my nobler reason 'gainst my fury
 Do I take part. The rarer action is
 In virtue than in vengeance. They being penitent,
 The sole drift of my purpose doth extend
 Not a frown further. Go, release them, Ariel.
 My charms I'll break, their senses I'll restore,
 And they shall be themselves.

(5.1. 17–32)

Shakespeare's reliance upon Florio's translation of Montaigne in this
speech was first pointed out by Eleanor Prosser in 1965 and now
seems self-evident.[12] "Though with their high wrongs I am struck to
th' quick/Yet with my nobler reason 'gainst my fury/Do I take part"
is clearly indebted in phraseology as well as conception to Montaigne,
and "The rarer action is/In virtue than in vengeance" is particularly
indebted to Florio's phrase, "performe a rare action," which in the
original reads "feroit chose très-belle et digne de louange," "do a fine
and praiseworthy thing." These verbal parallels have been generally

accepted in Shakespeare criticism, but their larger implications for the characterization of Prospero and for much else in the play have been, I think, almost willfully neglected.[13] A figure of supernatural as well as patriarchal authority, Prospero has godlike attributes, including a disquieting measure of the kind of irritability and wrath that often characterizes the Lord God in the earlier books of the Old Testament, but he learns about his humanity in the course of the action,[14] and he transforms himself (as well as others) in a way that Montaigne specifically illuminates. His speech on compassion constitutes both an implicit acknowledgment of the difference between God's power and man's, a prologue to the adjuration of his "rough magic" that immediately follows, and an elucidation of the consequent strife that his human virtue entails. Many, if not most, of the traits and actions that in recent years have been thought to falsify Prospero's ostensible motives and to signify his intractably tyrannical, if not colonialist, mentality, are made immediately intelligible by Montaigne's essay. His impatience with his daughter, and with her suitor, the son of his enemy, his "beating mind," his insistent asperity, his marked reluctance in forgiving his brother, and his violence to Caliban: all are ultimately signs of the struggle of virtue that Montaigne describes. Rather than subverting Prospero's "project," they constitute and authenticate it. Touched and stung to the quick in the present as well as in the past, animated by a "furious," if not "furiously-blind desire of revenge," Prospero "in the end after a great conflict, yeeld[s] himselfe master over-it" (2:108). The emotional keynote of the play is precisely this sense of Prospero's labor pains, of the "sea-change," to paraphrase Ariel's luminous song, that he "suffer[s],"[15] of his "groan[ing]" "Under [the] burthen" of his "sea-sorrow" (1.2.401, 156, 170) to give birth to new and resolved feelings. The action of the play dramatizes this process. The ordeals to which Prospero subjects others on the island are at once recapitulations of his beating memories and images of his effort to overcome them. His interruption of the wedding masque when he remembers Caliban (and perhaps thereby unconsciously expresses the threat of his own sexual desires)[16] is intelligible in just these terms, as is his ultimate and pained recognition that Caliban is native to him, has been made, indeed, partly in his image: "this thing of darkness I/Acknowledge mine" (5.1.275–6). The play's unusual obedience to the classical unities intensifies the sense of Prospero's struggle and is exactly appropriate to the presentation of the minute-to-minute pulsations, *le passage*, of a mind in the throes of accepting and forgiving.

Shakespeare also explores what makes compassion possible in *The Tempest*, and the whole of "Of Cruelty" is germane to this exploration, not just the introductory passage from which Shakespeare directly borrows. In the subsequent argument of the essay Montaigne reiterates the proposition that to be "simply stored with a facile and gentle nature" may "make a man innocent, but not vertuous," a condition "neere unto imperfection and weaknesse," and adds that "the verie names of Goodnesse and innocentie are for this respect in some sort names of contempt" (2:113). He goes on, however, to identify his own temperament with precisely such "a facile and gentle nature," and this identification is the essay's core subject. It is what makes the whole of it coherent, what connects it with "Of the Cannibals," whose essential subject is also cruelty,[17] and what forms the deepest ligament, I think, between both essays and Shakespeare's *Tempest*. "My vertue," Montaigne writes, "is a vertue, or to say better innocencie, accidentall and casuall . . . a kinde of simple-plaine innocencie, without vigor or art." "Amongst all other vices," he continues, announcing the theme of this essay, "there is none I hate more, than crueltie, both by nature and judgement, as the extremest of all vices" (2:115, 117). Montaigne's conjunction of his "innocence" and his hatred of cruelty has wide implications for an understanding of *The Tempest*. Montaigne says that he "cannot chuce but grieve" at seeing a "chickins neck puld off, or a pigge stickt," and "cannot well endure a seele dew-bedabled hare to groane, when she is seized upon by the houndes; although hunting be a violent sport" (2:117). His response is the same to cruelty to human beings. He protests that "Let any man be executed by law, how deservedly soever, I cannot endure to behold the execution with an unrelenting eye," and he condemns the "extreme point whereunto the crueltie of man may attaine," in which men torture others "onely to this end, that they may enjoy the pleasing spectacle." "I live in an age," he continues, "wherein we abound with incredible examples of this vice, through the licentiousnesse of our civill and intestine warres: And read all ancient stories, be they never so tragicall, you shall find not to equall those, we see daily practised" (2:119, 121). The contemporary civil wars in France elicit Montaigne's compassion, but they do not create it. The premise as well as the conclusion of Montaigne's response to cruelty is the recognition of his own inherently sympathetic nature: "I have a verie feeling and tender compassion of other mens afflictions, and should more easily weep for companie sake, if possiblie for any occasion whatsoever, I could shed teares. There is nothing sooner moveth teares in me, than to see others weepe, not onely fainedly, but howsoever, whether truly or forcedly" (2:119).

The discrimination of such compassionate impulses lies close to the heart of Montaigne's definition of himself in the *Essais* as a whole. In an addition made in 1588 to the opening essay of the first volume, when the full direction of the *Essais* must have become clear to him, he announces, "I am much inclined to mercie, and affected to mild-nesse. So it is, that in mine opinion, I should more naturally stoope unto compassion, than bend to estimation. Yet is pitty held a vicious passion among the Stoicks. They would have us aid the afflicted, but not to faint, and co-suffer with them" (1:18). This opposition between compassion and detachment, as Jean Starobinski has sug-gested,[18] is part of the central dialectic of the *Essais*. Montaigne goes on to deprecate his mildness as effeminate and childish, but the Stoic self-sufficiency that at once animates his project and is its ostensible goal is always balanced, in this essay and in the *Essais* as a whole, by his disposition to sympathize and "co-suffer" with others. One critic has argued that in "[p]utting cruelty first" among vices, ahead even of the seven deadly sins, Montaigne in effect repudiates Christian theol-ogy.[19] But that issue is at least open to debate. Montaigne has plenty to say about pride in *Sebond* and elsewhere, and his extraordinary ca-pacity to "co-suffer" with other human beings, remarkable for his age, but not unlike Shakespeare's, can just as aptly and interestingly be understood as an internalization, if not embodiment, of Christian charity.

In *The Tempest*, in any event, cosuffering, compassion, is a tonic chord in the whole of the action, not just the work of Prospero alone. It is revealed throughout the play in the "piteous heart" of Miranda, who is animated by "the very virtue of compassion," as well as in Gonzalo. Gonzalo's "innocence," like Miranda's, is "simple-plaine ... without vigor or art," and like Montaigne's also, it is com-posed of a "verie feeling and tender compassion of others mens af-fliction" (2:117, 119). It is the sight of "the good old Lord Gonzalo" and others in tears, "Brimful of sorrow and dismay" (5.1.14–5), that prompts Ariel's sympathy for the courtiers, and through him, the movement toward compassion in Prospero. "[I]f you now be-held them, your affections/Would become tender," Ariel says to Prospero, "Mine would, sir, were I human" (5.1.18–9). And Prospero answers, as we have seen, that if Ariel, who is but air, can have a "feeling/Of their afflictions," shall not he, "One of their kind," who relishes passions as sharply as they, be "kindlier moved," take the part of "reason 'gainst [his] fury," and find the rarer action in virtue than in vengeance (5.1.21–6).

Prospero, of course, emphatically does not have the innocence that nourishes Miranda's "virtue of compassion," nor does he have the in-nocent nature of Gonzalo, though he has from the first understood and responded to both. They can forgive instinctively, he cannot. But in this speech, the decisive moment in the action, Prospero is able to emulate them. He speaks of his reason in the struggle of virtue, as

Montaigne does, but the speech more importantly suggests another faculty as well. "Kind," as often in Shakespeare, denotes humankind as well as human kindness, and it is in the first instance Prospero's ability to imagine what others feel and to understand what he has in common with them—including, especially, Caliban—that enables him to sympathize with Alonso and to forgive Antonio and Sebastian despite the wrongs that continue to anger him.

It is particularly significant that it should be Ariel, associated throughout the play with Prospero's imaginative power, who prompts this movement, because human imagination is finally the deepest preoccupation of Shakespeare in *The Tempest* and a central filament in Montaigne's thoughts on compassion as well. In an apparent digression in the midst of the discussion of forgiveness in "Of Cruelty," Montaigne suggests that a lack of imagination can "*sometimes counterfeit vertuous effects*" and that the Germans and the Swiss, for example, appear brave in war because they have "scarce sense and wit" to imagine their danger, whereas the "subtiltie of the Italians, and the vivacitie of their conceptions" is so great, that they foresee "such dangers as might betide them . . . far-off" and can provide for their safety even before they actually see the danger (2:114). Montaigne's remark may be ironic, but it is nonetheless to such "sense and wit," such "vivacitie" of imagination, that he relates his own innocence and susceptibility to the suffering of others.

That imaginative susceptibility also subsumes the indictment of the cruelty of European culture in "Of the Cannibals," and it appears as well in interesting ways in another essay, "Of Cato the Younger," in which Montaigne writes,

> I am not possessed with this common errour, to judge of others according to that I am my selfe. I am easie to beleeve things differing from my selfe. Though I be engaged to one forme, I doe not tie the world unto it, as every man doth. And I beleeve and conceive a thousand manners of life, contrarie to the common sort: I more easily admit and receive difference, than resemblance in us. I discharge as much as a man will, another being of my conditions and principles, and simply consider of it my selfe without relation, framing it upon it's owne modell. Though my selfe be not continent, yet doe I sincerely commend and allow the continencie of the Capuchins and Theatines, and highly praise their course of life. I doe by imagination insinuate my selfe into their place: and by how much more they bee other than my selfe, so much the more doe I love and honour them.
>
> (1:243)

Montaigne discusses an analogous imaginative "insinuation" in "Of Diverting and Diversions," where he relates cosuffering to the creation as well as effects of rhetoric and art:

> An orator (saith Rhetorick) in the play of his pleading, shall be moved at the sound of his owne voice, and by his fained agitations: and suffer himselfe to be cozoned by the passion he representeth: imprinting a lively and essentiall sorrow, by the jugling he acteth, to transferre it into the judges, whom of the two it concerneth lesse: As the persons hired at our funerals who to aide the ceremony of mourning, make sale of their teares by measure, and of their sorrow by waight . . . *Quintilian* reporteth, to have scene Comedians so farre ingaged in a sorowful part, that they wept after being come to their lodgings: and of himselfe, that having undertaken to move a certaine passion in another: he had found himselfe surprised not only with shedding of teares, but with a palenesse of countenance, and behaviour of a man truly dejected with griefe.
>
> (3:59–60)

Quintilian's remark is a commonplace of the period, but Montaigne's mention of it in "Of Diversions" has a special suggestiveness because, like *The Tempest,* the essay associates the virtue of compassion not only with the salutary effects of the imagination but also with its illusoriness.[20] Right after mentioning Quintilian, Montaigne remarks that no cause is needed

> to excite our minde. A doating humour without body, without substance overswayeth and tosseth it up and downe. Let me thinke of building Castles in *Spayne*, my imagination will forge me commodities and afford me meanes and delights wherewith my minde is really tickled and essentially gladded. How ofte do we pester our spirits with anger or sadnesse by such shadowes, and entangle our selves into fantasticall passions which alter both our mind and body? what astonished, flearing and confused mumpes and mowes doth this dotage stirre up in our visages? what skippings and agitations of members and voice, seemes it not by this man alone, that he hath false visions of a multitude of other men with whom he doth negotiate; or some inwarde Goblin that torments him? Enquire of your selfe, where is the object of this alteration? Is there any thing but us in nature, except subsisting nullity? over whom it hath any power?
>
> (3:61)

In a well-known passage in "An Apology of *Raymond Sebond*," Montaigne remarks that "We wake sleeping, and sleep waking . . . Our reason and soul, receiving the phantasies and opinions, which sleeping seize on them, and authorising our dreames actions, with like approbation, as it doth the daies. Why make we not a doubt, whether our thinking, and our working be another dreaming, and our waking some kind of sleeping" (2:317).

The same consciousness both of the force of human imagination and of its evanescence in human existence haunts Shakespeare's *Tempest* as well. Caliban expresses it with the greatest immediacy in his moving speech about the magic of the island and of his own dreams:

> Be not afeard, the isle is full of noises,
> Sounds, and sweet airs, that give delight and hurt not.
> Sometimes a thousand twangling instruments
> Will hum about mine ears, and sometimes voices,
> That if I then had waked after long sleep,
> Will make me sleep again, and then in dreaming
> The clouds methought would open and show riches
> Ready to drop upon me, that when I waked
> I cried to dream again.
>
> (3.2. 133–41)

Prospero conveys a similar apprehension of imaginative impalpability and wonder, in a more metaphysical key, in his famous speech to Ferdinand after the interruption of the masque. He is enraged with Caliban, but in that very process, he incorporates Caliban's dreaming as well as interprets it. "You do look, my son, in a moved sort," he tells Ferdinand,

> As if you were dismayed. Be cheerful, sir;
> Our revels now are ended. These our actors,
> As I foretold you, were all spirits, and
> Are melted into air, into thin air,
> And, like the baseless fabric of this vision,
> The cloud-capped towers, the gorgeous palaces,
> The solemn temples, the great globe itself,
> Yea, all which it inherit, shall dissolve,
> And, like this insubstanial pageant faded,
> Leave not a rack behind. We are such stuff
> As dreams are made on, and our little life
> Is rounded with a sleep.
>
> (4.1. 146–58)

The *topos* of life as a dream is of course very common in the Renaissance, but its collocation in *The Tempest* with the impalpable realities of the imagination as well as with Prospero's achievement of compassion, suggests the particular matrix of ideas found in Montaigne's essays. If not a source, Montaigne's association of these ideas is an explanation. One tendency in recent criticism of *The Tempest* has been to see Prospero's magnificent speech and the play itself as an expression of Shakespeare's disenchantment with the limitations of theatrical illusion.[21] But Caliban's dreaming and Prospero's incorporation of it in his reflection on the "baseless fabric of this vision" do not so much question the value of the theatre, as characterize the dream-like nature of the human experience it imitates; and what the analogues to Montaigne should make clear is that Shakespeare's sense of this insubstantial pageant, of the subsisting nullity both of human existence and of the theatre, is not ironic, but the "stuff" of wonder and a motive to charity.

The idea of imaginative insinuation and compassion is given a final, hauntingly expansive, turn in the epilogue to *The Tempest*, when Prospero, still the character but now also an ordinary human being, an actor, asks the audience for applause. He speaks at precisely the moment in a play when we too are midway between our own world and the world of the theatre.[22] "Let me not," he says to us,

> Since I have my dukedom got,
> And pardoned the deceiver, dwell
> In this bare island by your spell,
> But release me from my bands
> With the help of your good hands.
> Gentle breath of yours my sails
> Must fill, or else my project fails,
> Which was to please. Now I want
> Spirits to enforce, art to enchant;
> And my ending is despair
> Unless I be relieved by prayer,
> Which pierces so that it assaults
> Mercy itself, and frees all faults.
> As you from crimes would pardoned be,
> Let your indulgence set me free.

(5.1.323–38)

Jan Kott[23] as well as other critics and directors have wished to place the entire stress in this epilogue on "despair." The emphasis is more naturally placed, if we attend to the syntax, on the "piercing" power of prayer, a phraseology common in Shakespeare but never in this self-consciously theatrical context. Montaigne, very appositely, uses the word "pierce" in his essay, "Of the Force of the Imagination," to describe his vulnerability to the suffering of others: "I am one of those that feels a very great conflict and power of imagination . . . The impression of it pierceth me . . . The sight of others anguishes doth sensibly drive me into anguish; and my sense hath often usurped the sense of a third man" (1:92). The same thought and the same image of piercing inform Montaigne's description of the moving power of poetry, and especially of plays, in "Of Cato the Younger," the essay in which he talks of imaginatively insinuating himself into the place of others. "It is more apparently seene in theatres," he writes, "that the sacred inspiration of the Muses, having first stirred up the Poet with a kinde of agitation unto choler, unto griefe, unto hatred, yea and beyond himselfe, whither and howsoever they please, doth also by the Poet strike and enter into the Actor, and [consecutively] by the Actor, a whole auditorie or multitude. It is the ligament of our senses depending one of another." "Even from my infancie," he concludes, "Poesie hath had the vertue to transpierce and transport me" (1:246).

The religious reverberations of the allusion to the Lord's prayer in Prospero's epilogue may be peculiarly Shakespearean (though Montaigne too repeatedly identifies the verse "forgive us our trespasses" with the virtue of forgiveness), but the correspondences between the sympathetic illusions of the theatre and of life, between theatrical imagination and human compassion, are essentially the same as they are in Montaigne. *The Tempest*, of course, calls attention to theatrical imagination not only in its evident meta-theatrical references but also in the distinctive manner in which it moves us. It begins with the depiction of a storm that captures Miranda's imaginative sympathy as well as ours, and then immediately makes us understand that the storm was not real, that it was an illusion of an illusion; and this exponential consciousness of our own imaginative work in the theatre informs our response throughout the action. We are thus peculiarly receptive to Prospero's epilogue. For what the actor playing Prospero suggests, in his grave and beautiful plea for our applause, is a recapitulation and crystallization of what the experience of the play itself has all along induced us to feel: that the illusory and evanescent passions of the the-atre are like those of actual life, and that both can be cosuffered, that the imaginative sympathy which animates our individual responses to the play also binds us together, "our senses depending one of another." He suggests, in a plea which is like a prayer, that an audience's generos-ity to the fictions of the actors is like mercy itself, and that the com-passionate imaginative ligaments which form a community within the theatre can also compose a community, in Montaigne's words, "void of all revenge and free from all rancour" (1:365), outside of it. There is no more spacious and humane a justification of the theatre in all of Shakespeare.[24]

NOTES

1. All references to *The Tempest* are to the New Oxford edition, ed. Stephen Orgel (Oxford: Clarendon Press, 1987) and will be cited parenthetically in the text by act, scene, and line numbers.

2. *Montaigne's Essays,* trans. John Florio, ed. L. C. Harmer, 3 vols. (London: Everyman's Library-Dent, 1965), 1:220. Subsequent references to Montaigne's essays are to this edition and will be cited parenthetically in the text by volume and page number.

3. For a discussion of Shakespeare's affinities to Montaigne in *All's Well That Ends Well* and *Othello*, see Arthur Kirsch, *Shakespeare and the Experience of Love* (Cambridge: Cambridge Univ. Press, 1981), pp. 121–7, 38–9.

4. Leo Salingar, *Dramatic Form in Shakespeare and the Jacobeans* (Cambridge: Cambridge Univ. Press, 1986), pp. 107–33. See also Kenneth Muir, ed., New Arden edition of *King Lear* (Cambridge MA: Harvard Univ. Press, 1959), pp. 249–53.

5. D. J. Gordon, "Name and Fame: Shakespeare's *Coriolanus*," in *The Renaissance Imagination: Essays and Lectures by D. J. Gordon,* ed. Stephen Orgel (Berkeley and Los Angeles: Univ. of California Press, 1980), pp. 203–19.

6. Robert Ellrodt, "Self-Consciousness in Montaigne and Shakespeare," in *ShS* 28 (1975): 37–50, 42.

7. See also W. H. Auden's brilliant interpretation of *The Tempest* in *The Dyer's Hand and Other Essays* (New York: Random House, 1962), pp. 128–34.

8. For the most comprehensive and elegant instance of contemporary interpretations of *The Tempest*, see Stephen Orgel's introduction to his New Oxford edition of the play, pp. 1–87. For discussions of the subject of colonialism, specifically, see, e.g., Stephen J. Greenblatt, "Learning to Curse: Aspects of Linguistic Colonialism in the Sixteenth Century," in *First Images of America: The Impact of the New World on the Old,* ed. Fredi Chiapelli, vol. 2 (Berkeley and Los Angeles: Univ. of California Press, 1976), pp. 561–80; Francis Barker and Peter Hulme, "Nymphs and Reapers Heavily Vanish: The Discursive Con-texts of *The Tempest*," in *Alternative Shakespeares,* ed. John Drakakis (London and New York: Methuen, 1985), pp. 191–205; Terence Hawkes, "Swisser-Swatter: Making a Man of English Letters," in *Alternative Shakespeares,* pp. 26–46; and Paul Brown, "'This thing of darkness I acknowledge mine': *The Tempest* and the Discourse of Colonialism," in *Political Shakespeare: New Essays in Cultural Materialism* (Ithaca and London: Cornell Univ. Press, 1985), pp. 48–71. For a full consideration of the scholarship on colonialism and *The Tempest* and a decisively trenchant criticism of it, see Meredith Anne Skura, "Discourse and the Individual: The Case of Colonialism in *The Tempest*," *SQ* 40, 1 (Spring 1989): 42–69.

9. See Arthur C. Kirsch, *Jacobean Dramatic Perspectives* (Charlottesville: Univ. Press of Virginia, 1972), pp. 7–15.

10. See, e.g., William Strachey, "A true repertory of the wreck," Appendix B, *The Tempest*, ed. Orgel, pp. 212–3.

11. "Il me semble que la vertu est chose autre et plus noble que les inclinations à la bonté qui naissent en nous. Les ame reglées d'elles mesmes et bien nées, elles suyvent mesme train, et representent en leurs actions mesme visage que les vertueuses. Mais la vertu sonne je ne sçay quoi de plus grand et de plus actif que de se laisser, par une heureuse complexion, doucement et paisiblement conduire à la suite de la raison. Celuy qui, d'une douceur et facilité naturelle, mespriseroit les offences receus, feroit chose très-belle et digne de louange; mais celuy qui, picqué et outré jusques au vif d'une offence, s'armeroit des armes de la raison contre ce furieux appetit de vengeance, et après un grand conflict s'en redroit en fin maistre, feroit sans doubte beaucoup plus. Celuy-là feroit bien, et cettuy-cy vertuesement; l'une action se pourroit dire borné; l'autre, vertu; car il semble que le nom de la vertue presuppose de la difficulté et du contraste, et qu'elle ne peut s'exercer sans partie. C'est à l'aventure pourquoy nous nommons Dieu bon, fort, et liberal, et juste; mais nous ne le nommons pas vertueux: ses operations sont toutes naifves et sans effort" (Michel Montaigne, *Oeuvres Completes*, ed. Albert Thibaudet et Maurice Rat [Paris: Pléiade-Gallimard, 1962], pp. 400–1).

12. Eleanor Prosser, "Shakespeare, Montaigne, and the 'Rarer Action,'" *ShakS* 1 (1965): 261–4.

13. For a notable exception, see John B. Bender, "The Day of *The Tempest*," *ELH* 47, 2 (Summer 1980): 235–58, 250–1.

14. See Jack Miles, *God: A Biography* (New York: Alfred A. Knopf. 1995), pp. 240–4, for a suggestive discussion of the changing faces of God Himself in the Old Testament, including in Second Isaiah, the movement, through His participation in human experience, from an inhumane (because first inhuman) God to a God of "loving pity."

15. For an illuminating explication of Ariel's song and particularly the transformational resonance of the word "suffers," see Stephen Orgel, "New Uses of Adversity: Tragic Experience in *The Tempest*," in *In Defense of Reading: A Reader's Approach to Literary Criticism,* ed. Reuben A. Brower and Richard Poirier (New York: Dutton, 1962), pp. 110–32, 116.

16. See Skura, p. 60.

17. See David Quint, "A Reconsideration of Montaigne's *Des Cannibales*," *MLQ* 51, 4 (December 1990): 459–89. Quint argues that Montaigne is less interested in investigating the new world in "Des Cannibales" than in criticizing the old and concludes that Montaigne "may not so much create the figure of the noble savage" in the essay "as disclose the savagery of the nobility" (p. 482).

18. Jean Starobinski, *Montaigne in Motion*, trans. Arthur Goldhammer (Chicago and London: Univ. of Chicago Press, 1985).

19. Judith N. Shklar, *Ordinary Vices* (Cambridge MA and London: Harvard Univ. Press, 1984), pp. 7–44.

20. For a discussion from a different perspective of the possible relevance of "Of Diversions" to *The Tempest*, see Gail Kern Paster, "Montaigne, Dido, and *The Tempest*: 'How came that widow in?'" *SQ* 35, 1 (Spring 1984): 91–4.

21. See, e.g., Alvin B. Kernan, *The Playwright as Magician: Shakespeare's Image of the Poet in the English Public Theatre* (New Haven and London: Yale Univ. Press, 1979), pp. 129–59.

22. See Michael Goldman, *Shakespeare and the Energies of Drama* (Princeton: Princeton Univ. Press, 1972), pp. 147–8.

23. Jan Kott, *Shakespeare Our Contemporary*, trans. Boleslaw Taborski (Garden City NY: Anchor Books—Doubleday, 1966), pp. 237–85.

24. An abbreviated version of this essay was presented in a talk at a symposium on "Cultural Exchange between European Nations" in Uppsala, Sweden and published in *Studia Acta Universitatis Upsaliensia Anglistica Upsaliensia 86*, ed. Gunnar Sorelius and Michael Srigley (Uppsala, 1994), pp. 111–21.

"Virtue, Vice, and Compassion in Montaigne and *The Tempest*" first appeared in *Studies in English Literature* 37:2 (Spring, 1997): 337–52.

Problems of Stagecraft in
"The Tempest"

Stanley Wells

This essay is offered as a tribute to Jan Kott in appreciation of all he has done to stimulate international enthusiasm for Shakespeare's plays.

THE TEMPEST is a play that commands great admiration as a poem in dramatic form. As is well known, the editors of the First Folio gave it pride of place in that volume; and as Shakespeare's last unaided play, it is often regarded as the culmination of his career as a poetic dramatist: a final, highly personal, even visionary utterance concerned at least in part with the relationship between life and art, and having at its centre a figure who has often been regarded as Shakespeare's shadowing forth of himself.

Its plot is comparatively slight, having none of the density and complexity of the plays that immediately preceded it in Shakespeare's output such as the immensely intricate *Cymbeline*. Its language, on the contrary, is very substantial—far more so than would have been necessary to project the story in naturalistic terms; the poetry is rich, dense, suggestive, complexly resonant; wonderfully integrated yet also, because of the way the play is constructed, falling often into set pieces (Prospero's "Our revels now are ended" is only the most obvious example) that are detachable and can almost be considered as poems in their own right.

Nevertheless, in spite of all its poetical power, the play has often "proved curiously resistant to successful theatrical realization,"[1] and indeed has been subjected over the centuries to various kinds of adaptation in the attempt to increase its theatrical viability; and when it is performed in relatively unadapted form it often fails to live up to the expectations raised by the impression it creates, in reading, on the theatre of the mind. In short, this is a play that exemplifies more than most the tensions between literature and drama.

In this paper I want to examine certain aspects of the play in the light of the various kinds of problems posed by their theatrical realization: not simply practical problems such as may be posed by any playscript, but problems that derive particularly from features of dramatic style which, if they are not unique to this play, are at least characteristic of the mode in which it is written. And I will start with the opening scene, which in practice has proved one of the most problematical.

THE OPENING SCENE

Representing a shipwreck caused by a storm at sea, this scene provides obvious opportunities for theatrical spectacle, opportunities which the theatre has not been slow to exploit. The opening stage direction of the original text, written to be performed on the bare boards of the Globe or the Blackfriars, refers only to sound: *"A tempestuous noise of thunder and lightning heard."* No doubt the actors entering upon the stage would have been able to convey through gestures and bodily movements the impression that they were reeling around on a storm-driven vessel, and conceivably some properties were used to add to the atmospherics, but there could have been nothing like the visual effects demanded half a century later when the play was given at the Duke of York's theatre in an adaptation by Dryden and Davenant.

There, as the overture played, a curtain rose to reveal a new, emblematic "frontispiece" with behind it

> The scene, which represents a thick Cloudy Sky, a very Rocky Coast, and a Tempestuous See in perpetual Agitation. This Tempest (suppos'd to be rais'd by Magick) has many dreadful Objects in it, as several Spirits in horrid shapes flying down amongst the Sailors, then rising and crossing in the Air. And when the Ship is sinking, the whole House is darken'd, and a shower of Fire falls upon 'em. This is accompanied with Lightning, and several Claps of Thunder, to the end of the Storm.

The scene that follows, though it retained much of Shakespeare's dialogue, made lengthy additions to it, including a lot of nautical language indicating stage business designed to increase the impression of a storm at sea. At the end of the scene, in the midst of a shower of fire, the scene changed, the theatre darkened, and "when the Lights return discover that Beautiful part of the Island, which was the Habitation of Prospero."[2]

The emphasis on spectacle inaugurated by the Dryden-Davenant adaptation reached its apogee in Charles Kean's production at the Princess's Theatre in 1857, in which the shipwreck was represented with extraordinary vividness but in which not a word was spoken. Shakespeare was being translated into a different medium from that in which he wrote: drama was replaced by spectacular mime; the play came close to the condition of ballet.

As this production continued, one triumph of spectacular staging succeeded another, but the text throughout was so severely shortened as to incur the condemnation even of the theatre historian G. C. D. Odell—no purist in these matters—who remarked that "the Shakespearian enthusiast must have left the theatre with a feeling of disappointment, not to say resentment and disgust, resolving hereafter to seek his poetry at Sadler's Wells, where scenery was less in evidence."[3]

Those are the terms in which Odell writes about the production when he is discussing the text; but when he comes to describe the production itself he reveals a distinct ambivalence in his reactions to it, describing it as "probably the most beautiful and astonishing ever put on the stage." "Purists then, like purists now," he writes—implicitly aligning himself with those who are not purists–"lamented their lost fragments of Shakespeare; but the average theatregoer simply revelled in the show for a long succession of performances."

TEXT VERSUS SPECTACLE?

These conflicting judgements are symptomatic of a constant ambivalence in the reactions of audiences to poetic drama: a feeling on the one hand that the text is what most matters, that the highest pleasures offered by the play are those that come through language; and at the same time a somewhat guilty feeling that in the theatre *other values may supervene*, even that the play's poetic integrity may be subverted by the more physical pleasures provided in its theatrical realization.

In recent times we have perhaps become a little more tolerant of adaptation, more receptive to the notion that each attempt to put a play on the stage must differ from every other one, and that it is ultimately impossible to define an essence which only is the play itself; we may respond to the pleasures of productions that alter the text, that substitute theatrical for verbal effects, that use the text as a jumping-off ground for an experience very different from that conveyed by reading alone, even a reading that is fully informed by consciousness of theatrical values.

Nevertheless there are many directors who work with full texts, and many audiences who are interested in the efforts that can made to be faithful to these texts; they present a challenge, and even if the challenge is finally evaded it is worth discussing the nature of this challenge and the terms in which it may be faced.

To return to Scene One of *The Tempest:* although the theatres of Shakespeare's time offered far less opportunity for spectacular staging than those of later ages, the mode in which this scene is composed is not conspicuously poetical. Most of the dialogue is written in prose. This may seem a mere technicality, because Shakespeare's prose can itself be very poetical, but here the prose is relatively naturalistic, colloquial in diction, often subservient to the bustling action that it serves:"Hey, my hearts! Cheerly, cheerly, my hearts! Yare, yare! Take in the topsail. Tend to the master's whistle…" and so on. In spite of a few antiquated expressions, it conveys an impression of modernity; and much of it could stand without alteration in, for instance, a television script.

If this were all, nothing might be lost by submerging it by action, or even by abandoning it altogether in the manner of Charles Kean. But if we look at it closely, and especially in the light of what is to come in later scenes, we may begin to feel that the impression of naturalism is illusory, that the dialogue is not simply atmospheric in the manner that spectacular productions (of any age) emphasize, and that neither is it simply expository of action, setting up the initial situation of the plot.

Rather, the scene is one in which what is represented has emblematic as well as narrative significance, and in which what is said is no less important than what is represented: it is expository of the play's ideas as well as of its plot, and introduces us to what it is perhaps too unfashionable to call the "themes" of the play—to those ideas that enrich its texture and that have caused it to be regarded not just as a stimulus to theatrical effect but also as one of the more important documents in our literary as well as our theatrical heritage. Let us try to look at the scene not from a single point of view but as a whole, a piece of poetical drama.[4]

THE SHIP AS MICROCOSM

We may note first that, as the play is to take place on an island, so this scene takes place upon a ship—itself a kind of island, giving the scene some of the aspects of a microcosm of the whole play. As I have remarked, it opens not with dialogue, but with sound—the ominous sound of thunder and of lightning (I'm not entirely clear what lightning sounds like). In the shorthand of drama, this sound of the elements threatening human life can immediately establish a mode in which symbol is important, in which anything that is heard or seen has significance beyond the mundane. The opening dialogue of the scene, and therefore of the play, gives us an image of authority—the authority exercised by the master of a ship as he gives orders to his crew: it introduces us to the concept of authority as an instrument of control: the master is controlling the crew's efforts which themselves are directed to control the ship so as to withstand the onslaught of forces mysteriously inimical to human life.

Having given us a glimpse of one kind of authority, Shakespeare rapidly juxtaposes it with another. On the ship the master has the kind of authority that a king exercises over the country that he rules. And the next characters to enter are a king—Alonso, King of Naples—and members of his court. It must be one of the minor problems in producing the play that these characters are not named in the dialogue of the scene, and that their offices, so important to our understanding of what is happening, are only implicitly alluded to: this is something that can be at least partially solved by costuming, but it is symptomatic of one of the more awkward aspects of the play's technique.

The King, having entered upon the scene, immediately starts trying to exert an authority that is irrelevant to the circumstances in which he finds himself. On board, the ship's master is king: Alonso's assumption of authority is irrelevant, is indeed subversive of the authority of the true ruler of this little kingdom: and the play that follows is to be much concerned with usurpation, both in the past and in the present.

The Boatswain's rebukes of Alonso and his fellows—at first polite ("I pray you, keep below"), then more insistent ("You mar our labour. Keep your cabin—you do assist the storm")—show two kinds of authority in collision, resulting in danger to each, as the Boatswain points out: "you do assist the storm." We are shown vividly and verbally that in some circumstances the higher power may be at the mercy of a lesser one; a parallel image might be that of a king having to submit to a medical authority. We are shown this through words: "What cares these roarers for the name of king?" asks the exasperated Boatswain, in a simple, direct, and memorable sentence that epitomizes the situation—and that has resonances characteristic of the play in that the word "roarers" could mean not only roaring winds and waves but also rioters, that is those who try to subvert authority. Significant too is the formulation "the name of king," the power of a king derives partly from the name of the office that he occupies, from a word which in itself has no power to quell the inimical forces of thunder and lightning—a theme that Shakespeare had already memorably explored in both *Richard II* and *King Lear*.

The Boatswain expands upon his rebuke in response to Gonzalo's injunction "yet remember whom thou hast aboard." "None that I love more than myself," he replies; "You are a councillor; if you can command these elements to silence, and work the peace of the present, we will not hand a rope more—use your authority. If you cannot, give thanks you have lived so long, and make yourself ready in your cabin for the mischance of the hour, if it so hap."

As the brief scene progresses, we see that the clash between two systems of authority produces reactions that are expressive of character. Sebastian and Antonio are harsh, insolent, and uncharitable—everything that they themselves accuse the Boatswain of being. Gonzalo, on the other hand, is good-humoured, tolerant, and humane. In the face of increasing disaster both the mariners and the more sympathetic members of the King's party abandon all claims to authority and resort to prayer—and if we know the play in advance we will remember that it is to end with a request for the audience's prayers. But two characters—Antonio and Sebastian—seem entirely resistant to the idea that their fate depends upon any power beyond that of the sailors: "We are merely cheated of our lives by drunkards," says Antonio—and we may remember that there will be drunkenness, a condition in which self-control is as it were voluntarily abnegated, in the play, too.

So far as we know at the end of the scene, as the ship splits apart, the storm has won, though Shakespeare cunningly provides a transition with Gonzalo's closing words:

> Now would I give a thousand furlongs of sea for an acre of barren ground—long heath, brown furze, anything. The wills above be done, but I would fain die a dry death.

There are, then, several different sorts of problem in this scene. One is for the actors to establish the characters in the audience's imaginations on the basis of relatively little information. Another is to determine the appropriate balance between naturalism and stylization. And most important, at least for a director who seeks (granted the changes in theatrical conditions between Shakespeare's times and ours) to achieve Shakespeare's effects in his own way, is to allow the ideas that the scene articulates to make themselves apparent: if elaborate sound effects are used, and if visual spectacle is to play its part in the presentation of the scene, the orchestration of these effects must be such that the words carrying the scene's ideas are not lost.

The problem is similar to that of the storm scenes in *King Lear*, though there it is more apparent because Lear so obviously must be heard: even Charles Kean—assuming he was playing Lear himself—would not have totally eliminated words there.

PROBLEMS OF NARRATIVE AND CHARACTER

The opening scene shows us something of the struggle that man has to exert to impose order on his universe, and at the beginning of the next scene we see a man who does literally have power, albeit a limited power, to exert control over the forces of nature. I say at the beginning of the second scene, but directors have frequently chosen to bring Prospero—and even (as in Sam Mendes's 1993 Stratford production) Ariel too—on stage at the very beginning of the play to show us that the storm is of Prospero's making. To do this runs the risk of diminishing the impact of the storm; foregrounding narrative over symbol, it suggests from the start that man *can* control the elements, and so reduces the scene's emblematic quality. It also adds yet another unidentified character to the scene, at least for audiences who are unfamiliar with the play.

The second scene is very much of a contrast with the first in both verbal style and dramatic mode, and taken together the two scenes represent a variation upon a technique of double exposition that Shakespeare uses elsewhere—notably in, for instance, *Hamlet* and *Macbeth*, where too a vividly atmospheric scene or episode is followed by one that lays out information essential to our understanding of the action in a more leisurely, amplificatory style.

In *The Tempest* Prospero's narrative is so long, so relatively free from interruption, so obviously literary, that it is often seen as un-dramatic and in need of theatrical pepping up; but this perhaps underestimates the theatrical force of spoken narrative. An actor inevitably imbues the lines with his own personality, and, as he relives it, Prospero's account of his past can compel our interest.

Prospero's long narration, addressed to Miranda, and his subsequent interchanges with Ariel and Caliban, firmly establish him as the play's central character; indeed there is even a sense in which he might be described as the play's only fully realized human character. I don't mean by this that, as some have maintained, the entire play takes place in Prospero's mind; but it does seem to me that one of the major theatrical problems of the play lies in Shakespeare's use of what we might call foreshortening and symbolical techniques in his presentation of certain characters.

Shakespeare's techniques of characterization vary from play to play, even from phase to phase of his career. In some plays, such as *Coriolanus* and *Antony and Cleopatra,* he is clearly very much interested in the quirks of individual personalities; in others, characterization tends to be more stylized, projecting only selected aspects of a personality and leaving the actor freedom either to maintain some detachment from the character, or to suggest hidden depths not apparent in the dialogue. One may think for example of Don John in *Much Ado About Nothing,* who can be played as a melodramatic villain but for whom some actors try to supply psychological motivation; or of the good and bad Dukes in *As You Like It,* defined largely by contrast.

The plays in which this technique predominates tend to be those in which the emphasis is on ideas rather than on human psychology. Shakespeare is particularly inclined to use such devices in his late plays (especially *Cymbeline* with, for example, its wicked, Snow White-type

Queen), but there is no other play in his output in which they are so predominant as *The Tempest*. In the storm scene Shakespeare rapidly establishes a contrast between Gonzalo on the one hand and, on the other, Antonio and Sebastian—this play's Rosencrantz and Guildenstern, or Tweedledum and Tweedledee—by juxtaposing the idealism of the former with the cynicism of the latter.

DRAMATIZING MORAL CONTRASTS

These are the tips of the icebergs of their personalities, all the actor has to work with at this stage of the play. And as the action continues the same techniques may be observed at work in both these and other characters. It causes particular problems, I think, in the court characters. Prospero names the more important of these in his narration, and it was perhaps in response to the shadowiness of their textual characterization that Mendes, in the production I have referred to, caused each of them to step forward from behind a screen as he did so, helping to fix their identities in our mind. Directorial devices like this, while they may sometimes seem like unnecessary impositions on a play, may also represent relevant and justifiable criticisms of it.

The difficulties with the courtiers come to a head in Act Two, Scene One, in the first part of which we witness their reactions to the shipwreck and to the island on which they find themselves, and in which contrasts between these reactions help to define them: Gonzalo again, and the very subsidiary lord Adrian—a dramatic nonentity if ever there was one—are full of idealism, especially in Gonzalo's Montaigne-inspired description of an ideal commonwealth; whereas Antonio and Sebastian take a jaundiced, cynical view of all they see.

In my experience, the audience's attention is all too liable to sag during this scene, with its somewhat obscure dialogue, its arid witticisms, and its two-dimensional characters. Roger Warren writes of it that "It is ... one of the most difficult for actors to perform and for audiences to concentrate upon," while feeling nevertheless that its problems are soluble—and were solved in Peter Hall's National Theatre production of 1988, largely as the result of subtle acting that found a psychological subtext to motivate the apparently stylized utterances. The actors, we may feel, were baling Shakespeare out; but of course a playwright can legitimately expect help from his interpreters. Another way of tackling the problems, however might be to accept the scene's artificialities and to play it in a consciously stylized fashion.

The dramatic mode of romance within which Shakespeare is working in this play encourages the presentation of moral absolutes, and this is very apparent in *The Tempest*. The moral contrasts within the court party are mirrored in other relationships in the play, most strongly perhaps in that between Ferdinand, the King's son, and Caliban. Here Shakespeare employs a symbolical method of characterization which helps both to distinguish between the two characters and to point to similarities between them. Before we see Caliban, Prospero tells Miranda

> He does make our fire,
> Fetch in our wood, and serves in offices
> That profit us,

and Caliban's first words, spoken "within", are "There's wood enough within." The carrying of wood is a symbolical burden, in Caliban's case a punishment imposed on him for the crime of attempted rape. The uncontrolled sexual urge is easily seen as part of that destructive disorder of which thunder and lightning had been the initial symbols. And it is a clear aspect of the play's self-conscious design that Shakespeare immediately follows the exit of the lustful figure of Caliban with the entrance of the play's romantic lover, Ferdinand.

Where Caliban resists control, Ferdinand, who enters under the magic control of Ariel (and thus of Prospero, whose agent Ariel is), willingly accepts it as a means of winning Miranda. For him love is a power, a bondage, but one that illustrates the Christian paradox that in some kinds of service lies perfect feedom:

> My spirits, as in a dream, are all bound up.
> My father's loss, the weakness which I feel,
> The wreck of all my friends, nor this man's threats,
> To whom I am subdued, are but light to me,
> Might I but through my prison once a day
> Behold this maid. All corners o'th'earth
> Let liberty make use of—space enough
> Have I in such a prison.

THE LOVE-TEST AND BETROTHAL

And Prospero imposes on Ferdinand a love-test, a task such as those to which heroes of chivalric romances were customarily subjected. In some stories, such love-tests involved heroic feats such as the subjugation of giants. Ferdinand's is less arduous: like Caliban, he has to fetch and chop Prospero's firewood. The opening stage direction of Act Three reads "Enter Ferdinand bearing a log," and his subsequent soliloquy, followed by the dialogue between him and Miranda, bases itself on his attitude towards his task, along with Miranda's concern that he "Work not so hard." Whereas the first words we have heard Caliban speak are a complaint against his task—"There's wood enough within"—Ferdinand accepts his "mean task" gladly because "The mistress which I serve quickens what's dead,/And makes my labours pleasures."

One of the problems in staging the play is to determine the nature and quantity of the wood to be carried by Ferdinand; it may seem a small enough point, but the decision will have a considerable effect on the tone of the scene and on the way we react to Ferdinand. If the logs are too heavy, Miranda's offer to relieve him of the task will seem absurd, and Prospero will seem to be punishing rather than testing him; if they are too light, the scene will be trivialized.

Nicholas Hytner hit the right note; I thought, when, placing this scene after the interval, he showed us Ferdinand repeatedly going to and fro in a spirit of rueful acceptance of his lot, bearing logs weighty enough to cause him moderate discomfort, before the house lights went down. The audience's amusement was channelled off before the play proper resumed. The significance of the symbolism is brought home at the end of the scene when Ferdinand, betrothing himself to Miranda, declares himself her husband "with a heart as willing/As bondage e'er of freedom."

Prospero has been an unseen witness of the conversation between the lovers, and at the end of the scene declares his satisfaction at their betrothal. But he is constantly concerned to sustain the distinction—not always an easy one to maintain—between lust and love, as symbolized in Caliban's uncontrolled desire and Ferdinand's acceptance of the need for self-restraint. Giving Miranda to Ferdinand, he says:

> All thy vexations
> Were but my trials of thy love, and thou
> Hast strangely stood the test. Here, afore heaven,
> I ratify this my rich gift.

Yet still he insists on the importance of control:

> If thou dost break her virgin-knot before
> All sanctimonious ceremonies may
> With full and holy rite be ministered,
> No sweet aspersion shall the heavens let fall
> To make this contract grow,

and again,

> Look thou be true; do not give dalliance
> Too much the rein. The strongest oaths are straw
> To th' fire i' th' blood.

The explicit moralizing here is unusual for Shakespeare, though it has its parallels in other late plays; it may be seen as an aspect, perhaps even an unpleasant one, of the characterization of Prospero, but it certainly also relates to the play's overriding concern, adumbrated in the opening scene, with man's attempts to control and tame the potentially anarchic forces of nature both within and outside of himself. Thus, both the importance of sexual self-control and the rewards that it may reap are the very themes of the masque that Prospero conjures up as his entertainment for the lovers.

MASQUE AS MEDIUM—AND AS MESSAGE

No one would question, I suppose, that the staging of the masque ranks high among the problems that this play presents to modern interpreters. In his essay on *The Tempest* Jan Kott speaks of Shakespeare's plays as "a system of mirrors, as it were, both concave and convex, which reflect, magnify, and parody the same situation."[5] In more than one respect the masque mirrors, the opening scene of the play. It is Prospero who conjures up both the storm and the masque; both episodes represent an exercise of the powers he has learnt from his books, and both are ultimately beneficent in effect. Both present technical problems to their performers; but for present-day performers the most difficult aspect of the masque rests not in the mechanics of its staging but in the outdatedness of the conventions upon which it draws.

The problem is both literary and theatrical. Even the more highly educated members of a modern audience are likely to be less familiar than their Jacobean counterparts with either the mythological or the poetical traditions on which Shakespeare draws in his representation of Iris, Ceres, and Juno. And the framework in which he presents them, the formal structure of a masque, is one that, highly topical at the time of the play's first performances, went out of fashion during the next few decades and now requires a major exercise of the historical imagination before it can convey anything of the excitement that it must have had in the early seventeenth century—the great age of the court masque, represented at its finest in the collaborative work of Ben Jonson and Inigo Jones.

In *The Tempest* Shakespeare provides for the audiences of the public theatres at least a shadow of the glory that the form achieved at the court of King James, where it stood at once as a symbol of power and wealth—frequently used as such in the game of power politics—and as a celebration of the highest achievements of civilization, in which the arts of music, dancing, painting, poetry, and acting combined in entertainments whose splendour was enhanced by their folly—for immense amounts of money were lavished upon a single evening's entertainment by those who did not have the good fortune, like Prospero, to be able to command unpaid spirits to enact their fancies.

An attempt on the part of a modern director to reproduce the conventions of the Jacobean masque is likely to mean little or nothing to members of a modern audience, and is rarely attempted. More commonly an effort is made to reproduce the effect of these conventions through other means. It is not particularly difficult to convey a sense of the splendour of the masque, as a "vanity" of Prospero's art designed to divert the lovers. Often it has been sung, sometimes adopting the musical and theatrical conventions of a particular operatic style of the past—that of Monteverdi or Cavalli, for instance. Sam Mendes, in his 1993 production, flew down a large model of a Victorian toy theatre and represented the goddesses almost as mechanical figures.

The difficulty, as with the storm, is to convey the sense of the words that the goddesses utter, to convey the moral message that underpins the spectacle and that relates it to the system of ideas embodied in the play. Prospero is certainly present throughout this performance, and we see him here in multiple functions—as father to Miranda, as an artist capable of devising this show, as a kind of surrogate playwright, as a magician, and also as a monarch with power (like James I) to create a lavish entertainment to be attended only by his personal guests.

But we see him also as teacher. Just as Ben Jonson's masques, for all their splendour, often carried a moral message—the "more removed mysteries" of which he speaks in the preface to *Hymenaei*—so Prospero's is very much designed to reinforce the injunctions to pre-marital chastity that precede it. Iris alludes explicitly to the temptations with which Venus and Cupid have beset the lovers, and praises the strength of will—the self-control—with which these temptations have been resisted:

> Here thought they to have done
> Some wanton charm upon this man and maid,
> Whose vows are that no bed-right shall be paid.
> Till Hymen's torch be lighted; but in vain.
> Mars's hot minion is returned again;
> Her waspish-headed son has broke his arrows,
> Swears he will shoot no more, but play with sparrows,
> And be a boy right out.

The masque will lose its point unless the director ensures that its message is not submerged in spectacle. In the printed text of *Hymenaei*, Jonson says:

> Nor was there wanting whatsoever might give to the furniture
> or complement, either in richness, or strangeness of the habits,

delicacy of dances, magnificence of the scene, or divine rapture of music. Only the envy was that it lasted not still, or, now it is past, cannot by imagination, much less description, be recovered to a part of that spirit it had in the gliding by.

Here Jonson describes his awareness of the transience that Prospero is soon to acknowledge: if the masque is a fitting symbol of the greatest splendour that man can achieve, it is a fitting symbol too of the impermanence of all human effort; the visions of a Prospero are at the mercy of the Calibans of this world; power that can create can also destroy, and so, when Prospero recalls "that foul conspiracy/Of the beast Caliban and his confederates" against his life, the vision vanishes, leaving not a rack behind.

CRISIS, CALCULATION—AND RENUNCIATION

One last problem that I want to mention briefly is a matter of interpretation rather than of stagecraft in the more limited sense, but it is crucial to the presentation of the play. While the masque is being performed, the King and his followers are prisoners, unable, as Ariel says, to "budge" until Prospero releases them. Prospero finds himself in a position of complete power over his enemies, and Ariel tells him:

> Your charm so strongly works 'em
> That if you now beheld them, your affections
> Would become tender.

It is a moment of crisis in the portrayal of Prospero, and it is also a moment that is subject to varied interpretation. "Dost think so, spirit?" asks Prospero, and Ariel replies: "Mine would, sir, were I human." Prospero may well pause for thought before his next speech.

> And mine shall.
> Hast thou, which art but air, a touch, a feeling
> Of their afflictions, and shall not myself,
> One of their kind, that relish all as sharply
> Passion as they, be kindlier moved than thou art?
> Though with their high wrongs I am struck to th' quick,
> Yet with my nobler reason 'gainst my fury
> Do I take part. The rarer action is
> In virtue than in vengeance. They being penitent,
> The sole drift of my purpose doth extend
> Not a frown further. Go, release them, Ariel.

This is certainly a speech of self-examination. The interpretive question is whether it also represents a moment of crisis at which

Prospero's intentions towards the shipwrecked men undergo a radical change.

Is it only now that Prospero decides upon forgiveness? Or, at the other extreme, can the whole action of the play be seen as essentially benevolent, the result of a desire to bring his enemies to a state of self-awareness which could naturally lead on their part to penitence and reconciliation? Or does the truth lie somewhere between these extremes? Or has Shakespeare deliberately left the question open?

Many arguments could be adduced on both sides of the question, and I doubt if any definitive answer can be found. I would ask only that the style in which the speech is written be taken into account. To me, Prospero does not sound here like a man going through a crisis of the soul, being wrenched from one course of action to another that is fundamentally different. There is not here the sense of anguish that we hear in, for example, Macbeth's "If it were done when 'tis done...." If the actor is going to suggest conversion, he will have to do so not through the words he speaks but between the lines—in, perhaps, the silence between Ariel's "Mine would, sir, were I human" and Prospero's "And mine shall."

In any case, it is after this final test, or demonstration, of his self-mastery that Prospero is able to describe his intention to renounce his supernatural powers. The speech in which he does so—"Ye elves of hills, brooks, standing lakes, and groves"—is remarkable for the way it offers a verbal recreation of the powers that Prospero has been able to exert at the very moment that he renounces them. "But this rough magic I here abjure"—it's as if, in some paradoxical way, the greatest of his achievements was not the exercise of power but the capacity to give it up. It is an acknowledgement of limitation, of humanity, and of mortality. In exercising, not vengeance, but virtue, Prospero is able to reveal to Alonso that his son, Ferdinand, is alive, and to bring about their reunion. When he reveals the lovers, they are playing chess—yet another symbol, surely, of self-control.

The final paradox of a play that has been so deeply concerned with control and restraint is that it ends in liberty. Ariel, who has done the services required of him, is freed. All the travellers are freed from the island to which they came unwillingly; and finally Prospero himself, freed from the responsibility of exerting his power, appeals to the audience to free him from the stage.

There are of course many more problems in the staging of *The Tempest* of which I could have written—problems in the visual representation of Ariel and Caliban, for instance, or in the integration into the masque of the nymphs and reapers, in the staging of the magical banquet and the "spirits in shape of dogs and hounds" who torment

Caliban, Stephano, and Trinculo. But whichever I had chosen, they would all need to be related to questions of interpretation, to the projection through theatrical means of the significances that we can derive from the play's text.

It is in the nature of the transmission of Shakespeare's plays that we can conjecture far more about the literary than the theatrical impact that they made in their own time, whether in reading or in performance. Critics and scholars may be inclined to overemphasize the literary; though the theatre can do something to redress the balance, it can never hope to arrive with any certainty at the solutions found in Shakespeare's day; but it may at least find ways of projecting the text which will work in terms of today's audiences.

NOTES AND REFERENCES

1. Roger Warren, *Staging Shakespeare's Late Plays,* p. 13. Quotations from *The Tempest* are from Stephen Orgel's Oxford Shakespeare edition (Oxford, 1987).
2. Cited from the New Variorum edition, ed. H. H. Furness (Philadelphia, 1892, reprinted 1964), p. 392, 395.
3. G. C. D Odell, *Shakespeare from Betterton to Irving* (New York, 1922 reprinted 1963), Vol. 2 p. 294.
4. The original staging of the scene is examined in detail in Andrew Gurr, "*The Tempest's* Tempest at Blackfriars," *Shakespeare Survey* 41 (Cambridge, 1989), pp. 91–102.
5. Jan Kott, *Shakespeare our Contemporary* (London, 1964), p. 183.

"Problems of Stagecraft in *The Tempest*" first appeared in *New Theatre Quarterly* 40:10 (November, 1994): 348–57.

"Noises, / Sounds, and Sweet Airs": The Burden of Shakespeare's *Tempest*

Michael Neill

> He fords
> his life by sounding.
> Soundings.
> —"Seamus Heaney, "Gifts of Rain""[1]

When Caliban, responding to his companions' terror at the sound of an invisible pipe and tabor, reassures them that "the isle is full of noises" (3.2.133),[2] he draws attention to an aspect of Shakespeare's dramaturgy that is easily disregarded: uniquely among the plays of its time, *The Tempest* is equipped with an elaborate sound track, in which episodes of violent, discordant, and chaotic noise are set against the harmonious songs and instrumental music performed by Ariel and his consort of spirits.[3] Following the work of Enid Welsford and, more recently, Stephen Orgel, it has been usual to connect these effects to the play's conspicuous affiliations with the masque.[4] But insofar as *The Tempest* constitutes a challenge to the spectacular attractions of this courtly genre, it does so not by offering to meet the court theatre on its own ground—the Blackfriars could never hope to match the extravagant resources that Inigo Jones was able to exploit at court—but by insisting on the superiority of the aural tradition. Early modern playgoers, after all, went to "hear" a play rather than to see it; they were "auditors" or "audience" before they were "spectators." Instead of seeking to gratify the eyes of its public, *The Tempest* reasserts the primacy of their ears.

It is not, of course, that this play entirely eschews spectacle; indeed, *The Tempest* begins with a scene of storm and shipwreck that might appear calculated to vie with the scenic extravagance of masque. The storm called for in the opening stage direction—one for which there are very few precedents in the canon[5]—can easily seem to be ushering in a display of spectacular theatricality; however, in a printed text that is unusually punctilious in its attentiveness to stage effects, what is particularly striking about the wording is its emphasis upon the aural: "*A tempestuous noise of thunder and lightning heard*" (1.1 s.d.). In stark contrast to the lavish evocations of visual magnificence that preface Ben Jonson's masque texts, for example, this direction imagines a storm primarily in acoustic terms—so that even lightning is something to be *heard* rather than seen.[6] It is true that we have no means of knowing for certain to what extent the stage directions in the Folio were scripted by the dramatist himself; it seems likely that in their present form they were supplied by the scribe—probably Ralph Crane—who prepared the *Tempest* manuscript for the printer. But, whatever their origin, there is general agreement that the stage directions consistently attempt to recreate the experience of actual performance.[7] The island world they evoke is one whose landscape is, as it were, mapped by sound. As though advertising the superior power of hearing over seeing, Shakespeare's language repeatedly calls attention to acoustic effects, underlining the extent to which the meaning of his play— what, to use its own terminology, we might call its "burden"—is expressed through the orchestration of inarticulate sound as much as through the eloquence of speech.[8]

> She tries a test that seems to work when she is writing: to send out a word into the darkness and listen for what kind of sound comes back. Like a foundryman tapping a bell.
>
> —J. M. Coetzee,
> *Elizabeth Costello*[9]

In the final scene of *The Tempest,* as he prepares to "discase" himself before his erstwhile enemies (5.1.85), Prospero famously renounces the "rough magic" (l. 50) that has sustained his authority on the island:

> I'll break my staff,
> Bury it certain fathoms in the earth,
> And deeper than did ever plummet sound
> I'll drown my book.
>
> (ll. 54–57)

The sheer familiarity of these lines, combined with their apparent simplicity, easily disguises the complex allusiveness of their verbal play: as the carefully placed "bury" suggests, Prospero's promise to break his staff, while it involves the symbolic evacuation of its magical power, also recalls the ritual performed by the officers of great households at their masters' interment, when, breaking their staffs of office over their heads, they would throw them into the grave to signify release from the burden of office and the surrender of their authority to the power of death.[10] Thus, the promised gesture emphasizes how, even as he prepares to resume the weight of his ducal responsibilities, Prospero simultaneously engages in an act of unburdening, readying himself for the self-mortification of an old age in which "Every third thought shall be my grave" (l.311). At the same time, his use of "fathoms" (a measurement more usually applied to water than to earth) anticipates the "plummet" and "drown" of the following lines, setting up a cluster of associations that reaches back to the shipboard world of the opening scene, to the apparent drowning of its frantic passengers and crew and to the transformative magic wrought in the mysterious aquatic depths of Ariel's "Full fathom five" (1.2.397–404). That song, as it plumbs the depth of Ferdinand's grief, "sounds" in the same double sense that may be glimpsed when the "deeper... sound[ing]" of Prospero's plummet gives way to the deep sound of the *"Solemn music"* that ushers the "spell-stopped" courtiers into Prospero's charmed circle (ll. 389, 406; 5.1.56, 58 sd, 61).[11] The elaborate braiding of puns and quibbles that links these episodes does not stop there; for Ariel's song, as it "remember[s]" Ferdinand's "drowned father," imitates the tolling of Alonso's death knell (1.2.403–6), its heavy note anticipating the weight of the king's own grief for his lost son in the following scene (2.1). It is from this sorrow, and the guilt that precipitated it, that Prospero will finally liberate his penitent captive:

ALONSO
But O, how oddly will it sound that I
Must ask my child forgiveness!

PROSPERO
                  There, sir, stop.
Let us not burden our remembrances with
A heaviness that's gone.

                       (5.1.197–200)

The unburdening that Prospero offers to his former enemy is inseparable from that which he plans for himself: only when Alonso is released from the "heaviness" of his past crime can Prospero himself be freed from the weight of his "sea-sorrow" (1.2.170) and from the burden of vindictive remembrance that he—like those revenge protagonists whose plots he at once repeats and redirects—has carried through the play. Thus, the unburdening of Alonso looks forward to the final release for which Prospero will appeal in the epilogue, where his longing to be *"relieved* by prayer" (5.1.4) involves not merely the "free[ing]... from sorrow" with which *The Oxford English Dictionary* glosses this passage, but the "[freeing] from ... any task or burden" which is another meaning of "relieve."[12]

The seemingly accidental conjunction of "sound" and "burden" in Prospero's exchange with Alonso picks up a conspicuous, but largely unremarked, piece of wordplay from the first three acts. The motif of burdens and unburdening is given particular prominence in two scenes

(2.2 and 3.1), one carefully mirroring the other, that are at the exact center of the play's action. In these scenes, Caliban and Ferdinand (characters linked by their common desire for Miranda) are shown laboring under the penitential tasks that Prospero has imposed upon them. Each hefts a bundle of logs, firewood designed for their master's cell; each receives unexpected succor in his labors; and each concludes his scene by claiming a species of enfranchisement. Act 2, scene 2, opens with the entry of Caliban, bowed under "*a burden of wood*" (2.2.1 s.d.) and ends with his defiant repudiation of bondage in a song that, in performance, traditionally announces the discarding of his load:

> A plague upon the tyrant that I serve!
> I'll bear him no more sticks....
> No more dams I'll make for fish,
> Nor fetch in firing
> At requiring,
> ... 'Ban, 'Ban, Ca-Caliban
> Has a new master—get a new man!
> Freedom, high-day! High-day, freedom! Freedom, high-day, freedom!
>
> (ll. 156–57, 175–77, 179–81)

If Caliban's burden is imposed on him as a penance for his rebellion against Prospero's authority and his attempted violation of Miranda's maidenhead, Ferdinand also suffers under the weight of past crime and present desire: his father's complicity in Antonio's palace coup opens him to the charge of being a usurper and a traitor (1.2.454, 461, 470), while his fascination with Miranda's virgin body (ll. 428, 448) exposes him to the suspicion that he may be no better than his monstrous counterpart: "To th' most of men this is a Caliban," declares Prospero, "And they to him are angels" (ll. 481–82). Ferdinand enters at the beginning of 3.1 visibly bound in the same condition of "wooden slavery" (l. 62) as Caliban, *"bearing a log"* (3.1 sd)—a "mean task" that would be "heavy" to him (in both senses of the word), did not Miranda's sympathetic tears lighten its "baseness" (ll. 4, 5, 12). Just as Caliban claims his "freedom" by transferring his allegiance to the "wondrous" Stephano (2.2.181–82, 158), so Ferdinand plights his troth to the "wonder," Miranda, "with a heart as willing / As bondage e'er of freedom" (1.2.427, 3.1.88–89).

The significance of these two carefully juxtaposed episodes seems to answer (at first sight, anyway) to a straightforwardly emblematic reading. Such a reading is suggested partly by the recollection of an Old Testament episode in which another powerful patriarch, Joshua, condemned the deceitful inhabitants of Gibeon, who had offered themselves as his "servants," to become "hewers of wood, & drawers of water" (Josh. 9:8–27, esp. 11, 23); it is reinforced by Shakespeare's self-conscious troping of the Christian paradox of freedom-in-service.[13] This paradox is turned on its head when Caliban's determination to free himself from "the tyrant that I serve" (2.2.156) results in his subjection to an even more humiliating servitude, as he swears to follow the drunken Stephano, minister to his needs, and "get [him] wood enough"(ll.154). Ferdinand yields to a different form of subordination, but the parallel between the two logbearers is emphasized when the prince makes a "humble" gesture of submission, kneeling before his chosen "mistress" (3.1.87, 86) in a repetition of Caliban's gesture of subservience to his "new master" (2.2.180). However, Ferdinand's loving submission to Miranda transforms the degrading servitude imposed on him by Prospero into an expression of the voluntary self-abasement that a chivalric lover owed to his lady—a form of "service" resembling the "perfect freedom" promised to the faithful by the Book of Common Prayer:

> The very instant that I saw you did
> My heart fly to your service, there resides
> To make me slave to it, and for your sake
> Am I this patient log-man.
>
> (3.1.64–67)

The prince's insistence on Miranda's ability to transmute his "heavy … labours" into "pleasures" (ll.5–7) recalls Christ's reassurance that "my yoke is easie, and my burden light" (Matt. 11:30), while her reciprocal determination to "be [his] servant" and to "bear [his] logs the while" (ll.85, 24) is reminiscent of St. Paul's injunction that the faithful should "beare … one anothers burden" (Gal. 6:2).[14]

If the contrasting liberations of Caliban and Ferdinand look forward to the decisive manumissions and psychological unburdenings of the final scene, they also glance back at Prospero's account of his initial deliverance after he and his small daughter were cast adrift by his usurping brother. In the course of his protracted exposition, Prospero remembers the near despair from which the young Miranda saved him, as the winds drove their "rotten carcase of a butt" (1.2.146) toward the island:

> Thou didst smile,
> Infused with a fortitude from heaven,
> When I have decked the sea with drops full salt,
> *Under my burden groaned,* which raised in me
> An *undergoing* stomach to *bear up*
> Against what should ensue.
>
> (ll.153–58)

"Undergoing" here has the double sense of "suffering" or "enduring," as well as "bearing" a load;[15] if the metaphoric "burden" recalls
the burdens of sin and punishment so frequently invoked in scripture,[16] Prospero's wording suggests that their rescue by "providence
divine" (l.159) fulfills the promise announced in the Geneva Bible's
headnote to the first epistle of John: "God will bee mercifull unto the
faithfull, if *groning under the burden of their sinnes,* they learne to flee unto
his mercie."

So far, at least, these interlaced tropes appear to conform to the
emblematic interpretation I have been outlining. Their significance is
complicated, however, by the way in which Prospero's talk of burdens
willingly borne is punningly echoed by Ariel's song later in 1.2, with
its call for "sweet sprites [to] bear / The burden" (ll.379–80). As the ensuing stage direction—*"Burden, dispersedly"* (l.381 s.d.)—makes clear,
Ariel's intention is that his fellow spirits should take up the chorus,
or "burden," of his song; but in the context of a music that allays the
fury both of the wild waves and of Ferdinand's passionate grief for his
father (ll.376–77, 392–94), a recollection of Prospero's burden of grief
is unavoidable. Although etymologically distinct, these two senses of
"burden" had long been assimilated: "burden" in the musical sense
(otherwise *bourdon* or *burdoun)* could still carry its original meaning
as the bass or undersong accompanying the melody in a choral work.
Because this low undersong usually continued when the main singer
paused at the end of a stanza, it typically supplied the tune for any
chorus or refrain, so that "burden" was extended to refer to the refrain
itself; and since the undersong was thought to be "heavier" than the
air, the vocal chorus, like Ariel's sprites, were said to "bear the burden"
of a song, as though carrying the weight of it.[17] Moreover, because the
words of the refrain so often paraphrased the pervading sentiment of
the lyric, "burden" also came to mean the "'gist' or essential contents"
of a work.[18] With these punning connections in mind, it is easy to see
how the tolling of the funeral bell that concludes Ariel's second song,
"Full fathom five" (ll.397–404), constitutes its "burden" in a triple
sense, as a refrain or undersong whose deep notes match both the
watery depths of Alonso's supposed tomb, as well as the emotional
depths of his son's grief, thereby concentrating the meaning of the
entire lyric and the scene of mourning on which it comments. "The
ditty," responds Ferdinand (using a word that could mean "burden"
or "theme," as well as "the words of a song"[19]) "does remember my
drowned father" (l.406).

The low register of the sounds that typically express human misery
makes low notes in music seem a natural correlative for the "heaviness"
of "deep" mourning; thus, the diverse burdens borne by the groaning

Prospero, the enslaved Caliban and Ferdinand, and the bereaved Alonso resonate with the play's emotional and somatic vocabulary, linking that language to an extensive sequence of musical episodes through the "burden" borne by Ariel's spirit chorus. In 2.1, for example, Ariel's *"solemn music"* transforms the heaviness of Alonso's grief into the "wondrous heavy" drowsiness into which the shipwrecked King and his loyal followers "sink" (ll.183 s.d., 196, 99). As a result, it is impossible to escape the suggestion that the task of Ariel's spirit chorus, like Miranda's effect on Prospero in the earlier storm described in 1.2, is to assist in an emotional unburdening—so that, by some mysterious transfiguration, the bearing of one "burden" will assist in the lightening of the other, just as this second "sinking" undoes the first.

A further, more oblique version of this musical wordplay occurs in the scene where Ariel, in harpy guise, removes the magical banquet set before Alonso and his entourage: disrupting the scene's *"Solemn and strange music"* with the threatening noise of *"Thunder and lightning,"* the harpy claps its wings and causes the banquet to vanish *"with a quaint device"* before the astonished eyes of the courtiers (3.3.20 s.d., l.53 s.d.). After a speech in which Ariel, as the harpy, urges "heart's sorrow" upon Prospero's enemies, the spirit disappears amid peals of thunder that give way to *"soft music,"* as the *"strange shapes"* of his "living drollery" return (ll.81, 83 s.d., 20 s.d., 21). The contrast here between thunder and music belongs to the pattern of alternating discord and concord around which the play is structured. In this case, however, the simple contrast between cacophony and polyphony is confused by the ironic *"mocks and mows"* (l.83 s.d.) of the spirits' eldritch ballet, and by the way in which the peals of thunder resound in Alonso's ear like music—albeit an ominous "Musick of Division,"[20] whose notes serve only to remind the king of his exclusion from the harmony that music exemplifies:

> Methought the billows spoke and told me of it,
> The winds did *sing* it to me; and the thunder,
> That *deep* and dreadful *organ-pipe,* pronounced
> The name of Prosper: it did *bass* my trespass.
>
> (ll.96–99)

For its complete effect, Alonso's vocabulary depends upon its subtle resonance with the "burdens" exemplified in Ariel's first musical performance—the two lyrics he sings for Ferdinand, with their accompanying spirit choruses. Properly speaking, the deep organ pipe that basses Alonso's trespass, like the spirit choruses of Ariel's lyrics, should be called a "bourdon" (variously rendered *burdoun, burden,* and *burthen).* Originally denoting the low drone of a bagpipe or hurdy-gurdy and apparently cognate with the term for bass, undersong, or refrain—by the seventeenth century the word *bourdon* had come to refer to the bass stop on an organ.[21] So the thunder's harsh music of accusation punningly articulates the burden of the king's offense.

A more intricate version of the same pun occurs in Prospero's masque, where Ceres' song calls down the blessings of fertility upon the betrothed couple, including the benison of "Plants with goodly *burden* bowing" (4.1.113). Since the burden imagined here is that of laden branches, "bowing" (doing obeisance) evidently plays on "boughing" (sending out branches);[22] but the juxtaposition with "burden" in a context of Orphic invocation, suggests that—as in Sonnet 102's "wild music burthens every bough" (102.11)—musical "bowing" (as of a stringed instrument) is also involved. The implication here, as in Caliban's description of an island "full of noises, / Sounds, and sweet airs" (3.2.133–34), is of a harmony intrinsic to the very order of nature itself, one that Prospero's masque identifies with the providence incarnated in Juno and Ceres, who "sings her blessing" (4.1.109) on the betrothed couple.

Of course, Alonso responds to the bass notes of the thunder's *bourdon,* as they sound the base depth of his trespass, as if they too were expressions of a providential design; they are linked, by a further chain of puns, to what Alonso feels must serve as the necessary expiation for his crime—"I'll seek him *deeper* than e'er plummet *sounded,* / And with him there lie mudded" (3.1.101–2). His words will be echoed, like a refrain repeated in some musical composition, in another speech full of both "rattling thunder" and "heavenly music" (5.1.44, 52)—Prospero's farewell to his magic, with which I began this essay. The word-play in that speech consigns the magician's arts (as it will ultimately consign the contrivances of his enemies) to a realm of profound silence, beyond sounding, which is another way of describing the play's movement from the vindictive or remorseful torments of memory to the blessed oblivion announced by Prospero when Alonso prepares to humble himself before his new daughter-in-law: "Let us not burden our remembrances with / A heaviness that's gone" (ll.199–200). In terms of the recurrent variations on the motif of the Fortunate Fall to which the wondering Gonzalo now returns his interlocutors— "Was Milan thrust from Milan that his issue / Should become kings of Naples?" (ll.205–6)—it is evident how such intimations of a harmony lying deep within the apparent confusion of the natural world fit with a providential understanding of the protagonist's plotting. Although analyses of the play's music have often addressed the providential aspect of its symbolic design, it is not always easy to separate this kind of providence from the more politic "provision in mine art" (1.2.28) of which Prospero boasts. While the patterns I have been tracing make complete sense only within the context of the play's larger treatment of concord and discord, they invite a less univocal interpretation than Prospero seeks to impose.

2

Freedom is a word, less than a word, a noise.
—J. M. Coetzee, Foe[23]

If the island world of *The Tempest* is given its sensuous immediacy and physical presence primarily by the dramatist's manipulation of sound effects, the idea for such a soundscape[24] may have been planted in Shakespeare's mind by a contemporary text which has been widely proposed as a partial inspiration for his play, William Strachey's *True Reportory of the Wreck and Redemption of Sir Thomas Gates*, an account of the catastrophic hurricane experienced off the Bermudas by an English fleet headed to the newly established Virginia colony in 1609.[25] Strachey's narrative stresses above all the terrible clamor of this tempest, its dire assault upon the mariners' hearing:

> *swelling and roaring* as it were by fits,… [the storm produced] horror and fear… to overrun the troubled and overmastered senses of all, which, taken up with amazement, the *ears* lay so sensible to the terrible *cries and murmurs* of the winds … as who was most armed and best prepared was not a little shaken…. [F]ury added to fury…. Sometimes strikes in our ship amongst women and passengers, not used to such *hurly* and discomfort,… [that] our *clamours* drowned in the winds, and the winds in *thunder*. Prayers might well be in the hearts and lips, but drowned in the *outcries* of the officers; nothing *heard* that could give comfort…. [T]he glut of water, as if throttling the wind erewhile, was no sooner a little emptied … but instantly the winds, as having gotten their *mouths* now free and at liberty, *spake more loud* and grew more *tumultuous* and malignant… Winds and seas were as mad as fury and rage could make them.[26]

Things were little better when the survivors of the shipwreck struggled ashore in the Bermudas, islands that were reported to "be so terrible to all that ever touched on them, [because] such tempests, *thunders,* and other fearful objects are seen and *heard* about them that they may be called commonly the Devil's Islands."[27] Not only was their precarious refuge "often afflicted and rent with tempests, *great strokes of thunder, lightning, and rain in the extremity of violence,*"[28] but to its

317

dreadful hubbub were added the weird cries of seamews—the very birds whose fledglings Caliban gathers from the rocks (2.2.166).[29] The birds made a *"strange hollow and harsh howling"*—one that the castaways themselves learned to mimic, *"holloing, laughing and making the strangest outcry* that possibly they could," in their efforts to trap the birds.[30]

Strachey's is the same *"strange hollow and confused noise"* (4.1.138 s.d.) with which Shakespeare fills his Mediterranean island: the "assaultive" cacophony described by Bruce R. Smith that begins with the wild tumult of a hurricane in which "all the physical attributes that make speech possible ... are dissolved in a loud, inflectionless confusion"[31] and concludes with the hollowing *"noise of hunters... dogs and hounds"* (l.256 s.d.) as Caliban and his fellow conspirators are driven roaring from the stage. In the opening scene, Smith suggests, these chaotic sounds are pitched against the vain efforts of Alonso and his courtiers to reassert the ordered regimen of speech, efforts that are finally overwhelmed by the fury of nature, when *"A confused noise within"* (1.1.60 s.d.) announces their vessel's foundering.[32] This noise itself, however, consists partly of human cries—"'Mercy on us!'—'We split, we split!'—'Farewell, my wife and children!'— 'Farewell, brother!'—'We split! we split! we split!'" (ll.60–62)—so that the hollowing of the storm is barely distinguishable from the "howling" of the terrified passengers which seems "louder than the weather" itself (ll.36–37). Indeed, Antonio and Sebastian denounce the boatswain as a "bawling, blasphemous, incharitable dog . . . [an] insolent *noise*maker" (ll.40–41, 43–44), as if identifying him with the anarchic frenzy of the elements, whose leveling "roarers" (crashing breakers punningly imagined as noisy rioters) care nothing "for the name of king" (l.17).

The theatrical emphasis upon sound that characterizes the play's opening is underlined in the language of the second scene, where Prospero's reiterated injunctions foreground the importance of hearing: "The very minute bids thee ope thine *ear.* / Obey, and be *attentive.* . . . Dost thou *attend* me? . . . Dost thou *hear* . . . *Hear a* little further" (1.2.37–38, 78, 106, 135). Ultimately, it is Prospero's ability (one that he shares with, and exercises through, Ariel) to "charm" the "ears" of his adversaries (4.1.178) that ensures his success; the subsequent action repeatedly asserts the imaginative power of hearing over the specious seductions of vision—whether these seductions are exemplified by the banquet that tempts and then cheats the Neapolitan courtiers in 3.3 or by the specious "trumpery" (4.1.186) of the *"glistering apparel"* (l.193 s.d.) that lures Stephano and Trinculo to their humiliation. By the same token, the one conspicuous check to Prospero's design involves the lavishly staged betrothal masque that he devises for Miranda and Ferdinand, who (he insists) are to become "All eyes" for the performance (l.58). Even here it is the harmonies of Juno and Ceres, rather than the "majestic vision" itself, to which Ferdinand attributes the magical charm of the performance (ll.118, 119). The masque comes to a sudden end when its *"graceful dance"* (l.139 s.d.) of nymphs and reapers is interrupted by Prospero's recollection of the "foul conspiracy / Of the beast Caliban and his confederates" (ll.139–40); then, *"to a strange hollow and confused noise,* [the dancers] *heavily vanish"* (l.138 s.d.).

Prospero's ensuing remarks about "the baseless fabric of this vision" (l.151) suggest an unwitting truth in the magician's self-deprecating reference to the "vanity" of his spectacular artifice (l.41).[33] At the same time, the audible clash between the masque music and the *"confused noise"* (l.138 s.d.) into which it disintegrates, with its echo of the *"confused noise within"* (I.1.59 s.d.) that announced the imminent sinking of the king's ship in the opening scene, serves as a reminder of how the moral conflict here is repeatedly figured and played out in aural terms. Thus, in the second scene, the compelling power of Prospero's tale, which Miranda insists, "would cure deafness" (1.2.106), is implicitly contrasted both with the insinuating rhetoric of his usurping brother, which "set all hearts i'th' state / To what tune pleased his *ear,"* and with the evil spells of Caliban's mother, the "damned witch Sycorax," who was banished from Algiers "For . . . sorceries terrible / To human *hearing"* (ll.84–85, 263–65). Furthermore, although the scene is quiet by comparison to the chaotic "roar" of "wild waters" that so terrified Miranda (l.2), or the "thunder-claps" and "cracks / Of sulphurous roaring" of which Ariel boasts (ll.203–4),[34] Prospero's didactic narrative is filled with the remembered noise of the sea and the answering sounds of his own despair on the voyage to which he and his infant daughter were abandoned:

> There they hoist us
> To *cry* to th' sea that *roared* to us, to sigh
> To th' winds, whose pity, *sighing* back again,
> Did us but loving wrong....
> When I...
> Under my burden *groaned.*
>
> (ll.148–51,155– 56)

These inarticulate sounds of woe and terror are echoed not only in the "sighs" of the bereaved Ferdinand but in the memory of the "groans" and "howls" vented by Ariel during his imprisonment in Sycorax's "cloven pine" (ll.222, 280, 296, 277) and in the "din" and "roar" of pain that Prospero threatens to extract from the recalcitrant

Caliban (ll.369–70), as well as the animal incoherence of the "gabble" attributed to his once-languageless condition (l.355).

Again and again, the chaotic tumult of the elements and the inarticulate cries, groans, and sighs of suffering creatures are offset by the strange harmonies of *The Tempest's* several musics: these include not just the songs of Ariel—whose elemental name puns on the "airs" he performs—but the melodies played by offstage instruments at key points in the action.[35] Thus, the discordant hubbub of the storm is counterpointed by the harmony of Ariel's music as he enters, "*playing and singing*" (l.373 s.d.)—producing a "sound" so mysteriously powerful that it not only "remember[s]" (and imaginatively remembers) Ferdinand's "drowned father" (ll.405–7) but overcomes the violence of the elements themselves. "This music," Ferdinand wonderingly remarks, "crept by me upon the waters, / Allaying both their fury and my passion / With its sweet air" (ll.392–94). On an island governed by "airy charm[s]" (5.1.54), whose sounds are orchestrated by an "ayrie spirit,"[36] sweet airs are, as both Ferdinand and Caliban observe, "i'th' air" (3.2.134, 1.2.388), tempering the rough air of ocean tempest.

The magic influence of harmony is felt once more in the following scene, when Ariel's "*solemn music*" lulls Alonso and his courtiers to slumber (2.1.182 s.d.), and then again when his "*music and song*" awake the "snoring" sleepers to the conspiracy of Antonio and Sebastian (ll.294 s.d., 305 s.d.). Its notes are almost immediately followed, however, by a recurrence of the fearful "*noise of thunder*" (2.2.3 s.d.) and wind that opened the play and that accompanies the early action of 2.2, where the terrified Caliban, his imagination haunted by the tormenting sounds of Prospero's spirits—the chattering of apes and hissing of adders (ll.9, 13–14)—is discovered cowering beneath his gabardine by Stephano and Trinculo. In 3.2 and 3.3, music reasserts itself twice more, first with the tune that Ariel "*plays... on a tabor and pipe*" (3.2.122 s.d.) to lure this trio of drunken conspirators across the island, and then in the "*Solemn and strange music*" of the banquet scene (3.3.17 s.d.). Alonso and Gonzalo marvel at the "harmony" of this "Marvellous sweet music," a "sound expressing, / . . . a kind / Of excellent dumb discourse" (ll.18–19, 37–39), as though it were vehicle to a meaning that transcends mere words; but their musings are almost immediately interrupted by the fresh outburst of "*Thunder and lightning*" (l.52 s.d.) that rings so ominously in Alonso's ears.

"*Soft music*" is called for again in the following scene when Prospero launches his "harmonious" betrothal masque for Miranda and Ferdinand, with its songs and dances (4.1.58 s.d., 119, 105 s.d., 109, 138 s.d.), only for the performance to be cut short by that "*strange hollow and confused noise*" to which the masquers "*vanish*" (l.138 s.d.)—an alarming sound later matched by the noise of the hunt that reduces Caliban and his confederates to howling animality (ll.255 s.d., 262). In the final scene, Prospero's great farewell to magic recollects the "roaring war" and "dread rattling thunder" of the storms he has conjured, before he abjures their violence in favor of an appeal for "heavenly music" (5.1.44, 52)—a harmony realized in the "solemn air" with which he ministers to the tormented minds of his "spell-stopped" enemies (ll. 58, 61) and in the song that accompanies Ariel's reinvestiture of Prospero in his ducal attire (l.87 s.d.). With that final lyric, the play's soundtrack effectively comes to an end, although the chaotic noise of the opening is remembered one last time in the boatswain's account of his miraculous release from his shipboard prison:

> ... even now with strange and several noises
> Of roaring, shricking, howling, jingling chains,
> And more diversity of sounds, all horrible,
> We were awaked, straightway at liberty.
>
> (ll. 232–35)

Where he was once terrorized by the story of his "monstrous . . . trespass" against Prospero, of which "the billows spoke and told me" (3.3.95, 99, 96), Alonso now looks forward to hearing his former adversary rehearse the story of his life—a narrative that, like *The Tempest* itself, promises to "take the ear strangely" (5.1.312–13). Then, in the epilogue, the "heavenly music" of his courtiers' release has its faint, theatre-bound equivalent in the sounds of intercession which Prospero begs from the audience—not only the rhythmic sound of clapping that takes the place of the storm's "dreadful thunderclaps" (1.2.202) and the threatening "*claps*" of Ariel's wings on the banqueting table (3.3.52 s.d.), but the "gentle breath" (5.1.329) of prayer, a last air that must replace the tormented sighing and whistling of the island winds.

This sequence of contrasting acoustic effects has typically been explained by reference to the early modern habit of imagining the created order of things in musical terms.[37] According to this Neoplatonic tradition, the principles of harmony that governed the macrocosm should be mirrored in every aspect of creation, the sublime music of the spheres, to which the planets themselves danced, forming the ideal pattern to which the orders of society and government, like those of the human microcosm itself, were intended to conform. In the discord of a fallen world, it is the constant task of government to strive for the restoration of harmony to the body politic. Thus, Sir John Davies, whose poem *Orchestra* is perhaps the best-known contemporary expression of such ideas, imagined the regulation of colonial disorder in language that Prospero would immediately understand. In his reformatory tract on Ireland, Davies looked forward to a future in which the wild "hubbub" of which Spenser and others complained would be reduced to musical perfection: "The strings of this Irish Harpe, which the Ciuill Magistrate doth finger, are all in tune . . . and make a good Harmony in this Commonweale: So as we may well conceiue a hope, that *Ireland* (which heertofore might properly be called the *Land of Ire. . .*) will from henceforth prooue a Land of *Peace* and *Concorde*."[38] The same figure is elaborated in Ben Jonson's 1613–14 *Irish Masque,* where "a *solemne musique of harpes,*" replacing the wild racket of bagpipes, represents the harmonious order to which the king's uncivil subjects are brought by the magic of his regal authority.[39] James here becomes a royal Orpheus—the power of whose lute to command nature itself Shakespeare remembered in the lyric "Orpheus with his lute made trees" (*Henry VIII,* 3.1.3–14)—or he resembles Amphion, founder of Thebes, the sound of whose harp was sufficient to raise the mighty walls of his city.

It is obviously no accident that Antonio should be made to parody these ancient allegories of political harmony when he sarcastically compares Gonzalo's consolatory speeches (designed as they are to rescue his king from the discord of grief) to the music of Amphion's "miraculous harp" (2.1.85);[40] Prospero can indeed be seen as the civil[izing] magistrate of Shakespeare's drama, conjuring concord out of the chaotic violence of the storm and replacing the false "tune" to which his usurping brother "set all hearts i'th' state" (1.2.85, 84) with the *"solemn music"* (5.1.57 s.d.) that announces his own imminent restoration. As "the best comforter / To an unsettled fancy," he promises to settle the tumult that "boil[s] within [the king's] skull" (ll. 59, 60). The magus whose "art" summons the harmonies of a betrothal masque to banish "discord" (4.1.20) from his daughter's marriage bed implicitly offers himself as the Orphic conductor of the play's music. If his score stands for the political, social, and psychological harmony for which he yearns, the storm with which he opens the play bodies forth both the political chaos resulting from his brother's usurpation and the turbulent passions stirred up by that disorder—notably, of course, the vindictive emotion by which he himself is tormented. This is the tumult that Prospero attempts to "still" in his *"beating* mind" after Caliban's conspiracy has disrupted the music of his carefully orchestrated masque (l. 163)—an inner storm that recalls the "tempest" that "beats" in Lear's head even as its pelting violence "invades [him] to the skin" (*King Lear,* 3.4.12,14, 7). The same punning trope is deployed when Miranda feels the "sea-storm" "still... *beating* in [her] mind" (1.2.177,

176) and when Alonso's experiences "infest [his] mind with *beating* on/ The strangeness of this business" (5.1.246–47).

Unlike Lear's storm, however, the "direful" roaring of the island's "wild waters" (1.2.26, 2) proves to be less a direct expression of the disordered violence of unregulated nature, than a kind of antimasque (as Orgel's approach has enabled us to see),[41] merely mimicking such chaos, since all its effects have been so "safely *ordered*" by its presenter that there is "Not a hair perished" among those creatures whose terrified cries appeared to signal their mortal destruction (ll. 29, 217). The fierce "beating" of winds and waves (l.176) may be echoed in the desperate force of Ferdinand's struggle to "beat the surges under him" (2.1.112) and in the slapstick violence of the various blows and beatings meted out to Trinculo in 3.2. But the distempered noise of the drunken Stephano, Trinculo, and Caliban "beat[ing] the ground / For kissing of their feet" (4.1.173–74) is immediately followed by the sound of Ariel "beat[ing] his tabor" (l. 175)—the same rhythmic percussion that accompanied his piping in 3.2—which makes them "lift... up their noses / As they smelt music" (4.1.177–78). There appears to be a strange consonance between the choreographed movements of the betrothal masque and the chaotic flight that leaves these rebels "*dancing* up to th' chins" "I' th' filthy-mantled pool beyond [Prospero's] cell" (ll. 182–83). Moreover, Ariel's beating of musical time has its somatic echo in the "beat" of the human pulses to which he draws Prospero's attention (5.1.103, 113–14)—the rhythm with which the human body keeps its own time—underlining the suggestive etymological link between "tempest," *tempus,* and musical tempo explored by Douglas L. Peterson.[42]

In details of this kind, the simple opposition between music and noise, concord and discord seems deliberately blurred, as though Shakespeare were elaborating a set of more profound variations on the paradox of "musical confusion" with which he had played in *A Midsummer Night's Dream* (4.1.110, 118; 5.1.60).[43] If there is a musical tempo to be discovered even in the most distempered noise, music itself can sometimes threaten to disintegrate into mere clamor, contrasting with ideal harmony just as the rough bagpipes of the wild Irish contrast with the civilizing notes of the harp in Jonson's masque. The "scurvy tune[s]" of the drunken Stephano and Caliban in 2.2, for example, lie somewhere between music and noise, Caliban's song of freedom sounding to Trinculo like mere "howling" (ll. 43, 174), while the raucous catch they share with Trinculo provokes even the musically challenged Caliban to complain "That's not the tune" (3.2.122), until an invisible Ariel sounds out its true melody on his "*tabor and pipe*" (l. 122 s.d.).

It is Caliban himself, however, who is made to draw attention to the soothing effect of a very different island music—"noises, / Sounds, and sweet airs" that, as he explains to the alarmed Stephano and Trinculo, "give delight and hurt not. / Sometimes a thousand twangling instruments / Will hum about mine ears; and sometimes voices" (ll. 133–36). Commenting upon Caliban's response to the soundscape of his island, Bruce Smith suggests that "within the broad acoustic horizons of *The Tempest,* between noise and music, Caliban stands dead center."[44] But it is telling that, despite the lyrical language in which he evokes the sounds that haunt him, Caliban himself does not really seem to distinguish between the island's different kinds of sound— "noise" on the one hand, and music's "sweet airs" on the other. In this context, it is probably significant that among the available meanings of "noise" in Shakespeare's time—a clamor or din, a "loud, harsh, or unpleasant" sound—were "a pleasant or melodious sound" and "a company or band of musicians."[45]

But, while *The Tempest* may capitalize on this paradoxical semantic, its repeated blurring of the distinction between the orchestrated concord of music and the discordant confusion of mere "noise" also seems likely to represent Shakespeare's imaginative response to a detail from Strachey's *Reportory.* In Strachey, the arrival of the storm is heralded by winds that are described as "singing and whistling" around the ship.[46] It is a casual touch, but one that nevertheless appears to color the moment at which Trinculo recognizes "another storm brewing" as soon as he hears it "sing i' th' wind" (2.2.19–20), just as it seems to be recalled later when "The winds did sing" "The name of Prosper" to the despairing Alonso (3.3.97, 99). This last episode, in particular, suggests that Shakespeare may have found in Strachey's metaphor the suggestion of an unexpected consonance between the terrifying uproar of the storm and the mysterious providence by which "it pleased our merciful God to make even this hideous and hated place both the place of our safety and means of our deliverance."[47] This consonance is mirrored in the "loving wrong" (1.2.151) that Prospero and Miranda suffer from the winds that lash the rotten boat carrying them to the island, as well as in Ferdinand's recognition that "Though the seas threaten, they are merciful" (5.1.178). So, just as hellish suffering can be the instrument of redemption, it is as if some mysterious melody were hidden in the wildest, most incoherent racket—a melody that, like the music of the spheres, is either inaudible to fallen creatures or, if heard at all, perceived only by the dispensation of grace.

Some such intuition appears to underlie the differing accounts of the mysterious "*music and song*" (2.1.294 s.d.) by which Alonso and his loyal followers are awakened, just in time to save them from assassination by Antonio and Sebastian. To the virtuous Gonzalo this ethereal music resembles a melodious "humming" (l. 315); but the conspirators claim to have been terrorized by a very different kind of noise.

SEBASTIAN
... we heard a hollow burst of bellowing,
Like bulls, or rather lions—did't not wake you?
It struck mine ear most terribly.
ALONSO   I heard nothing.
ANTONIO
O, 'twas a din to fright a monster's ear,
To make an earthquake. Sure, it was the roar
Of a whole herd of lions.

(ll. 309–14)

If music can be presented as a monstrous din or else be drowned out by chaotic hubbub, by the same token, the most inharmonious uproar can sometimes appear to resolve itself into mysterious harmony.[48] Thus, the "sweet air" of Ariel's first song, in which the dancing feet of his fellow sprites "kissed / The wild waves" into silence, is accompanied by a chorus of harsh animal noises, the barking of dogs and crowing of cocks (1.2.394, 376–77).[49] The burden of Ariel's second song imitates the grim tolling of a funeral bell, while his last resounds with the cry of owls (5.1.90). For Aristotle, Lucretius, and other classical theorists it was the rational, ordering power of human speech—as opposed to the purely emotive force of the inchoate sounds uttered by animals—on which the very existence of the *polis* and its social order depended.[50] But in *The Tempest* that distinction is less secure. Thus, in the first and last of Ariel's songs—depending on how they are performed—we might think of the bestial chorus either as being absorbed into a music that allays both the fury of the waves and Ferdinand's passion of despair, or (contrariwise) as a residue of confusion that resists all such comforting reconciliation.[51]

The ways in which musical order itself sometimes threatens to disintegrate into acoustic confusion—as, for example, when the consort that accompanies the "graceful dance" of nymphs and reapers in the betrothal masque gives way to *"confused noise"* (4.1.138 s.d.)—seem to suggest that the reforming power of art, by some entropic principle, is in constant danger of reverting to the disorder of fallen nature. Prospero's magic, moreover, is always tainted by the suspicion that it traffics in the forbidden, and that for all its benevolent professions, it may constitute a kind of Faustian overreaching—something that in the end will have to be renounced, like his magician's staff and book, and consigned to the oblivious silence, "deeper than did ever plummet sound," of that "abyss of time" from which his vindictive memories first surfaced (5.1.56, 1.2.50). From this perspective, the animal chorus of barking and crowing that constitutes the burden of Ariel's first song can seem to resemble the lunatic cacophony of birds and beasts that erupts in Middleton and Rowley's *The Changeling*,[52] vocalizing the violently discordant passions that seethe beneath the ordered surface of society.

The ambivalence of such an episode, combined with the uncertain status of his magical practice, may encourage the conjecture that, far from being a transcendent sage whose studies have put him in tune with the deep harmonies of nature, Prospero has merely mastered the arts of politic manipulation more effectively than the brother who, by controlling "the *key*/Of officer and office," once contrived to "set all hearts i' th' state/To what *tune* pleased his *ear*" (1.2.83–84). Prospero's metaphors, after all, give a more sinister valency to music, seeming to endow Antonio with the power to effect his own baleful meta-morphoses, "new creat[ing]" the "creatures" of Prospero's court (ll. 81–82) in parodic anticipation of the transformations wrought by the art of the magician-prince at the end of the play. Striking a similar note, Ferdinand primly remembers a time when "Th' harmony of [ladies'] tongues" sounded a dangerous siren song that "into bondage/ Brought my too diligent ear" (3.1.41–42). In a play where bondage (whether for Ariel, Caliban, or Ferdinand himself) typically follows transgression, this seemingly casual conceit carries a more powerful resonance than it otherwise might—especially coming, as it does, in a scene where this "patient log-man" interprets his "wooden slavery" as a form of chivalric service to Miranda, a "bondage" more desirable than "freedom" (ll. 67, 62, 89).

From one perspective, as we have seen, Ferdinand's experience amounts to a profane yet mysteriously consoling version of the Chris-tian paradox of freedom-in-service; but the tune that seduces Steph-ano and Trinculo with the prospect of "a brave kingdom . . . where I shall have my music for nothing" (3.2.142–43) is a different matter. "[C]harm[ing] their ears" with its "lowing," only to lure them "calf-like" into "Toothed briars, sharp furzes, pricking gorse, and thorns" and then into a "foul lake [that] / O'er-stunk their feet," it finally betrays the rebels to the threatening "*noise of hunters... dogs and hounds*," who pursue them until they "roar" at the "cramps" and "dry convulsions" that "grind their joints" (4.1.178–80, 83–84, 255 s.d., 259–62), consign-ing them to humiliating subjection even as their principal tormentor is promised that he may "have the air at freedom" (l. 266). In contrast to the curative "heavenly music" (5.1.52) that heralds the release of the "spell-stopped" courtiers (l. 61), Prospero's music is exposed here as an agent of sensual deception and an instrument of oppressive discipline.[53] Once the orchestrating power of the magician's "potent art" (l. 50) is questioned in this way, it raises the possibility that, deeper than the sounding measure of his plummet, there are other measures that he cannot hear: the noises and sounds, to which Caliban responds with such uncharacteristically tender lyricism, may be of quite another order than those that "rough magic" (l. 50) can summon, just as the "sweet air[s]" (1.2.394) of Ariel's real music will sound only when he achieves the liberty suggested by his name, becoming free as air. Caliban's song of liberation, significantly enough, ends in a pair of chanted lines that are surely designed as its "burden"—"'Ban, 'Ban, Ca-Caliban/Has a new master—get a new man!" (2.2.179–80)—in which his very name fragments into inarticulate cries that resemble cursing ("'Ban, 'Ban"). This is perhaps how freedom sounds, when the slave casts off the burden of his imposed language ("my profit on't/Is I know how to curse" [1.2.362–63]).

The implications of such a conclusion for our understanding of Prospero are, of course, entirely in accord with postcolonial readings of the play—most conspicuously with that offered in Aimé Césaire's *Une tempête*. In this irreverent reworking of *The Tempest*, Prospero is a ruthless agent of empire, an "old colonial addict" who justifies his appropriation of Caliban's and Ariel's island by presenting himself, in exactly Shakespeare's metaphor, as the orchestrator of sublime order, although the real music of the play belongs to the creatures of the island, above all to Caliban and the African spirit beings of his disorderly pantheon:

> Understand me well.
> I am not, in the ordinary sense,
> the master, as this savage thinks,
> but rather the conductor of a boundless score:
> this island.
> Drawing out voices, myself alone,
> and mingling them at my pleasure,
> arranging out of confusion
> the sole intelligible line.
> Without me, who would be able
> to draw music from all this?
> Without me, the island is dumb.[54]

In Shakespeare's play, it is difficult to avoid the self-reflexive implications of the patterns I have described. These implications, needless to say, expose the author as complicit in the very hubris that the magician's farewell to his art ("Ye elves of hills, and brooks" [5.1.33]) at once renounces and celebrates. The "burden" under which the tempest-tossed Prospero groans, as a laboring mother might groan under the "burden" of her pregnancy,[55] is not simply the weight of his past sins, but the burden of revenge with which his history has charged him—a burden linked not just to the "fardels" of tormented memory in Hamlet's "weary life" *(Hamlet,* 3.1.75, 76) but to the "monstrous birth" of Iago's vindictive scheming *(Othello,* 1.3.404). By extension, however, it is also the burden of the dramatic narrative itself; if we take it in that sense, it may be colored by the use of "burden" in the English bible to translate the Hebrew *massā,* meaning "lifting up (of the voice), utterance, oracle" or "prophecy" or "heavy doom"[56] —the use suggestively exemplified by "The burden of Tyrus [and Zidón]" as the prophet Isaiah announced it: "for the sea hathe spoken, *euen* the strength of the sea.... Howle ... ye that dwell in the yles" (Is. 23:1, 4, 6). Steeped as it is in the language and motifs of scripture, *The Tempest* is a play that might easily be read as trespassing on sacred ground; it is partly for this reason that the magician-dramatist who orchestrates its action is required to abjure his art. At this moment of ceremonious unburdening, as Prospero flourishes his magic staff one last time before breaking it, we may wish to remember (as the more alert members of Shakespeare's audience might have done) that an old but still-extant synonym for "staff" was "bourdon," "burdon," or "burdoun," and that—perhaps significantly for a poet who never tired of punning on his own name—the word could also mean "spear or spear-shaft."[57]

In the light of this wordplay, Sir John Gielgud's famous *coup de théâtre* in Peter Hall's 1973 production may deserve revisiting, as something more than a mere throwback to sentimental Victorian fantasy. Just as he prepared to speak the epilogue, Gielgud's Prospero doffed his ducal bonnet to reveal a startling resemblance to the Droeshout engraving of Shakespeare. Spoken by an actor who has performed the role of a playwright-magician, one whose "charms" (Epilogue, 1) have visibly shaped the plot of the play the audience has just witnessed, the epilogue is largely responsible for the long-lived reading of the play as Shakespeare's public farewell to his craft.[58] The burden that Prospero seeks to discard, when—like Caliban, Ferdinand, and Ariel before him—he claims the indulgence of freedom, resembles that of the theatrical artist seeking manumission as one of His Majesty's Servants. That, too, is part of the "burden" of *The Tempest.*

FOOTNOTES

1. Seamus Heaney, "Gifts of Rain," in *Opened Ground: Selected Poems, 1966–1996* (New York: Farrar, Straus and Giroux, 1998), 51–53, esp. 51.

2. Citations from *The Tempest* will be from the edition prepared by Stephen Orgel (Oxford: Clarendon Press, 1987). For the quotation in the title of this essay, see 3.2.133–34. Throughout, emphases added to quotations (in boldface italic type for stage directions or in italic type for running text) are my own.

3. For a good analysis of the play's elaborately patterned aesthetic, see Mark Rose, *Shakespearean Design* (Cambridge, MA: Belknap Press of Harvard UP, 1972).

4. See Enid Welsford, *The Court Masque: A Study in the Relationship between Poetry and the Revels* (Cambridge: Cambridge UP, 1927); Stephen Orgel, *The Jonsonian Masque* (Cambridge: Harvard UP, 1961); and David Lindley, ed., *The Court Masque* (Manchester: Manchester UP, 1984).

5. Typically, Shakespeare's plays begin with a simple entry for the characters who are to initiate the dialogue: apart from the martial music that introduces *Coriolanus* and several of the history plays and the "dying fall" of the consort that opens *Twelfth Night* (1.1.4), the only precedent for such a nonverbal opening is provided by the *"Thunder and lightning"* at the beginning of *Macbeth* (1.1 s.d.). With the exception of *The Tempest* (see n. 2 above), quotations from Shakespeare's works follow *The Riverside Shakespeare,* 2d ed., gen. ed. G. Blakemore Evans (Boston: Houghton Mifflin, 1997).

6. Orgel's note in the Oxford edition insists that the wording "need not imply that no visual effects accompanied the sound of thunder," since we know that "Jacobean theatres had lightning machines" (97n); so that here, as in *Macbeth,* the spectacle of the storm was to be as important as its sound. It is difficult to believe, however, that such machines can have been particularly effective in a theatre where darkness had to be imagined by the audience; and Lindley (citing Andrew Gurr) suggests that "the SD's *heard* may accurately reflect a performance in which only off-stage noise was employed." See *The Tempest,* New Cambridge Shakespeare, ed. David Lindley (Cambridge: Cambridge UP, 2002), 1.1 s.d. note.

7. See Orgel, ed., 56–58; and Peter Holland, "The Shapeliness of *The Tempest,*" *Essays in Criticism* 45 (1995): 208–29, esp. 208. In their Arden3 edition of *The Tempest* (Walton-on-Thames: Thomas Nelson, 1999), Virginia Mason Vaughan and Alden T. Vaughan discuss Crane's role and conclude that, while the directions appear to be the work of someone less familiar with theatrical technicalities than Shakespeare must have been, they nevertheless give a good sense of the play's original staging (126–30).

8. For further commentary on the play's sound effects, see Vaughan and Vaughan, ed., 9, 17–18; and Lindley, ed., *The Tempest*, 18–25.

9. J. M. Coetzee, *Elizabeth Costello* (New York: Penguin Books, 2003), 219.

10. Michael Neill, *Issues of Death: Mortality and Identity in English Renaissance Tragedy* (Oxford: Clarendon Press, 1997), 279.

11. For a general account of the relationship between sound, sounding, and "deep subjectivity" in early modern culture, see Wes Folkerth, *The Sound of Shakespeare* (London: Routledge, 2002), 25–33.

12. *The Oxford English Dictionary*, 2nd ed. (Oxford: Oxford University Press, 1989), s.v. "relieve, *v.*," 3a, 4c. *OED Online*, http://dictionary. oed.com.libproxy.library.wmich.edu (accessed 7 January 2008).

13. Michael Neill, *Putting History to the Question: Power, Politics, and Society in English Renaissance Drama* (New York: Columbia UP, 2000), 13–48, esp. 24. The paradox of service as "perfect freedom," which received its classic expression in the Second Collect for Morning Prayer from Crammer's prayer book, is discussed at length by David Evett in *Discourses of Service in Shakespeare's England* (London: Palgrave Macmillan, 2005), 1–16; and David Schalkwyk in "Between Historicism and Presentism: Love and Service in *Antony and Cleopatra* and *The Tempest*," *Shakespeare in Southern Africa* 17 (2005): 1–17, esp. 13–15.

14. All biblical citations are taken from the Geneva Bible, the version best known to Shakespeare, and are made parenthetically in the text. See *The Geneva Bible: A Facsimile of the 1560 Edition*, intro. Lloyd E. Berry (Madison: U of Wisconsin P, 1969).

15. *OED Online*, s.v. "undergo, *v.*," 5.

16. See, e.g., Ps. 38:4; Is. 13:1; and Gal. 6:4–5.

17. *OED Online*, s.vv. "burden, burthen, *n.*" IV, 9; and "bourdon[2] , burdoun, *n.*" 1. See Margaret's wordplay in *Much Ado About Nothing*: "Clap's into 'Light a' love'; that goes without a burden" (3.4.44– 45); the joke is elaborated later in the play when the dirge sung at Hero's supposed tomb is given the burden "Heavily, heavily" (5.3.18, 21). See also *The Two Gentlemen of Verona*, 1.2.79–81.

18. *OED Online*, s.v. "burden, burthen, *n.*," IV.9–11.

19. *OED Online*, s.v. "ditty, *n.*," 3.

20. The phrase is borrowed from Sir Walter Raleigh's grimly witty descant on death, "The Life of Man"; see *The Poems of Sir Walter Ralegh: A Historical Edition*, ed. Michael Rudick (Tempe: Arizona Center for Medieval and Renaissance Studies, 1999), 70 (poem 29c, I. 2).

21. *OED Online*, s.vv. "bourdon[2], burdoun," 1–2; and "burden, burthen, *n.*," 9–10. See also *New Grove Dictionary of Music and Musicians*, ed. Stanley Sadie (London: Macmillan, 2001), vol. 3, s.vv. "bourdon," 1; and "organ stop," 2.

22. *OED Online*, s.vv. "bow, *n.*[1]," 6; and "bough, *v.*[1]."

23. J. M. Coetzee, *Foe* (London: Secker & Warburg, 1986), 100.

24. For a discussion of the Shakespearean "soundscape" and the need to "listen ... closely to Shakespeare himself listening to the world around him," see Folkerth, 7–11, 14–25, esp. 9.

25. Strachey's letter was not published until Purchas included it in his *Hakluytus Posthumus* (1625), and there is no way of being certain that a manuscript version was accessible to Shakespeare. As a result, some scholars, including Lindley *(The Tempest,* ed., 31) have recently questioned its plausibility as a source. The fullest of these attacks has been mounted by Roger Stritmatter and Lynne Kositsky in "Shakespeare and the Voyagers Revisited," *Review of English Studies* 58 (2007): 447–72. The authors argue that the *Reportory* uses material that cannot have been available to Strachey until after the supposed arrival of his letter with Sir Thomas Gates's ship in July 1610, but a forthcoming article by Alden C. Vaughan challenges the alleged historical grounds for Stritmatter and Kositsky's conclusions. The only significant textual parallels in the Bermuda section of Strachey's narrative are with Silvester Jourdain's *Discovery of the Barmudas* (London, 1610). Stritmatter and Kositsky think that Strachey must have copied this material at a later date from Jourdain's published work; but since Jourdain himself returned from Virginia with Gates, there is every reason to suppose that he would have had access to any material sent home by Strachey, elements of which he could then have incorporated into his own text. There is, of course, good evidence that Shakespeare was familiar with a number of New World texts, including Montaigne's "Of the Cannibals" and Peter Martyr's *De Orbe Novo* in Richard Eden's 1555 translation, *The Decades of the Newe Worlde.* (Stritmatter and Kositsky's as-yet-unpublished essay, "'O Brave New World': *The Tempest* and Peter Martyr's *De Orbe Novo"* gives a detailed analysis of important parallels.) However, no other account of storm and shipwreck seems as close to Shakespeare's as Strachey's. Stritmatter and Kositsky, in another unpublished essay, argue for the influence of Erasmus's *Naufragium,* while Arthur F. Kinney, in "Revisiting *The Tempest,*" *Modern Philology* 93 (1995): 161–77, identifies James Rosier's voyage narrative *A True Relation* (London, 1605) as a probable alternative to Strachey's text, noting that Rosier's narrative too begins with a storm. However, no proposed source gives so much emphasis as Strachey's to the terrifying sound of the storm, nor does any other offer so rich a collection of verbal parallels with *The Tempest.*

26. Strachey, quoted in Orgel, ed., 209–10.

27. Strachey, quoted in Orgel, ed., 213.

28. Strachey, quoted in Orgel, ed., 213.

29. I follow Malone's orthographically plausible emendation of "scamels" to "sea-mels" (a variant of *seamews),* since F's "Scamels," despite the heroic conjectures of editors, makes no convincing sense. See Orgel, ed., 2.2.166n; and *The First Folio of Shakespeare,* prep.

Charlton Hinman (New York: W. W. Norton, 1968), through-line number (TLN) 1216.

30. Strachey, quoted in Orgel, ed., 215.

31. Bruce R. Smith, *The Acoustic World of Early Modern England* (Chicago: U of Chicago P, 1999), 337, 336.

32. The fullest treatment of noise in Shakespeare is Kenneth Gross's *Shakespeare's Noise* (Chicago: U of Chicago P, 2001). However, although he includes an extended discussion of the storm scene in *Lear* (176–84), Gross's primary concern is with noise conceived as "violent or disorderly forms of speaking: slander, defamation, insult, vituperation, malediction, and curse" (1); my interest here is in forms of more or less inarticulate sound.

33. Lindley sees the play as "grow[ing] out of [a] general disquiet [with the court masque], and attempt [ing] itself to grapple with the problems it raises." See David Lindley, "Music, Masque and Meaning in *The Tempest*," in *The Court Masque* (see n. 4 above), 47–59, esp. 54.

34. Holland, 220–25, discusses the noise of the storm and the insistent recurrence of "roaring" in the play's language, relating the alternation of music and noise to the order/disorder pattern of masque and antimasque.

35. The description is from the list of characters printed at the end of the Folio text; see *The First Folio of Shakespeare*, fol. 19.

36. See, for example, John P. Cutts, "Music and the Supernatural in 'The Tempest': A Study in Interpretation," *Music and Letters* 39 (1958): 347–58; Theresa Coletti, "Music and *The Tempest*," in *Shakespeare's Late Plays*, ed. Richard C. Tobias and Paul G. Zolbrod (Athens: Ohio UP, 1974), 185–99; and Robin Headlam Wells, *Elizabethan Mythologies: Studies in Poetry, Drama and Music* (Cambridge: Cambridge UP, 1994), 63–80, esp. 63. In his essay on "Music in Shakespeare," by contrast, W. H. Auden insists that while *"The Tempest* is full of music of all kinds,... it is not one of the plays in which, in a symbolic sense, harmony and concord finally triumph over dissonant disorder." See *The Dyer's Hand and Other Essays* (New York: Random House, 1962), 500–27, esp. 526.

37. Edmund Spenser, *A View of the Present State of Ireland*, ed. W. L. Renwick (London: Eric Partridge, 1970), 70, 72. Sir John Davies, *A Discoverie of the True Causes Why Ireland Was Never Entirely Subdued...* (London, 1612), sig. Nn3ᵛ. See also Richard Hooker, *Of the Laws of Ecclesiastical Polity.* "Where the *King* doth guide the state and the lawe the *King*, that commonwealth is like an harpe or melodious instrument, the stringes whereof are tuned and handled all by one hand, following as lawes the rules and canons of Musicall science." See *The Folger Library Edition of the Works of Richard Hooker*, gen. ed. W. Speed Hill, 4 vols. (Cambridge, MA: Belknap Press for Harvard UP, 1977–82), 3:342. For the possibility that Prospero's island was

conceived as a figure for Ireland, and Caliban for the so-called
"wild Irish," see Paul Brown, "'This thing of darkness I acknowledge mine': *The Tempest* and the Discourse of Colonialism," in
Political Shakespeare: New Essays in Cultural Materialism, ed. Jonathan
Dollimore and Alan Sinfield (Ithaca: Cornell UP, 1985), 48–71;
and David J. Baker, "Where Is Ireland in *The Tempest?*," in
Shakespeare and Ireland: History, Politics, Culture, ed. Mark
Thornton Burnett and Ramona Wray (London: Macmillan,
1997), 68–88.

38. *The Irish Masque at Court* in *Ben Jonson: The Complete Works,* ed.
C. H. Herford, Percy Simpson, and Evelyn Simpson, 11 vols. (Oxford:
Clarendon Press, 1925–52), 7:403, l. 141 s.d.. See also Michael Neill,
"Broken English and Broken Irish: Nation, Language, and the Optic
of Power in Shakespeare's Histories," *Shakespeare Quarterly* 45 (1994):
1–32.

39. For parallels between Prospero, Amphion, and Orpheus as orchestrators
of a music that has power to conjure harmonious order out of the wild
confusion of nature, see Lindley, ed., *The Tempest,* 19.

40. Orgel, ed., 47.

41. See Douglas L. Peterson, *Time, Tide and Tempest: A Study of Shakespeare's
Romances* (San Marino, CA: Huntington Library, 1973), 3–70, 214–54.

42. See also *All's Well That Ends Well,* 1.1.172: "His jarring concord, and
his discord dulcet."

43. Smith, 337.

44. *OED Online,* s.v. "noise, *n.*" 2b, 3.

45. Strachey, quoted in Orgel, ed., 209.

46. Strachey, quoted in Orgel, ed., 213.

47. The role of music becomes even more ambiguous, as David Lindley
argues in "Music, Masque and Meaning," in *The Court Masque* (see
n. 4 above), when it is remembered that, according to contemporary
theories, music had the capacity to "delude or spur illicit passions
as well as cure, heal, and restore" (47). Lindley writes that the play
"exploits and explores the tensions" between the conventions of the
court masque, in which the symbolic power of music was "firmly
controlled and directed" (47), and those of the playhouse, where its
function was more varied and unpredictable. See also his discussion
of audience response in *Shakespeare and Music* (London: Thomson
Learning, 2006), 218–33.

48. Here, I assume that Orgel and other editors are correct in assigning
the cockcrow at 1.2.387 (like the barking at ll. 381–83) to the chorus
of sprites indicated by F's earlier stage direction *"Burthen dispersedly"*
(*First Folio,* TLN 525 s.d.). Howell Chickering, "Hearing Ariel's
Songs," *Journal of Medieval and Renaissance Studies* 24 (1994): 131–72,
esp. 155, suggests that the raucous chorus of these songs links them
with the discordant catches of Stephano and Trinculo.

49. For a full discussion, see Deborah Levine Gera, *Ancient Greek Ideas on Speech, Language, and Civilization* (Oxford: Oxford UP, 2003).

50. For Lindley, the barking and crowing of the choric sprites creates a discomfort with the sublime metamorphoses of Ariel's "sea-change," to "make ... us uneasily conscious of the compromise with truth that Prospero's designs necessitate." What Shakespeare dramatizes is a clash between the traditional Neoplatonic view of music as an instrument of transcendental harmony and a newer account of it as primarily rhetorical in its effects. The audience is left, Lindley suggests, divided between skepticism and a nostalgic regret at the dissolution of those Platonic theories that once sustained "a Sidneyan belief in art's golden world" ("Music, Masque and Meaning," 49, 58).

51. After the entry of "MADMEN *above, some as birds, others as beasts*," Isabella explains, "Sometimes they imitate the beasts and birds, / Singing, or howling, braying, barking—all / As their wild fancies prompt 'em." See Thomas Middleton and William Rowley, *The Changeling*, 3d rev. ed., ed. Michael Neill (London: A. and C. Black, 2006), 3.2.184 s.d., 189–91.

52. Observing these contradictions, Lindley argues that "by stressing the essentially rhetorical nature of music and dramatising the way in which it is used to manipulate and control, Shakespeare questions the traditional view of its God-derived power.... The music of the island is not Prospero's ... but Ariel's [and] in this respect the play seems to suggest that music is of itself morally neutral" (*The Tempest*, Lindley, ed., 19, 22).

53. My own translation, adapted from Aimé Césaire, *A Tempest (Based on Shakespeare's "The Tempest"; Adaptation for a Black Theatre)*, trans. Richard Miller (New York: Ubu Repertory Theatre Publications, 1992), 73.

54. *OED Online*, s.v. "burden, burthen, *n.*" 4a. See also Orgel, ed., 1.2.156–57n.

55. *OED Online*, s.v. "burden, burthen, n.," 3.8; and Alexander Cruden, *A complete Concordance to the Holy Scriptures of the Old and New Testament...* (New York: M. W. Dodd, 1854), s.v. "burden."

56. *OED Online*, s.v. "bourdon¹, burdoun, *n*," 2.

57. This approach goes back to at least 1838, when Thomas Campbell declared *The Tempest* marked by "a sort of sacredness as the last work of the mighty workman. Shakespeare, as if conscious that it would be his last, and as if inspired to typify himself, has made its hero a natural, a dignified, and benevolent magician." See the *New Variorum* edition of *The Tempest,* ed. Horace Howard Furness (Philadelphia: J. B. Lippincott, 1892), 356.

"'Noises,/Sounds, and sweet airs': The Burden of Shakespeare's *Tempest*" first appeared in *Shakespeare Quarterly* 59.1 (2008): 36–59.

FOR FURTHER READING, VIEWING, AND LISTENING

Auden, W. H. *The Sea and the Mirror: A Commentary on Shakespeare's* The Tempest. Ed. and intro. Arthur Kirsch. Princeton, NJ: Princeton UP, 2003. Print.

Baily, Roger, and Christy Desmet. "The Shakespeare Dialogues: (Re)producing *The Tempest* in Secondary and University Education." *College Literature* 36 (Winter 2009): 121-40. Print.

Barker, Francis, and Peter Hulme. "'Nymphs and reapers heavily vanish': The Discursive Contexts of *The Tempest.*" *Alternative Shakespeares.* Ed. John Drakakis. NY: Routledge, 1985. 191-205. Print.

Berger, Karol, "Prospero's Art." *Shakespeare Studies* 10 (1978): 211-39. Print.

Bevington, David, and Peter Holbrook. *The Politics of the Stuart Court Masque.* Cambridge, U.K.: Cambridge UP, 1999. Print.

Briggs, John C., "Catharsis in *The Tempest.*" *Ben Jonson Journal* 5 (1998): 115-32. Print.

Cartelli, Thomas. "Prospero in Africa: *The Tempest* as Colonial Text and Pretext." *Shakespeare Reproduced: The Text in History and Ideology.* Ed. Jean Howard and Marion O'Connor. NY: Routledge, 99-115. Print.

Cobb, Hal. "The Pursuit of Character." PEN American Center website. http://www.pen.org/viewmedia.php/prmMID/4923. Web.

Cox, John D. "Recovering Something Christian about *The Tempest.*" *Christianity and Literature* 50:1 (Autumn 2000). 31-51. Print.

Esolen, Anthony M. "'The isles shall wait for His law': Isaiah and *The Tempest.*" *Studies in Philology* 94 (1997): 221-47. Print.

Fulton, Robert C., III. "*The Tempest* and the Bermuda Pamphlets: Source and Thematic Intention." *Interpretations* 10 (1978): 1-10. Print.

Graff, Gerald, and James Phelan. Eds. *The Tempest: A Case Study in Critical Controversy.* NY: Bedford/St. Martin's, 2001. Print.

Greenblatt, Stephen. *Learning to Curse: Essays in Early Modern Culture.* NY: Routledge, 1990. Print.

Grant, Patrick. "The Magic of Charity: A Background to Prospero." *Review of English Studies* 27 (1976): 1-16. Print.

Hulme, Peter, and William H. Sherman. Eds. '*The Tempest*' and Its Travels. Philadelphia: U of Pennsylvania P, 2000. Print.

Hunt, Maurice. Ed. *Approaches to Teaching Shakespeare's 'The Tempest' and Other Late Romances.* NY: MLA, 1992. Print.

Hunter, R. G. *Shakespeare and the Comedy of Forgiveness*. Cambridge, U.K.: Cambridge U P, 1965. Print.

Iselin, Pierre. "'My Music for Nothing': Musical Negotiations in *The Tempest*." *Shakespeare Survey* 48 (1995): 135-45. Print.

James, D. G. *The Dream of Prospero*. Oxford, U.K.: Clarendon Press, 1967. Print.

Knight, G. W. *The Crown of Life*. London: Methuen, 1948. Print.

———. *The Shakespearean Tempest*. 1932. Reprinted London: Routledge, 2002. Print.

Kastan, David Scott. "'The Duke of Milan/ And His Brave Son': Old Histories and New in *The Tempest*." *Shakespeare after Theory*. Ed. David Scott Kastan. NY: Routledge, 1999. 183-200. Print.

Kott, Jan. "Prospero's Staff." *Shakespeare Our Contemporary*. Trans. Boleslaw Taborski. 1964. Reprinted NY: Norton, 1974. 163-205. Print.

Leininger, Lorie Jerrell. "The Miranda Trap: Sexism and Racism in *The Tempest*." Carolyn R. S. Lenz, Gayle Green, and Carol T. Neely. *The Woman's Part: Feminist Criticism of Shakespeare*. Champaign-Urbana: U of Illinois P, 1980. 285-94. Print.

Marx, Leo. "Shakespeare's American Fable." *The Machine in the Garden: Technology and the Pastoral Ideal in America*. Oxford, U.K.: Oxford U P, 1964. Print.

Morse, Ruth. "Monsters, Magicians, and Movies: *The Tempest* and the Final Frontier." *Shakespeare Survey* 53 (2000): 164-74. Print.

Mowat, Barbara A. "Prospero, Agrippa, and Hocus Pocus." *English Literary Renaissance* 11 (1981): 281-303. Print.

Nelson, T. A., *Shakespeare's Comic Theory: A Study of Art and Artifice in the Last Plays*. Mouton: The Hague, 1973. Print.

Orgel, Stephen. "Prospero's Wife." *Representations* 8 (1984): 1-13. Print.

Pierce, Robert B. "Understanding *The Tempest*." *New Literary History* 30 (1999): 373-88. Print.

Reid, Robert L. "Sacerdotal Vestiges in *The Tempest*." *Comparative Drama* 41:4 (Winter 2007-8): 493-513. Print.

Retamar, Roberto Fernández. *Caliban and Other Essays*. Trans. Edward Baker. Minneapolis: U of Minnesota P, 1989. Print.

Robinson, James E. "Caribbean Caliban: Shifting the 'I' of the Storm." *Comparative Drama* 33:4 (Winter 1999-2000): 431-53. Print.

Rodó, José Enrique. *Ariel*. 1900. Austin: U of Texas P, 1988. Print.

Rogerson, Hank. *Shakespeare Behind Bars*. Los Angeles, CA: Shout! Factory, 2006. DVD.

Sanchez, Melissa E. "Seduction and Service in *The Tempest*." *Studies in Philology* 105:1 (2008): 50-82. Print.

Schneider, Ben Ross, Jr. "'Are We Being Historical Yet?': Colonialist Interpretations of Shakespeare's *Tempest*." *Shakespeare Studies* 23 (1995): 120-45. Print.

Shakespeare, William. *The Tempest*. Dir. John Gorrie. BBC, 1980. DVD.

Simonds, Peggy Muñoz. "'My Charms Crack Not': The Alchemical Structure of *The Tempest.*" *Comparative Drama* 31:4 (Winter 1997-98): 538-570. Print.

Smith, Hallett, *Shakespeare's Romances: A Study of Some Ways of the Imagination.* San Marino, CA: Huntington Library P, 1972. Print.

Sokol, B. J., *A Brave New World of Knowledge: Shakespeare's 'The Tempest' and Early Modern Epistemology.* Madison, NJ: Fairleigh Dickinson U P, 2003. Print.

Tiffany, Grace, *Ariel.* NY: HarperCollins, 2005. Print.

———. "Eden and the New World in Shakespeare's *The Tempest.*" *Critical Essays on the Myth of the American Adam.* Ed. María Eugenia Díaz-Sanchez and Viorica Patea. Salamanca: Ediciones Universidad de Salamanca, 2001. 45-53. Print.

Tillyard, E. M. W. *Shakespeare's Last Plays.* London: Chatto and Windus, 1938. Print.

Traversi, Derek. *Shakespeare: The Last Phase.* London: Hollis and Carter, 1954. Print.

Velie, A. R. *Shakespeare's Repentance Plays: The Search for an Adequate Form.* Cranbury, NJ: Associated U P, 1972. Print.

Visconsi, Elliott. "Vinculum Fidei: *The Tempest* and the Law of Allegiance." *Law and Literature* 20:1 (March, 2008): 1-21 Print.

Walter, James. "From Tempest to Epilogue." *PMLA* 98 (1983): 60-73. Print.

William, David, "*The Tempest* on the Stage." *Jacobean Theatre.* Ed. John Russell Brown and Bernard Harris. Stratford upon Avon: Stratford upon Avon Studies 1, 1960. 133-57. Print.

Wilson, J. Dover. *The Meaning of 'The Tempest.'* Literary and Philosophical Society: Newcastle upon Tyne, 1936. Print.